Why You Need this New Edition

5 good reasons why you should buy this new edition of *Developing the Public Relations Campaign!*

1. **The revised introductory chapter** provides more basic information about the public relations profession, making the book suitable for introductory as well as advanced courses.

2. **A new chapter** deals with interactive media, including the Internet, the World Wide Web, podcasting, and social media.

3. **Additional case studies** highlight public relations campaigns, including those surrounding Hurricane Katrina, the 2006 Duke Lacrosse case, the movie *We Are Marshall*, and the 2007 tragedy at Virginia Tech.

4. **A new real-world sample campaign**, "Tracking the Case of College Students and Credit Card Debt," illustrates concepts discussed in Chapters 3 through 10.

5. **New detailed discussion problems** in the ethics chapter ask students to think about the most ethical courses of action in real-world situations.

PEARSON

SECOND EDITION

DEVELOPING THE PUBLIC RELATIONS CAMPAIGN

A Team-Based Approach

RANDY BOBBITT

University of West Florida

RUTH SULLIVAN

Marshall University

PEARSON

Boston   New York   San Francisco
Mexico City   Montreal   Toronto   London   Madrid   Munich   Paris
Hong Kong   Singapore   Tokyo   Cape Town   Sydney

Acquisitions Editor: *Jeanne Zalesky*
Project Manager: *Lisa Sussman*
Marketing Manager: *Suzan Czajkowski*
Production Editor: *Pat Torelli*
Editorial-Production Service: *Publishers' Design and Production Services, Inc.*
Manufacturing Buyer: *JoAnne Sweeney*
Electronic Composition: *Publishers' Design and Production Services, Inc.*
Cover Administrator: *Joel Gendron*

For related titles and support materials, visit our online catalog at www.pearsonhighered.com.

Between the time website information is gathered and then published, it is not unusual for some sites to have closed. Also, the transcription of URLs can result in typographical errors. The publisher would appreciate notification where these occur so they may be corrected in subsequent editions.

ISBN-13: 978-0-205-56990-8
ISBN-10: 0-205-56990-0

Printed in the United States of America

10 9 8 7 6 5 4 3 2 1   12 11 10 09 08

Photo Credits: p. 5: AP Images; p. 6: UPI/Corbis/Bettman; p. 15: Josh Sher/Photo Researchers; p. 27: Matt Rainey/Star Ledger/Corbis; p. 36: The New Yorker Collection 2001 Lee Lorenz from cartoonbank.com. All Rights Reserved; p. 43: Susan Van Etten/PhotoEdit; p. 68: Elrick & Lavidge Inc.; p. 70: Comstock; p. 82: Rudy Von Briel/PhotoEdit; p. 89: Stephen Jaffe/AFP/Getty Images; p. 102: Mark Richards/PhotoEdit; p. 120: Corbis/Bettman; p. 126: Geri Engberg Photography; p. 192: AP Images; p. 201: Robert Brenner/PhotoEdit; p. 242: Richard Drew/AP Images; p. 243: Getty Images/NewsCom; p. 245: Michael Newman/PhotoEdit.

To our students—past, present, and future—
who remind us every day why we became teachers.

CONTENTS

CHAPTER THREE

Planning: Background Research   31

CHAPTER FOUR

Planning: Primary Research   45

CHAPTER FIVE

Planning: Goals and Objectives, Messages and Themes, Channels and Strategies   75

CHAPTER SIX

Implementation: Traditional Media Channels   95

CHAPTER SEVEN

Implementation: Interactive Media Channels   125

CHAPTER EIGHT

Implementation: Nonmedia Channels   137

CHAPTER NINE

Implementation: Logistics   163

CHAPTER TEN

Evaluation   177

Part III PROFESSIONAL RESPONSIBILITY

CHAPTER ELEVEN
Legal Considerations   195

CHAPTER TWELVE
Ethical Considerations   209

CHAPTER THIRTEEN

International, Multicultural, and Gender Issues   233

PREFACE

This book is targeted for students at advanced or "capstone" courses in public relations that typically carry such titles as Advanced Public Relations, Public Relations Campaigns, or Public Relations Program Development. Although it was written with such classes in mind, it was also tested in introductory classes and includes some material general enough to be used in programs in which there is only one omnibus public relations course. The various "discussion starters" at the end of each chapter can be used for either an introductory or advanced public relations course.

The subtitle of the book makes reference to a teaching method known as the competitive agency model. Professors teaching public relations and advertising classes often find a campus organization or local nonprofit organization to serve as the "client," then divide the class into teams that compete against each other to develop campaign proposals in the same way that real-world agencies compete for the business of prospective clients.

In addition to serving as a practical tool to assist students working on team projects and the professors who supervise them, one of the new ideas introduced in this book is the simplification of the public relations process. The traditional formula often taught in public relations classes has for many years been based on the "four-step process" of research, planning (sometimes described as action), communication, and evaluation. In developing this textbook, however, we discovered through conversations with working professionals that the four-step (or RACE) process is not the magic formula it was once thought to be, and in the "real world" it is often difficult to diagram the process. We found that the research and planning steps are often muddled together, with little or no visible dividing line.

Another problem with the RACE formula is that it oversimplifies the four-step process as one that proceeds from left to right through the four stages, as though a public relations planner could not return to the research phase after moving into the planning stage. In fact, the public relations process is seldom that linear.

For this book, however, we have instead consolidated the research and planning stages, and the result is a three-step process: planning, implementation, and evaluation (PIE). We believe, as do many working professionals we have spoken to, that this three-step model more accurately describes the campaign development process used in the "real world."

The PIE formula, as detailed in Chapters 3 through 10, recognizes that the three components are not watertight compartments that require the program developer to move through the process in a straight line. For example, there may be a case in which public relations planners get to the implementation stage and realize they do not have all the information needed to choose the most effective tactics. Thus, they must return to the planning stage (in this case, for more primary research) to determine the media habits of the audiences.

Like most endeavors of this complexity, this book would not have been possible without the help and inspiration of other people in our lives. We thank the following friends, professors, colleagues, work supervisors, and mentors who have provided guidance and encouragement over the years: Donna Dickerson, Roger Dyer, Jim Foust, Dennis Hale,

Don Harrison, John R. Jones, Larry Leslie, Steve Ludd, Eileen Perrigo, Barbara Petersen, Terry Rentner, Hal Shaver, Raymond Smallwood, Bruce Swain, Frank Trimble, Vicki Vega, and Gary Werner. We also thank the faculties and staffs of the W. Page Pitt School of Journalism and Mass Communications at Marshall University, the Department of Communication Studies at the University of North Carolina at Wilmington, the Department of Communication Arts at the University of West Florida, the library and computer support staffs at all three institutions, and the hundreds of students who have taken our classes and provided valuable feedback on preliminary drafts of the book.

We also thank the following individuals who helped in the development of this book: Kristi Singer, research and editorial assistant; Carol Hemmye, proofreader; Kelli Matthews and Julie Peacock, UNCW student assistants; Sue Cody, UNCW reference librarian; Devan Ezzell Owens, a former student who helped us reconstruct the sample found in Chapters 3 through 10; and Lisa Sussman, Jeanne Zalesky, and Karon Bowers, Allyn & Bacon editors. We are also grateful to the following reviewers of the text: Eric Brown, Canyon College; Robert A. Carroll, York College of Pennsylvania; Don W. Stacks, University of Miami; and Beth Wood, Indiana University.

Randy Bobbitt
Ruth Sullivan

ABOUT THE AUTHORS

Randy Bobbitt is an assistant professor in the Department of Communication Arts at the University of West Florida. In addition to public relations, he has taught courses in journalism, communication law, and communication ethics. Prior to coming to UWF, he taught at the University of North Carolina at Wilmington, Marshall University, and the University of South Florida.

His research interests include public relations, political communication, popular culture, and communication law and ethics. Prior to college teaching, he worked professionally in both journalism and public relations. He is a past president of the West Virginia Chapter of the Public Relations Society of America and is a frequent speaker at professional and student public relations conferences. He holds a Ph.D. in communication law and policy from Bowling Green State University.

In addition to this book, Professor Bobbitt has published four other books on topics including public relations, communication law and ethics, journalism history, and political communication: *A Big Idea and a Shirt-Tail Full of Type: The Life and Work of Wallace F. Stovall* (1995), *Who Owns What's Inside the Professor's Head?* (2006), *Lottery Wars: Case Studies in Bible Belt Politics* (2007), and *Exploring Communication Law* (2008). He is currently working on a new book, *Us Against Them: The Political Culture of Talk Radio,* which he hopes to publish in 2009.

Ruth Sullivan is a public school teacher in Kenova, West Virginia, and an adjunct professor in the W. Page Pitt School of Journalism at Marshall University, where she has taught courses in public relations and print journalism for more than 25 years.

Prior to teaching, she worked in a variety of public relations management positions in both the education and corporate arenas. Her professional background includes work with the West Virginia coal and utility industries, where she focused on safety, environmental, and educational programs, and public education, where she focused on strategic planning and management issues.

Professor Sullivan is a past president of the West Virginia Press Women's Association, past president of River Cities Chapter of the International Association of Business Communicators, and past president of the W. Page Pitt Marshall University School of Journalism and Mass Communications Alumni Association. She earned a master's degree in mass communications from Marshall University and has won numerous national and state awards in communications competitions.

CHAPTER 1

PUBLIC RELATIONS AND PERSUASION

DEFINING PUBLIC RELATIONS

Definitions from the Past

Every public relations textbook begins with its own definition for *public relations,* and this one is no exception. But first, we begin by discussing some other commonly used definitions and the strengths and weaknesses of each.

One oversimplified definition compares public relations with advertising. Any publicity that is purchased, according to the definition, is labeled as "advertising," whereas other forms of publicity that do not involve a financial transaction can be labeled as "public relations." That shorthand definition simply does not work because public relations is more than just publicity. Publicity is a large part of public relations work, but true public relations also involves research, problem solving, long-term planning (publicity is short-term planning), and two-way communication instead of one-way communication.

A somewhat better definition was developed by public relations pioneer Edward Bernays, who defined public relations as "good work understood by the public." Bernays expanded on this definition using a two-part formula. First, a company or organization must do good work. It must produce quality products or provide a valuable service; it must have honest and productive relationships with its customers, employees, and other constituent groups; and it must be socially responsible. The second part of the formula requires letting people know about an organization's good work through various forms of communication, such as the news media, paid advertising, or in-house publications.

The converse of Bernays' definition is also true. When communicating about quality products or valuable services, good relationships with employees and customers, and the claim of social responsibility, all of that must be true. A popular cliche used in sports can also be applied here: "If you are going to talk the talk, you must also walk the walk."

A Modern Definition

We prefer the following definition, which combines the best features of various definitions currently used today. It will provide the basis for understanding the subsequent chapters of this text:

> Public relations is the *management function* that uses *two-way communication* to receive information from and give information to an organization's *various publics.*

What Public Relations IS

1. *Public Relations Is a Management Function.* In order to be as effective as possible, the public relations department must be part of an organization's management, not just a department that reports to management. Even though most organizations will have one or more employees with "public relations" in their job titles and a department labeled "public relations," the organization must consider the concept on a broader scale. Public relations must be part of the organization's everyday decision making, not just a department that carries out the results of those decisions.

2. *Public Relations Involves Two-Way Communication.* True public relations depends heavily on public opinion and public opinion research. This is the component that draws the clearest distinction between publicity and public relations—publicity is one-way communication that includes little or no research, measurement, or feedback; true public relations is built on two-way communication.

Effective public opinion research takes two forms: **formative research** to provide information necessary to develop persuasive campaigns, and **evaluative research** that measures the effectiveness of campaigns after their conclusion. Both forms of research use similar methods, such as media tracking, surveys, focus groups, field observation, and feedback gathered through the organization's website.

3. *Public Relations Deals with Various Publics (or Multiple Publics).* Instead of attempting to communicate with a broad, general audience using a "shotgun" approach, public relations professionals segment their audiences into the smallest units possible. Examples of **publics** include customers, potential customers, employees, suppliers, distributors, retailers, government regulators, competitors, media, environmental advocacy groups, and consumer advocacy groups. This part of the definition is what separates public relations from marketing—marketing deals with customers, potential customers, distributors, and retailers; true public relations deals with a broader array of publics.

What Public Relations Is NOT

1. *Public Relations Is Not Synonymous with Publicity or Event Planning.* What's the difference? Public relations, as previously indicated, consists mostly of two-way communication; publicity and event planning are forms of one-way communication. Further, public relations efforts generate long-term results; publicity and event planning yield short-term results. Publicity and event planning are two methods that public relations professionals use, but they are not public relations in themselves.

The terms *public relations* and *publicity* are far from interchangeable, and the fact that other people use them as such does not make it correct. A website associated with the public relations program at Syracuse University spoofs this matter as it asks the question, *Isn't public relations just another way of saying publicity?* "Often we find that students arrive at our door with misconceptions about public relations," the site reports. "Too often they think that public relations begins and ends with special events and news conferences. Ultimately, our students come to understand that public relations is a core management function for every type of organization."

The bottom line: When you create awareness for your student organization or one of its events by distributing posters across campus or chalking the sidewalks, you're doing **publicity,** not **public relations.**

2. *Public Relations Is Not a Synonym for Schmoozing, Spin, Deception, Manipulation, Distortion, or Disinformation.* Just because politicians and television commentators use various terms as synonyms for *public relations* does not mean it's correct. Similarly, *PR* should never be used as a verb (such as, "We have to PR this"), in a frivolous sense (such as, "That's just PR"), or in a derogatory sense (such as, "You're a good b.s. artist—you should consider going into PR").

3. *Public Relations Does Not Deal with Show Business News or Celebrity Gossip.* Your favorite singer has a new CD? A well-known celebrity is charged with drunk driving? Your two favorite movie stars are getting married (or divorced)? Good for them.

But that's publicity, not public relations. If a professional athlete fails a drug test or is arrested for an alleged crime, is it publicity or public relations? It's both. For the athlete, it's bad publicity (not "bad PR"). But it is a public relations issue for the team he or she plays for or the league in which he or she participates. For the athlete, it's *publicity* because how he or she is perceived by fans, reporters, or teammates is mostly a *short-term* issue. For the team or league, it's publicity (short-term) as well, but how they decide to deal with the *long-term* issue of drugs or criminal behavior is *public relations.*

Although it is true that some individuals and organizations in show business employ publicists, that is much different from public relations. Many professors and public relations experts consider show business publicity to be second-class work.

A BRIEF HISTORY OF PUBLIC RELATIONS

Public relations historians around the world often disagree about how, when, and where the profession began. In the United States, however, the field can be broken down into three general phases: The early period (the late 1700s and most of the 1800s); the transitional period (roughly between the late 1880s and 1970), and the modern period (the early 1970s through the present).

The Early Period

The early period began in the years leading up to the Revolutionary War and continued through the late 1700s and most of the 1800s. This period also included the first applications of public opinion in political campaigns, when the political leaders of what would eventually become the United States began to realize the importance of public opinion in shaping political and social movements.

No one used the term *public relations* during this stage—the concept was simply known as "public opinion" or "persuasion." The major persuasive event of the era was the Boston Tea Party, when angry colonists boarded British ships in Boston Harbor and dumped hundreds of pounds of tea overboard to protest an import tax. The event also served to call attention to the growing conflict with the British and to generate public support for the inevitable war ahead. The event was symbolic more than substantive—as many public relations events tend to be—but the event and the time period it symbolized were believed to represent the first organized application of public opinion science in this country.

Shortly after the war that gave America its independence from Great Britain, the science of public opinion and persuasion was applied to politics and political campaigns. Politicians realized the value of finding people who not only knew how to influence public opinion but also knew how to measure it. These pioneer political campaign operatives developed techniques for opinion polling that could measure the public mood and determine how that information could be used to develop appropriate political strategies.

In the late 1800s, P. T. Barnum, founder of the circus that bears his name, was one of the first individuals to apply public opinion and persuasive techniques in the entertainment industry. Later called *press agentry*, Barnum's idea was that promotional events (in Barnum's case, public parades of his animals through cities prior to the circus opening) would reach more people, generate more media attention, and be more cost effective than paid advertising. That way of thinking started with Barnum's circus and then spread to other forms of entertainment—first to Broadway, then to Hollywood. The thinking was that if a person wanted to be successful and famous in the entertainment industry, he or she had to employ a publicist, or at least an agent who knew how the publicity process worked.

The Transitional Period

As the label indicates, the transitional period was characterized by major changes in how public relations was practiced and how practitioners were perceived.

Even though the term *public relations* was not used until the 1920s, the first applications of what would eventually become modern public relations can be found as far back as 1889. Two companies—Westinghouse and Mutual Life Insurance Company—both claim in their corporate histories to have established the first corporate public relations departments in the country.

The concepts behind the field were not widely applied until after the turn of the century, however. The first industrywide applications of public relations in the business world were used by banks and railroads. Public relations historians say that public relations in this country "came of age" during the first three decades of the 1900s, beginning with banks and railroads and then expanding to the manufacturing and public utilities industries.

The early 1900s was also the period in which the profession saw its first "superstars." There were dozens of pioneers in the field, but the two most important were Ivy Lee and Edward L. Bernays. Lee did his most important work between 1910 and 1934, the year of his death. Bernays began his work during World War I and continued working until his death in 1995, but he is best known for his work in the 1920s and 1930s.

Both men were former journalists, and that began a trend that is still seen today—that of public relations representatives coming from the ranks of journalism. (Today, journalism is the most common former occupation for public relations professionals.) Lee also began the trend of public relations practitioners coming into the field with a college education. The press agents and the publicists that came before Lee had little or no formal education or professional training; most had high school diplomas (or less).

But Lee was a Princeton graduate and the first of the Ivy League–educated practitioners to become successful in public relations. He was a reporter for the *New York World,* which at the time was part of the Pulitzer newspaper chain. Lee is credited with being the first practitioner to use the "news release" as a tactic for presenting story ideas to the media, although at the time they were known as *handouts.*

Although he did not use the term *public relations,* Lee founded one of the country's first consulting firms, Parker and Lee, in 1905. One of the philosophies that he encouraged clients to follow was that of being accessible to reporters rather than secretive. One of his clients, the Pennsylvania Railroad, had a policy of denying reporters access to accident scenes. The result was a climate of mistrust that only motivated the reporters to be more aggressive in their pursuit of negative news about the company. Lee insisted that company representatives make themselves available to answer media questions and allow reporters access to the accident sites.

Lee's most famous client was billionaire oil magnate John D. Rockefeller Sr. Rockefeller amassed a fortune in the oil, coal, and natural gas industries, but while doing so suffered from a horrible public image. The Rockefeller image hit bottom in 1914 with labor problems and violence at company-owned mining operations in Colorado. By then, Rockefeller's son, John D. Rockefeller Jr., had taken over the family business. He hired Lee as an advisor to help the family recover from the Colorado situation, and later to help him and his father refurbish the family image on a broader scale.

Ivy Lee (1877–1934) was a former journalist who became famous by helping the Rockefeller family with its publicity problems.

Lee was followed a few years later by Edward L. Bernays. Like Lee, Bernays was a former journalist; he wrote for and edited a number of magazines in the entertainment and medical fields. He later became a Broadway press agent, but did not become famous until he began working for the U.S. government during World War I.

Bernays worked for the government's Committee on Public Information, headed by former newspaper reporter George Creel, who had been selected to direct the committee by President Woodrow Wilson. The committee generated public support for the war by promoting war bonds, using airplanes to drop propaganda leaflets behind enemy lines, and producing newsreels. The committee labeled its work as "information" or "propaganda"—with the latter term not carrying the negative stigma that it does today.

His work with the Committee on Public Information gave Bernays his first glimpse of fame, but he earned even more notoriety after the war when he began working in corporate public relations. Looking for a way to apply his wartime experience to civilian work, he opened an office on Madison Avenue in New York with his new wife, former newspaper reporter Doris Fleischman. At the beginning, they called their work "publicity direction," and their early clients were from the fields of manufacturing, public utilities, government agencies, and Broadway plays. After a few years, they realized the term *publicity direction* did not adequately explain what they did, so they developed a new term—*public relations*—and soon after many other professional communicators adopted the same term.

In addition to giving the field its name, Bernays is known for three other contributions to the field: (1) he was the first to teach public relations in a university setting (in New York University's business school), (2) he was an early advocate for ethical guidelines and standards of professional conduct, and (3) he was among the first practitioners to take the scientific approach to public opinion research. Bernays was the nephew of psychoanalyst

Edward Bernays (1891–1995) was one of the pioneers of the profession and among the first to use the term public relations.

Sigmund Freud, and in his writings gave credit to Freud for influencing many of his theories about human behavior and decision making.

Another significant highlight of the transitional period was the formation of two professional organizations: the Public Relations Society of America in 1945 and the International Association of Business Communicators in 1970.

The Modern Period

The final phase in the history of public relations consists of what happened in the field during the last three decades of the 1900s and continues through the present day.

One highlight of this time period is the development of public relations as a field of academic study. Colleges and universities across the country are enrolling an increasing number of undergraduate students in public relations degree programs. Although most are found in departments such as journalism or mass communications, a few are found in business schools. Some institutions take an interdisciplinary approach and offer degrees in "integrated marketing communications" that are joint ventures of business schools and communications programs. At the graduate level, some institutions offer master's and doctoral degrees with titles such as "corporate communications" or "public affairs."

Related to the growth of the academic study of public relations is the rapid growth in the literature associated with the field. The number of books and professional journals has grown exponentially over the last 40 years. Another significant highlight of the modern era is a greater emphasis on two-way communication, especially in the area of public opinion research. There is also more attention paid to the concept of crisis communications or crisis management, due mostly to widespread media attention generated by incidents such as Three Mile Island (1979), the Tylenol tampering case (1982), the Exxon-Valdez oil spill (1989), the crash of TWA flight 800 (1996), the Firestone tire recall (1999–2000), the terrorist attacks of September 11 (2001), the Enron and Worldcom financial scandals (2001–2002), and the Federal Emergency Management Agency's slow response to Hurricane Katrina (2005).

The modern period has also given birth to the trend of large corporations merging their advertising, public relations, and marketing functions into one department. The buzz-phrase used to describe this trend is **integrated marketing communications (IMC).** One of the primary advantages of the IMC approach is the prevention of potential embarrassments that occur when a company's advertising messages appear to be inconsistent with the messages that the public relations representatives attempt to disseminate through media coverage. Another potential advantage is the reduction of tension, rivalry, or competition between employees assigned to the various functions. Advocates of the IMC approach claim that the closer together these individuals work, the less likely they are to attempt to undermine the work of others. One potential disadvantage to the IMC approach is the difficulty of merging together people whose professional training and strategic preferences vary widely.

Yet another aspect of this period is the growing influence of technology, including the impact of the Internet and the World Wide Web. The Internet offers organizations opportunities to communicate more effectively with employees, stockholders, potential stockholders, customers, potential customers, and the media. But the technology also presents a number of challenges, as organizations and their public relations staffs must deal with angry consumers and advocacy groups that launch their criticisms using a variety of "nontraditional media" such as websites, chat rooms, on-line discussion groups, and blogs.

THE NATURE OF PERSUASION

The term *persuasive campaign* should not be confused with its less admirable cousin, the *propaganda campaign.* By definition, legitimate attempts at persuasion differ from propaganda in several important ways. **Persuasion** is defined as "an effort to gain public support for an opinion or course of action." What is implied in the definition is that the effort is based on truthful and ethical methods. **Propaganda,** on the other hand, is "the attempt to have a viewpoint accepted on the basis of appeals other than the merits of the case." It often uses methods that could be labeled as unethical or manipulative.

Another attempt at drawing a distinction between the terms is to say that persuasion is based on truth, whereas propaganda is based on fiction or exaggeration; persuasion is based on consensus, whereas propaganda tries to set up adversarial relationships or "us against them" scenarios.

In their 1992 book, *Propaganda and Persuasion,* theorists Garth S. Jowett and Victoria O'Donnell pointed out that the intent of persuasion is to serve the interests of both the persuader and the audience; propaganda, however, generally serves only the interests of the person acting as its source. Jowett and O'Donnell's view is consistent with the long-standing philosophy of public relations programs producing results that are mutually beneficial or "win-win."

Jowett and O'Donnell's work was an expansion of that done during World War II by Columbia University Professor Clyde R. Miller, who founded the Institute for Propaganda Analysis. At first the emphasis was to study the use of propaganda in the war in Europe, but he quickly expanded its scope to include the study of propaganda from all sources, including the Ku Klux Klan, other extremist groups, and the U.S. advertising industry. The institute is still in operation today and identifies—in its publications and on its website—nine common propaganda devices:

1. *Name-calling* is the use of emotional labels that are offered in the place of logic or evidence. Examples of labels applied to individuals include "extremist," "radical," "liberal," "fundamentalist," and "racist." Examples of labels applied to ideas include "social engineering," "radical," "legislating morality," and "counterculture." For example, when critics wanted to generate opposition to President Clinton's proposed health care plan in the early 1990s, they did so in part by referring to Clinton and his wife, Hillary, as representing the "counterculture."

2. *Glittering generalities* represent the opposite of name-calling. Instead of wanting the audience to reject an idea without examining the evidence, a communicator resorting to glittering generalities wants the audience to accept an idea without requiring evidence. What results are generalizations so extreme that receivers disregard the lack of substance behind the appeals. Examples are claims that begin with "Everyone knows that . . ." and "It goes without saying that . . . ." In political campaigns, examples of glittering generalities include a candidate's charges that his or her opponent's proposals are "all style and no substance" or "based on ideas of the past."

3. *Transfer* is a device by which the communicator wants the audience to take the authority, sanction, or prestige of a respected idea and apply it to a new idea that the communicator wants the audience to accept. Examples include the use of symbols such as the cross, representing the Christian church, or Uncle Sam, representing patriotism and love of country. If a church publication shows the cross being used to promote helping the poor, it implies that helping the poor is something that Christians should do. If a cartoonist draws Uncle Sam in a manner in which he approves of a proposed new law, it implies that the entire country should be in favor of it.

Transfer is often used as a tactic in political campaigns. In the 2002 senatorial race in North Carolina, for example, the campaign of republican Elizabeth Dole aired television commercials emphasizing that democrat Erskine Bowles once served in the administration of former President Bill Clinton, expecting voters to "transfer" their negative perception of Clinton to Bowles.

The advertising industry often attempts to transfer the authority of science and medicine in making product claims, asking consumers to purchase certain brands because of their association with the latest techniques in science or medicine.

4. The *bandwagon* approach is one in which audiences are encouraged to adopt a certain behavior because "everyone else is doing it" and they "do not want to be left behind."

5. The *plain folks* approach suggests that audiences should adopt an idea because it comes from someone similar to them or reject an idea because it comes from someone unlike them.

6. *Testimonials* are appeals from influential celebrities or authority figures whose expertise may be irrelevant to the product being sold or idea being promoted. A common example is the use of professional athletes to endorse companies or products, including those that are unrelated to the sport for which they are known.

7. *Card Stacking* is a method that stacks the cards in favor of the desired result, presenting one-sided evidence or half-truths. For example, critics of a university's athletic program may point out the graduation rate for the school's athletes is only 45 percent (and therefore the athletic program should be eliminated), but not mentioning (or perhaps not knowing) that the graduate rate for nonathletes is only 42 percent.

8. The use of *fear or scare tactics* as devices to influence behavior is common in advertising and political campaigns. A communicator using this tactic typically pairs a negative result with the desired behavior required to avoid it. Examples include television commercials showing an accident scene followed by the suggestion of wearing seat belts, or the scene of a house fire followed by a pitch for smoke detectors.

9. *Euphemisms* are terms intended to obscure or soften the true meaning of behaviors or concepts. Examples include a company referring to employee layoffs as "early retirement opportunities" or the government referring to a tax increase as a "revenue adjustment."

CHARACTERISTICS OF LEGITIMATE PUBLIC RELATIONS CAMPAIGNS

There are three characteristics found in legitimate public relations campaigns. The first is that of *free choice,* meaning the audiences are able to choose freely among several actions: Adopt the ideas or behaviors being advocated by campaign organizers, adopt the ideas or behaviors of another party involved in the issue, remain committed to their previously held ideas or behaviors, or not take part in the issue at all. Free choice also means there is no coercion involved. Campaign organizers are allowed to be assertive in their work, of course, but in an ethical communications campaign the final choice must be up to members of the audience.

The second characteristic is *mutual benefit,* meaning that both the communicator and the audience must emerge from the transaction with some benefit. A campaign in which only the communicator benefits is manipulation rather than true public relations.

The third characteristic of a legitimate public relations campaign is that it takes a *multidisciplinary approach.* Instead of dealing only with the mass media, an approach typically used in advertising, true public relations campaigns may also apply theories and techniques from fields such as psychology, sociology, and education. For example, a company trying to sell cat litter may find success with traditional advertising and marketing techniques. However, an organization attempting to promote the importance of spaying or neutering cats will have to apply a variety of other communications techniques to be successful.

TYPES OF PERSUASIVE CAMPAIGNS

Persuasive campaigns are used either to resolve problems or to take advantage of opportunities. They can be placed into five categories: political, commercial, reputation, educational, or social action.

The category of **political campaigns** can be subdivided into those that are *candidate oriented* and *issue oriented.* Candidate-oriented campaigns are usually orchestrated by campaign managers and other professionals who use techniques other than those used by public relations professionals. Those techniques include scare tactics, deception, exaggeration, and other forms of communication commonly referred to as *spin.* Because we (and many other public relations professionals) prefer that such tactics not be confused with those used in the public relations profession, candidate-oriented campaigns will not be discussed here.

The tactics used in issue-oriented campaigns, although not completely free of "spin," are generally conducted on a higher ethical plane than those that are candidate oriented. Issue-oriented campaigns are often aimed at attempting to get a proposed governmental action passed or defeated. It could be at the federal, state, or local level. Examples of issue-oriented campaigns at the federal level include those that resulted in the passage of the Brady Bill (handgun control act), the Americans with Disabilities Act, the Family and Medical Leave Act, and the North American Free Trade Agreement. Recent examples of issue-oriented persuasive campaigns at the state level include those involving the spread of legalized gambling, changes to a state's workers' compensation laws, or an increase in the state's sales tax. At the local level, city and county governments often work with private interests to pass measures that either provide for a "local option" sales tax or the public sale of bonds to fund new schools, sports stadiums, or other public works projects.

Commercial campaigns are used to promote a company's new products or services (often called *rollout campaigns*) or a new company as a whole. They may include activities usually thought of as "advertising" or "marketing," but they include public relations techniques as well.

Reputation campaigns (sometimes called *image campaigns*) are those aimed at improving how a company or nonprofit organization is perceived by its publics. Reputation campaigns are different from commercial campaigns because they do not promote specific products or services; they instead deal with the organization as a whole. They often follow a major crisis or other situations generating negative publicity, such as Tylenol's recovery from a 1982 product tampering crisis, Exxon's attempt to recover from the 1989 oil spill in Alaska, or United Way's recovery from a 1991 financial scandal. More recent examples include Firestone's campaign that accompanied the recall of defective tires and United Airlines' effort to recover from a summer of flight delays caused by bad weather, equipment problems, air traffic control patterns, and labor conflicts.

In other cases, the decline in an organization's reputation may not have resulted from a specific incident, but rather from the accumulation of factors over a long period of time. One example involves the National Rifle Association, which financed a reputation campaign in the late 1980s after years of negative publicity—mainly caused by its opposition to gun control legislation—contributed to a decline in public perception.

Educational or public awareness campaigns are those conducted by nonprofit organizations or other advocacy groups. Many such campaigns involve medical conditions such as cancer, heart disease, and eating disorders, and attempt either to educate people of a medical condition's warning signs or to make behavioral changes. Other campaigns in this category deal with social concerns such as drunk driving, domestic violence, and child abuse.

In those cases in which the campaign is advocating a behavioral change, it often asks members of its audience to do one of two things: begin doing something they have never done before (such as examine themselves for signs of cancer) or stop doing something that they have done for a long time (such as smoking).

Social action campaigns are those that advocate a social issue or cause. They are similar to issue-oriented political campaigns and use many of the same techniques; the main difference is that they are generally long term in nature. For example, an issue-oriented campaign may be a short-term or closed-ended attempt to pass a specific gun control law, whereas a social action campaign would be a broader, open-ended campaign to continue the effort to pass additional gun control measures long after the initial victory was won (or lost).

Many campaigns fall into more than one category. One example is found in Case Study 1. Johnson & Johnson's "Campaign for Nursing's Future"—designed to enhance the reputation of the nursing profession and address the long-term nursing shortage—has elements of a reputation campaign, a public awareness campaign, and a social action campaign. Another example can be found in the debate over abortion: Advocates and opponents find themselves designing campaigns that are both issue-oriented political campaigns and social action campaigns. In fact, many amendments to the United States Constitution resulted from persuasive campaigns that were both political and social action causes, such as Amendments 18 (prohibition) and 19 (women's right to vote).

SERVICE LEARNING AND STUDENT PROJECTS

Public relations and advertising were among the first disciplines to use the idea of collaborative projects in which students develop campaign proposals either used to benefit a local charity and/or to be entered in national competitions. A popular trend today is for colleges and universities to expand the concept to other disciplines, using the label of *service learning*.

The term *competitive agency model*, which is used later in this book, refers to a pedagogical technique for organizing an advanced public relations class around such team projects. Professors teaching public relations and advertising classes often find a campus organization or local nonprofit organization to serve as the "client," then divide the class into teams that compete against each other to develop campaign proposals in the same way that real-world agencies compete for the business of prospective clients. Variations of the model include (1) selecting multiple clients, with each team working with a different one, and (2) selecting one client and having the entire class work to produce one proposal, dividing students into "committees" rather than "teams."

An advanced class in public relations may provide the first setting in which students work in teams. But it also provides students the opportunity to use many of the skills learned in other classes and participate in the start-to-finish process of a real-world public relations campaign. Even though some or all of the finished product may be used by a real client, the student project provides the safe atmosphere of the classroom. Even though instructors may be critical at times, they also provide encouragement and function as a "safety net."

Although there are always exceptions, most students find collaborative projects enjoyable and beneficial, especially when they are chosen to be team leaders or committee chairs. And since many of the students participating are close to graduation, it is not uncommon for students to impress clients enough to be offered employment or internship opportunities upon the project's completion.

Here are some things to keep in mind throughout the semester:

■ **Match Talents, Interests, and Strengths**
Few people are good at everything, but every member of a team is good at something. Assignments should be made according to each member's strength. The team member who volunteers to drive to an early-morning meeting at the client's office, for example, may not be the same person to pull an all-nighter in the computer lab.

■ **Proofread, Proofread, Proofread**
The team member who writes a piece of copy should not be the only one to proofread it. Team members, as many as possible, should proofread drafts for spelling, grammatical, and factual errors. Regardless of who wrote the copy, the entire team is responsible for its accuracy.

▪ Practice Effective "Disk Management"
Make multiple copies of work on multiple disks and store them in different places. Label one version as the "working copy" in order to keep track of which is the most current. Save each printout or draft until it has been replaced by a more recent version. Resist the temptation to toss the printout into the trash (or a paper recycling barrel) until the team is assured it will no longer be needed.

▪ Practice the Golden Rule
Do unto others as you would have them do unto you. No matter how stressful the situation, treat clients and teammates with respect.

▪ The Best Way to Eat an Elephant Is One Bite at a Time
When faced with a task that appears to be overwhelming, break it into smaller pieces and start chipping away. Waiting for what one assumes is enough time to tackle a large chore may mean it never gets started at all.

▪ Think Quality of Meetings, Not Quantity
Success is not determined by the number or length of team meetings, but by what is accomplished. Come to meetings prepared to participate. Show respect for other people's time by being on time.

▪ Use the Buddy System
Work in pairs or trios. Partners can encourage each other, bounce ideas off each other, and check each other's work.

▪ Late Warning Is Better Than No Warning at All
If a team member runs behind on his or her share of work, the person should notify the team leader and teammates as soon as possible. It is acceptable for a team member to ask for help when running behind on his or her piece of the puzzle.

TRENDS AND ISSUES

Flack, Hype, and Spin

In his book, *The Persuasion Explosion,* public relations educator Art Stevens uses the following parable to illustrate some common misuses and abuses of the term *public relations.*

Let's start with what public relations is not. A beautiful young woman runs an ad in a magazine accompanied by a photograph of herself in a bikini. The ad says, "Attention meeting and convention planners—I can be your public relations representative at your next event." That is not public relations.

A lonely senior citizen calls a travel agency and tells the travel agent that she plans a month's vacation to Europe and seeks a "public relations escort" to accompany her. That is not public relations.

Not long ago I was sitting in a restaurant nibbling on a sandwich. It was dry. I asked the waitress to bring me some mayonnaise on the side, and she did. When I thanked her, she said,

"Think nothing of it. I'm just practicing good public relations." But that is not public relations.

A Mafia chief instructs one of his lieutenants on the art of collecting protection money from neighborhood stores. "If they go two or three times without coughing up the money, throw a rock through their window. If they don't cough up the money by the fifth time, rough them up a little bit. That's Mafia public relations." But that, too, is not public relations.*

Stevens's humorous parable is not as far-fetched as it sounds. Every day, people outside the profession confuse and interchange words such as *advertising, marketing, promotion, publicity,* and *public relations* as though they were just all synonyms for what public relations professionals do. Although each of the five terms describe forms of communication that may appear to be similar and may indeed overlap each other, they should not be used casually or interchangeably. What's worse than confusion over the terms is the use of the acronym as a derogatory form of slang, such as "That's just PR," or the use of PR as a verb, such as "We have to PR this."

We, along with many other professionals, are also concerned about the growing use of catch-phrases or other terms in association with the public relations profession. Among these are negative terms such as **flack, hype,** and **spin**. The problem with associating buzzwords, such as *spin,* with the profession of public relations is that they are too often seen as euphemisms for lying, manipulation, and propaganda—all techniques that true public relations professionals abhor. Even worse is that public relations professionals themselves often use those terms as if they are unaware of the negative connotations they create.

Even advice columnist Ann Landers took a swipe at the profession in a 1988 column in which she predicted that a high school boy with a reputation for misleading and deceiving his female classmates had "a great future in public relations." Members of professional associations such as the Public Relations Society of America (PRSA) and the International Association of Business Communicators (IABC) flooded her mailbox with complaints, prompting her to apologize in a subsequent column in which she also mentioned some of the industry's accomplishments.

The profession has also drawn harsh words in recent decades from various consumer advocates and other critics. One of the field's most vocal critics is consumer activist John Stauber, who authored a 1995 book titled *Toxic Sludge Is Good For You: Lies, Damn Lies and the Public Relations Industry,* the title of which indicates its tone. Today, he continues his criticism of the field through publishing *PR Watch,* a quarterly newsletter that calls attention to what he describes as the misleading and unethical conduct of some public relations professionals.

The alternative political magazine *Utne Reader* also takes frequent shots at the public relations industry. In one 1994 article, it accused the public relations profession of "shaping public life in ways we're not supposed to notice" and commented that the profession is based on its belief that it is "easier to change the way people think about reality than it is to change reality."

Misunderstandings about the profession and criticisms of it were problems as far back as the 1970s and 1980s. Professional organizations such as PRSA and IABC have responded by promoting their codes of ethics and other aspects of the profession. Public relations executive Reg Rowe responded to the misperceptions and criticisms of the profession in a 1992 newspaper column:

> The perception of a public relations person as a glad-handing, backslapping, trinket-disseminating, let's-do-lunch, gets-along-well-with-people individual lingers even today in the public's mind. A few months back, Morley Safer of *60 Minutes* stated that public relations people believe they can "sell anything, given enough time, money and access to the media." That sends the wrong message.
>
> Safer's remark was a blatant attack on all professionals who practice public relations. I take offense. . . . [Public relations] is a far cry from the images in the mind of many. And it takes much more than "being good with people" to practice the discipline professionally.†

---

*Reprinted by permission of Art Stevens, public relations executive.

†Courtesy of Reg Rowe, APR.

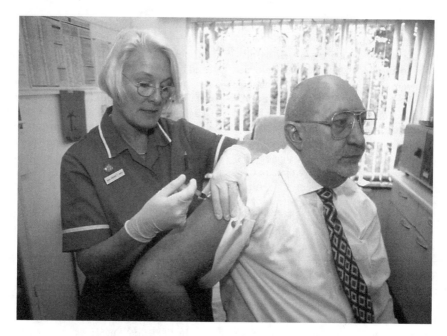

In 2001, Johnson & Johnson unveiled a multiyear, $30-million campaign to help the nursing profession improve its image and recruit the next generation of nurses.

CASE STUDY 1

Johnson & Johnson's "Campaign for Nursing's Future"

In late 2001, the U.S. health care system was experiencing one of the worst nursing shortages in its history. Industry experts estimated that more than 110,000 nursing vacancies existed across the country. To respond to the nursing shortage, Johnson & Johnson—the largest manufacturer of health care products in the world—launched the "Campaign for Nursing's Future," a multiyear, $30-million campaign to enhance the overall image of the nursing profession as well as to recruit new nurses and nurse faculty.

Components of the campaign included print and interactive advertising of real nurses in action, as well as a comprehensive website, www.discovernursing

.com, containing searchable links to hundreds of nursing scholarships, more than 2,000 accredited nursing educational programs, funding resources, and information on more than 100 specialties for individuals who are interested in pursuing a career in nursing. In 2007, the campaign expanded with a growing emphasis on nurse faculty recruitment and retention. Recent additions to the campaign include a new television advertising campaign, which will include nurse faculty ads for the first time, as well as a new website—www.campaignfornursing.com—designed to address nurse and nurse faculty retention with career training and professional development opportunities.

"Johnson & Johnson has always had a special relationship with nurses," said Andrea Higham, director of the campaign. "When we launched the campaign five years ago, we knew we had to act on a crisis that would not only greatly impact nurses, but the larger health care community as well. There is significant data which demonstrates that as nurse staffing levels decrease, or become over-burdened, patient health care quality declines, and patient mortality rates increase. This staffing crisis has a very real impact on anyone who needs health care."

"The nursing community is extremely grateful to Johnson & Johnson for their strong commitment to revitalizing interest in professional nursing careers," said Dr. Geraldine Bednash, executive director of the American Association of Colleges of Nursing (AACN). "Since the start of the Campaign for Nursing's Future, nursing schools nationwide have experienced significant increases in enrollment and graduations. Now we need to focus on preparing more qualified faculty to accommodate all those interested in entering the nursing profession."

Since its inception, the campaign has distributed more than 15 million pieces of recruitment materials to schools, health centers, and every high school career center in the country. Additionally, nearly 30 Promise of Nursing fund-raising galas—sponsored by Johnson & Johnson, and hosted in cooperation with local and regional hospitals and health care organizations in cities and regions where the nursing shortage is most acute—have raised in excess of $12 million, funding 800 renewable student scholarships, 250 renewable faculty fellowships, and 150 nursing school grants. All funds raised stay within the cities and regions where the galas have been held.

"We don't believe it to be a coincidence that more of today's students are choosing to major in nursing," Higham added. "Of the 10 most popular college majors, nursing has moved from nearly the bottom of the list into the fourth ranking over the last few years. We've made great progress, but much more work remains to be done."

In the program's first five years, more than 500,000 men and women have entered the nursing profession. Despite the early success of the program, however, Johnson & Johnson officials admit that much still remains to be done to stave off a long-term health care crisis, as the perfect storm of aging baby boomers, retiring nurses, and a critical shortage of nursing faculty still lead the U.S. Health Resources and Services Administration to forecast one million nurse staffing vacancies by 2020.

In 2006, the White House awarded the 2004–2005 Ron L. Brown Award for Corporate Leadership to Johnson & Johnson for the Campaign for Nursing's Future. This award is presented to companies demonstrating a deep commitment to innovative initiatives, which give back to the greater community at large.

DISCUSSION QUESTIONS

1. Word association: Write a brief list of words and phrases with which you associated the concept of public relations (before you read Chapter 1 of this book.) They can be either positive or negative.

2. Can you think of any alternative definitions for public relations? Is there anything missing from the definition discussed on page 2 of this chapter?

3. In addition to those examples listed in the "Trends and Issues" section in this chapter, find other examples of the misuse of the term *public relations* or use of the abbreviation *PR* as slang.

4. After reading the history part of this chapter, compare the careers of Ivy Lee and Edward L. Bernays. If you could interview one of these men as part of your research for a term paper, which would you choose, and why?

5. Who are some of the more visible nonprofit organizations in the community? How can they do a better job of reaching out to college students?

GLOSSARY OF TERMS

Commercial campaigns. Used to promote a company's new products or services or the entire company. Also called a "rollout" campaign.

Educational campaigns. Conducted mostly by nonprofit organizations or other advocacy groups. Also called "public awareness campaigns."

Evaluative research. A form of public opinion research that measures the effectiveness of campaigns after their conclusion.

Flack. A derogatory term for a public relations professional, usually used by journalists.

Formative research. A form of public opinion research that provides information necessary to develop persuasive campaigns.

Hype. From the mathematical term *hyperbole,* often used to refer to an effort to exaggerate the importance of a trivial or routine product or event.

Integrated marketing communications (IMC). The method of combining advertising, public relations, and marketing functions into one department within an organization.

Persuasion. An effort to gain public support for an opinion or course of action.

Political campaign. A campaign designed to promote a political candidate or issue.

Propaganda. The attempt to have a viewpoint accepted on the basis of appeals other than the merits of the case.

Public relations. A management function that uses two-way communication to receive information from and give information to an organization's various publics. Often confused with *publicity.*

Publicity. A form of one-way communication that involves providing information to the audience with no formative research done in advance nor evaluative research done afterward.

Publics. Constituent groups with which an organization has relationships.

Reputation campaigns. A campaign aimed at improving how a company or organization is perceived by its publics. Also called an "image campaign."

Social action campaigns. A campaign that advocates a social issue or cause.

Spin. First coined by *Time* magazine in 1988, this slang term is used in a derogatory fashion to describe an effort to exaggerate positives while downplaying negatives.

CHAPTER 2

AN OVERVIEW OF THE PUBLIC RELATIONS PROCESS

THE THREE-STEP PROCESS

The traditional formula often taught in public relations classes has for many years been based on the four-step process of research, planning, communication, and evaluation. The shorthand version of this formula is (1) find out what needs to be done, (2) decide how to do it, (3) do it, and (4) measure how well it was done. One variation of the formula used the term *action* instead of *planning* to describe the second stage, thus creating the *RACE* acronym.

In developing this textbook, however, we discovered through conversations with working professionals that the four-step, or RACE, process is not the magic formula it was once thought to be, and that in the "real world" it is often difficult to apply the process. We found that the research and planning steps are often muddled together, with little or no visible dividing line. Another problem with the four-step process is that it is an oversimplification to plot it as a process that proceeds from left to right through the four stages, as though one could not return to the research phase once into the planning stage. In reality, the public relations process is seldom that linear.

We recognized that the formula components are not watertight compartments that require a person to move through the process in a straight line. For example, there may be a case in which a public relations professional gets to the communication stage and realizes he or she does not have all the information needed to choose the most effective tactics. Thus, the person will have to return to the planning stage (in this case, for more primary research) to determine the media habits of audiences. One popular textbook deals with this problem by using the labels of *linear model* and *dynamic model,* the latter being more common because of the necessity sometimes to "step back" in the process. The book uses the analogy of the public relations process as a square dance rather than a conga line.

For this book, however, we have instead consolidated the research and planning stages, and the result is a three-step process:

1. *Planning.* Research and analyze the problem in order to determine how to most effectively respond to it.
2. *Implementation.* Execute the response.

3. *Evaluation.* Measure the effectiveness of the response and determine what needs to be done next.

This book refers to this new model as the *PIE chart.* We, as well as many working professionals, believe this three-step model more accurately describes the campaign development process used in the real world.

Of course, no public relations plan exists only in an abstract form. All plans—whether developed by a professional public relations firm or by students in a college class—must be put into written form so that they may be revised, approved, and eventually implemented. The following section provides a suggested outline for how a written plan can be developed. The first version of the written plan is often vague and tentative, but each time it is revised, it becomes more specific.

Beginning in Chapter 3 and continuing through Chapter 10, the summary of a real-world public relations campaign designed by students is included at the end of each chapter, with each entry illustrating the parts of the campaign discussed in that chapter.

THE WRITTEN PROPOSAL: PLANNING

The planning section of the campaign proposal results from the completion of six tasks. In written form, the planning section includes (1) a summary of background research gathered, (2) lists of priority audiences, (3) a description of proposed methods for primary research, (4) a description of goals and objectives, (5) lists of messages and themes, and (6) descriptions of channels and strategies chosen. As this list indicates, background research must be gathered and summarized before steps 2 through 6 can be taken. Depending on the timetable developed, steps 2 through 6 may be turned in to the instructor together or separately.

Background Research

Background research is the first stage of the information-gathering process. It consists of preliminary fact finding and the gathering of information from secondary sources. Depending on the preferences of the client (or in the case of a class project, the professor), this section of the written plan may either provide all of the background information, or provide only a brief summary of the background information with instructions to the reader to consult the appendices for the detailed version.

Priority Audiences and Opinion Leaders

The terms *publics* and *audiences* are often confused. The difference is that **publics** refers to groups that one communicates with on an ongoing basis, and **audiences** refers to groups that will be the targets of a specific campaign.

For a corporation, publics typically include employees, retirees, customers, suppliers, retailers, vendors, unions, competitors, government regulators, stockholders, stock analysts, residents of the community where the company is located (especially if there is an environmental, economic, or traffic impact), and journalists who cover the industry. For nonprofit organizations, typical publics include members, volunteers, charity watchdog groups, individual and corporate donors and sponsors, and journalists who cover the issues in which the group is involved.

When developing a list of key audiences for a specific campaign, campaign planners should begin by asking: *Who are they attempting to reach?* It is unlikely that there will be only one audience. Typical audiences for a campaign include customers, potential customers, stockholders, stock analysts, employees, members (of a nonprofit organization or professional association), consumer advocacy groups, and environmental groups. The categories should be as narrow and specific as possible. For instance, "government" is too vague a term to describe an audience; more specific labels would include individual public officials, elected governmental bodies, or regulatory agencies.

When determining priority audiences, it is often helpful to identify **opinion leaders** for each group. Opinion leaders are individuals in a position to influence others by speaking, writing, or modeling behavior that is copied by others. *Formal opinion leaders* are those in positions such as elected public officials or individuals chosen to head unions, special-interest groups, or nonprofit organizations. Journalists often ask these people to comment on issues in the news. *Informal opinion leaders* are those individuals who are not in elected or appointed positions, but are able influence others because of personal characteristics such as charisma or assertiveness.

Opinion leaders can be male or female and are found in every racial, ethnic, social, and political group. Paul Lazarsfeld, the communication researcher who first developed the opinion leader theory, first applied this model to how voters made decisions about candidates and issues in the 1940s, and public relations professionals soon began applying it to fields other than politics.

Today, public relations professionals use this model in other types of campaigns by first identifying target audiences for their messages and then determining who those groups consider their opinion leaders.

The expansion of technology over the twentieth century has changed the nature of opinion leaders. In the early 1900s, for example, opinion leaders were most likely the town bankers, retailers, clergy, union stewards, and schoolteachers. Some of those individuals may still play that role today, but for some groups, their opinion leaders are more remote—such as television personalities, popular authors, newspaper columnists, national political leaders, and those expressing their opinions to large audiences via the Internet.

Opinion leaders in today's society typically share five characteristics. The first is that they tend to possess a higher degree of education than people around them. The majority have attended college, and many have gone on to graduate school.

The second characteristic is that they consume more media than other individuals and are usually more informed about current events and social trends. They tend to rely on daily newspapers more than on television for news, and when they watch television, they do so for the purposes of information rather than entertainment.

The third trait shared by today's opinion leaders is that they tend to be active in politics and community affairs. The majority attend public meetings, write letters to newspaper editors and elected public officials, work for special-interest groups, and serve on the boards of community associations and nonprofit organizations.

The fourth characteristic is that they are early adopters of new ideas. Within a list of friends, coworkers, or other persons considered to be members of a peer group, the first individual on that list to use email, own a cell phone, or design his or her own website, is also likely to be the group's opinion leader.

The fifth and perhaps most important characteristic is that they have the ability to influence people around them, either because of position (such as in the case of parents, employment supervisors, or union stewards), or personal qualities such as charisma or assertiveness.

Proposed Primary Research Methods and Research Objectives

This section of the written campaign proposal refers to the research that takes place after a written plan has been developed, but before any formal communication takes place. The term **primary research** refers to the process of getting information directly from the source, as opposed to **secondary research**, which is information already published or otherwise gathered by someone else.

Primary research is sometimes called **verification research** because it often answers most or all of the questions that could not be answered in the background research. It provides an opportunity either to confirm or refute preliminary assumptions and presents additional information that will be used in selecting the proper channels of communication. Examples of primary research, which will be addressed in detail in Chapter 4, include surveys, focus groups, interviews, and field observation. In the preliminary version of a campaign proposal, this section is written in future tense and describes which of those research methods you intend to use. It should be supported by appendices, such as preliminary drafts of survey instruments or a list of focus group questions.

This is followed by an explanation of **research objectives.** This should not be confused with the term *program objectives,* which refers to the desired outcomes for the program as a whole. *Research objectives* refers to the questions raised by background research that you hope to answer in primary research—for example, "to determine what factors go into the customer's purchasing decisions" or "to determine the level of confidence that community residents have in the mass transit system."

After the primary research has been conducted, this section is revised and rewritten in past tense to describe the research methods that were used and a summary of what was learned. The summary of information is given in narrative form in the text, and graphs, charts, and tables may be either inserted into the text or submitted as appendices.

Many public relations campaigns fail because the primary research was done poorly or not at all. Rushing into a persuasive campaign without conducting the appropriate amount of research could result in ineffective and misdirected efforts. There is also the occasional problem of going to the opposite extreme of conducting too much primary research. Over-analyzing a situation and spending too much time, money, and energy on research and preparation could result in depleted resources and time when one finally reaches the implementation stage. Some public relations experts explain this problem by using a baseball analogy about a pitcher who takes so long in his wind-up that he never delivers the pitch. The problem has also been referred to as the *paralysis of analysis.*

Once the primary research has been conducted and analyzed, this section of the written proposal can be removed from the proposal binder and replaced with a summary of results, written in past tense. The text of this section should include summaries of the information gathered through interviews, surveys, and focus groups. If the research produces a great deal of detail, the complete results should be included in one or more appendices.

Goals and Objectives

Goals and *objectives* are two other terms often confused. **Goals** are the broader, general outcomes one wants to see as a result of one's persuasive efforts. Generally, goals are not quantifiable. **Objectives** are the specific and measurable indicators of whether or not one has met one's goals. An example of a goal for a public relations campaign is "to improve the image of a city-run public hospital." An example of objectives supporting that goal might include increasing the name recognition of the hospital by a certain percentage or increasing the number of positive news stories about the hospital in the local media. The relationship between goals and objectives is covered in more detail in Chapter 5.

Messages and Themes

Messages and themes are the basic ideas that a public relations professional wants members of the audience to remember as a result of receiving his or her communication. They are similar to the product messages used in advertising campaigns, such as "low prices," "product quality," and "company reputation." **Themes** are the overarching ideas that apply to all of the audiences. In a public relations campaign for the city's mass transit system, for example, **key messages** may include "passenger safety" and "on-time performance," whereas a possible theme might be "the safe and reliable way to go to work."

Strategies and Channels of Communication

This subsection serves as a transition from the planning section to the implementation section. **Channels of communication** refers to the broad categories of communication methods (sometimes called "tools" or "tactics") that will be used. Examples of communication channels include news media, advertising, donated media, events, philanthropy programs, internal/employee communications programs, marketing activities, in-person communication, inserts and enclosures, and interactive media.

It is important to select the channels that have the best chance of reaching the audiences previously identified. One would obviously not buy radio advertising time during the morning drive time if research showed that the target audience works at night and is still asleep in the early morning. Likewise, one would not spend much time trying to attract the attention of newspaper reporters if they are dealing with audiences that get their news primarily from television.

The specific tools or tactics to be used from each broad category will be listed in the implementation section of this chapter.

Strategies refers to how categories will be combined or prioritized. Examples include "By working through the public school system, we will first . . ." or "By using a combination of news media and paid advertising, we will . . . ." The strategies section of the campaign may also include any special circumstances uncovered during research that need to be taken into account. For example, if a campaign involves a wide variety of members, it is likely that each audience views the organization differently and expects different benefits from the relationship. That means that the implementation stage must include a variety of tactics designed to account for the various relationships.

THE WRITTEN PROPOSAL: IMPLEMENTATION

The implementation section of the campaign proposal consists of two subsections: tactics and logistics.

Tactics

The **tactics** subsection will be the bulkiest part of the implementation section, as it will list all of the possible ideas for communicating with audiences. This is more detailed than the list of channels of communication. Instead of listing "news media," for example, one would list specifics, such as news conferences, satellite media tours, and editorial meetings. This section of the written proposal should be supported by a variety of appendices, including mock-ups of brochures, preliminary drafts of news releases, and schedules for events. Chapter 6 deals with tactics related to traditional media outlets such as print and broadcast media. Chapter 7 deals with interactive media tactics, mostly those associated with the Internet. Chapter 8 deals with those tactics not related to traditional or interactive media.

Logistics

The **logistics** subsection deals with the process of how the tactics will be executed, including budgeting, staffing, and a timetable or calendar. These are covered in more detail in Chapter 9.

THE WRITTEN PROPOSAL: EVALUATION

Public relations campaigns are major investments of both money and staff time. In order to continue getting money and staff time allocated for future campaigns, a professional communicator has to be able to prove that he or she is getting results. Like most sections of the written proposal, the evaluation section of the written plan is subject to constant revision. In the preliminary version of the written plan, or any revision that takes place before it is executed, the evaluation section is written in future tense, such as, "We will evaluate the campaign by the following methods . . . ." That introduction is followed by a list of research methods you expect to use when measuring campaign results.

The future-tense version of your evaluation section may be subdivided into ongoing evaluation and summative evaluation. **Ongoing evaluation** refers to methods of evaluation that can be done while the program is underway in order to revise or fine-tune it to deal with unexpected problems or wrong turns. **Summative evaluation** refers to the evaluation that is done immediately after the program's conclusion; it is often the most detailed part of the evaluation section.

After the campaign has run its course and the evaluation has taken place, the evaluation section of the proposal is revised into past tense—for example, "We evaluated the campaign by the following methods . . . ." That introduction is followed by a list of the research methods used and a summary of the results.

The final evaluation often includes a subsection titled **formative evaluation**, which describes how the information gathered in the evaluation can be used to get the most benefit out of the success of the campaign or to lay the groundwork for future programs.

In the preliminary versions of the proposal, written in future tense, the evaluation section describes what methods will be used to evaluate the campaign and is supported by preliminary drafts of surveys, comment cards, focus group questions, or other evaluative instruments. The final version of the evaluation section is written in past tense and describes how it was evaluated and provides a summary of the results. Appendices in the final version should include the detailed results of that evaluation.

A communications program is not complete until the results have been measured—until the communicator has listened as well as spoken. This is one element that separates public relations from journalism. Journalists prepare their material for transmission to the audience and then execute the transmission, but rarely receive any feedback except for the occasional letter or phone call from a reader or viewer offering praise or criticism. Newspapers conduct readership studies and television and radio stations hire consultants to conduct audience research, but seldom are the results used to the same extent as they are in public relations work.

THE LAST STEP

After the program has been executed and evaluated, the entire written proposal is revised and placed into a **program book** that can later be used to show off the department's or agency's good work. It can also be used to enter national or regional competitions sponsored by professional groups such as the Public Relations Society of America or the International Association of Business Communicators.

TRENDS AND ISSUES

Applying the Three-Step Process to Crisis Situations

In addition to using the planning–implementation–evaluation (PIE) model for a formal persuasive campaign, one can also use it in responding to a crisis. The only difference is that each of the steps and substeps is done in an accelerated time frame, and a few may be eliminated. For example, in a crisis situation, one does not have time to conduct formal primary research, so more emphasis is placed on the fact-finding step. The implementation step is also executed in an accelerated time frame.

After the crisis has been resolved, move into evaluation—the only part of the formula that can be executed without the accelerated time frame. Results of the evaluation should be compiled into a final report to be distributed to all parties affected by the crisis—employees, stockholders and stock analysts, government regulators, and the media, for example. A shorter version written in lay terms may be appropriate for current and potential customers.

After the successful resolution of a well-publicized crisis, many companies take the final report a step further by publishing self-congratulatory materials to tell their story. Examples include colorful, glossy booklets with titles such as "The Tylenol Comeback," published by Johnson & Johnson following its 1982 product tampering crisis, and "The Pepsi Crisis: What Went Right," after the soft-drink maker's 1993 product tampering hoax.

CASE STUDY 2

When a Crisis Strikes Campus: The Three-Step Process at Work

Three times in the last two decades, public relations professionals employed by large universities applied the three-step process, as well as other rules regarding crisis communications, in dealing with tragedies and other potential threats to their institutions' reputations. The first occurred at the University of Florida when five students were murdered in their off-campus apartments. In 2006–07, Duke University was in turmoil for more than a year as it dealt with the negative publicity stemming from allegations that members of its lacrosse team raped a stripper at a team party. Then, in April 2007, a mentally unstable student at Virginia Technological Institute killed 32 students and faculty members and then himself.

Because the University of Florida and Virginia Tech cases unfolded so rapidly, the planning stage in both cases consisted mainly of preliminary fact finding rather than formal primary research. At the fact-finding stage, university officials at both institutions worked quickly to find out the basic information about what happened and worked with law-enforcement officials to prepare for the arrival of local and national media. And in both cases, priority audiences included not only students but also their parents.

At the height of the tragedy at Florida, university President John Lombardi used student records to generate a mailing list of the students' home addresses and wrote a letter to the parents of the university's 36,000 students, informing them that the school was taking the necessary steps to protect their children. The primary goals of the university's response to the multiple murders were to (1) reduce the level of anxiety among students and their parents, (2) serve the needs of the news media covering the crisis, and (3) protect the university's reputation. Specific objectives included getting positive messages about the university's response in news coverage of the crisis and reducing the number of students withdrawing from the university out of fear. Lombardi's letter to the parents was only one part of the implementation stage.

The university took a number of other measures to respond to the crisis. Administrators allowed students to use a bank of telephones in the alumni office (usually used for fund-raising calls) to make free phone calls home. And because the murders took place in off-campus apartments, the university assisted students in moving into on-campus housing. The institution made another smart move by including student government representatives on the crisis response team, and it was one of the students' ideas that turned out to be among the most valuable suggestions heard during the implementation stage.

When students left campus on Friday afternoon to go home for the Labor Day weekend, university officials feared that many would not come back. Student Government President Mike Brown suggested a major news conference be moved from Monday to Sunday in order for the news to reach students who had gone home. The idea, Brown contended, was that students would make their decisions on Monday night as to whether to return to the campus, so it was important to reach them with encouraging news before they made that decision. To provide further encouragement to return, the university moved registration, financial aid, and other administrative deadlines until later in the semester. At the evaluation stage, university officials compiled information from numerous sources to measure the effectiveness of their response to the crisis. They made note of both the positives and negatives and produced a final report that could be used in the future at UF and other institutions. Linda Gray, the university's media relations officer, reported that keeping a daily journal of the details and events during the crisis made it easier for her to participate in the evaluation process. Also included in the evaluation were recommendations on what needed to be done next, such as encouraging media to do positive follow-up stories, including those highlighting improvements to campus safety.

At Virginia Tech, the story unfolded even faster, as the entire tragedy unfolded in a matter of hours rather than days. The public relations process, including following the basic rules of media relations, was helpful in dealing with an onslaught of national media coverage at a time when many university employees and students were themselves still in shock regarding what had happened. In the first two days after the tragedy, the media were praised for demonstrating restraint, good taste, and sensitivity. University officials, law-enforcement personnel, and media critics thanked the print and broadcast journalists and their employers for respecting the privacy of the families affected. Many critics commented that the media appeared to have learned from the mistakes they made in covering previous tragedies.

The university was closed for a week following the tragedy, and when students returned, the media became more aggressive in attempting to interview students who would have preferred to put the matter behind them and concentrate on resuming their education. A few days after their return to campus, many students posted signs on campus that read "Media go away."

In the aftermath of the tragedy, the administration of Virginia Tech established the Office of Recovery and Support to coordinate grief counseling services for students and family members, process the millions of dollars in donations that poured in to the university's fund-raising offices, and make decisions regarding what should be done for the long term to honor the students and faculty members who lost their lives. In all three areas, the ORS was able to take advantage of one communication channel that didn't exist at the time of the University of Florida tragedy—the Internet. Links on the university's website connected students and family members with sources for counseling and up-to-date information, gave alumni and other potential donors suggestions for directing their gifts toward specific projects, and provided numerous photo galleries that illustrated memorial services and other campus events related to the tragedy.

The Duke lacrosse case was different from both the UF and Virginia Tech cases in that the crisis unfolded over a period of several months. It began when an African American woman hired to perform as an exotic dancer accused three athletes of assaulting her

Students at Virginia Tech held a candlelight vigil to honor the 32 students and faculty members killed on April 16, 2007. Virginia Tech was one of several U.S. universities rocked by tragedy in recent years.

at an off-campus party. Those three athletes were arrested and charged with kidnapping and sexual assault. School officials cancelled the remainder of the lacrosse season, and the team's coach resigned.

In the months following the initial incident, stories in the national media mentioning the university increased from 3,700 per month to more than 33,000. Many of the media stories portrayed the case as one of contrasts—rich white students at an elite university against a lower-income African American student who attended a historically black institution in the same city. In the year that followed, the case against the athletes was dismissed after investigators found numerous inconsistencies in the accounts of the incident that were provided by the alleged victim and witnesses. In addition, the prosecutor in the case was forced to resign and was convicted of prosecutorial misconduct.

But the damage to Duke's reputation was already done. Both fund-raising and student-recruiting challenges became more difficult, and the term "Duke lacrosse case" became a regular part of the national vocabulary. However, university officials believe that, like Florida and Virginia Tech, the school will eventually recover. "I think the general public understands that this is a great institution and it's going through a tough period in a media frenzy," Vice President for Public Affairs John Burness told the Associated Press. "The ultimate test of Duke is how people perceive six months or a year from now how we dealt with this saga and how we handled it."

DISCUSSION QUESTIONS

1. A typical community organization is concerned with four major publics: its members, local media, local government, and residents of the community who are not members. But what if you worked for one of these other organizations?

2. If you worked for a public utility such as the telephone company or electric company, who would your publics be?

3. If you worked in the public affairs office at your university, who would your publics be?

4. Think about the student organizations you belong to or other campus activities in which you participate. What elements of the planning–implementation–evaluation formula do those groups use? If they do not apply any of these elements, from which do you think they might benefit?

    Find examples of persuasive campaigns through local media coverage. See how many components of the PIE formula you can spot.

GLOSSARY OF TERMS

Audience. A group designated as the target of a communications or persuasive campaign. Often confused with *public.*

Channels of communication. The broad categories of communication methods that will be used in a campaign.

Formative evaluation. The final stage of evaluating a program in which the evaluator describes how the information gathered can be used to get the most benefit out of the success of the campaign or to lay the groundwork for future programs.

Goals. The broad, general outcomes hoped for as a result of a persuasive campaign. Often confused with *objectives.*

Key messages. The basic ideas that campaign organizers want members of their audiences to remember as a result of receiving the communication.

Logistics. The process of how communication tactics will be executed, including budgeting, staffing, and timing considerations.

Objectives. The specific, measurable indicators of whether or not the goals of the program were met.

Ongoing evaluation. The methods of evaluation that can be done while a communication program is underway in order to revise or fine-tune it to deal with unexpected problems.

Opinion leaders. Individuals in a position to influence other members of an audience by speaking, writing, or modeling behavior copied by others.

Primary research. The process of seeking information directly from the source. Examples include surveys, interviews, focus groups, and field observation.

Program book. The finished version of a written campaign proposal, usually presented in a ringed binder or similar device.

Public. A group that affects, or is affected by, the actions taken by an organization. Often confused with *audience*.

Research objectives. The questions raised by background research that one hopes to answer in the primary research.

Secondary research. Informal methods of background research in which one gathers information that has already been published elsewhere.

Strategies. A description of how categories of communication tactics will be implemented, combined, or prioritized.

Summative evaluation. The evaluation of a campaign performed immediately after its conclusion.

Tactics. Specific methods of communication used to reach audiences of a persuasive campaign.

Theme. An overarching idea or principle on which a persuasive campaign is based.

Verification research. An alternative term for the type of primary research that takes place after a written plan has been developed, but before any formal communication takes place.

CHAPTER 3

PLANNING

Background Research

PRELIMINARY FACT FINDING

The initial step in planning any public relations campaign is to conduct background research. The information gathered is then used to determine key audiences and to set research objectives for the primary research to follow.

The first background research activities conducted are known as *preliminary fact finding*, which will include an initial client interview and archival research, which are then followed by one or more forms of secondary research. **Secondary research** refers to the types of research in which one gathers information that has been conducted by someone else. College students should already be familiar with this type of research because it is similar to the types of research conducted in most liberal arts courses, such as those dealing with history, psychology, and literature. This form of research must be done quickly, but it is more important that it be done correctly.

Initial Client Interview

Once a company or organization has chosen a public relations agency or given its current agency a new assignment, representatives of the agency meet with the client to discuss the task ahead. It is unlikely that any concrete decisions will be made at such a meeting; its purpose is to allow the opportunity for representatives of both sides to get acquainted and agree on general goals for the campaign. The meeting can take place at the agency's office, but it is better for agency representatives to visit the client's location in order to get a "feel" for the atmosphere. In the case of projects being conducted by an internal public relations department rather than an external agency, a preliminary meeting with the management of the company or organization takes the place of the client interview.

Archival Research

Archival research may include *external* documents, such as newsletters, annual reports, and other publications, or *internal* documents, such as memoranda, board meeting minutes, and information that summarizes the results of previous campaigns. Archival research will help in gathering the information necessary to answer the following questions:

> What is the client's history?
>
> What kind of products and services does this company or nonprofit organization provide? Of these, which is it best known for?
>
> How is the company organized in terms of management and leadership?
>
> Is the company privately held or publicly held?
>
> Is the organization government regulated? If so, what is the regulatory climate?
>
> Are the company's employees unionized?
>
> What is the competitive environment?
>
> What share of the market does the company hold?
>
> Is the organization a leader or follower in its industry?
>
> Does the company have a mission statement or an organizational philosophy?

Clients are sometimes reluctant to allow agency representatives to have access to internal documents because of security concerns, but most reputable agencies have confidentiality policies that prohibit employees from releasing a client's sensitive information. Many agencies take this idea a step further by providing confidentiality agreements—written assurances that the agency will take reasonable precautions to prevent the leaking of sensitive information. In addition, the ethical codes of the Public Relations Society of America and International Association of Business Communicators remind practitioners about their obligation to protect confidential information and materials.

Mass Media Sources

Mass media sources include articles from newspapers and magazines as well as transcripts and recordings of radio and television news broadcasts. The client may be able to provide some of this material, but additional research could uncover materials of which the client is not aware. Newspaper and magazine articles can be located at university or public libraries or through the Web, and reference librarians can help with the search. The best sources of general business information include publications such as *The Wall Street Journal, Business Week, Nation's Business, Time, Newsweek*, and *U.S. News and World Report*. For other topics, locate indexes that deal with the appropriate specialty publications. Most are available through search engines such as Lexis-Nexis, ProQuest, and EBSCOhost (discussed later in this chapter).

Television and radio news broadcasts are more difficult and costly to obtain (one must know the date of the broadcast in order to find and purchase transcripts or recordings). Also, the information seldom provides information not included in newspaper and magazine articles on the same topic.

Historical Research and Case Studies

The historical or case study approach involves locating problems or situations similar to the one facing the client or employer. Entire textbooks have been written on the famous cases in the history of public relations, and many include chapters dealing with categories such as crisis communications, issues management, government planning, health communications, environmental communications, customer relations, and employee relations. There are also monthly and quarterly public relations publications that chronicle the successes and failures of public relations programs in a similar variety of categories.

This form of research can also be conducted at a university or public library, but is more likely to be found in books than in newspapers or magazines. Case studies are often more valuable than mass media sources because in addition to the basic facts, they also include analysis and commentary from experts. Sources for case studies include academic journals in the field of business and communications, news and business magazines, and *CQ Researcher* (discussed later in this chapter).

Databases and Internet Sources

Research companies and other organizations can provide demographic, economic, and scientific information in databases that can be purchased on either a one-time basis or by annual subscription. The data can be provided on disks. In addition, other research companies provide information through their websites. Many provide a summary of the information at no cost and charge a fee for more detailed versions. A number of research companies provide access to their password-protected databases by annual subscription. Many public and university libraries have on-line sources for similar information, but it is typically not as detailed or current as the information available from research companies.

The Web and other Internet sources may be helpful in tracking social issues and trends. These sources can provide easy access to free or inexpensive information and can produce valuable leads for other sources of information on the same topics. Internet research is only one part of a well-designed research plan. Many professional and industry publications and databases are still available only in bound books or on CD-ROMs.

Although the Internet may reduce the amount of time spent visiting the library in person, it cannot take the place of it. Relying solely on the Internet for background research is shortsighted and dangerous. Information on the Internet is often unreliable because it has not gone through the same editorial process as more traditional published sources. As a result, information gathered from the Internet must be scrutinized and examined for evidence of bias and distortion.

The best information on the Web comes from sites sponsored by universities, government agencies, and professional and industry associations. Although perhaps not subject to the same scrutiny as published sources, the information tends to be of high quality. Public relations representatives must be cautious in using information from websites or bulletin boards sponsored by special-interest groups and so-called think tanks. The information is often slanted to support the sponsoring organization's point of view, and it is often too difficult to separate fact from opinion in the content provided.

Government Sources

Many state and federal governmental agencies provide demographic, economic, and scientific information either on paper, computer disk, CD-ROM, or microfilm. They also provide their data on-line by annual subscription.

University and Scientific Studies

Universities and other institutions often publish the results of their research on paper, CD-ROMs, or microfilm. The best way to locate such information is through organizations' websites.

IDENTIFYING PRIORITY AUDIENCES

After the preliminary fact finding is complete, the information can be used to develop a list of priority audiences for the campaign. When the implementation and evaluation sections of the preliminary proposal are complete, it is helpful to keep referring to this list to make sure each of those audiences is involved throughout the campaign. Some ideas for identifying and reaching audiences are discussed next.

Using Demographics and Psychographics

The terms *demographics* and *psychographics* are often confused, but they refer to different methods for categorizing individuals. **Demographics** is the science of grouping individuals by characteristics over which individuals have little or no control, such as age, gender, race, and ethnicity. **Psychographics** is the science of grouping individuals by their lifestyle choices over which they do have control, such as level of education, occupation, income, housing choice, marital status, family size, religion, and recreational and entertainment choices.

In recent years, the marketing research industry has focused its attention on five significant demographic groups.

1. *Seniors* represent a category of individuals roughly defined as those aged 50 and over, although some observers contend that because life expectancy keeps increasing, "60 and over" may be a more accurate dividing line. In terms of media habits, seniors tend to prefer daily newspapers and lifestyle magazines over television and radio. They have more leisure time, travel more, and perform more volunteer work. They are also brand loyal, more resistant to change, and less likely to buy on impulse than younger audiences. Within this category is a subcategory called the *elderly,* roughly defined as those aged 80 and older. They share many of the same characteristics as the larger group, except many have more limited incomes and greater health care costs. They are highly sought after by providers of health insurance and pharmaceutical products.

Until recently, this segment of the consumer market was largely ignored by companies selling computer hardware and software, but now those same companies indicate that it is the fastest-growing segment of their customer base, as seniors are purchasing computers and computer-related services. According to market research, seniors use the Internet for much the same reasons as their younger counterparts—email, Web surfing, shopping, bill paying, discussion groups related to public affairs and their hobbies, and social networking.

One of the smallest demographic subcategories in the United States—but the fastest growing—is the *very elderly,* those aged 100 and older and who, in many cases, have outlived their children.

2. *Baby boomers* is a term originally used to describe the 78 million Americans born between 1946 and 1964. Although that definition is still used occasionally, most demographers and market researchers now limit its application to those individuals born in the 1950s and early 1960s (otherwise, persons born in the late 1940s would be both "baby boomers" and "seniors"). When this category was first recognized, marketers realized that their tastes in music, food, and fashion could influence popular culture, but now politicians, many of whom consider themselves part of that group, are feeling their influence. Facing retirement, they are concerned with issues such as health care and financial security, and they vote in large numbers. As of early 2008, that age group represents about 40 percent of the U.S. population but accounts for more than 60 percent of consumer spending.

3. *Midlifers,* sometimes called "thirty-somethings," are those individuals born between the mid-1960s and early 1970s. Most are recently established in their careers, have started families, and do not have as much leisure time as seniors. They are also facing financial concerns such as paying off student loans, purchasing their first homes, planning for retirement, and, in some cases, caring for aging parents. Midlifers tend to consume both entertainment and news media and are politically active.

4. *Generation X,* sometimes called "twenty-somethings," are typically the children of the early baby boomers. They are the demographic group most sought after by advertisers because they purchase automobiles and clothing in large quantities. Because they watch more hours of prime-time television (including music video channels and reality programs) than the other three groups, advertisers spend a great deal of their budgets on that medium.

Recent demographic research indicates a number of trends concerning this age group. According to researchers, these individuals are less likely to become pregnant, commit crime, or use tobacco products and illegal drugs; they are also more interested in performing volunteer work; and they tend to work at two or more jobs simultaneously and delay marriage until later in life. Another interesting aspect of this age group is that the percentage of college graduates moving back in with their parents nearly doubled (from 11 percent to 20 percent) between 1970 and 2006. According to demographic researchers, the most common reasons behind the trend are the increasing amount of student loan debt and the increase in their level of uncertainty about their futures. Those who do not move back into their parents' homes are nevertheless unsettled, as nearly 25 percent had four or more addresses in the first five years following college graduation.

When asked about the news events having the most impact on their lives, most Generation Xers respond, "September 11 (terrorist attacks)" and "the war in Iraq." Demographers also describe this group as more cynical about politics (yet ironically, more likely to vote than in past generations) and more focused on instant gratification and the short-term results of their work and behaviors. Employers interviewed about the work habits of their

Generation X employees report that the major weakness in their work habits is their inability to think long term.

5. *Generation Y* refers to the children of the late baby boomers and are mostly teenagers and preteens. They tend to spend their money on clothing and entertainment. This group consumes a large quantity of entertainment media and are easily influenced by advertising messages, especially those delivered by their pop-culture idols. They consume news media to a lesser degree than the other four groups, however. Much like their older brothers and sisters, many Generation Y children tell market researchers their life goals are "to be rich and famous." Children of Generation Y also tend to be more optimistic than their older siblings and parents. Opinion researchers report that more than 80 percent of children in this age group say they are optimistic about their futures, whereas for older children the percentage is typically 60 to 70 (for adults, the percentage is 50 to 60). Child psychologists report that many of today's teenagers focus more on themselves than others, a phenomenon that many describe as "it's all about me."

*"Take a load off, Leonard—we're watching
Generations X and Y duke it out."*

Looking at demographic categories based on age—as well as those based on race or nationality—are helpful to some extent, but doing so is not without its drawbacks. Professional communicators are sometimes guilty of making three incorrect assumptions regarding demographic categories.

The first false assumption is that all members of a demographic category share the same beliefs and behaviors. Examples include all seniors are tight with their money and skeptical about new technology, and younger individuals are selfish and more interested in themselves than others. In extreme cases, excessive dependence on generalities may result in stereotyping, an issue dealt with in more detail in Chapter 13.

The second false assumption is that demographic characteristics are the sole factor influencing an individual's behavior. An example would be concluding that the 142 college students (out of a sample of 200) reporting they did not vote in the last presidential election was due solely to their age and therefore the results reinforced the belief that college students were politically apathetic. In reality, the failure of those 142 students to vote may have been based on a number of factors unrelated to their age.

The third incorrect assumption is that there is such a thing as an "average" or "typical" member of any demographic group. Therefore, when presenting the results of background research (either orally or in writing), a professional communicator should avoid saying or writing that "the average teenager listens mostly to rap music" or "the typical Asian American quickly adapts to new technology."

Demographic information is available from government sources such as the United States Census Bureau and various state and county agencies. Also, an annual reference book titled *Sourcebook of Zip Code Demographics* provides information on every zip code in the country, listing percentages of the population by age, gender, race, and ethnicity.

In the area of psychographics, public relations professionals are able to capitalize on the research produced by the advertising and marketing industries. Much of this research is based on determining two factors: how individuals consume media and how they make purchasing decisions. One of the more common systems was developed in the 1980s by SRI International and is currently run by SRI Consulting Business Intelligence (SRIC-BI). The VALS™ system segments U.S. adult consumers into eight primary groups on a grid called a VALS Chart. This information is provided in Case Study 3 at the end of this chapter.

Using Existing Groups and Networks

Public relations professionals often use the term **prepackaged** to refer to audiences that can be reached through their affiliations. Students can be reached through their school groups; professionals such as doctors, lawyers, and teachers can be reached through associations to which they belong; business leaders can be reached through the local chamber of commerce; and seniors can be reached through groups such as the American Association of Retired Persons. Working through the leadership of such groups, one can attend meetings, place information in the groups' publications, and gain access to membership mailing lists. This can facilitate two-way communication by using such connections to gather information during the primary research and evaluation stages, and disseminate information during the implementation stage.

Including the Media

The media will always be an important audience because they serve as the connection to many other audiences. Rather than just using the broad category of "media," it is more effective to categorize the media by their specialty areas: sports writers, business writers, health care reporters, or editorial page editors.

PROPOSED PRIMARY RESEARCH METHODS AND RESEARCH OBJECTIVES

The next step in conducting research for your public relations campaign is to choose which primary research methods to use for finding additional information from the designated key audiences. Examples of primary research include surveys, questionnaires, focus groups, interviews, and field observation, which are covered in more detail in Chapter 4. In the preliminary version of the campaign proposal, this section is written in future tense and describes which of those research methods you intend to use. This section should be supported by appendices such as preliminary drafts of survey instruments or lists of focus group questions.

Next is an explanation of research objectives. This should not be confused with the term **program objectives**, which refers to the desired outcomes for the program as a whole. **Research objectives** refers to the questions raised by the background research that will be answered in the primary research. Research objectives tend to fall into four broad categories:

1. *Consumer Habits and Purchasing Decisions.* What does the audience do? Why does the audience do it? What would motivate the audience to change?
2. *Media Habits.* Which types of media does the audience consume? How much credibility does the audience attach to each type of media?
3. *Attitudes, Beliefs, and Opinions.* What are the audience's opinions? How are those opinions influenced? Who are the audience's opinion leaders (family, friends, professionals, political leaders, coworkers)?
4. *Existing Knowledge.* How much do the audiences already know about the product or issue?

SOURCES OF BACKGROUND INFORMATION

The most popular sources for background research can be divided into two categories: traditional news sources (available free to everyone) and specialized sources (available by subscription). Traditional news sources for public relations professionals most commonly include national daily newspapers (the most influential being *The Wall Street Journal*) and weekly magazines such as *Time, Newsweek, U.S. News & World Report,* and *Business Week.* Another example is *CQ Researcher*, a weekly publication of *Congressional Quarterly* magazine. Once titled *Editorial Research Reports, CQ Researcher* deals with a variety of controversial topics facing society and does so from an unbiased perspective. For each topic, it provides background information about the controversy, a summary of the arguments made by both sides, and sources of additional information

Specialized sources available on a subscription basis include InfoTrac, Lexis-Nexis, and ProQuest. InfoTrac is an on-line library providing access to millions of full-length articles from scholarly and popular periodicals since 1980. Professors and students can access the database via the Internet (www.infotrac.com). Lexis-Nexis provides access to more than 7,000 newspapers, newsletters, magazines, trade journals, wire services, and broadcast transcripts on general, business, legal, and trade news. LEXIS, the legal part of the database, provides access to federal and state case law, statutes, and secondary sources. Many documents are available in full text (www.lexisnexis.com). ProQuest provides the user with access to thousands of full-text periodicals and newspapers since 1986. Billions of pages are added daily as the interface digitalizes its microfilm collection (www.proquest.com).

Two national polling organizations provide information on a subscription basis. The Gallup Organization (www.gallup.com) is best known for providing polling data on political issues, but it also includes a variety of other topics, including those related to business, sports, and entertainment. In addition to the most current polls, an annual subscription also provides access to several decades worth of polling data. A feature on the company's website titled "Gallup A–Z" provides an alphabetical listing of every topic on which the company has polled in recent decades in reverse chronological order. A researcher wishing to examine how public opinion on a specific issue has changed over the last 30 years can access a number of polls taken over that time period and will be able to spot trends and shifts in opinion on that issue. Similar services are provided by the Pew Research Center (www .pewresearch.org).

WRITING THE BACKGROUND RESEARCH SUMMARY

There are two important keys to writing an effective summary of the preliminary fact finding. The first is to emphasize any information discovered that runs counter to common belief or that is likely to surprise clients or others who read the proposal. Here are three examples:

1. A public relations professional is conducting research on the issue of missing children to plan an informational campaign for a nonprofit organization working on that problem. Because of the issue's media coverage, many people believe that missing children are abducted by sinister figures or child molesters. Through her research, however, the professional discovers that only a small percentage of missing children are abducted by strangers; the majority are taken by separated or divorced parents involved in custody battles.
2. Because of effective public service campaigns developed by the National Park Service ("Only you can prevent forest fires"), the majority of Americans believe that careless campers are responsible for starting forest fires. But government reports and scientific studies indicate that lightning is the leading cause of forest fires, and careless campers are a distant second.

3. Shoplifting remains a serious problem for retailers, but crime statistics reveal that retailers lose far more of their merchandise to employee theft or "inside jobs" than they do to theft by outsiders.

The second key to writing effectively is to use lay terms. Even if the campaign deals with a complex topic, the research summary should not read like an academic research paper. The majority of people reading the proposal will not be doctors, scientists, or engineers, so you should avoid medical, scientific, or technical vocabulary. Also avoid footnotes, endnotes, or other formal types of attribution. It is better to use less formal attributive phrases, such as *wrote, said*, and *according to*. Use *wrote* if quoting from an article or book, *said* if quoting from an interview or speech, and *according to* if quoting from a source with no specific author, such as a government report or university study.

Regardless of how and where the information is found, credit must be given to the proper sources. Quoting from government or university studies is common in public relations research; it saves time and helps avoid "re-inventing the wheel." Few sources will object to the use of their scientific studies (most will be flattered), but readers of the proposal should be aware of the source of the information and not led to believe that it was conducted by the public relations professional.

TRENDS AND ISSUES

Lifestyle Trends of the Twenty-First Century

In addition to the five categories listed earlier in this chapter, demographers have also noted five "lifestyle trends" of the 1990s and early 2000s that affect consumer behavior.

1. *Larger Families with More Children.* Unlike the 1970s and 1980s, a time during which advances in the science of contraception led to fewer children being born and families being smaller, the 1990s and early 2000s have seen a trend toward young couples having more children. The result is the need for more schools and the development of larger markets for products such as children's clothing and toys as well as services such as child day care and pediatric medicine.

2. *Two-Career Couples.* A trend that began in the 1980s, this phenomenon is almost the norm in most communities. The result is the need for companies to develop policies regarding maternity leave and other forms of long-term leave (in addition to those mandated by federal law) and an increase in the need for child day care and related services.

3. *Blended Families.* Portrayed in popular culture as far back as the 1960s (by television programs such as *The Brady Bunch* and movies such as *Yours, Mine, and Ours*), this trend is now common in society, as divorcées with children marry other divorcés with children. The result is increased need for family counseling services and the potential for companies to develop or expand their employee assistance programs to include family-related counseling services.

4. *Parents Living with Their Children.* First portrayed on television by the 1990s television comedy series *Frasier*, the reality of the role reversal is no laughing matter. The rapid growth of the senior demographic category, and in some cases their inability to care for themselves, means that more midlifers and baby boomers will soon be caring for their aging parents. Many seniors resist the traditional nursing home environment, which means the need for more modern medical services such as "independent living" and "assisted living" facilities and similar services is likely to decrease.

5. *Exurbia.* This term was recently coined to refer to residential communities that are too far away from metropolitan areas to be called "suburbs" but not so far that they have separate identities. Exurbs are typically located 20 to 50 miles outside of major cities and have populations of 10,000 to 70,000. They are large enough to have their own local governments and law-enforcement agencies, but are still dependent on the larger city for employment, entertainment, and recreation. Examples include Sanford, Florida (near Orlando), Marietta, Georgia (near Atlanta), and Murfreesboro, Tennessee (near Nashville). Once called "bedroom communities," these cities often lack major employers of their own; therefore, the majority of their residents work in the larger cities nearby. The results of this trend include longer commutes, less leisure time, and more stress on families.

CASE STUDY 3

The Eight Types of Americans*

TYPE	PURCHASING HABITS	MEDIA HABITS
Innovators	Skeptical of advertising. Enjoy the "finer things." Receptive to new products, technologies, and methods of distribution.	Frequent readers of a wide variety of publications. Light television viewing.
Thinkers	Above-average consumers of products for the home. Little interest in image or prestige.	Watch educational and public affairs programs. Read widely and often.
Achievers	Attracted to premium products; prime target for variety of products.	Average TV watchers. Read business, news, and self-help material.
Experiencers	Spend much of disposable income on socializing. Pay attention to advertising. Buy on impulse. Follow fashion and fads.	Listen to rock music. Heavy consumers of fashion magazines.
Believers	Buy American. Slow to change habits. Look for bargains.	Watch TV more than average; read retirement, home/garden, and general interest magazines.
Strivers	Limited discretionary income, but carry credit card balances. Spend on clothing and personal-care products.	Prefer TV to reading.
Makers	Shop for comfort, durability, value. Not impressed by luxuries; buy the basics.	Read auto, home mechanics, fishing, and outdoor magazines. Listen to radio.
Survivors	Use coupons and watch for sales. Trust advertising. Brand loyal.	Watch TV. Read tabloids and women's publications.

The C-BI website features an on-line test consisting of 44 multiple-choice questions that visitors can take in order to determine which VALS ™ group they belong to. The web address is www.sricbi.com/VALS/ presurvey.shtml. This address changes periodically, so if the address does not work, you can find the site using a keyword search with the search terms "values and lifestyles."

TRACKING THE CASE: COLLEGE STUDENTS AND CREDIT CARD DEBT

Chapters 3 through 10 each include segments of a hypothetical student-produced public relations campaign proposal. The student team, as part of an advanced public relations class, spent the semester researching the problem of credit card debt among college students for a fictional nonprofit organization, Credit Counselors of Mason County.

Planning—Background Research

Initial Client Interview.   The team invited the director of the Credit Counselors of Mason County (CCMC) to come to campus and make a presentation about the problem of credit card debt in the general population. The director admitted that she had no specific information concerning how credit card debt affected college students, but told the group she suspected that demographics was likely to be one contributor to the problem. Later, the team visited the offices of the CCMC to ask follow-up questions and meet other staff members. During this meeting, the director mentioned that in addition to other nonprofit organizations providing similar services, there were also a number of for-profit companies involved in the business. Although some of those were reputable, there were a number of others that were not, and many charged large up-front fees and delivered questionable results.

Archival Research.   On their visit to the agency's offices, the students were given access to a variety of additional materials, including some information from other agencies that gave detailed demographic data regarding individuals seeking help from credit card counseling services. Consistent with the information provided by the director, there was no helpful information regarding the college audience. Some of the data referred to the 18–25 age category (many of whom would be college students), but there was no information to indicate if college students were any different from nonstudents in the same age group in respect to their vulnerability to credit card debt.

Mass Media Sources.   The team collected a number of articles from mass media sources such as national news magazines and business publications. The students were able to locate one recent article in a national professional journal read by professors and university administrators. The article provided some of the statistical data the team sought, and was also pertinent because it spread the blame for the problem of college students accruing credit card debt among three parties: the students themselves (for not being more responsible), the credit card companies (for their "predatory" practices), and the university administrators (for allowing credit card companies to solicit on campus, both in-person and through applications inserted into bookstore shopping bags). The articles reported that credit card debt is a growing problem among college students and is likely to become a greater problem as tuition continues to rise. The articles also mentioned that credit card debt, as reported on an individual's credit report, is a factor that may reflect negatively on new college graduates as they are subjected to pre-employment screening during the job-hunting process.

Historical Research and Case Studies.   The team found no examples from this category dealing directly with the issue of credit card debt among college students, but did find a number of case studies regarding how college students respond to other campaigns related to their personal behavior, such as those related to study skills, dating behavior, and physical and mental health.

Database and Internet Sources.   The team found no examples from this category (and the heading was eliminated from the proposal).

Government Sources.   The team found no examples from this category (and the heading was eliminated from the proposal).

Credit card debt is a major problem for college students in today's economy. "Tracking the Case: College Students and Credit Card Debt" presents a hypothetical public relations campaign aimed at addressing the problem.

University and Scientific Studies. The team located one university study addressing the issue that included data regarding college students. The study, published in a journal widely read by university administrators and education researchers, indicated that as a whole, college students are more likely (than nonstudents in the same age group) to accrue credit card debt because of their exposure to on-campus credit card promotions and the temptation to use credit cards to pay their college-related expenses.

Priority Audiences
The team established that the university's students would be the obvious priority audience, but it also saw the need to include other individuals with whom students interact on a daily basis, such as professors and residence hall advisors; and those they seek out for advice on academic and personal problems, such as academic counselors and employees in the university's student counseling service.

The students' written product for the above sections included summaries of the results of each of the research activities (including a source list) and a list of the priority audiences. Appendices included photocopies of the most pertinent news articles and reports.

DISCUSSION QUESTIONS

1. What research skills have you learned in college (writing term papers, etc.) that you believe will be helpful in public relations work?

2. This chapter provided three examples of information gathered during the planning phase that run counter to common belief. Do you know of other examples?

3. Either at home or in your school's computer lab, take the VALS™ test that is described in Case Study 3 and be prepared to discuss the results with the class. The web address changes periodically, so if the URL is not current, find the site using the search engine of your choice and the key word *VALS*.

GLOSSARY OF TERMS

Archival research.   Research such as newsletters or meeting minutes to help with gathering information needed to answer research questions.

Demographics.   A method of categorizing people by grouping individuals by characteristics over which individuals have little or no control such as gender.

Prepackaged.   Refers to audiences that can be reached through their affiliations, such as their school groups.

Program objectives.   The desired outcomes of the program as a whole.

Psychographics.   A method of categorizing individuals by grouping individuals by their lifestyle choices over which they have control, such as the level of education.

Research objectives.   Questions raised by the background research that one hopes to answer during the verification research.

Secondary research.   Informal methods of background research in which one gathers information that has already been published elsewhere.

■ ■ ■ ■ ■

CHAPTER 4

PLANNING

Primary Research

PRIMARY RESEARCH METHODS

Artemus Ward, an eighteenth-century English educator and humorist, once said, "It ain't what we don't know that hurts us. What hurts us is what we think we know that ain't so."

Bad grammar aside, Ward's quote is valuable for public relations professionals. Paraphrased, it means that it may be dangerous to operate with an absence of information, but it may be even worse to operate on information believed to be correct that is actually false. Applying that quote to the public relations field warns of the dangers of not conducting effective primary research prior to conducting a campaign.

One illustration of this danger is an anecdote about a retail business owner who hired a public relations agency to help expand his customer base. In the initial client interview, the retailer told the account executive that the decline in his business was due to the bad grooming habits of his employees; he wanted the agency to design a campaign to encourage employees to pay more attention to their clothing and appearance. The agency skipped over the primary research stage (since the client had already pinpointed the problem) and proceeded directly into the campaign. After the campaign ran its course and was evaluated, there was no improvement in the store's business. It turned out that the decline in customers was not due to the employees' appearance; it was because the store was located in an unsafe neighborhood, its parking lot was covered with litter, it was not open during the right hours, and its aisles were always cluttered and disorganized. But because the agency did not conduct the type of primary research that would have indicated those other problems, the campaign addressed the wrong problem and was a failure.

Employees of public relations agencies are trained to listen to their clients and to take their opinions and observations into consideration, but it is dangerous to assume that the client's perspectives are accurate. Agency employees should include the client's assumptions in their preliminary fact finding, but should always double-check those assumptions using primary or verification research.

An effective research program can measure and evaluate the credibility of information that is in circulation about an organization, the benefit of positive information, and the potential for damage caused by negative information. Research can help an organization spend its resources wisely and avoid spending them addressing nonexistent issues.

There are two general categories of research that public relations professionals deal with: qualitative and quantitative. **Qualitative research** is a category of research methods that are used when general information, rather than specific results, is needed. The results are expressed in words. **Quantitative research** is a category of research tools used when precise results are needed. The results are expressed in numbers or statistics.

QUALITATIVE RESEARCH

In-Depth Interviews

In-depth interviews are conducted one on one with a sample of a target audience. Generally, they are impractical for large audiences because a small sample would not provide a reliable result, and too large a sample would be too costly and time consuming to interview. They are, however, effective in cases in which audiences are extremely small and a few representatives may speak for the group, such as government officials or leaders of special-interest groups. Other possible applications include dealing with highly personal topics, such as personal finances, sexual behavior, or drug use; interviewing persons reluctant to speak openly because of the discussion of confidential business information; or dealing with a topic that is too complex to be discussed within the time limitations of a focus group.

Focus Groups

A **focus group** (short for "focused group interview") is a meeting with 10 to 12 members of a target audience in a conference room setting, conducted by an experienced moderator. Focus groups are not only relatively inexpensive (compared to other research methods) but they can also save money for a client or organization when used effectively. In advertising and marketing research, for example, a focus group may cost a few thousand dollars to implement, but it may save a company hundreds of times that amount by preventing the implementation of advertising or marketing campaigns that are either ineffective or offensive to an audience.

For nonprofit organizations, focus groups can help define problems, gather reaction to proposed solutions to those problems, and identify underlying reasons for differences that exist between an organization and its publics. For companies, focus groups can also be used to gather feedback on proposed products and services, test proposed changes in packaging, measure reaction to proposed advertising messages, and seek answers to other marketing-related questions.

Because of their shortcomings, focus groups are seldom used as the sole method for collecting information; they are most effective when combined with other research techniques. They can be used to help refine proposed survey questions or to interpret the results of a survey if they seem ambiguous, contradictory, or otherwise unclear.

History of Focus Groups.   Focus groups are often associated with marketing research, but they were not widely used for that purpose until the 1960s. The methodology actually began in the early 1940s, when media theorist and researcher Paul Lazarsfeld began group interviews as part of a Columbia University research project to measure how and why people listened to the radio, and how much influence radio news and radio entertainment had on audiences. One of his assistants, Robert K. Merton, then used similar methods on behalf of the Army during World War II. Merton and his researchers used the group interview method to help the Army evaluate the effectiveness of its training and morale films.

By the late 1940s and early 1950s, other researchers, including Edward L. Bernays, used similar techniques to help nonprofit organizations and social service agencies improve their images. Market researchers began using focused group interviews (later shortened to "focus groups") in the late 1950s. Today, it is estimated that researchers conduct more than 150,000 focus group research projects a year. The bulk of the research is still related to marketing objectives, but focus groups are also popular among public relations professionals dealing with problems unrelated to the marketing function.

Focus group research has an image problem today, caused by the deceptive practice of using focus group invitations to lure unsuspecting persons to attend thinly disguised sales presentations. Real estate companies sometimes invite individuals to meetings by describing them as "focus group research to determine people's attitudes toward vacations and leisure time," but many turn out to be sales pitches for time-sharing properties. Some pharmaceutical companies invite doctors to meetings labeled "focus group sessions," but many turn out to be sales pitches for those companies' products.

Although no one is claiming that the problem has reached crisis proportions, researchers who make their living by organizing legitimate focus group sessions are concerned that if the image problem gets worse, the potential pool for focus group participants may dry up. In the interim, the only step that legitimate focus group researchers can take is to promise participants that when researchers issue the invitation, the session is legitimate public opinion research and not a sales presentation in disguise.

One of the most common and legitimate applications of the focus group method is **gap research**. Nonprofit organizations, membership associations, and social service agencies conduct gap research among members or constituents to help measure strengths and weaknesses and determine what must be done to better serve those audiences. The three basic questions asked are: What are we doing well? What are we not doing well? What is it that we should be doing that we are not doing now?

Who Uses Focus Groups?   Focus group methodology has a wide variety of applications for a wide variety of clients. Among the most common applications are testing the potential of proposed new products, generating ideas for improving existing products, and choosing questions to be used in quantitative studies.

One example of the product-testing application of focus groups involves the use of that methodology to improve the written instructions that accompanied child safety seats used in automobiles. After realizing that many parents found the directions confusing, a major manufacturer organized focus group sessions during which parents were asked to strap their children into the seats and then advise researchers as to how the directions could have been better written. As compensation, participating couples were given free car seats for their children's use.

Other examples of clients and their applications of focus group research follow:

CLIENT	RESEARCH OBJECTIVES
Membership organizations	Positioning studies; evaluating recruitment and retention strategies; gap research
Charities	Determining fund-raising potential among target audiences
Social service agencies	Needs assessment studies; gap research
Colleges and universities	Evaluating student recruiting strategies; measuring alumni attitudes and perceptions
Advertising and marketing departments	Evaluating potential for new products, product names, packaging, slogans, and jingles; learning about customer habits and usage; improving existing products
Public relations departments	Measuring public perception; measuring employee morale; evaluating publications
Newspapers and magazines	Evaluating content and design; measuring readership habits and attitudes
Public utilities	Evaluating factors such as quality of service and billing procedures
Television consultants	Evaluating on-air talent
Movie studios	Testing audience reactions to possible endings of unfinished films
Political candidates	Testing potential campaign strategies
Jury consultants	Using "mock juries" to develop trial strategies (see Case Study 4B)

Advantages of Focus Groups.   Focus groups have their limitations, but many public opinion researchers believe their positives far outweigh the negatives. Advantages include:

1. *Cost and Speed.* Focus groups are cheaper and faster than formal opinion polls; they are relatively inexpensive and can be assembled on short notice. The client can get information directly from members of the target audience without waiting for results to be processed by third parties.
2. *Opportunity for Probing.* Focus groups provide researchers the opportunity to ask follow-up or clarifying questions.
3. *Breadth and Depth of Responses.* Focus groups provide the range and depth of feeling and emotions that are not possible with written questionnaires.
4. *Effectiveness with Special Audiences.* Focus groups are effective for working with children, the elderly, and the illiterate, or other audiences who might be unable or unwilling to complete a written questionnaire.
5. *Visual Stimuli.* Focus groups provide the opportunity to use visual stimuli such as product samples, printed images, video, or other audiovisual presentations.
6. *Sense of Security.* Even though they typically call for the discussion of issues in a room full of strangers, many participants are remarkably candid and will often

provide information they might not tell an individual researcher. Experts believe this effect is due to participants feeling that their opinions are similar to others in the group, and they are not fearful of rejection or confrontation.

7. *Serendipity and Spontaneity.* Ideas will sometimes seem to come out of nowhere. Even though this seldom happens with specifics, such as the development of new products, ideas with less tangibility, such as suggestions for new services or policies, may emerge from a well-run focus group session.

Disadvantages and Limitations of Focus Groups. Critics of focus groups (usually those who prefer more quantitative methods) point out the following negatives:

1. *Lack of Quantifiable Results.* Unlike surveys, the results of focus groups cannot be quantified and applied to the larger population.
2. *Tendency to Overinterpret the Results.* Focus groups are not a panacea that can solve all of the client's problems in 90 minutes.
3. *Domination by a Few Participants.* One or two members may dominate a poorly moderated focus group.
4. *Courtesy Bias.* Participants sometimes tend to provide answers they know will please and/or not offend the moderator or other participants.
5. *Possible Sampling Errors.* A focus group represents a relatively small group of individuals, and their opinions might not accurately represent the potential users of a product or service being discussed. This problem can be reduced or eliminated, however, if the participants in the group are carefully chosen and screened.

Mechanics of Focus Groups. The timing and location of focus group sessions are critical to their success. For a general adult population, weekday evenings are generally the most convenient. For professionals, such as doctors and lawyers, invitations to meet for breakfast at 7:30 A.M. are usually successful. For seniors and retirees, midafternoon often works best.

In marketing research, when participants should not know the identity of the client, focus group sessions can be held at the office of the agency conducting the research. Sessions can also be conducted in office conference rooms, community centers, hotel conference rooms, restaurant meeting rooms, or specially designed focus group meeting rooms. Hotel conference rooms and restaurant meeting rooms are recommended because they make food service more convenient, and because many hotels and restaurants will waive their standard charge for using their meeting room if the researcher purchases a minimum amount of food.

If an audience consists of doctors or nurses, a hospital may provide a conference room. Some research firms will conduct focus group sessions at airports by arranging to use membership lounges and recruiting travelers with ample time between flights.

Videoconferences represent a possible alternative to in-person focus group sessions. One obvious advantage to this method is client savings. Although more technical equipment is needed, the money saved in travel expenses and staff time will offset the cost of purchasing or renting it. Disadvantages include the lack of direct interaction among the participants and between the participants and the moderator, and the loss of information picked up by nonverbal communication.

When recruiting participants for any type of focus group session, the following guidelines should be used:

1. Participants should be representatives of one of the program's target audiences.

2. Participants should not be acquainted with each other. The ideal group consists of 10 to 12 individuals who do not know each other. That is why "prepackaged" groups do not work. When participants arrive in pairs, couples, or other groupings, they should be separated into different groups.

3. Participants should be close together in age. With adults, the general rule is to have no more than a 15-year spread between the youngest and oldest person in the group. If the spread is more than 15 years, the older participants tend to defer to the younger ones. With children, the spread should be no more than 3 years. If the spread is greater than 3 years, younger children tend to defer to the older ones.

4. In market research, the participants should not be regular users of that product brand, unless the researcher is looking specifically for ideas on new applications for existing products. Current users of a product may not contribute much in a focus group session because they are likely to be satisfied with the product being discussed. Although it is helpful for clients to hear positive comments about a product, it is more helpful if focus group participants can offer opinions about what is wrong with a product or how it can be improved. Therefore, researchers should seek focus group participants who are occasional users, former users, potential users, or users of competing products.

5. Groups should be as homogenous as possible, meaning they should be similar in characteristics that may affect how they communicate with others. For example, if college students are invited to participate in focus groups to provide feedback on the content and format of the student newspaper, there is no need for them to be separated into male and female groups, as their opinions of the newspaper is unlikely to differ because of their gender. But if the subject of the focus group is sexual assault or acquaintance rape, separate groups for men and women would be required because of the sensitive nature of the topic.

6. Researchers should screen out "professional participants." People who participate in focus groups on a regular basis tend to dominate the discussion and give answers they believe the moderators or clients want to hear.

7. Researchers should conduct multiple sessions. The carpenter's axiom is to "measure twice, cut once." If time and budget allow, multiple focus groups should be conducted until all possible constituent groups have been included.

8. It is advantageous to overrecruit. Most experienced focus group organizers invite more participants than are actually needed. Not only does this address the problem of no-shows but it also allows organizers to be selective in choosing participants based on their age, race, or gender. When working with ordinary consumers, focus group organizers typically overrecruit by 25 percent. When dealing with college students or business professionals, the no-show rate is substantially higher, so overrecruiting by 50 percent may be necessary.

9. Avoid participants with known hostilities toward the topic. Although some level of disagreement may be productive, researchers should avoid inviting participants with sharply divergent points of view. The goal of a focus group is to gather information, not stage a debate. Some companies dealing with customer dissatisfaction or other contentious issues find focus groups an effective way to allow participants to "blow off steam," but that should not be their primary purpose.

In addition to these guidelines for participants, the moderator should be chosen with care. Qualities of a good moderator include good listening skills, diplomacy in dealing with interruptions or problem participants, the ability to anticipate the flow of discussion, and the skill to project a presence of being in charge without being overbearing or bossy. The moderator must be able to give license to different points of view and remind participants that it is permissible to disagree. Conversely, a biased or unskilled moderator may skew the results by wording questions inappropriately or responding to comments in a way that inhibits discussion.

The role of the moderator is obviously to ask the questions, but also to encourage everyone to contribute, make sure the conversation stays on the subject, practice effective time management, and handle problem participants. Problem participants include those who attempt to dominate the conversation, believe they are experts on the topic, or become overly negative or hostile. In extreme cases, the moderator may call for a break and ask that disruptive individuals be excused from further participation, but compensated for their time.

In addition to the moderator, there are often assistants in the room to function as observers and note-takers. The number of observers should be kept to a minimum, however, as an abundance of extra people in the room may inhibit the discussion. It is also important for observers to avoid exhibiting any negative body language or making inappropriate remarks.

If the session is being audio/video recorded, participants must be informed before the session begins.

Types of Questions.   In general, moderators should ask open-ended questions that lead to meaningful responses rather than yes/no questions or other questions that lead to dichotomous answers. Questions advance from general to specific—beginning with warm-up questions and then proceeding through detail questions, probing questions, and wrap-up questions.

EXAMPLES

Warm-Up Questions
How often do you use *X?*
How do you feel about *X?*
When do you use your *X?*
Think back to the last time that you . . .

Detail Questions
What do you like about *X?*
What do you not like about *X?*
How do you feel about the safety of *X?*
Where do you get your information about *X?*
What was your reaction the first time you saw *X?*
Do you think the spokesperson in this commercial is believable?
Would this commercial motivate you to buy *X?*
What did you learn from this commercial that you did not know before?

Follow-Up or Probing Questions
Has anyone had a similar experience?
What is it about *X* that makes you say that?
Would you explain further?
Give me an example.
Describe what you mean.

Summary or Wrap-Up Questions
Is there anything else you would like to add?
If you could change one thing about *X,* what would it be?
If you could make one suggestion to the president of the *X* Company, what would it be?
Are there any other areas we need to cover?

Types of Analysis.   Focus group researchers can provide the information to the client in three forms. The simplest form is to provide raw data—a transcript, written summary, video, or audio. The second option is to provide a written summary that is organized either chronologically or by topic. The most complex form of analysis is a summary of the results followed by interpretations and recommendations.

When organizing the summary, researchers should take note of key themes or controlling ideas, the adjectives used, the context of the remarks, tone (sarcasm versus sincerity), consistency, consensus, and specificity ("I like it because . . .").

Errors in Interpreting Results.   Common errors in interpreting the results of focus group sessions include:

1. *Projecting Findings onto the Larger Population.* Generalizations cannot be made from a focus group like they can from a survey. When writing results, researchers should avoid using percentages or fractions that imply the results are representative of the larger population.
2. *Using Results Alone to Make Yes/No Decisions.* Researchers can use focus groups to confirm or disprove the results of other types of research—but not by themselves.
3. *Using Results to Predict Product Sales.* Researchers cannot interpret the results precisely enough to make such predictions.
4. *Expecting Participants to Produce Original ideas.* According to Florida State University Professor Jay Rayburn, one of the country's leading focus group experts, one of the misconceptions about focus groups is that they produce ideas for new products. Focus groups can be effective in evaluating the potential for products currently in

development or generating ideas for improving existing products, but they are not effective in suggesting ideas for new products that have not yet been developed.

Field Observation

In **field observation** research, the person gathering the information becomes an active or passive participant in the activity being studied, similar to working undercover. Edward Bernays was one of the earliest practitioners to use this form of research in the 1940s. Many of his clients were in the fashion industry, and one of his research strategies was to take a bag lunch to a public park near his office, watch people walking by, and make notes about their clothing.

Another more recent example of field observation is a 2007 study on hand-washing in public restrooms, conducted by a market research company on behalf of the American Society for Microbiology. Researchers spent more than a week observing more than 6,000 users (evenly split between male and female) of public restrooms. The researchers found that although 92 percent of individuals responding to previous telephone surveys claimed they always washed their hands after leaving a restroom, only 77 percent of those being observed did so. The latter figure represents a drop from 83 percent seen in a similar research activity conducted in 2005. In the 2007 study, women outwashed men by a margin of 88 to 66 percent.

The advantage of field observation is that it is inexpensive and in most cases requires little preparation. One weakness, however, is that the results are often superficial and cannot be quantified or generalized to a larger audience. Another significant problem occurs when individuals know they are being observed and therefore tend to act differently—most likely in a way they know will please the observer or not reveal bad habits or behavioral issues.

This phenomenon is known as the **Hawthorne effect**, which was first observed when researchers were studying work habits and productivity of employees at a manufacturing plant. When researchers changed factors such as lighting and background music, they found that productivity increased. But when they lowered lighting to its original level and eliminated the music, productivity increased again. Researchers eventually concluded that the result was not based in changes in lighting or background music, but that the employees increased their productivity based simply on the fact that they were being observed.

Direct Consumer Observation

Similar to field observation, **direct consumer observation** allows the researcher to closely watch consumers as they interact with a product or exhibit other behaviors. Unlike field observation, direct consumer observation often requires obtaining the consent of the individuals to be observed, as many observations take place within the home.

In 2004, for example, researchers at Ball State University used this method to track the media consumption habits of typical Americans. The researchers shadowed individuals during a typical 16-hour day and recorded the amount of time they spent reading print media, watching television, listening to the radio, and using the Internet. Researchers came to two important conclusions when compiling the results of their work: First, consumers spent more time consuming media than previously believed, and second, the direct observation method was far more accurate (at least for this topic) than either asking individuals to estimate their time spent on each activity or asking them to record those activities in a journal—the two forms previously used in research on media consumption habits.

When developing the company's new Vista software program, the Microsoft Corporation recruited hundreds of home computer users to participate in a similar research project. Researchers visited the homes of the participants at three-month intervals and filmed them using their computers for a variety of purposes. The company's engineers used the results of the study to improve the design of both the hardware and software products involved. The company later rewarded each of the participating families with a new computer loaded with the new Vista software.

Manufacturers of personal hygiene products employ similar tactics. Proctor & Gamble, for example, filmed men taking showers (wearing swimsuits) in order to improve its shower products, and Kimberly-Clark equipped mothers with goggles that featured tiny video cameras that recorded how they bathed and diapered their infants.

Telephone, Postal Mail, and Electronic Mail Monitoring

Although not as reliable as scientific public opinion polls, tracking incoming communications such telephone calls, letters, and email messages can provide researchers with a cheap and inexpensive method for measuring public opinion on issues. Public officials and organizations that receive large volumes of communication on controversial issues can measure the public mood informally by using this technique. It consists of keeping informal statistics concerning the "for" and "against" nature of telephone calls and mail received. It is far from a scientific method, but the process can still produce valuable information. Even though the results can be expressed in numbers and percentages, it is not considered quantitative research because the sample has chosen itself, as opposed to having been randomly chosen.

Another problem is that with yes/no or for-or-against issues, the majority of calls and mail received will be from persons either strongly for or strongly against the issue, with little input from those in between. Thus, the results may indicate where the extremes are in public opinion, but they cannot be projected with certainty onto the larger population.

Delphi Study

Named for the "Oracle at Delphi" in Greek mythology, this research technique was developed by scientists at the Rand Corporation in the 1950s. The most common form of a **Delphi study** involves mailing confidential surveys in multiple cycles. In the first cycle, a large pool of experts on a topic (sometimes 100 or more) is selected to complete questionnaires and return them to the researcher. Subsequent rounds are used to debate the ideas, challenge the points of view of the other panelists, and ultimately seek some level of consensus. Variations of the Delphi method involve a series of in-person meetings, but most are done by fax, postal mail, or email.

Most Delphi studies are "blind," meaning that respondents do not know each other's identity. For the second cycle, the results of the first cycle are summarized and mailed to the respondents, who are then asked to comment on or clarify the information. The process is repeated for as many cycles as are necessary to reach consensus. An effective Delphi study may require four to six cycles, with each cycle taking 60 to 90 days.

Its anonymous nature makes the Delphi method effective for gathering information on controversial or emotional issues. Generally, Delphi studies have an excellent track record of being highly accurate in forecasting long-range trends. For example, a local chamber of commerce or other organization may conduct a Delphi study in order to predict the future of the community in areas such as economics, employment, education, transportation, and the environment. When such a study was conducted in a small community in Florida in 1987, its goal was to predict what the community would be like 10 years hence. Looking at the report more than a decade later, community officials described many of the predictions as "right on the money" and most others as "very close."

Another example is a Delphi study conducted for the Charleston County (South Carolina) public school system. The purpose of the survey was to gather opinions on how to handle issues such as student conduct and the vandalism of school property. A wide variety of suggestions were collected and incorporated into a proposal that earned a multiyear government grant of more than $1 million per year.

One of the advantages of the Delphi technique is that it helps avoid the problem of "groupthink" that often results from focus groups. Another advantage is that by not allowing the participants to interact directly, researchers can better handle conflict and disagreement among the panelists. There is also less chance of the discussion being dominated by one or more strong personalities and less chance of peer pressure influencing the results.

One obvious drawback associated with Delphi studies is that they may take 12 to 18 months to complete. Therefore, they are mainly effective with long-range strategic planning efforts when the results can be gathered over an extended period of time. Another disadvantage of this method is that participants who are not highly motivated or interested in the topic tend to drop out along the way. Researchers using the Delphi method often begin with a larger number of participants than they expect to complete the process.

QUANTITATIVE RESEARCH

Survey Research

The survey is, by far, the most common form of quantitative research used in public relations work. The most effective surveys are related to only one topic, but in some cases researchers find an omnibus or "piggyback" survey effective.

An **omnibus survey** is one in which questions are asked on a variety of topics. This type of research most often results from national opinion research companies that combine questions of interest to multiple clients in the same survey or poll. For example, during a 10-minute telephone survey, a researcher may ask five questions about the environment on behalf of a chemical company, three questions about shopping habits on behalf of a national retail chain, and six questions about food safety on behalf of a national grocery store chain. This is practical for both the research firm and its clients, as many clients need responses to only a few basic questions.

The terms *survey* and *questionnaire* are often confused, but they should not be used interchangeably. **Survey** is a noun referring to the beginning-to-end process of conducting this type of research, such as "We conducted a survey of our members." It can also be used as a verb, as in "We will survey our members." The term should not, however, be used to describe a list of questions, which is more accurately known as a **questionnaire** or **research instrument**.

Research instruments ask two types of questions: open-ended and closed-ended. **Closed-ended questions** provide to the respondents a list of responses (such as adjectives or adverbs) from which to choose, whereas **open-ended questions** allow the respondents to choose their own adjectives or adverbs.

Open-ended questions can be effective with a small number of responses because they typically provide more information than closed-ended questions. They are impractical for large audiences, however, because of the difficulty of coding and tabulating the responses.

The advantages of closed-ended questions (over open-ended questions) include the ease of compiling the results and the ability to produce cross-tabulations. **Cross-tabulations** are the division of research results by demographic and psychographic categories. For instance, in addition to determining how many of the respondents purchase brand X and how many purchase brand Y, the number of people under the age of 18 who purchase brand X and how many purchase brand Y (and the same information for other age groups) can also be determined.

The six most common categories for cross-tabulations for general consumer surveys are age, gender, race, income level, education level, and residence. Age brackets are generally narrow for younger age groups (such as 13–15, 16–18, 19–21) and wide for older age groups (for example, 50–59, 60–69, 70–79). Income brackets are generally framed in $5,000 increments (such as $20,000–$24,999, $25,000–$29,999). Typical education categories offered are "less than high school," "high school graduate," "some college," "college graduate," and "graduate degree." Questions about residence usually ask respondents to indicate either "urban," "suburban," or "rural," and/or "own home" or "rent."

In political polling, there are three additional psychographic questions: party affiliation, registered to vote/not registered, and likely to vote/not likely to vote.

Many computer software programs are available that make cross-tabulations easy. One of the most popular is the Statistical Package for the Social Sciences (SPSS), which also offers a variety of formats in which to present data, including bar charts and scatter plots.

Closed-ended questions take two forms: **demographic/psychographic questions** that ask for factual information and **substantive questions** that ask for opinions. Both types of questions can be either closed ended or open ended. Various forms of the closed-ended questions are discussed next.

Dichotomous.   **Dichotomous questions** are followed by a list of only two possible answers (yes or no, for or against, male or female).

Multiple Choice.   **Multiple-choice questions** are followed by a list of three or more possible answers. When used to ask demographic or psychographic questions, there are three criteria for developing a list of possible choices.

1. First, the list of choices should be as *detailed* as possible. For example, when asking respondents to indicate their age or income, the brackets should be as narrow as possible.

When compiling the results, brackets can always be combined to create fewer ones, but when researchers begin with wide brackets, it is difficult or impossible to divide them later.

2. The list of choices should be *exhaustive,* meaning that they include all or most of the possible answers, and the number of respondents choosing "other" should be as small as possible. For example, for a question such as "Where were you born?" a researcher would likely list all 50 states (and perhaps other continents) in order to have an exhaustive list. A list of choices such as "California," "Texas," and "other" would not be exhaustive because the majority of respondents would likely choose "other."

3. The list of choices must be *mutually exclusive,* meaning that it would not be possible for anyone to mark more than one choice. For example, for a question that asks "Where do you live?" a list of choices such as "on campus," "off campus," "inside city limits," "outside city limits," and "with parents" is not mutually exclusive because many respondents would fall into more than one category.

Barometer Scale. **Barometer scale questions** ask the respondent to choose from a list of possible answers that moves upward or downward from a natural zero point.

EXAMPLES

How often do you attend church?

    0—never
    1—once a year
    2—once a month
    3—once a week
    4—every day

Describe your interest in your university's football team:

    4—extremely interested
    3—very interested
    2—somewhat interested
    1—very little interest
    0—none

In these two examples, a natural zero point is at one end of a scale because it would not be possible to attend church less than "never" or to describe your interest in the football team as less than "none."

Likert Scale. **Likert-scale questions** ask respondents to choose their answers from a list that includes two extremes and various degrees in between. Most offer choices such as "strongly agree," "somewhat agree," "no opinion," "somewhat disagree," and "strongly disagree." A typical Likert-scale question offers five possible answers, but sometimes offers seven or nine. Odd numbers of possible answers are preferred over even numbers so that there will always be a neutral center mark, such as "no opinion." Also, the scale must be balanced so that the two extremes, such as "strongly agree" and "strongly disagree," are the same distance from the center mark. An example of a poorly designed Likert scale is one that offers five positive answers to the left of neutral and only two negative answers to the right.

Ranking Scale.   **Ranking-scale questions** ask respondents to rank-order items from a list, such as first preference, second preference, and third preference; or most important, second-most important, and third-most important. These questions are effective when exploring how members of an audience make certain decisions, such as purchasing habits and entertainment choices.

EXAMPLES

When you buy a new *X*, which of the following factors are most important? (rank-order 1 to 5):

_____ price
_____ appearance/packaging
_____ quality
_____ company reputation
_____ customer service

Which of the following entertainment choices do you prefer? (rank-order 1 to 6)

_____ movie
_____ live theatre
_____ comedy club
_____ sporting event
_____ television
_____ concert

For most audiences, the maximum number of choices to include in a ranking scale is seven. When asking respondents to rank-order more than seven items, they may have difficulty when they reach the bottom of the list and are trying to differentiate, for example, between their 12th, 13th, and 14th preferences.

Errors to Avoid in Wording Questions.   Here are some common errors made while developing questions.

ERROR	EXAMPLE
Leading questions	Do you agree that . . . ?
Ambiguous terms (more than one meaning)	Have you been in *contact* with . . . ?
Vague terms (uncertain as to degree)	Would you consider making a *large* donation to our organization?
Double-barrel questions	AIDS and crime are two of the most serious problems facing America today—do you agree or disagree?
Contradictory questions	Did you bring your lunch today, or did you ride the bus?

Researchers should avoid asking questions that are too hypothetical in nature. Although such questions are excellent for a focus group because participants have the opportunity to reflect on their answers before speaking, hypothetical questions seldom provide useful information for a written questionnaire or intercept survey because there is little time to ponder an answer. At best, questions such as, "How would an economic recession affect your family?" result in hypothetical answers. And by all means, serious researchers should avoid the far-fetched hypothetical, such as, "If you were a tree, what kind of tree would you be?"

It is also helpful to assign a time frame to most questions, such as, "In the last six months, have you . . . ?" or "In the last two years, have you . . . ?" One key to avoiding the **double-barrel question** is not to ask questions that include conjunctions, such as, "In the last six months, have you been to the movies or mowed your lawn?" Some people have done one or the other, some have done both, and some have done neither.

If the interviewer must ask questions that are sensitive or highly personal (such as those related to sexual conduct, family relationships, financial matters, or drug or alcohol usage), they should be placed at end of the questionnaire. This is recommended for two reasons. First, if the participant chooses to terminate the interview because of the nature of the personal questions, the answers from earlier questions may still be used. Second, having sensitive questions at the end allows the interviewer to establish a rapport with participants that may increase their level of comfort. Also, questions should not include acronyms, technical or specialized vocabulary, jargon that would not be known to the respondents, or new ideas or theories that are not explained well.

Methods of Administering Surveys.   The most common methods for administering survey instruments are mail, telephone, and in person (sometimes called an **intercept survey**), although surveys administered through email or the Web are gaining in popularity.

The *mail questionnaire* is impersonal, but it has several advantages. It is cheaper and faster than other methods, does not require training of personnel, provides the highest level of anonymity, provides respondents the opportunity to think about their answers before responding, and is effective for covering a wide geographical area. It also eliminates **courtesy bias**, which is the tendency of participants to provide answers that will please and/or not offend the interviewer, moderator, or other participants.

The disadvantages of a mail questionnaire are that it requires simple questions and answers, provides no opportunity for the researcher to ask clarifying or follow-up questions, and tends to have a low response rate. Researchers cannot control the conditions under which the questionnaire is completed. Some respondents will take their time and provide well thought-out answers; others will complete the questionnaire while distracted by other activities or obligations. The researcher also cannot assess the quality of the responses. For example, sincere respondents will complete most questionnaires; others will simply provide random answers as quickly as possible simply to receive the reward being offered. Also, the researcher has no idea who actually completed the survey—perhaps a child or teenager will find the questionnaire and write in a false age. But the largest weakness is the low response rate, and despite what some researchers claim, providing a stamped envelope results in only a minimal increase in the response rate—seldom enough to warrant the extra expense.

For a broad or general audience, an effective mail survey may provide a response rate of 20 to 40 percent. Response rates tend to be higher if the audience is narrow and its members are carefully chosen, or if the topic is controversial.

One popular method of increasing the response rate of a mail survey is to include a letter of endorsement from an influential person, such as a celebrity involved with a charity, or, in the case of a student project, the instructor supervising the research. Other ideas include sending a brief letter or postcard in advance of the questionnaire, advising potential respondents to "watch their mailboxes" for it, or sending a reminder letter or postcard (see Figure 4.1) weeks after the questionnaire.

Some researchers find the combination of follow-up postcards and duplicate questionnaires to be effective in increasing the response rate. For example, the first mailing of a questionnaire may result in a response of only 25 percent, but a follow-up postcard mailed a week or two later may result in another 10 to 15 percent response. The third mailing is a replacement questionnaire, sent two weeks after the postcard, and it may result in another 10 to 15 percent response. The final mailing is another replacement questionnaire, sent three weeks after the previous one, which may result in another 10 to 15 percent response. Cumulative response to the four mailings is 55 to 70 percent, making it well worth the additional printing and postage costs.

The advantages of the *telephone survey* include a moderate cost (not as cheap as mail, but cheaper than in-person interviews) and speed (a large number of responses in a short period of time). Although the response rate is generally high, researchers conducting surveys by telephone still have to deal with out-of-service telephone numbers, hang-ups, children who answer the telephone, and answering machines. Telephone surveys may also leave out individuals without telephones (8 to 10 percent of the population) or those with unlisted numbers (more than 15 percent of the population). Some researchers get around the latter

---

FIGURE 4.1   Follow-Up Postcard for Mail Survey

Customer Relations Department
XYZ Cable Company

Dear XYZ customer:

A few weeks ago we mailed to you a brief questionnaire designed to help us measure the quality of cable television service we provide.

Every completed survey is important to us, so if you have not already done so, please take a few minutes to complete the questionnaire and return it in the enclosed prepaid envelope. Your answers will help XYZ Cable Company monitor customer satisfaction and continue to improve our service.

Thank you.

problem by selecting common prefixes and using computer programs to generate random four-digit numbers to produce a list of random telephone numbers that will include those that are unlisted.

Researchers preparing for telephone surveys should first check state laws regarding telephone soliciting. Most state laws provide exemptions for legitimate public opinion polls and nonsales marketing research, but some laws limit calls to certain times and require callers to provide certain information at the beginning of the call.

Telephone polling has always had shortcomings, such as the difficulty of drawing representative samples. That problem has become worse with the trend of younger individuals using cell phones as their primary methods of communication, with many not even having traditional land-lines in their homes. Pollsters conducting research in the early stages of the 2008 presidential election, for example, admitted they were having difficulty including the under-30 voters in their samples because their cell phone numbers were not available.

Other disadvantages of telephone surveys include the respondents' reluctance to discuss sensitive or controversial topics and the difficulty of asking questions of children. In many states, it is illegal to conduct phone surveys with minors without permission of their parents. Another disadvantage of the telephone survey results from the habits and lifestyles of the respondents. The pool of respondents is typically top-heavy with older individuals (because they have more leisure time and are more willing to talk) and women (because they tend to answer the phone before men).

The response rate for telephone surveys can be increased by calling from a university telephone (because of caller-ID) and being honest about the length of time the survey will take. Some organizations will also send a postcard to potential respondents in advance, letting them know the value of their participation and, in some cases, assuring them that it is not a sales or fund-raising call (see Figure 4.2).

FIGURE 4.2   Advanced Notice Postcard for Telephone Survey

Office of Alumni Relations
XYZ University

Dear XYZ graduate:

In the next few weeks, a current student at XYZ University will call you to ask your opinions about services available to you as one of our graduates. Please be assured that this is an alumni survey and *not a fund-raising call.* Although financial contributions to the university are always appreciated, from time to time we just want to know how we're doing.

So please take a few minutes to answer the student's questions. Your answers will help the Office of Alumni Relations develop better programs and services for your benefit.

Advantages of conducting in-person or intercept surveys include the ability to maintain control over the interview situation, the opportunity to ask clarifying or follow-up questions, and a fairly high response rate. More complete information is received because there is more time and the person's attention can be maintained. In-person surveys are also the most effective method for dealing with children.

Disadvantages of the in-person survey include the limited audience and the difficulty of getting a good "mix." Surveys conducted at a shopping mall will measure the opinions of only those people who visit that mall; surveys conducted on a downtown street corner will measure the opinions of only those people who happen to walk by; surveys conducted in a college class will reflect only the opinions of students in that class. In-person surveys are also more expensive because of the costs associated with hiring and training the interviewers.

The biggest drawback of the in-person survey, however, is the lack of anonymity, which causes problems when the subject of the survey is controversial or sensitive. Other problems include courtesy bias and interviewer bias (poorly trained interviewers influencing responses through voice inflection or body language).

Web or *email surveys* represent a relatively new method of administering surveys, and researchers are still debating the strengths and weaknesses of such methods. The major advantage of web-based or email surveys is low cost. Some staff time will be required to configure the questionnaire into an electronic or web format, but it is less expensive than the costs of telephone calls, postage, and staff training required in other survey methods. Much like mail surveys, web or email surveys provide a high level of anonymity and are effective in reaching audiences spread over a wide geographic area. They also provide easy processing of the results, as computer software can be purchased (or custom designed) to compile the results as responses are received.

Email surveys tend to produce a higher response rate than most other methods, with the response rate increasing with the quality of the address list used. Like with traditional mail methods, more than half of those responding will do so shortly after receiving the questionnaire, and a second mailing—typically two weeks later—will result in a second wave of responses.

In addition to the higher response rate, other advantages to the email survey include low cost and the elimination of interviewer bias. Unlike in-person interviews, there is no need to transcribe handwritten results. In some cases, respondents can be asked to clarify their responses or provide additional information. Speed is another advantage. The majority of individuals responding to an email survey will do so immediately, whereas responses to mail surveys tend to dribble in over days, weeks, and sometimes months.

Disadvantages of the email survey include its partial anonymity, an abundance of incorrect addresses, and possible confusion with "spam" or other unsolicited email. Disadvantages of web-based or email surveys also include the exclusion of individuals without email accounts or Internet access. In the case of web-based surveys, the respondents must know the website's address and be motivated to take the time to find it. And as with mail surveys, the researchers have no assurance that the person completing the electronic questionnaire is actually a member of the target audience. In earlier times, both web-based and email surveys likely produced skewed results if any of the target audiences for the survey did not have Internet access. For example, using the Internet to administer a survey on television viewing habits would be a flawed method because viewers with Internet access were generally younger, better educated, and more affluent than those without Internet access. More important, their television viewing habits would be quite different, resulting in the loss of input from significant segments of the television viewing audience.

During the first decade of the Web's existence, its demographic profile was dominated by young males, a phenomenon that limited its effectiveness in reaching more diverse audiences. More recently, studies show that the Web audience is more inclusive in terms of gender and age. Women now make up approximately half of the audience, and older Americans represent the fastest-growing segment of the audience. The only remaining challenge is to make the Web more accessible to low-income Americans, but that, too, should be accomplished as the price of home computers continues to fall and Internet access is available at most public libraries.

Including survey instruments on an organization's website involves a number of other drawbacks. Some participants may complete the questionnaire more than once. Surveys that provide incentives, such as a product giveaway or contest entry, are especially vulnerable to multiple responses. The anonymous nature of the web survey also provides the opportunity for inaccuracies, exaggerations, and misrepresentations, but there is little evidence that this occurs more with on-line surveys than other anonymous research methods.

Content Analysis

A **content analysis** is a scientific study of the media coverage of a topic or issue. In its simplest form, such as merely counting the number of stories on a topic or the number of references to it, it can be considered qualitative, but when executed properly and in detail, it is generally considered quantitative. As the term implies, content analysis can be used to examine the content of materials being studied. Although a tedious and time-consuming process, content analysis is highly effect in describing trends and changes in content over time.

As a research method, content analysis has a long and somewhat controversial history. For example, during World War II, the extent of German military casualties was estimated by a content analysis of German newspaper articles. In the 1980s, futurist John Naisbitt was able to make predictions about American life in the 1990s by analyzing the content of more than 2 million articles from hundreds of American newspapers.

Steps in the content analysis process are (1) define the purpose of the study, (2) define the communication to be studied, (3) define the coding categories to be counted, (4) sample and categorize the messages, and (5) analyze and interpret the results. Examples of content analysis in researching media include print and broadcast news stories (the latter being in the form of audiotapes, videotapes, or scripts), opinion columns, editorials, letters to the editor, cartoons, and photographs. On the Internet, content analysis can be used to measure mentions of an issue or organization on websites, on bulletin boards, and in chat rooms. Apart from measuring the media, content analysis can be used to measure the content of news releases, brochures, quarterly and annual reports, and other company publications.

Examples of content analysis used in the study of popular culture include research on music lyrics, entertainment television, television and radio talk shows, fiction and nonfiction books, theatrical productions, and even subway and restroom graffiti. A common example of popular culture research involves sex and violence on television. Researchers choose the content analysis method to make inferences about the effect of such content on television audiences. Examples of coding labels for sexual content might include noncriminal sexual acts, criminal sexual acts, and sexual language or innuendo, whereas examples of coding labels for violence might include violent acts that appear to result in punishment of the offender, those that appear to result in rewards for the offender, and those for which neither punishment or reward is apparent.

In more personal forms of communication, content analysis can be used to measure the content of letters, speeches, and personal and telephone conversations. Psychologists have even drawn inferences about the thought processes of patients by analyzing the content of personal diaries and suicide notes.

In public relations work, content analysis can be used as formative research in the planning stages of a public relations program or as a measurement tool in the evaluation stage. Specifically, a content analysis might help researchers to (1) describe the content of messages disseminated, (2) make inferences about the motives of the individuals or groups sending those messages, and (3) make inferences about the effects of those messages on the intended recipients.

On a superficial level, an organization can conduct a content analysis by having employees examine newspaper clippings and broadcast news stories and note both the quantity and quality of the terms used. On a scientific level, a formal content analysis would more specifically categorize the content of the news coverage through the tone (positive or negative), the duration (number of words in a print story or length of a broadcast story), the presence of key messages, the nature of negative terms, and whether competitors were also mentioned.

In evaluative research, content analysis can be used to determine how many of a public relations program's "key messages" show up in news coverage resulting from the program, and in what context they appear. For example, if a company's public relations program includes supporting local schools through providing employees as student mentors and sponsoring school activities such as science fairs and athletic teams, a content analysis of newspaper and television stories can measure not only the number of times those efforts were mentioned but also whether those mentions were positive, negative, or neutral.

If a company has received considerable news coverage because of its environmental problems, a content analysis can measure the number of times such problems are mentioned, as well as whether the tone is positive, negative, or neutral. In assembling a content analysis of how a company or its products are mentioned in the media, possible contexts would be positive, negative, or neutral; and categories of product messages might include safety, reliability, customer service, advantages over competition, warranty, and maintenance costs.

INTEGRITY AND VALIDITY IN PRIMARY RESEARCH

In both qualitative and quantitative research, practitioners must follow a number of rules related to the thoroughness and ethical considerations of conducting the research and interpreting the results. These considerations include:

1. Avoid invalid claims or comparisons (twisting or distorting results to make them appear to say something that they do not). Politicians and special-interest groups often release the results of studies that support their causes, but such research is often poorly conducted. Examples include questions that are intentionally worded to produce the results desired or omission of details that are not consistent with the sponsor's cause. Because of the misuse of research results by many politicians and special-interest groups, the Associated Press has established guidelines for journalists using the results of polls and surveys in their reporting. These guidelines are listed later in this chapter.

2. Ensure a proper sample size and composition. A **random sample** is a sampling method in which all members of the audience have an equal chance of being chosen for the sample. It is used when demographic characteristics of the sample are not important. A **quota sample**, or "representative sample," is a sampling method in which demographic groups are equally represented in the sample chosen. It is used when characteristics such as age, race, or gender may influence answers.

A **convenience sample** is a sample chosen because its members are easy to find and are willing to cooperate, even though they may not be as random as the researcher might prefer. An example is asking a college class to complete a questionnaire or participate in a focus group to discuss issues pertinent to college life. Even though the class might consist of students generally interested in the issues raised on the questionnaire or in the focus group, the class chosen might not accurately reflect the diversity of campus in terms of gender, race, or other characteristics. Another example is found in the typical shopping mall, or intercept survey. As discussed previously, such a survey reflects only the opinions of those who happen to walk by. Although they may not be the "perfect" sample, they are chosen because they are easy to find.

3. Provide incentives for participating. Money and food are often effective incentives for individuals agreeing to participate in a survey, focus group, or other research activity, but researchers have found the most effective reward is one that is intangible: the participant's level of confidence that this information collected will be used for an important purpose. A company or social service agency that promises participants that their responses "will help us improve our services" will realize more cooperation than if they provide no incentive whatsoever. Most individuals are flattered by the opportunity to provide an opinion or help with a problem, especially if they will also benefit. Even busy individuals who are unlikely to participate in a commercial marketing survey will agree to participate in a survey conducted by college students working on a class project. Conversely, when companies conduct annual employee morale surveys but fail to implement any of the suggestions, employees will eventually become skeptical and unwilling to participate in subsequent surveys.

In mail surveys, it is often helpful to include an endorsement letter. For example, a survey conducted by students may include a cover letter from the professor, explaining the importance of the survey and thanking the participants for their time. Nonprofit organizations and charities often find it effective to include with their surveys a cover letter from a celebrity or other well-known person associated with the cause.

4. Ensure confidentiality to the respondents. This is difficult to do with focus groups and interviews, but easy to do with a survey. Many companies that conduct employee morale surveys ask respondents to submit their questionnaires to the personnel office in a sealed envelope or to mail them to a public opinion research firm hired to conduct the survey. For interviews and focus groups, some researchers use a method known as the **third-party question**, in which they ask respondents to describe behaviors of a larger peer group rather than their own personal behavior. Questions such as "Could you please describe the drinking behavior of your peer group?" or "Could you please describe the sexual behavior of your peer group?" allow respondents to give more truthful answers, even though they may actually be talking about themselves.

5. Weight the results. Although results should never be deliberately "slanted" to show results favorable to a cause, in some cases it is appropriate to "weight" results to provide a more realistic picture. As an example, a company with 500 male employees and 500 female employees might expect that of the 200 employees responding to a morale survey, 100 would be male and 100 female. But what should the researcher do if 150 are male and only 50 are female? For questions in which the gender of respondents is unlikely to affect their answers (such as issues of parking and building cleanliness), the results can be reported as is. But for questions in which the gender of the respondent is likely to affect answers (such as those dealing with sexual harassment, promotion opportunities, building security, and maternity leave policies), the results must be weighted to reflect the gender breakdown of the employees. In the preceding scenario, women's answers would be multiplied by 3, then matched against the responses from male employees and then computed as a percentage. When explaining the results, however, the researcher should provide the results both ways— raw data and based on weighted results—and allow the individual or company requesting the research to decide which data to use. The researcher should then also consider why one group or the other is overrepresented or underrepresented in the sample and consider it as a possible "red flag" that there may be a larger problem.

Working with Human Subjects

For any research projects conducted by university professors or students, a higher ethical standard applies, especially if it involves human subjects. When institutions first developed their research policies in the 1970s and 1980s, they were concerned with the physical and emotional welfare of the subjects involved in experiments dealing with reactions to various stimuli. Today, many institutions apply those policies to all methods of research—even those such as focus groups discussing nonpersonal or noncontroversial topics. Most universities have oversight committees with titles such as Human Subjects Review Board or Institutional Review Board that must approve all research before it begins.

TRENDS AND ISSUES

Associated Press Guidelines for Reporting Research Results

Because of the proliferation of surveys conducted or sponsored by political organizations, special-interest groups, and other parties with an interest in the outcome (and journalists' fascination with survey results), the Associated Press provides the following guidelines for journalists who include such results in their print and broadcast stories as well as those appearing in on-line stories. The intent of the guidelines is to provide readers and viewers the information necessary to place survey results in their proper context. Public relations representatives should abide by these same guidelines in releasing the results of research for which they are responsible.

Who Conducted the Poll?

Was the poll done by a professional public opinion research firm, a political candidate's staff, or an organization's own public relations staff? Journalists recognize the significance of research conducted by firms such as the Gallup Corporation, the Harris Poll, or Yankelovich Partners. Many media outlets are conducting their own opinion research and forming partnerships to share both the costs and the results. Examples include the USA Today/CNN Poll, the NBC News/Associated Press Poll, and the CBS News/Wall Street Journal Poll.

Sample Size and How the Sample Was Chosen

A survey with a small sample size is not as reliable as one with a larger sample. The time and place selected to sample is also important. For example, if one were to conduct a survey to determine which sport is more popular—football or baseball—using a sample chosen from a crowd of people leaving a stadium after a football game would not be an appropriate sample. That is obviously an exaggerated example, but some researchers draw their samples using methods and locations that are almost as questionable.

Who Was in the Sample?

At the level of absolute certainty, survey research reflects only the opinions of those in the sample; but at the level of probability, the results can be projected onto the larger audience from which the sample was drawn. Many media consumers do not understand the complexity of survey research, so care must be taken when the results are announced.

Methodology

Was the survey conducted by telephone, mail, email, or in person?

Timing

When was the research conducted? Opinions can change overnight. A poll taken the day after a presidential speech is going to give a different result than one taken a week later. For example, accurate reporters will write in a story: "The poll was taken the week of March 3 . . . ."

Sponsorship, If Any

Reporters are skeptical of any poll that is privately sponsored, and for good reason. Effective reporters may mention those results of privately sponsored research in their stories, but will identify the sponsor so that readers can put the results in context.

Margin for Error

A poll's margin for error is determined by a mathematical formula and expressed in a percentage related to the sample size. The larger the sample is, the smaller the margin of error; the smaller the sample is, the larger the margin for error.

How Were the Questions Worded, and in What Order Were They Asked?

It is unlikely that the exact wording of the questions will appear in the newspaper story, but most polling companies provide reporters with a copy of the questions.

CASE STUDY 4A

Lawyers Use Focus Groups to Design Trial Strategies

Although the technique had been in use for more than a decade, the idea of using focus groups to help trial lawyers design their courtroom strategies came to the attention of the media and the public during the 1995 murder trial of O. J. Simpson.

Forensic Technologies, a California-based research firm, conducted four surveys of Los Angeles residents (potential jurors) to gauge public attitudes toward Simpson during pretrial proceedings. The company then used two focus groups of mock jurors to help defense attorneys prepare for the juror screening process and determine what qualities they should look for in prospective jurors. During the trial itself, the company conducted additional focus groups in which they asked participants to react to videotaped segments showing the defense lawyers so they could adjust their presentation style.

Today, many defense attorneys in both criminal trials and civil trials (such as product liability cases) use focus groups to help them with both jury selection and trial strategy. One of the reasons for their popularity and success is the similarity of the group dynamics involved in focus group discussions led by a moderator and jury deliberations led by a foreperson.

Potential customers of a new product participate in focus group "taste tests." Focus groups are a popular way to test new products, but research firms use focus groups for gathering information for a variety of other purposes, including evaluating the content of newspapers and television programs, testing political campaign strategies, and setting up mock juries to test trial strategies.

CASE STUDY 4B

Field Observation and the Science of Shopping

Paco Underhill, founder of a New York–based marketing research firm called Envirosell, describes the perfect uniform for his employees: a polo shirt, khaki pants, thick socks, comfortable walking shoes, and no heavy aftershave or perfume.

An inconspicuous uniform is necessary in Envirosell's line of work because much of it involves field observation in which those being observed must not notice the observers. Underhill refers to his company's work as "retail anthropology." Every workday, his employees go into restaurants, grocery stores, department stores, and other retail establishments armed with high-tech devices such as laptop computers, tiny video cameras, and 8mm film cameras for time-lapse photography. They take low-tech devices as well: clipboards and their own eyesight.

Envirosell's clients include a number of Fortune 500 companies. Since 1989, his operatives have spent thousands of hours examining the interaction between people and products and between people and commercial spaces, and then putting the resulting information into context for clients. Among the company's findings are the following:

A market researcher uses the field observation method to note foot traffic in a retail store.

1. The shopping experience does not begin at an establishment's front door, but in the parking lot. Parking lots must therefore be clean, well lighted, and safe.
2. Most retail stores have a "decompression zone" immediately inside their front doors—open space that allows shoppers to adjust to the change in environment. Most merchandise placed in the decompression zone will go unnoticed.
3. Most shoppers tend to move to the right of the store upon entering. Retailers can take advantage of this tendency by putting their "hottest" merchandise on that side of the store.
4. Shoppers like to "pet" merchandise and are more likely to purchase items they can touch, as opposed to those items wrapped in plastic or other material.
5. Shoppers are uncomfortable shopping in narrow aisles because of the potential contact with other customers. Underhill's employees observed what they call the "butt brush" effect of people leaving an aisle if there are too many other shoppers passing in front of them or behind them.

CASE STUDY 4C

How to Lie with Statistics

In her job as the editor of *The Wall Street Journal* "Marketplace" page, Cynthia Crossen receives the results of hundreds of surveys a year—not all of them having honorable intentions. Many are generated either by special-interest groups with cause or by public relations agencies representing major companies trying to generate interest in their products.

By 1994, Crossen had become so skeptical of those surveys that she began work on *Tainted Truth: The Manipulation of Fact in America* (Simon and Schuster, 1996). Starting with those she received at *The Wall Street Journal* and adding hundreds gathered from other sources, Crossen authored a searing condemnation of the research and public opinion industries.

Crossen urges both citizens and the reporters who provide them with news to be more skeptical of survey results. She points out that although Americans are already skeptical and sometimes cynical about both political and commercial advertising, they can still be easily fooled by claims involving both numbers. "Information, however persuasive, is never neutral, and the purpose of this book is to expose the interests that underlie the 'truths' we have come to trust," she wrote. Crossen suggests tighter controls on the practices of the research industry and greater awareness on behalf of the public. Her book is cynical in places, but her examples indicate that her cynicism is warranted.

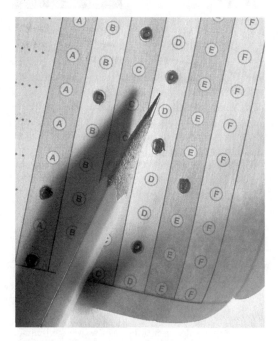

Email and Web surveys are growing in popularity, but the pencil-and-paper or "bubble sheet" questionnaire is still a commonly used research instrument.

One of the two "bottom lines" to Crossen's book is that privately sponsored studies have far less credibility than those generated by universities and similar sources because they are funded by companies or special-interest groups that have a vested interest in the outcome. But even university-based studies or others from supposedly "credible" sources can be misleading.

Crossen's best examples are from the pharmaceutical, tobacco, and consumer product industries. Proving the adage that "Statistics can be made to show whatever you want them to show," Crossen documents the case of competing market studies about diapers. One study funded by the manufacturers of brand names Pampers and Luvs disposable diapers found that disposable diapers are better for the baby's health and safer for the environment than conventional reusable cloth diapers; another study funded by manufacturers of cloth diapers reached the opposite conclusion.

Other examples include a study touting the benefits of eating white bread that was funded by Wonder Bread, and another promoting the benefits of eating chocolate that was funded by Mars. One of Crossen's few political examples involves how the Supreme Court nomination of Clarence Thomas was pushed through the Senate Judiciary Committee based on faulty and manipulated poll results showing public support behind the nomination.

But Crossen's other "bottom line" contains a much more serious criticism. She points not only at the public's gullibility in believing such polls but also at the media's failure to scrutinize polls on the public's behalf. "The more the study defies common wisdom, the more likely it is to enjoy wide acclaim," she wrote. "It would be comforting to think that the media protect us from the flood of dubious information we face every day." Crossen harshly criticizes the journalism profession for its lack of diligence, mentioning specific examples of media that have been duped. She even mentions examples from *The Wall Street Journal*—choosing not to spare her own newspaper from criticism.

Crossen's book is not the first to document the manipulation of fact. Michael Wheeler's *Lies, Damn Lies, and Statistics* (Liveright, 1976) made the same charges about survey research using different examples, and to a lesser extent, so did Daniel Boorstin's *The Image: A Guide to Pseudo-events in America* (Harper and Row, 1961).

Wheeler, a professor at the New England School of Law, found the title to his book in a famous quote, "There are three types of falsehoods: lies, damn lies, and statistics," attributed to both British Prime Minister Benjamin Disraeli and American novelist Mark Twain. His book includes examples of both unintentional errors in polling caused either by sloppiness or incompetence and the intentional manipulation of survey results. His best examples of the former are the polls that predicted the elections of "President" Alf Landon in 1936 and "President" Thomas Dewey in 1948. His best examples of intentional manipulation of results are those originating from the Nixon White House and the television network's use of Nielsen ratings to set advertising rates.

Sociologist Christina Hoff Sommers has studied how statistics are exaggerated and misused by feminist groups. In her 1994 book, *Who Stole Feminism: How Women Have Betrayed Women,* Sommers uses examples such as the statistic that "more than 150,000 women die each year of anorexia" (the real number is fewer than 1,000) and that "domestic violence causes more birth defects than all medical causes combined." The March of Dimes is often cited as the source for the latter statistic, but it claims to have never made such a statement or conducted such a study. Sommers wrote that numerous other sources of health information agree that the statistic has no scientific basis.

Sommers also devotes an entire chapter in her book to debunking a 1991 study by the American Association of University Women that indicated that girls lose self-esteem when they enter high school. The study reports that in studies of elementary school students, 60 percent of girls and 69 percent of boys say they are "happy with the way I am." But when they reach high school, the study contends, the number for girls drops 31 points to only 29 percent, while for boys it drops only 23 points, to 46 percent. Sommers examined the questionnaire more closely and found that researchers counted only those cases in which girls replied "always true," but the majority answered "sometimes true" and "sort of true." Sommers criticized the validity of the study and accused the AAUW of using only the portion of the results that supported its position that girls were being shortchanged in the educational system and that teachers needed more training in concepts such as "gender equity."

There are actually two separate problems described by the Crossen and the Sommers books. One is the intentional misuse or manipulation of polls and surveys by people with vested interests in the outcome of the research. The second problem is the inaccuracies and misleading results that are generated by bad surveys that are unintentional; they result not from malice or lack of ethics, but rather sloppiness or incompetence. The latter could consist of something as simple as poorly designed survey instruments and incorrectly chosen samples. In both cases, however, Crossen's second bottom line holds true—because most citizens lack the resources to understand and verify polls and survey results on their own, the media must do a better job of doing it for the general public.

TRACKING THE CASE: STUDENTS AND CREDIT CARD DEBT

Planning—Primary Research

Chapters 3 through 10 each include segments of a hypothetical student-produced public relations campaign proposal. The student team, as part of an advanced public relations class, spent the semester researching the problem of credit card debt among college students for a fictional nonprofit organization, Credit Counselors of Mason County.

After conducting background research, including an interview with the director of the Credit Counselors of Mason County (CCMC), archival and historical research, a review of relevant sources in the mass media, and case studies, the students moved on to the primary research phase.

The team chose to conduct both focus groups and surveys. The surveys were aimed at measuring the students' awareness of the problem and their awareness of the availability of counseling services such as those provided by CCMC. The surveys asked questions regarding current credit card usage (impulse purchases, school-related expenses, luxury items, etc.). The focus groups were used to determine which methods of communication were most effective in creating awareness and in motivating students to change their behavior.

The students conducted five focus group sessions: one each consisting of freshmen, sophomores, juniors, seniors, and graduate students. Once the results were compiled, the team used the data to develop a 16-question survey instrument that was emailed to 1,000 students chosen at random from a list of email addresses provided by the university. The team hoped for a response rate of at least 20 percent.

In the preliminary version of this segment, the team provided separate drafts of the questions it proposed to use in the survey and focus group sessions. After those research activities were conducted, the proposal was revised to reflect those results.

DISCUSSION QUESTIONS

1. Suppose you were to conduct a survey, using a ranking scale, among first-year students at your university. Your research objective is to determine the most common reasons why those students chose your university over other institutions. List some of the factors you would ask the participants to rank-order.

2. Think about the last time you participated in a research activity (opinion poll, marketing survey, or focus group—not an informal customer comment card). Describe the experience. Did the person conducting the research (interviewer or focus group moderator) follow the guidelines described in this chapter? Explain in detail. What incentive were you offered? How do you feel about the experience? How competent, professional, and/or courteous was the person conducting the research?

3. In addition to the ideas listed in this chapter, how can you deal with the problem of unlisted telephone numbers to make sure those individuals have an equal chance to be selected for your sample?

4. Would a focus group be an effective research method for an employee morale survey? Why or why not?

5. You have spent most of your adult life working for other people; now you have decided to work for yourself. Encouraged by your spouse and soon-to-be-former coworkers, you quit your downtown job and begin to pursue your life-long dream of running your own restaurant. Because your soon-to-be-former coworkers are always complaining about the lack of quality eating establishments downtown, you decide that the target market for your restaurant will be the downtown business crowd, including executives, middle-managers, and clerical staff.

Your first task is to find a suitable location. Your real estate agent shows you three locations—each with its own positives and negatives. Location A is on the edge of downtown and not within walking distance of the larger office buildings, but it has an abundance of free parking nearby and has a nice view of a nearby river. It is a ground-floor location with wheelchair access.

Location B is in a part of downtown with no free parking nearby and only a per-hour parking lot several blocks away. However, it is located within walking distance of many downtown office buildings and also has a nice view of the river. It is on the top floor of a three-story building with stairs but no elevator, meaning that potential customers in wheelchairs would be unable to visit.

Location C is a bit closer than location A to large downtown office buildings and would be within walking distance for some—but not all—of your customers. There is no free parking nearby, but a per-hour parking lot is across the street. It is a ground-floor location with wheelchair access. The only view from the windows is of a nearby widget factory.

Your second task is to develop a tentative menu.

Which research methods will you use to approach these two tasks—choosing a location and developing a tentative menu? You should employ at least two; you can use one method for the first task and a different method for the second, or you can use two methods that each will deal with both tasks.

6. Visit a variety of local restaurants (or any businesses that use customer comment cards) and bring the samples to class. Which ones are well designed and which ones are not? How can they be improved?

7. Find what types of research your school conducts among students in order to improve its programs, facilities, and recruiting methods. Discuss in your group how those methods can be expanded or improved.

8. Suppose you are setting up a focus group and the client not only wants to be in the room but also insists on being a co-moderator. What do you do?

9. One sentence in this chapter states that part of a focus group moderator's goal is to remind the participants that it is OK to disagree, but another sentence states that one of the goals of a focus group is to seek consensus. Is this a contradiction?

10. Does anyone conduct student focus groups at your university? Who are moderators? What kinds of questions are asked? What are the group's research objectives?

11. What is the best incentive you can provide to individuals to participate in a research project (in the real world) by either completing a survey or participating in a focus group?

GLOSSARY OF TERMS

Barometer scale questions. Research questions that ask the respondent to choose from a list of possible answers that moves upward or downward from a natural zero point.

Closed-ended questions. Research questions that provide a list of responses to choose as answers.

Content analysis. A scientific study of the content of communications.

Convenience sample. A sample chosen largely because the individuals are easy to find and willing to cooperate even though they may not be the most appropriate respondents.

Courtesy bias. The tendency of those being surveyed to provide responses that will please and/or not offend the interviewer, moderator, or other participants.

Cross-tabulations. The division of research results by demographic and psychographic category.

Delphi study. A research technique that involves mailing confidential surveys in multiple cycles.

Demographic/psychographic questions. Research questions that ask for factual information.

Dichotomous question. A survey question with only two possible answers.

Direct consumer information. A form of research that allows the researcher to closely watch consumers as they interact with a product or exhibit other behaviors.

Double-barrel question. A research question that contains the error of including more than one question combined to ask for one answer.

Field observation. A form of research where the person gathering the information becomes an active or passive participant in the activity being studied.

Focus group. A focused group interview or a meeting with 10 to 12 members of a target audience in a conference room setting with an experienced moderator.

Gap research. A form of research conducted by an organization or agency, usually through focus groups, to help measure its strengths and weaknesses and determine what it must do to better serve its publics.

Hawthorne effect. The tendency of research subjects to act differently as a result of knowing their behavior is being observed or recorded.

In-depth interviews. One-on-one interviews with a sample of a target audience.

Intercept surveys. Interviews conducted in person with the ability to maintain control over the interview situation.

Likert scale questions.   Research questions that ask respondents to choose their answers from a list that includes two extremes and various degrees in between.

Multiple-choice questions.   Questions that are followed by a list of three or more possible responses.

Omnibus survey.   The method of including questions related to two or more topics in the same survey.

Open-ended questions.   Research questions that allow the respondents to choose their own answers.

Qualitative research.   A category of research methods that are used when general information, rather than specific results, is needed. The results are expressed in words.

Quantitative research.   A category of research tools used when precise results are needed. The results are expressed in numbers or statistics.

Questionnaire or **research instrument.**   A list of questions used in research.

Quota sample.   A sampling method in which demographic groups are equally represented in the chosen sample. It is used when characteristics such as age, race, or gender may influence answers.

Random sample.   A sampling method in which all members of the audience have an equal chance of being chosen for the sample. It is used when demographic characteristics of the sample are not important.

Ranking-scale questions.   Research questions that ask respondents to rank-order items from a list, such as first preference and second preference.

Substantive questions.   Research questions that ask for opinions.

Survey research.   A noun referring to the beginning-to-end process of conducting this type of research.

Third-party question.   A method for conducting interviews or focus groups in which respondents are asked to describe the behavior of their peer group rather than their personal behaviors.

CHAPTER 5

PLANNING

Goals and Objectives, Messages and Themes, Channels and Strategies

GOALS AND OBJECTIVES

The terms *goals* and *objectives* are often confused, but they are not the same. **Goals** are the broader, more general outcomes one wants to see as a result of persuasive efforts. Generally, they are not quantifiable. **Objectives** are the specific and measurable indicators of whether the goals have been met. Objectives such as "to solve our company's problems" or "to increase our sales" are not specific enough to be objectives; with some revision they may be used as goals.

An example of a goal for a hospital's public relations campaign might be "to improve perception of our hospital in the community." Examples of objectives supporting that goal might include increasing name recognition of the hospital by a certain percentage and increasing the number of positive news stories about the hospital in the local media. Nonprofit organizations and social service agencies often use the term *targets of opportunity* in place of *objectives.*

Objectives can be categorized either by time frame (short term and long term) or by end result, such as informational, motivational, financial, or statutory. **Short-term objectives** are those expected to be accomplished either during the campaign or immediately upon its conclusion, whereas **long-term objectives** are those expected to be completed long after the program's conclusion.

Informational objectives refer to what one wants members of audiences to know as a result of a campaign; they do not necessarily require any action on the part of the members. Examples include "for people to become more aware of our company's products," and "for people to understand the dangers of not wearing seatbelts."

Motivational objectives refer to what one wants audience members to do as a result of receiving a message, such as buy a product, conserve water, vote for or against a proposed law or ordinance, or write their congressional representatives about a certain topic.

Statutory objectives refer to influencing the policy decisions of governmental bodies and agencies or persuading voters to pass or defeat proposed laws or ordinances.

Financial objectives refer to an increase in product sales for a profit-making company or an increase in donations for a nonprofit organization or charity. Many public relations professionals object to stating financial objectives because doing so places too much emphasis on the "bottom line" and suggests that financial results are the ultimate benefit from public relations activities, which they are not.

Another possible way of categorizing objectives is to label them as process objectives and outcome objectives. **Process objectives** refer to the quantifiable actions taken in executing a public relations program, such as the number of news releases distributed, the number of employee orientation meetings conducted, or the number of public events organized. **Outcome objectives** describe the results desired, such as an increase in sales or financial contributions, an increase in number of members joining an association, or an increase in name recognition.

Well thought-out objectives have the following characteristics:

1. *Objectives Should Be Realistic.* The objectives for a public relations program should be easy enough to be attainable but not so simple that they do not represent a challenge. In describing the art of setting objectives, experienced public relations professionals often cite two comparisons—one from poetry and another from politics. The first is Robert Browning's famous poem, "Andrea del Sarto," in which he wrote that "a man's reach should always exceed his grasp." The other comparison is a parable often included in the speeches of President John F. Kennedy. Kennedy was fond of the story about a man who was walking around town wearing his best hat when he came to a wall that at first glance appeared to be too high to climb. The man threw his hat over the wall and then spent the rest of the day finding a way to retrieve it. Kennedy's reference was to humankind's attempt to reach the moon.

The same high ideals should apply to communications programs. One should not, however, set objectives that are unreasonably high. Doing so may be a setup for failure. Instead of setting extremely high objectives, it is often more effective to concentrate on taking smaller incremental steps toward meeting goals.

2. *Objectives Should Be Clearly Defined.* Objectives should be specific and concrete rather than vague and abstract. Objectives should not be based on clichés or buzzwords. Ideas such as "improving our image" are too vague to be good objectives and are better used to describe goals.

3. *Objectives Should Be Measurable.* If there is no way to measure a result, it is a weak objective, because there will be no way to check it at the evaluation stage. Not every objective lends itself to being measured or quantified, but the majority should be.

Setting objectives is a critical part of the planning process. Objectives that convey meaningful results are better than those consisting of only gibberish. Before the campaign, it is the only way to justify the time, effort, and expense required. Afterward, it is the only way to prove it was worth doing. Meaningful objectives are especially important when proposing a high-budget campaign. Before company leaders or clients will approve a proposed budget, they will want some sense of what is hoped to be accomplished.

Grammatical Construction

The preferred construction of a written objective consists of an infinitive phrase (the word *to* followed by an active verb), the desired result, the relevant target audience, a quantification (the amount or degree of change expected), and a target date or deadline.

EXAMPLE

To increase	*Infinitive phase*
use of the mass transit system	*Desired result*
by downtown employees	*Target audience*
by 10 percent	*Quantification*
by June 1, 2009.	*Target date*

As objectives are written, they should be considered in light of whether they can be easily evaluated; the more specific and quantifiable they are, the easier they will be to evaluate once the program has been completed.

There are two possible ways to establish objectives that can later be measured (in the evaluation stage) by making before-and-after comparisons. The first is by establishing a desired percentage of increase or decrease, which is preferable when dealing with numbers that are already large. As an example, if a hospital desires to increase the number of individuals participating in its annual health fair, it may choose to establish an objective of increasing participation by 10 percent. If the goal of a campaign is to improve workplace safety, quantifiable objectives might be to decrease the number of workplace accidents by 20 percent or the number of missed workdays by some other measurable percentage.

An alternative method for expressing a quantifiable objective is to identify the desired increase or decrease in total numbers rather than percentages. This is preferable when dealing with smaller numbers. For example, if the objective is to increase the number of students participating in volunteer service activities—and the current number of students doing so is 2—it would be meaningless to seek an increase of 10, 20, or even 50 percent, as even a 50 percent increase would represent only one additional student. It would therefore be more meaningful to write an objective seeking "at least 50" student volunteers.

MESSAGES AND THEMES

Messages are the basic ideas that one wants members of audiences to remember as a result of receiving a communication. These are similar to the product messages used in advertising campaigns, such as "low prices," "product quality," and "company reputation."

Themes are the overarching ideas that apply to all of the audiences. In a public relations campaign for the city's mass transit system, for example, key messages may include "passenger safety" and "on-time performance," and a possible theme might be "The safe and reliable way to go to work," or something to that effect. Themes must be consistent through all forms of communication used. When developing a campaign for a hospital, for example, the television commercial used to communicate to senior citizens and the radio commercial used to communicate to teenagers will obviously be quite different, but the theme should be the same.

CHANNELS AND STRATEGIES

This subsection of the written proposal serves as a transition from the planning section to the implementation section. **Communication channels** are the broad categories of communication tactics selected to reach audiences. Those tactics are often categorized as media channels, nonmedia channels, and interactive media channels. **Strategies** is a catch-all term that refers to other decisions made on how the program will be implemented.

Media channels are associated with broad dissemination through print, and broadcast, media, including news media, institutional advertising, and donated media. **Nonmedia channels** include events, community involvement and philanthropy programs, in-person communication, and direct mail. **Interactive media channels** include email, the Internet, blogs, and social media, and the list keeps growing. Each channel consists of several tactics, and those tactics are discussed in detail in the next three chapters.

Some factors to consider when choosing communication channels include the following:

1. *Who the Client Is.*   Even though a specific budget will not be developed until later in the process, planners must keep in mind whether they are working for a company, a nonprofit organization, or a governmental agency as well as the level of funding likely to be available.
2. *Who the Audiences Are.*   Planners should refer to the list of audiences and determine where members of these audiences are most likely to get their information. Much of this should be revealed by primary research.
3. *Time Available.*   Various channels take varying lengths of time to convey messages to the audiences, and expectations should be phrased accordingly.

As a "bonus," planners should look for opportunities to use channels that provide for two-way communication so they can solicit feedback from the audiences through the same channels used to transmit information to them.

The decision as to which channels to use can be based not only on the information gathered in the background and verification research but also on information previously known, such as that learned through the evaluation of past campaigns. For example, if comment cards distributed at last year's event asked respondents to indicate where they heard about the event (news stories, advertisements, posters, word-of-mouth, etc.), those results would influence which of those channels and tactics should be used for the following year.

Because the implementation section will describe those specific tactics, the "communication channels" portion of the proposal needs to list only the channels without being specific about tactics. One or two sentences explaining why each channel was chosen would be helpful, however.

Strategies refer to the overall concept, approach, or general plan for the program. The term should not be confused with *tactics,* which refer to the operational level: the actual events, media, and methods used to implement the strategy.

The list of strategies may include explanations of how those categories will be combined, prioritized, or applied in a specific way. An example is "By working through the public school system, we will first . . ." or "By using a combination of news media and paid advertising . . . ."

Another example of a strategy is to take different approaches to each audience based on factors uncovered in the research. For instance, in developing a communications program for a university's alumni association, focus group research might indicate that alumni from different years would have much different expectations and perceptions of the association. Recent graduates would be interested in the alumni association as an opportunity to socialize with former classmates and as a source of business contacts and job leads. They might be very interested in social and networking activities, but would be unable to make a financial donation due to their employment status. Older alumni who are established in their careers, might be in a better position to support the organization financially. A strategy statement in this case might read, "Because alumni have a variety of perceptions and expectations of the association, these differences must be taken into account when communicating to them about their potential involvement."

Another example of a strategy statement is related to how the audiences receive information. Research might reveal that one or more of the audiences speak languages other than English, so an appropriate strategy would be to issue campaign or other informational materials in those other languages.

For nonprofit organizations, an example of a strategy is to partner with media organizations. Many newspapers and broadcast outlets have community service policies through which they sponsor community events and provide levels of free publicity and news coverage.

Strategies may also include rhetorical appeals, such as those taught by the Greek philosopher Aristotle. He taught that there are three basic appeals used to persuade audiences: *ethos* (because it is the right thing to do), *pathos* (feeling sympathy or empathy for someone who will benefit from the desired behavior), and *logos* (because something makes sense to do). Generalizations about logical and emotional appeals include the belief that communicators on the offense should use emotional appeals (pathos), whereas those on the defense will be more successful with logical appeals (logos). Another common generalization is that emotional appeals can be made more effectively through the broadcast media, and logical appeals can be made more effectively through the print media. Still another generalization is that logical appeals tend to be more effective in dealing with better-educated audiences, whereas emotional appeals tend to be more effective with audiences with a lower education level. Other experts simply contend that the combination of logical and emotional appeals is more effective than either approach used exclusively.

Yet another example of a strategy is to recommend a change in management policy that goes beyond just the communications methods to be used. For example, suppose the public relations department of a hospital is developing a program to address public criticism of its policy regarding treatment of uninsured patients. Obviously, the most effective way to eliminate the criticism is to change or eliminate the policy. Thus, a recommended strategy in the communications plan would be "to implement a policy change concerning uninsured patients."

GENERALIZATIONS ABOUT MEDIA

The following generalizations about media channels apply to both news coverage and advertising.

Decades of research into media habits have concluded that although audiences report receiving the majority of their information from television, they retain much more of what they read in newspapers and magazines. That may be partly due to the fact that reading newspapers and magazines requires more intellectual involvement than watching television or listening to the radio.

One popular generalization about selecting media is that print media are better for logical appeals, and broadcast media are better for emotional appeals. Another is that television and radio are effective for providing information, but newspapers are better for generating a call to action.

According to a number of research studies, the majority of Americans (50 to 70 percent, depending on which study is being looked at) identify television as their primary source of news. Newspapers are a distant second at 20 to 30 percent. Radio comes next at 10 to 15 percent and magazines last at 5 to 10 percent.

According to a 2005 study, conducted by Roper Public Affairs and Media, the average American adult spends more than 272 minutes per day watching television, 122 minutes listening to the radio, 73 minutes using the Internet, 29 minutes reading newspapers, and 19 minutes reading magazines. There's little variance in the number across age groups, except in the case of those age 65 and over, in which case television viewing increases to 322 minutes, newspaper and magazine reading increases to 60 minutes and 30 minutes, respectively, and Internet usage drops to 33 minutes.

Media researchers have coined the term **convergence** to refer to the trend of newspapers, television stations, and on-line news services originating from one source, sometimes referred to as the "common newsroom." Federal Communications Commission rules once prohibited cross-ownership between television stations and newspapers, but those restrictions were relaxed in the 1990s. While the television news covers mostly stories that have visual elements and produces shorter stories with less details, the newspapers cover more complex stories and provide more detail. The on-line editions include many of the same stories, and are also more interactive because they allow readers to post comments to discussion boards and respond to polls and other interactive features based on news content.

Contrasting News and Advertising

The two advantages of communicating to audiences through the news media are credibility and low cost. Credibility results from a process known as **filtering or validation**, meaning that audiences attach more importance to information presented in the form of news because it is assumed the information has been verified. Getting media coverage for a product, event, or issue costs much less than advertising; the only costs involved are related to production of publicity materials and the amount of staff time necessary to organize news conferences and other events.

Relying on the news media comes with a trade-off, however, in that control of the message is lost. The media take control of the message and determine how much of it gets through to the audience and when and where it will get through.

The main advantage of advertising is complete control over the message. Robert Morley, a British film director who was upset over negative reviews of his work, once called advertising "the only thing we have left where we can always be assured of a happy ending."

The main negative associated with advertising is its high cost. Regardless of whether an organization advertises through newspapers, magazines, television, radio, or billboards, it will likely be the largest budget item in the public relations program. The second problem is a lack of credibility, as advertising is presumed by the audience to be one-sided.

Selecting which forms of advertising to use involves the consideration of both frequency (the number of times the message will be seen or heard) and reach (the number of individuals exposed to the advertisement). Advertising professionals suggest an audience should be exposed to a product message a minimum of six times; the audience's retention and understanding of the information will increase with repetition.

In *The Fall of Advertising, the Rise of PR,* authors Al and Laura Ries explain that the difference between advertising and public relations is the same as the difference between the wind and the sun:

> Advertising (the wind) is perceived as an imposition, an unwelcome intruder who needs to be resisted. The harder the sell, the harder the wind blows, the harder the prospect resists the sales message.
>
> The harder an advertiser tries to force its way into the mind, the less likely it will accomplish its objective. Once in a while a prospect drops his or her guard and the wind will win. But not often.
>
> PR is the sun. You cannot force the media to run your message. It is entirely in their hands. All you can do is smile and make sure your publicity material is as helpful as possible.

Newspapers

Even though circulation figures for most national and daily newspapers have been declining steadily for almost a decade, research consistently shows that newspapers remain an influential source of information for Americans who are college-educated and in the middle- and higher-income brackets.

One problem with national newspapers is how they react to information provided by public relations sources. *USA Today* is one of the most difficult newspapers in which to get a story; its reporters and editors accept few news releases and story ideas from public relations people because they prefer to find news on their own.

One exception to this generalization about national newspapers is the *Wall Street Journal.* Because of its business focus, its reporters are highly dependent on public relations representatives for story ideas. Often there appears to be a love-hate relationship between the *Wall Street Journal* reporters and the public relations profession: The reporters love PR people when they supply good story ideas, but those same reporters gripe when PR professionals clog their mailboxes, fax lines, and email servers with news releases that they cannot use.

Another problem with national newspapers is the high cost of advertising space. Local daily and weekly newspapers are much less expensive and can target audiences much better.

In the 1980s, journalism professor John Merrill developed a list of what he labeled "intellectually elite newspapers." He said that in every country of the world, there might be thousands of daily newspapers, but only a handful that have national circulation and that appeal to a largely intellectual audience. For the United States, he listed these four: *New York Times, Los Angeles Times, Washington Post,* and *Christian Science Monitor.* If the better-educated and more affluent individuals are in one's target audience, one should keep those papers in mind if a campaign is nationwide in scope. The national newspapers of that type are likely to pay more attention to major social issues and are read by people who are

Even in the age of the Internet, the daily newspaper remains an effective method to reach educated audiences.

decision makers and opinion leaders. The equivalent on television would be *The News Hour* weekday evenings on PBS and *Morning Edition* and *All Things Considered* on National Public Radio, as they also appeal to the intellectual audience.

One of the significant qualities of newspapers is pervasiveness. Including both home delivery and single-copy sales, more than 450 million newspapers are sold daily in the United States, and total readership numbers are even higher because most newspapers are read by more than one person. Known as the **pass-along rate**, it is believed that there are approximately 2.2 readers per copy. (The figure varies by geography and day of the week.) As of 2005, more than half of Americans reported reading a newspaper every day, with more than 60 percent reading a Sunday newspaper.

However, both circulation and total readership numbers represent an annual decline of 2 to 4 percent since 2000, as the medium has lost market share to the Internet. When the decline first became noticeable, organizations and industries that depended on newspapers to reach their audiences took some solace in the fact that although the total amounts were down, the numbers still showed that the most important audiences—opinion leaders and decision-makers in fields such as business and politics—still read newspapers in large numbers. More recently, however, even those individuals responding to media consumption surveys indicated a shift away from print media and toward the Internet.

In response to this decline, nearly every major daily newspaper in the United States publishes an on-line version. In some cases, the papers include every word of every news item in their on-line editions, whereas others include either abbreviated versions of every story or the complete versions of only selected items. (Some features such as comic strips, editorial cartoons, and syndicated columns are not included because of copyright restrictions.)

For public relations professionals, one helpful element of on-line newspapers is the archive feature that allows users to access stories from past editions, with the most recent issues (from the past week or so) available for free and older stories available for a modest fee.

Those newspapers have no intention of abandoning their print products and producing their products only in the on-line format, however. Instead, they use their two products to promote each other, using the on-line version to tout the benefits of their print edition, and vice-versa. As a result of this trend, media researchers have coined the term *aggregated readership* to refer to combining the readership of the print product with the number of consumers using the on-line edition.

In addition, national publications such as the *New York Times*, the *Wall Street Journal*, and *USA Today* are attempting to keep their print editions viable by working with universities to make their print products available to students either for free or at a substantial discount from the regular subscription costs. Representatives of those newspapers conduct workshops on how teachers can incorporate newspaper readership into their classes. Similarly, many local daily newspapers have developed "newspapers in education" programs designed to increase readership among teenage audiences.

Newspapers have a broad appeal in terms of adults and are effective in handling complex or in-depth material that television cannot adequately cover. Another factor in favor of newspapers is permanence; one can cut an article out and save it.

A drawback of newspapers is their lack of appeal to youth; readership among youth is low. In 1965, teenage newspaper readership was 67 percent. By 2000, it had dropped to 30 percent.

One problem that public relations representatives occasionally experience with daily newspapers is skepticism. Whether intentional or not, newspapers and the reporters who work for them often display anticorporate and antipublic relations biases. It is not as much of a problem as it was 20 years ago, but it is still noticeable. One example of this problem is the reluctance of some newspaper reporters and editors to cover certain business news stories because they do not like the concept of promoting specific products for fear they will be accused of providing news sources with free publicity.

Many communities have weekly or monthly business publications that could take the form of either newspapers or magazines, and they are excellent venues for either news items or paid commercial messages. And, of course, the leading national business publication is the *Wall Street Journal,* which is widely read by business executives and other opinion leaders.

Magazines

The advantage of magazines for either news coverage or advertising is their ability to target specific audiences. The growth of the magazine industry has produced at least one publication for every industry, lifestyle choice, entertainment preference, or recreational interest found in U.S. society. Editors of these publications tend to look more favorably at publicity materials than do the editors of newspapers, and advertising space is much less expensive than space in general-interest magazines such as *Time* or *Newsweek*. Most magazines can provide prospective advertisers with detailed demographic profiles of their readers; that information is also available to public relations representatives. There are four types of magazines:

1. General or news magazines are those such as *Time, Newsweek,* and *U.S. News & World Report.*
2. Alternative magazines cover many of the same issues as general news magazines, but have much smaller readerships. Examples include *Village Voice* and *Utne Reader.* Many communities have their own alternative publications that focus mainly on entertainment and cultural issues but occasionally address local politics.
3. Content-specific magazines are those related to specific sports and leisure activities, such as *Baseball Digest* and *Gardening.*
4. Audience-specific magazines are those that target specific demographic groups according to gender, age, and race, or combinations thereof. Examples are *GQ, Esquire, Cosmopolitan, Mademoiselle, Seventeen, Jet,* and *Ebony.* Magazines targeted at housewives or stay-at-home moms are known in the publishing industry as the "seven sisters." They are *Better Homes and Gardens, Family Circle, Good Housekeeping, Ladies Home Journal, McCall's, Redbook,* and *Woman's Day.*

The advantages of the content-specific and audience-specific publications (over the general/news magazines) include well-defined audiences, lower advertising rates, and editorial staffs that are more receptive to news items submitted by public relations representatives. Another advantage of magazines is that the demographic information about their readership is often more detailed and more accurate than the information available for newspapers, whose readers are more difficult to profile. Researchers know, for example, that the median age of readers of *Time, Newsweek,* and *U.S. News & World Report* is 43 to 47, whereas the median age for readers of lifestyle publications such as *InStyle* and *Maxim* is 32 to 33.

One drawback is that magazines work on a long lead time, which can be anywhere from 30 to 90 days for monthlies and six to nine months for quarterly publications. Public relations representatives who send information that is time sensitive must be working several months ahead.

Magazines charge higher advertising rates than newspapers, but have a longer shelf life than newspapers and have greater pass-along readership because they remain in waiting rooms and on library shelves for longer periods of time.

Many communities have at least one "alternative" magazine, usually a weekly, which focuses on entertainment and culture but also addresses local political and social issues. Alternative weeklies and monthlies experienced major growth in the 1990s and continue to grow today. The advantages of such publications include low advertising rates, more room to publish news related to nonprofit organizations, and the ability to reach younger audiences that are unlikely to read more traditional dailies.

Trade Publications

Every industry or profession has its own trade journal or specialty publication that may take the form of a newspaper or magazine and may be published weekly, monthly, or quarterly. Publications with titles such as *Construction News* and *Grocery Store Monthly* are not sold on newsstands, but they can reach specific audiences in ways that the *New York Times* and the *Wall Street Journal* cannot.

The most effective way to get stories into trade publications is to be familiar with their contents and formats by thoroughly examining sample copies before sending news releases. Before attempting to contact a publication's editors, public relations representatives must understand the needs of that publication as well as know the companies and products the publication promotes.

The emphasis in many trade publications is new products, trends, and issues, but they are also open to lighter news such as profiles of company leaders. Public relations representatives should approach such a publication in the same manner that a freelance journalist would: first by query letter, then by follow-up telephone call.

Public relations representatives attempting to interest trade publications in a story must make three successful matches. The first is to match the purpose and content of the information one sends with the purpose and content of the publication.

The second is to match the target audience for the campaign with the readership of the publication. If a public relations representative is uncertain about whether a specific publication has the right readership, he or she can contact the publication's research department and ask for a readership profile. Most trade publications employ research departments or demographers to study their readership, compile the results, and tell them who their readers are. That information is used mainly by the publication's advertising sales representatives, but the publication will often share the information with anyone who asks for it, including public relations representatives considering including that publication on their media list.

The third match is timing. For both news and advertising, business publications and trade journals have editorial calendars that describe the topics covered at a certain time of year. Early in the year, January and February issues will likely focus on new products. In the spring, the emphasis may be on financial matters because of upcoming income tax deadlines. Summer issues may offer vacation options for business people. Fall issues often provide information about conventions and meetings specific to the field. If a public relations representative submits a news release about a new product after the new products issue has come out, it may not be published until the following year, if at all. One must be aware of when special editions are coming out and when their deadlines are and plan several months in advance.

Here is another example of an editorial calendar, taken from *Wilmington* (North Carolina) *Business Journal:**

January	Health and fitness
February	Financial planning
March	Golf and tennis
April	Travel
May	Retirement planning
June	Legal issues
July	Marine trades
August	Higher education
September	Housing market
October	Construction
November	Health
December	Technology

*Reprinted with permission of Greater Wilmington Business (Joy Allen, publisher).

Television

A major advantage of television is access. More than 99 percent of U.S. households have a least one television and many have more than one, according to Nielsen Media Research. In major metropolitan areas, more than 90 percent of homes are wired for cable, and cable service is standard offerings in most hotel rooms, restaurants, and bars. In rural areas, approximately 70 percent of homes are either wired for cable or receive their television programming from satellite services. In the United States, television sets, on average, are on for 7.5 hours a day. In addition to being most Americans' primary source of news, television is also reported to be the most authoritative and credible source of advertising information.

In prime time, one-third of all television viewers watch cable and two-thirds watch network programming. In terms of television advertising, one advantage is that the advertiser has complete control of the message. That is true of any form of advertising, but it is likely more significant with television because an organization can choose the time of day and which programs on which it wants to place its spots.

Another positive is that television is very effective for making emotional appeals. If an organization has chosen an emotional appeal rather than a logical route to persuade its audience, television will be more proficient than print media in helping to do that. Television is also effective at reaching the broad consumer audience, including teenagers who do not read the newspaper.

Studies show that traditional evening newscasts are declining in popularity and credibility with the audience, but network newsmagazines such as NBC's *Dateline*, CBS's *60 Minutes*, and ABC's *20/20* remain solid. Cable news channels such as Cable News Network (CNN), MSNBC, and the Fox News Channel are growing in popularity for coverage of national issues. On the local level, audiences report preferring their local television stations for news, even in communities in which newspaper readership is high.

Market researchers have found that the link between television viewing habits and purchasing habits is stronger than the link between newspaper readership and purchasing. A 1998 study found that for each hour per week spent watching television, total household expenditures increase proportionately.

Television's negatives include a lack of retention, which research shows to be quite low. Audiences hear the message but do not remember it for very long. The exception is when an organization pays for advertising and can repeat the commercial enough times. But nonprofit organizations cannot afford to buy enough television time to repeat the message, and in the case of one-time news stories on television, retention is extremely low.

Also, a limitation of television is its bias toward visual stories and toward style over substance. Some good stories may go unreported because they are not visual enough. Another disadvantage with television news is its emphasis on brevity; reporters are given only brief slots in which to fit their stories and are therefore unlikely to go into great depth in any story. That problem is especially apparent on evening newscasts. A decade ago, individuals involved in television news stories would complain about 10-minute interviews reduced to one-sentence sound bites. Now, video editors sometimes cut them even shorter, using only fragments of sentences spoken by interviewees. *Dateline, 60 Minutes,* and *20/20* can go into detail, but those stories are usually negative rather than positive.

Yet another limitation of television is a lack of appeal to highly educated audiences. There are two characteristics media researchers have about highly educated audiences: (1) They watch television less than other audiences and (2) their viewing patterns are inconsistent. Lesser-educated audiences, conversely, tend to watch television to a greater degree and with fairly consistent viewing habits—favoring reruns, game shows, daytime dramas, and tabloid-format talk shows.

Unlike newspapers and magazines, in which one has little influence over which page an advertisement appears on, with radio and television the time of day and specific program one wishes to advertise during can be selected.

Radio

In the last decade, many public relations professionals have begun to view radio in a more positive light. When public relations researchers conduct comparative studies of which forms of media are the most accurate and do the best job of covering certain issues, they find that radio news consistently outperforms all other forms of media in terms of accuracy and thoroughness. One form of radio that is frequently highlighted in media studies is National Public Radio (NPR), which is especially strong in the area of public issues. According to media researchers, the majority of NPR listeners are over the age of 45.

Therefore, if an organization is working on a campaign that involves an issue—for or against a proposed government regulation or law, for example—NPR can be an effective channel to reach audiences. Many communities have local public radio stations that are affiliated with both NPR and nearby universities. Its reporting may not take the organization's side and agree with the cause it is promoting, but NPR has a stronger reputation than other forms of media for accurate and thorough reporting.

One of the positives of radio is pervasiveness. More than 98 percent of U.S. households own at least one radio, and most own more than one, according to Arbitron, a media research company specializing in researching radio listening patterns. The average listener spends more than 3 hours and 15 minutes per day listening to radio, more than half of which takes place outside of the home (mostly at work or while driving).

Another positive for radio is its appeal to the youth audience. Arbitron reports, for example, that more than 98.1 percent of teenage girls listen to radio. But 25- to 34-year-old men listen the most—an average of almost 26 hours per week.

Yet another benefit of radio is specialized timing. Radio stations do a better job than television stations of researching their audiences and can make that information available to prospective advertisers and news sources. Not only can radio stations provide a demographic profile (like a magazine can with its subscribers) but they can also break down such a profile by time of day (which age groups listen during morning commutes, during the day on the afternoon drives, and late at night and overnight). An additional advantage of radio advertising involves money and time. It is relatively inexpensive to produce radio spots and purchase the time, and an advertiser can also quickly produce or update a series.

The main limitation of radio is an inability to cover visual stories. Another negative is limited news staff. Much of radio news is taken from daily newspapers. It may be difficult to persuade radio news reporters to come to a news conference when they can simply summarize the newspaper story they read the next day.

Yet another drawback to radio is the difficulty of measurement. Clip files cannot be created like with newspapers, and there are few monitoring services like there are for television news.

PUBLIC RELATIONS ON THE INTERNET

For public relations professionals, the Internet offers organizations opportunities to communicate more effectively with employees, stockholders, potential stockholders, customers, potential customers, and the media. But the technology also presents a number of challenges, as organizations and their public relations staffs must deal with angry consumers and advocacy groups that launch their criticisms using a variety of "nontraditional media" such as websites, chatrooms, on-line discussion groups, and blogs.

More detail on the use of the Internet as a communication channel is found in Chapter 7, but for comparison purposes, some of the major advantages of the Internet include immediacy and convenience. One example is found in the ability of organizations to offer on-line news conferences for journalists spread over a wide geographic area, thus reducing or eliminating travel costs. The major disadvantage is the inability of the Internet-based communication programs to reach audience members without computers in their homes—a problem that social scientists refer to as the "digital divide." However, as the retail prices of home computers continue to drop, and more public libraries expand their computer laboratories to meet the increased demand, this becomes less of a problem.

One weakness of the Internet is that many organizations do not take their websites seriously, and as a result the information on their sites is either outdated or superficial and fails to provide to audiences a current and accurate picture of what the company does and the principles by which it operates. Public relations departments are especially guilty of website neglect. When journalists searching for background information visit a company's website and navigate their way toward the public relations department's page, for example, they draw negative impressions when they "click here to read our latest news releases," only to find that the most recent item is six months old.

Another potential weakness of the Internet is the ongoing uncertainty over what types of information Internet users are seeking, especially the 18- to 24-year-old demographic category. Before politicians and policymakers embrace the Internet as a new magic weapon for reaching that demographic, they should know that research shows the 18- to 24-year-old age group uses the Internet for news and information about the entertainment industry and popular culture far more than they do for more serious topics such as political news and public affairs. The rare exceptions, media researchers have concluded, are news stories that have a more immediate impact, such as those involving employment or student loans. For more "big picture" issues such as the national economy and health care, however, the 18–24 demographic remains largely apathetic.

TRENDS AND ISSUES

News Values and Interests

When attempting to influence journalists to provide coverage of a story or issue, public relations professionals should understand how potential story ideas are evaluated. The concept of *newsworthiness* includes consideration of both news values and news interests.

Common **news values** are timeliness, consequence, proximity, and prominence. *Timeliness* means that it is bigger news if it just happened, is about to happen, or was recently discovered. Most of the news reported in tomorrow's newspaper will be based on events that happened today. For public relations representatives, that means associating a potential news story with events already happening. For example, if you are working for a defense contractor and one of the company's products played a part in a recent military victory overseas, a news release about that product would be timely. Even if it had been rejected by the media before, an old release about the device can be dusted off and revised by emphasizing the timeliness in the lead.

Consequence refers to the importance or significance of the story being proposed. If an individual donates $10 to a local charity, few people care. If a client donates $50 million to the same charity, it results in a front-page news story. If a storm turns over an individual's garbage can, he or she may be the only one to notice. When a larger storm disrupts electrical power for 200,000 customers, the media notice right away.

Proximity refers to how close the news story is to the audience. In his book, *Coups and Earthquakes,* journalist Mort Rosenblum explained that a "dogfight in Brooklyn makes more news than a civil war in Africa." One of the major complaints gatekeepers have about news releases they receive through the mail is "no local interest." If you want a story in a newspaper outside of the city in which the story takes place, you must find a tie-in with that other community and make sure it is clear in the headline and lead. News releases distributed nationally about something happening at corporate headquarters will be tossed unless there's a local angle for each community.

Prominence refers to the inclusion of well-known individuals, companies, or organizations in the story.

The media will seldom cover the grand opening of a small business unless a celebrity is involved. Even though the focus of the story will be the celebrity rather than the business, the business will still receive at least a secondary mention because the journalist will indicate in the story the circumstances in which the appearance took place. Prominence is not limited only to people; it also applies to the organization itself. A new product from IBM or Apple is more newsworthy than one from a computer company with less name recognition. The grand opening of a new Macy's department store will attract more attention than that of Joe's Hardware Store.

Here are some of the major **news interests** that public relations writers should keep in mind when considering the worthiness of news stories they promote. This list is not as complete as those found in journalism textbooks, but it includes the ones with which public relations professionals will have the most success.

Public relations writers should keep in mind the newsworthiness of stories they promote. News values consist of timeliness, consequence, proximity, and prominence.

Self-Interest

Journalists often pursue stories that will help their readers make good decisions and improve their lives. Examples include stories that help them improve their health, protect themselves as consumers, or pursue better employment opportunities.

Other People

Human interest story is a vague term that is overused and misused by people outside of the news business. A better term is *other people,* because readers are drawn to stories about other people doing interesting things. A person does not have to be a hero or a world champion to be the subject of a news story. In many cases, the biggest celebrities to emerge from the Olympic Games are not the winners, but those who finish well behind; they capture the attention of the media because of their perseverance and competitive spirit in the face of overwhelming odds.

Conflict

American media audiences are more interested in conflict than harmony, and the journalism industry caters to this preference by publishing and broadcasting stories involving individuals and organizations that disagree with each other. It need not be a physical confrontation; a philosophical difference of opinion, such as a company criticizing a government agency for a change in regulation or policy, is just as newsworthy. Journalists are also interested in stories about how such conflicts are resolved, but to a lesser degree.

Progress

Examples of "progress stories" include those about nonprofit organizations taking steps to improve their services to clients or their communities. Other examples include stories about government agencies introducing new programs or changing their procedures in order to better serve citizens.

Novelty

Novelty refers to stories that show what is different about the company's products or services. One indicator of news value can be found in modifiers. Any time a modifier can be attached to a news story, such as *first, youngest, oldest,* or *largest,* it should be emphasized. Modifiers should not be buried at the bottom of the release; work them into the lead—for instance, "The Richardson County School System will become the first school system in the country to . . . ."

Ragan's Media Relations Report lists a few additional examples of adding interest to potential feature stories:

- *Find a Way to Involve Others.* Instead of positioning the potential feature story as one that simply advances the client's or employer's interests, find a second party to share the spotlight, such as a charity or nonprofit organization that will also benefit.
- *Look for a Milestone.* The anniversary of a product's debut or the millionth (or ten millionth) to roll off the assembly line makes a story more timely.
- *Relate to the Season.* This is also known as "calendar connections." Spring is a natural time of year for news stories on home improvements; summer is good for stories on exercise and fitness, and fall is a good time for stories on family holiday gatherings. Also look for opportunities to relate to quasi-holidays, such as Valentine's Day, Mother's Day, Father's Day, and Administrative Professionals' Day.
- *Find an Inspiring Character in the Organization.* In most organizations there is an "unsung hero" or other newsworthy individual who does an unusual amount of volunteer work, has a special talent, or some other newsworthy attribute worthy of a news story that will also mention his or her role in the organization.

CASE STUDY 5

Dixie Chicks: Shut Up and Sing!

Check any blog or news list of music controversies, and the Dixie Chicks, a popular country-western music group, will be included for their utterance of 15 spontaneous words during a London concert in 2003. As support for the war in Iraq continues to decline and as President Bush's approval ratings continue to drop, the famous words become less important and more of a joke or point for discussion. Even a *Dancing with the Stars* judge made a play on the famous words.

Over time, country music fans have forgotten about the controversy, and the group continues to be one of the highest-selling female groups in any genre and the only female group to earn back-to-back Diamond Awards for sales.

"Just so you'll know, we're ashamed the president of the United States is from Texas," said Natalie Maines, the group's outspoken lead singer, at the concert just nine days before the war in Iraq began.

For Maines, the comment showed how difficult it is to stop a reaction, how important timing can be, and how poor public relations, planned or unplanned, is remembered as long, or often longer, than good public relations.

The story made front-page news even as the country headed into war. Some country music radio stations boycotted the group from Texas, angry fans reacted with threats and destroyed CDs, and many spoke out publicly against the group. Conservative talk radio host Neal Boortz referred to the group as the "Ditsy Twits" and his callers labeled the group the "Dixie Sluts."

Some radio networks that owned stations across the Southeast ordered their stations not to play Dixie Chicks songs, and the controversy became part of the debate on the Federal Communications Commission's rules on multiple radio station ownership and the potential influence that results from networks owning too many stations.

As Associated Press and other media outlets picked up the story, Maines tried to do damage control. "As a concerned American citizen, I apologize to President Bush that my remark was disrespectful," Maines said. She defended her right to speak out but said it was the wording she used and the way she said it "with genuine emotion and questions and concern

behind it." She spoke strongly of the group's support of the troops.

The country singers often make comments on stage and prefer to work without a script. "This keeps the show fresher," said a tearful Maines in an interview with Diane Sawyer on a special ABC's *Primetime,* with the title, "Landslide: The Dixie Chicks." The word *landslide* refers to a song by the Dixie Chicks. Maines said there was no thought behind the comment and she would like to say she had learned to think before she talked.

Sisters Emily Robinson and Martie Maguire defended their partner and friend and expressed hurt as a result of the criticisms and backlash. While admitting to Sawyer that they had paid a price for the mistake, the singers spoke strongly of their patriotism, their role as humans who make mistakes, and their likeness to their fans, and they said the punishment had gone overboard and crossed the line.

Fearing the worst in the summer of 2003, the concert organizers arranged for metal detectors and extra security personnel at concert venues. Although the trio faced picket lines outside some of the venues and some minor heckling inside, in most cases, their fans outnumbered their critics once they began performing.

Continuing to perform and continuing to tour, the Dixie Chicks sent fans media-released information saying rumors to cancel concerts were untrue and the group persevered. The group continued to make number-one hits with songs such as "Vote for Change" in 2004. In addition, they earned numerous nominations and awards, including a Grammy for Best Country Performance by a Duo or Group for "Top of the World" in 2005. They were presented the Rock the Vote Patrick Lippert Award in 2004 and given media honors, including *Country Weekly,* one of the most popular magazines covering the industry. They urged fans to support efforts to stop global warming and gave song benefits to the Hurricane Katrina relief.

Their seventh studio album, released in the United States in May 2006 and worldwide in June 2006, titled "Taking the Long Way," won five Grammy Awards and has been called a global smash. Song lyrics address the controversy. "Not Ready to Make Nice" refers to the group's purpose and "The Long Way Around" talks about nonconformity.

TRACKING THE CASE: COLLEGE STUDENTS AND CREDIT CARD DEBT

Goals and Objectives, Messages and Themes, Channels and Strategies

Chapters 3 through 10 each include segments of a hypothetical student-produced public relations campaign proposal. The student team, as part of an advanced public relations class, spent the semester researching the problem of credit card debt among college students for a fictional nonprofit organization, Credit Counselors of Mason County.

After conducting primary research with regard to students and credit card debt, the team set its goals and objectives.

Goals and Objectives

The team established the overall goals of (1) increasing the awareness of the problem of credit card debt and its effect on college students, professors, counselors, advisors, and administrators; and (2) increasing the awareness of available services, such as those provided by the CCMC, among the same audiences.

The team chose to categorize its objectives for the campaign into two categories: process objectives and outcome objectives.

Its *process objectives* included (1) having credit card debt included in the series of seminars presented in new student orientation programs, ongoing residence hall programs, and for-credit classes taken by new students; and (2) providing information on credit card debt to academic and mental health counselors.

Outcome objectives included (1) increasing the number of members of all audiences aware of the problem of credit card debt by 20 percent by the end of the academic year and (2) decreasing the number of students self-reporting problems with credit card debt on confidential surveys. The students were careful not to use before-and-after comparisons related to the number of students seeking the services of the CCMC. If the number of students seeking services increased, the team would have no way of knowing if that meant the campaign was unsuccessful because the number of students in credit card debt had actually increased or it was successful because the students

seeking services were already in debt but were now aware of the program.

Messages and Themes

The team chose the following messages for the campaign:

- Credit card debt is a growing problem among college students and universities and is likely to become more of a problem as tuition continues to rise.
- Credit card debt, as reported on an individual's credit report, is a factor that may reflect negatively on new college graduates as they are subjected to preemployment screening during the job-hunting process.
- College students should not be embarrassed about seeking the services of agencies such as Credit Counselors of Mason County.

The theme for the campaign was "Graduate From College—Footloose and Debt Free." Team members believed the theme would effectively play on the cliche, "footloose and fancy free" and convey to students the importance of beginning their postcollege years with a clean financial slate.

Strategies and Channels of Communication

The team identified two strategies that it believed would be crucial to the success of the program. The first was to utilize the technique of prepackaged publics—in this case, existing opportunities to reach students through programs such as new student orientation, residence hall programming, and a course required for all entering freshmen and transfer students, Introduction to College Life.

The second strategy was to involve university employees at all levels, including the president of the institution. As one example, the president would be encouraged to support the effort by issuing an executive order prohibiting the bookstore from inserting credit card applications in shopping bags and also prohibiting credit card companies from soliciting on campus.

DISCUSSION QUESTIONS

1. Consider each communications channel mentioned in this chapter. Which ones have changed the most during the time you have been communicating with people outside your family? How were these communications channels different when your parents were growing up? Which ones will be different when your children begin communicating with others?

2. Think back about the purchases (or other decisions) you made in the last week. Which ones were influenced by some of the tactics listed in this chapter, and to what degree?

3. Read the lists of "shalls" and "shall nots" in Chapter 12. What are some of the limitations these ideas place on setting objectives for a public relations campaign?

4. What is your opinion of how the Dixie Chicks controversy was addressed (by all participants)? If you had been a participant in the controversy, what would you have done differently? Consider the public relations concepts discussed in this chapter: goals, objectives, messages, themes, strategies, and channels. Which of those concepts can be applied to this case?

GLOSSARY OF TERMS

Communication channels. The broad categories of communication tactics selected to reach audiences.

Convergence. The trend of newspapers, television stations, and on-line news services to originate from one source, sometimes referred to as the "common newsroom."

Ethos. A persuasive appeal based on a course of action being the right thing to do.

Filtering or validation. A process that gives credibility because audiences attach more importance to information presented as news because it is assumed to be verified.

Financial objectives. An increase in product sales for a profit-making company or an increase in donations for a nonprofit organization or charity.

Goals. Broad, general outcomes sought as a result of persuasive efforts.

Informational objectives. What a public relations professional wants members of their audiences to know as a result of a campaign.

Interactive media. Refers to nontraditional media channels such as the Internet.

Logos. A persuasive appeal based on logical appeals.

Long-term objectives. Objectives expected to be completed long after the program or campaign's conclusion.

Media channels. Refers to traditional forms of media.

Messages. Basic ideas that a public relations professional wants members of his or her audiences to remember as a result of receiving a communication.

Motivational objectives. What a public relations professional wants audience members to do as a result of receiving a message, such as buy a product.

News interests. Qualities possessed by news stories that affect whether they will attract the attention of the audience. Examples include self-interest, conflict, humor, and novelty.

News values. Factors that influence the degree to which audience members will find a news story compelling, including timeliness, consequence, proximity, and prominence.

Nonmedia channels. Refers to forms of communication other than media, such as events, speeches, public debates and forums, and other examples provided in Chapter 8.

Objectives. Specific and measurable indicators of whether goals have been met.

Outcome objectives. An objective based on actual results of a communications program.

Pass-along rate.   A term used in newspaper circulation to refer to the average total number of persons who read one copy of the newspaper.

Pathos.   A persuasive appeal based on sympathy or empathy for someone who will benefit from the desired behavior.

Process objectives.   Objectives that refer to the specific actions taken as part of a communications program.

Short-term objectives.   Objectives expected to be accomplished during the campaign or immediately upon its conclusion.

Statutory objectives.   Influencing the policy decisions of governmental bodies and agencies or persuading voters to pass or defeat proposed laws or ordinances.

Strategies.   Decisions made on how the program will be implemented.

Themes.   The overarching ideas that apply to all of the audiences. Themes must be consistent through all forms of communication used.

■ ■ ■ ■ ■

CHAPTER 6

IMPLEMENTATION

Traditional Media Channels

WORKING WITH THE NEWS MEDIA

Compared to buying advertising space, persuading a reporter to write a news story is fairly inexpensive. A news story resulting from a news release costs only the paper, postage (or electronic resources), and staff time involved in the preparation of the release and follow-up work; however, the sender of the message loses control of it.

So, if one can afford to advertise, why use news instead? Because of the enhanced credibility that comes with news coverage. Research consistently shows that consumers attach far more importance to information received through news stories than through advertising. Most consumers understand that before the information reaches them, it has been scrutinized or "filtered" on their behalf. According to public opinion polls, respect for the news media has gradually declined over the last two decades, yet for many Americans it is still more credible than paid advertising messages. What is most important for public relations professionals is that news media carry a high degree of credibility among opinion leaders, many of whom trust journalists to be reliable gatekeepers and interpreters of information.

News Releases

News releases are standard tools in public relations work. A news release is a formal instrument used to communicate to the media that regularly cover an organization or the industry in which it operates. The release provides a summary of a story idea to a reporter or editor and enough information for the individual to make a decision about whether he or she wants to pursue it. Entry-level account executives or assistant account executives at public relations agencies spend a majority of their working time writing, editing, and seeking approval for news releases.

In the case of shorter news items, such as announcements of organizational events or personnel changes, newspapers and magazines often run news releases as submitted, with perhaps only minor changes to improve grammar, clarity, style, and conciseness. Most newspapers and magazines employ news clerks (usually college interns or entry-level employees) to condense routine news releases into "community calendars," "business profiles," or similar daily or weekly features.

More detailed news releases that introduce complex or significant news items are seldom published as written. Although smaller daily newspapers and weeklies with limited news staffs may run them verbatim, larger newspapers and magazines will use releases only as starting points in researching stories.

News releases customarily include the names, phone numbers, and email addresses of contact persons knowledgeable enough about the topic to respond to media follow-ups and requests for interviews. If the persons identified are outside of the public relations department, they should receive copies of the release, or approve them in advance, in order to better prepare them to be contacted.

When reporters receive such releases, they often respond in one of three ways: pursue the stories themselves, pass them along to other reporters whom they feel may show more interest, or discard them. When editors or broadcast news directors receive releases, they first decide whether the story is newsworthy, and if so, to which reporter the story should logically be assigned. Publications and broadcast outlets have preferences on who news releases should be addressed to—and those preferences should be respected. In some cases it is more effective to address releases to specific reporters, in some cases to editors or news directors, and in the case of routine calendar items and personnel items, to the news clerks who compile the appropriate columns or features.

Methods of Delivering News Releases and Other Materials.   Journalists have a variety of attitudes and preferences with respect to how they prefer to receive news releases and other publicity materials. Depending on which survey is reviewed, the media's most preferred methods for receiving news releases are by email, first-class or "regular" mail, or fax.

Many reporters and editors prefer regular mail for news stories that are not urgent. With breaking news stories and information that is time sensitive, it is more practical to send via fax or email. Bulky media kits that cannot be sent by email or fax may be sent by overnight mail if timeliness is a consideration. Follow-up phone calls are recommended one or two days later to make sure the package arrived.

Many fax machines are capable of **broadcast faxing** in which a document can be sent to numerous recipients after being fed into the machine only one time. Unfortunately for the public relations industry, other types of businesses also use the broadcast fax method, including restaurants sending lunch menus, office-supply companies promoting their products, and other service providers sending sales information. As a result, faxed public relations materials often end up getting thrown out with the commercial clutter. It is therefore a good idea to send materials only to journalists who have expressed an interest in a specific item. This method is called **fax-on-demand**. It's also a good idea to ask permission before sending.

Today, many journalists prefer to receive news releases and public relations materials via email. Since reporters and editors spend most of their working day at their desks, receiving publicity materials via email is more convenient than walking to the fax machine and sorting through the pile. Emailed releases can easily be printed if the reporter prefers a hard copy on which to make notes. One benefit to emailing press materials is that the reporter can instantly reply to the message, request more information, or arrange for an interview.

The United States Postal Service, Federal Express, and United Parcel Service all offer overnight and two-day guaranteed service on both letters and packages, so they can be used for both news releases and news kits. It is unlikely that overnight delivery would be appropriate for a simple news release, as a fax machine or email could deliver it quicker and cheaper. Overnight service might be appropriate, however, for media kits and other bulky items for which the fax or electronic mail would not be practical.

Most communities also have messenger services, but much like overnight delivery services, they are seldom worth the expense except in extraordinary circumstances. Some public relations professionals like the "personal touch" of hand-delivering news releases themselves.

Getting News Releases to the Right Decision Makers. Communicators who work for hospitals should send news releases to the health care reporters at the newspaper—not just to the publication or broadcast outlet with the hope that it will find its way to the right person. Likewise, a communicator for a computer software company should send the company's news releases to the reporter in the business section who writes about computers.

Although few broadcast journalists are specialists, newspaper reporters often are—especially those who write for the business section. This level of specialization is somewhat new in business journalism. Prior to the 1980s, business journalists were generalists rather than specialists, and a typical business staff might consist of six reporters who dealt with all types of business issues. Today, those same newspapers might still have six reporters, but each is a specialist—one writes about banking and finance, one writes about computers and technology, one writes about the stock market, one writes about real estate, one writes about agriculture and manufacturing, and one writes about small business.

Structuring Releases Like News Stories. As much as possible, the news release should read like a news story—not an attempt at free publicity. The four key factors that news releases share with news stories are newsworthiness, timeliness, brevity, and format.

Newsworthiness means getting away from "hype" or any characteristics that make the copy read like an advertisement or promotional copy.

Timeliness means that news releases have to be current and deal with news stories while they are still fresh. Many companies set up cumbersome approval processes for news releases that require drafts to go all the way up the chain of command for people to approve and revise it—sometimes all the way to the president's office. Releases dealing with controversial issues or topics subject to government regulation (such as news about company stock that will be carefully examined by the Securities and Exchange Commission, or new product news that will be scrutinized by the Federal Trade Commission) must be reviewed by the company's legal counsel. Many public relations representatives become frustrated with such a process because by the time the news item goes way up the ladder and all the way back down, the story may not even be news anymore.

Another impediment to timeliness is what occurs when public relations departments post news releases on their companies' websites. Many corporate home pages will include a link labeled either "public relations" or "media information." Beyond that link is another link labeled "click here to read the latest news releases." But reporters or interested persons who click on that link may find that the latest news release is six months old. That makes the public relations department look inefficient. When deciding to post news releases on a website, public relations professionals or companies should post them either the same time they are distributed on paper, or shortly thereafter.

When Ashland Inc., a chemical company based in Kentucky and Ohio, began posting news releases on its website in the mid-1990s, company leaders instructed the public relations staff to post releases within one hour of their release on paper. If reporters make frequent visits to a company website and find it is often outdated, they will eventually stop checking it for information and a valuable communications opportunity will be lost.

Brevity means keeping news releases down to a manageable number of pages. One or two pages (500 words or fewer) is a common standard that will be appreciated by those receiving them. Occasionally, companies announce new products with news releases of 20 pages or more, but journalists seldom have the time or interest to read a release that long. Releases should be as detailed as possible, but not include so much detail that they run in excess of two pages. If a great deal of information needs to be conveyed, a more practical method is to provide a summary of 1 or 2 pages and provide the detail in appendices or fact sheets.

Format refers to structuring a news release in the same manner as a print reporter would write a news story. The most common format for news releases is a model borrowed from newspaper journalism called the **inverted pyramid**. This model places the most important details of a story in the first one or two paragraphs; subsequent paragraphs provide further details in descending order of importance. In the early days of journalism, the inverted pyramid was important because news stories were transmitted by teletype—and if there were problems in transmission, some of the bottom paragraphs could be lost. Today, the pyramid format is still important for both newspaper stories and news releases because readers may just stop reading—and communicators want to be sure readers get the major details before they stop reading.

Types of News Releases.   Most releases fall into one of the following categories:

■ *Institutional.* These releases are intended to enhance the reputation of a company or organization rather than deal with a specific product, service, or event.

■ *Upcoming Events.* These releases promote or announce an upcoming event. In most parts of the country, the Associated Press administers a **datebook** organized by state or city that serves as a calendar of upcoming business and community events. Public relations representatives can have an event listed by sending news releases to the AP office nearest them.

■ *Past Events.* These releases describe or summarize a recent event for the benefit of the journalists unable to attend the event in person.

■ *Consumer Information.* These releases are designed to assist consumers in their purchasing or to provide them with information about significant trends in the marketplace.

■ *Timely Topics.* These releases are designed to motivate audiences to think about public issues.

■ *Features.* These releases are about a company, organization, or person that are of a "lighter" nature than typical news stories.

■ *Prepared Statements.* As the term indicates, a **prepared statement** is one that provides an organization's official response to a situation, often a fast-breaking news story, such as a workplace problem, an environmental crisis, or a transportation accident. One advantage of the prepared statement is that it serves as an alternative to granting an interview to a potentially hostile interviewer or a news conference that may be difficult to control in volatile situations. Such statements are often sent by fax or email rather than regular mail. They are usually short and to the point—meaning the inverted pyramid format is even more important.

Quite often, a prepared statement will not include much substance or detail; instead it merely acknowledges that a situation has taken place (or is taking place) and that it is being addressed.

The statement should also include an indication of when and how more information will be available. Prepared statements are those offered in situations in which an organization must respond quickly but briefly to certain situations. One example is the response to a controversial or emergency situation, such as an environmental accident, labor dispute, product defect, or similar occurrence.

A prepared statement can also be used as an alternative to dealing with potentially negative interviewers. By providing a prepared statement, company representatives can avoid being drawn into a hostile situation in which they may be misquoted, quoted out of context, or otherwise presented in a negative light. Providing a prepared statement should not be done to avoid such interviews in their entirety, but instead to provide more time for company representatives to gather information and develop a rational response rather than attempting to "wing it."

■ *Research.* If newsworthy enough, survey results often become news stories in themselves. Publicly released surveys can generate news, focus attention on an issue important to the client, or position an issue or topic in a favorable way.

Often referred to as a **target-topic poll**, the most common example of releasing research results occurs when the results of a survey conducted during the planning phase of the campaign process are later released as part of the implementation phase, with a news release or cover letter to summarize the information. One example is the series of surveys conducted by the Dehere Foundation, one of the country's leading advocates of gun control legislation. The foundation conducts frequent opinion surveys on the issue and uses the results not only to plan its informational campaigns but also as evidence to support its lobbying efforts in Congress and state legislatures.

Public relations agencies are able to generate positive publicity for their clients using this method. For example, an agency representing a national temporary help agency might conduct a survey of personnel directors about what skills office workers will need in the upcoming decade. The keys to making such polls work are to (1) find a subject that is timed to the client's area of interest and is also of interest to the client's key publics and (2) find a news "peg" based on the time of year or recent or upcoming events. An example of using a news peg would be to release the results of the survey mentioned above during National Administrative Professionals' Day (formerly National Secretaries' Day).

Journalists are often fascinated by the results of polls and surveys, but prefer those conducted by impartial public opinion research firms rather than companies or special-interest groups with an interest in the outcome of the research. Journalists occasionally quote from privately funded research results, however, and public relations representatives can improve the chances of having results published if they follow the Associated Press guidelines by providing key information in a news release or cover letter that accompanies the results.

■ *Media Advisories.* **Media advisories** are brief written communications that serve either to invite media to a news conference, media availability, or other event, or to announce a cancellation or schedule change.

Media Kits

A **media kit** is a collection of public relations materials arranged in a pocket folder, envelope, or other device. An effective media kit should include a cover letter summarizing the contents (and in the case of a complicated kit, perhaps a table of contents), one or more news releases and/or fact sheets, and optional items such as backgrounders, biographies, event schedules, photographs, point-of-purchase brochures, annual reports, newsletters, or other company publications.

Newspapers prefer black and white photographs, whereas magazines prefer 35mm color slides from which they can make color separations. Newspapers use black and white photographs more often than color, however there are times when color artwork is preferred. This usually depends on the story's placement and importance. If budget allows, public relations representatives should provide both a black and white and a color photo and leave the decision up to the editor. Editors prefer a variety of artwork options to a limited range of choices, and they also may keep the extra photos on file for use in future stories. Most newspapers can work with standard photographs as well as slides.

Artwork can also be sent via email to editors, but it is important to notify them first because of the generally large file size.

Many media kits include product samples, especially those that are flat and can fit easily into the folder or envelope. When Weyerhaeuser Company's Personal Products Division introduced its new Soft-Stretch diaper, for example, its news kits included a neatly folded sample. In the entertainment field, media kits normally include a news release, one or more black and white glossy promotional photographs of the artist or performer(s), a brief biography, and the business card of the publicist or contact. In the case of musicians, a CD is often included.

Sometimes even the nature of the folder can attract attention. When International Business Machines unveiled its PS/2 laptop computer in 1991, the news kit was packaged inside a cardboard mock-up of the product. Concorde Brands, marketers of a candy product called Laffy Taffy took its news kit a step further. When the company began sponsoring its annual National Joke-Writing Contest in 1992, the news kit announcing the first competition included a battery-operated device that emitted a laughing sound when the kit was opened.

Article Reprints

Most major newspapers and magazines allow companies that have been the subject of positive news stories (such as reviews of new products) the opportunity to purchase high-quality reprints of those articles for distribution in media kits or other publicity materials. Most publications charge a modest permissions fee (in addition to the cost of the actual printing) that allows such usage for a limited time (usually 6 to 12 months, subject to renewal). In most cases, the only restriction is that the articles must appear in their complete form, with none of the text or photographs deleted or altered. Although it would be much cheaper to make photocopies, to do so in large quantities would violate federal copyright law. In addition, reprints are of a much higher quality, especially in cases in which color photographs are included.

News Conferences

Another effective method of delivering news is the **news conference**, but it is a tool that tends to be overused and misused. Reporters often complain about being invited to news conferences labeled as "major announcements," only to find out that the news value of the announcement was trivial and could have been better handled with a simple news release. Experienced public relations professionals and journalists know many news conferences are unnecessary; in nonemergency situations, individual interviews with reporters are often more effective. But in those circumstances (possibly under the influence of a boss or client) of trying to decide between holding a formal news conference or simply issuing a news release, the factors that would support the choice of a news conference include:

▪ *The News Being Announced Must Be Newsworthy in Nature.* In order to warrant a news conference, the news must be significant enough that a simple news release would be insufficient.

▪ *The Story Must Be Too Complicated to Explain with a Simple Written Announcement.* A news conference can be very effective when a large amount of information from two or more viewpoints has to be assembled. That is why the two sides in a conflict situation usually hold a joint news conference when they announce the resolution of a conflict. That makes it much easier for the reporters than trying to explain it on paper and expecting reporters to visit one location and conduct one interview and then a second location to conduct another. Journalists attending the news conference will still receive a news release that provides background information, but the news conference provides the opportunity for reporters to be there in person and ask their own questions of both sides.

▪ *There Should Be Visual Elements, Not Just People Talking.* For newspaper photographers, think in terms of still photography—most likely black and white. For television, think in terms of color video, preferably involving motion. So if a company is announcing that it will construct a new building, a scale model or artist's rendering should be placed in the background with enough copies to distribute to those attending. If a company is introducing a new product, have a prototype of it there for the journalists to examine close-up.

News conferences are an effective way to release information to all media simultaneously.

In an agency-client situation, sometimes the client wants to have a news conference when the agency that represents them does not think it is a good idea. Deanne Roberts, founder of Roberts Communications, a public relations agency in Tampa, Florida, employs a standard technique for talking clients out of a news conference when her staff realizes that the topic is not appropriate. She suggests setting up a practice session in which the client meets with the account team to develop a list of sample questions. Before the client arrives, Robert instructs her staff to develop a list of what she calls the "toughest, meanest, nastiest" questions they can think of—questions they know the client would not want to address. By the time the practice session is over, the client often changes his or her mind about holding a news conference.

But when a news conference is truly warranted, its advantages over an ordinary news release include:

■ *The Release of Information Is Immediate and Simultaneous.* Everybody attending the news conference gets the information at the same time. That way, one cannot possibly be accused of playing favorites or leaving anyone out. When mailing or faxing the information, there is the possibility of it getting lost.

■ *Opportunity Exists for the Media to Ask Follow-Up Questions.* It is much easier for a journalist to do this in person than to receive a news release on paper and then attempt to do follow-up interviews either in person or by telephone.

■ *Opportunity Exists for Still and Video Photographers.* News publications will sometimes use photographs provided by public relations representatives, and their broadcast counterparts may use video provided, but in most cases they prefer to shoot their own. Their philosophy is that if the story is important enough to be accompanied by a photograph or video, it is important enough for them to send their own photographers or camera crews.

■ *Opportunity Exists to "Take the Pulse" of the Media.* For all their shortcomings, news conferences remain the best available method for two-way communication between company leaders and the journalists who cover that company or industry. Not only can the organization use the news conference to release information and emphasize its message but it can also analyze the types of questions asked and determine the attitudes of the journalists and their audiences.

When inviting the media to a news conference, avoid giving them too much notice, as the timing must be precise. Give the media enough notice so that they have time to prepare for it, but not so much notice that they can cause problems. Television reporters need to book the camera crew or the mobile news van, and print reporters need to schedule photographers. Thus, public relations representatives need to provide a half-day or perhaps a full day of lead time.

But two problems arise when reporters are given *too much* advanced notice of a major news conference. First, reporters who cover a client, organization, or industry regularly may try to exploit the working relationship they have (or think they have) with the public relations representative and ask for an exclusive interview prior to the event. Second, more aggressive journalists will simply contact other sources (who may or may not be knowledgeable about this specific story) and try to piece together the story. As a result, the "major announcement" being planned for a Friday news conference may be reported in Wednesday's paper as "speculation." And although the reporter may get in trouble with his or her editor if the story is wrong, the pubic relations representative in charge of the Friday announcement may come under scrutiny as well, regardless of his or her degree of responsibility for the inaccuracies.

If there is concern that a formal news conference may be unnecessary or poorly attended, an alternative is a tactic known as **media availability**. It differs from a news conference in that instead of announcing a specific time for the media to attend, organizers instead provide a time frame ranging from a few hours to a half-day for which one or more organizational spokespersons will be available. When an individual journalist shows up, a one-on-one interview takes place. If a substantial number of media representatives show up at or about the same time, the meeting can become slightly more formal and resemble an actual news conference.

Editorial Meetings

An **editorial meeting** is a variation of the news conference, and it is a fairly new strategy in public relations, becoming popular in the last few decades. The idea behind the editorial meeting is to focus attention on one newspaper at a time; such meetings take place between companies and newspapers as well as nonprofit organizations and newspapers.

If a public relations representative believes the newspaper has been too negative about a certain topic or is biased against a client or an organization, he or she can suggest a face-to-face meeting between representatives of the organization and the newspaper in question. On one side of the table might be the president or CEO, a public relations representative, and perhaps one or two other key executives. Sometimes those representing the newspaper will be its actual editorial board, and other times it is a team assembled to deal with a specific issue, such as the managing editor, business editor, editorial page editor, and one or two reporters.

Such a "let's-clear-the-air" session is often effective in reducing tension and resolving misunderstandings. The newspaper will learn more about the organization and why it does what it does, and the organization will learn more about the newspaper and why it has published articles about the organization or the issue involved. The editorial meeting is therefore a step above holding a news conference.

The public relations side may use audiovisual presentations or other supplementary materials, but the newspaper side often dictates the tone and pace of the meeting—what topics are to be covered, the availability of audiovisual equipment, and the time allotted.

Public relations representatives should provide the newspaper representatives with as much advanced information as possible, including annual reports, relevant news releases and fact sheets, and biographies of company representatives who will be present. Public relations professionals should also take the initiative to set up these meetings; newspaper representatives seldom do because they do not have as much to gain. Occasionally, the newspaper representatives will go to the public relations representative's location, but more often, one of the newspaper's conference rooms will be the venue.

Media Guides and Referral Services

A **media guide** is a publication that an organization provides to journalists assigned to cover it, or the industry in which it operates, on a regular basis. The idea began when college and professional sports teams prepared such publications for local reporters, as well as those following the visiting team. A sports team's media guide includes information on the team's players and coaches (and in the case of professional teams, its ownership and management), statistics from previous years, a description of the stadium or arena in which the team plays, the current season's schedule, and contact names and phone numbers.

Corporations produce publications that are analogous to the media guides published by sports teams, although they may not use that label. The corporate form of the media guide might include information on the company's history, purpose, structure, and leadership. Journalists can use these publications as reference sources for basic information, eliminating the need to contact the company to ask routine questions. These publications are easy to prepare, as much of the information has already been gathered for annual reports and other publications.

Some media guides are industrywide in nature. In the mid-1980s, for example, corporations within the nuclear power industry became concerned over the quality of media coverage the industry received, so they worked together to produce *A Journalist's Guide to Nuclear Energy,* a 61-page booklet that provides a history of the nuclear power industry, a "crash course" in understanding the science at the heart of it, a glossary of terms, and a list of other reference sources and industry officials available to respond to media inquiries. In

2000, the National Safety Council's Environmental Health Center produced for journalists covering the chemical industry a similar media guide titled *Chemicals, the Press and the Public.* In the same field, the Dow Chemical Company provides a service that features a toll-free number that journalists can call to ask questions not only about matters related to Dow but also any matter within the chemical industry as a whole.

A related strategy is to provide a **referral service** for media. One common example is a university's listing of faculty members who volunteer to be interviewed by journalists on topics in their area of expertise. At the University of South Florida, for example, the communications staff produces a publication titled *Ask the Experts,* which provides a listing of the institution's faculty members, organized first by broad subject area and then by specific area of expertise. A journalist researching a story on domestic violence, for example, could first use the referral service to find a listing of faculty members in the sociology department, then specifically find one person who teaches or conducts research on domestic violence. Faculty are given the option of providing their office or home telephone numbers (or both).

At Marshall University in West Virginia, the communications office produced a similar publication after being swamped with interview requests from local journalists wanting more information about the tragic deaths of the school's football team. The university contracted with the school's Public Relations Student Society of America (PRSSA) chapter to produce the booklet as a service project.

Universities with medical schools find these publications helpful because of the high volume of requests they receive from medical journalists researching stories on the latest health issues and medical discoveries.

At the University of South Florida, Marshall University, and other universities, such publications are updated periodically to allow for the addition of new faculty members or the deletion of retired faculty.

The State University of New York at Stony Brook took the idea a step further when it organized PROFNET, an on-line referral service that arranges for on-line interviews between journalists and experts from hundreds of U.S. universities and companies. The service is now part of PR Newswire, which provides reporters with access to a variety of credible sources that include experts from more than 1,200 universities, 4,000 corporations, 1,200 public relations agencies, 1,000 nonprofit organizations and government agencies, and 100 scientific associations and "think tanks."

Some public relations agencies publish "resource guides" that provide a list of clients who are available for media interviews and a list of topics on which they are qualified to comment.

Freelance Solicitations

Most states have freelance writers associations that publish lists of their members, organized by their interests and specialties. Public relations representatives can use these directories to locate freelance writers, suggest story ideas, and offer to provide background information and interview leads. The advantage of finding a **freelancer** to pursue a story is that he or she may have better contacts with publications and may have more success in getting a story placed. Also, the freelancer is paid by the publication to which the story is sold, not the organization suggesting the story.

A successful relationship with a freelancer creates a win-win situation in that free-lancers are as interested in finding good story ideas as public relations staffs are to find new sources of news coverage. Newspaper and magazine editors may be more receptive to a pitch from a knowledgeable freelancer than they are to an inquiry from an organization's public relations department. In addition to using organizational directories, qualified free-lancers can be located by skimming the by-lines of the appropriate publications or by con-tacting the professional associations to which they belong.

Position Statements

Position statements are formal letters or documents by which a company, industry associ-ation, nonprofit organization, or special-interest group communicates directly to persons or organizations they are trying to influence. Also known as "position papers" and "white papers," position statements travel directly from the source to the receiver, rather than being transmitted through the media. In many cases, however, excerpts from position statements are included in news stories when copies are distributed to the media, which is the main rea-son they are being discussed in this chapter rather than the next.

Organizations involved in public issues often use position statements to ask govern-ment officials to vote for or against proposed federal laws, state laws, or county or city ordinances. In addition to public officials, they can also be used to communicate to other special-interest groups asking them to take (or not take) some specific action.

Like any other form of professional writing, position statements must be well written in order to receive the attention they deserve. A well-written piece has a much greater chance of being accepted than one with an equally important message that is not well writ-ten.

Position statements can take many forms, but two of the most common approaches are the brief but formal business letter and the more detailed argumentation paper. As its label implies, the *business letter approach* uses an organization's stationery and includes the recipient's address, date of release, a salutation, body copy of one or two pages, and signa-ture line.

One tactic that makes these position statements more effective is to provide copies to local journalists covering that topic or issue. Many journalists will include excerpts from the position statement in their stories, and because conflict is a basic news interest, many will also call the person to whom the statement was sent and ask them for a reaction, which will also be included in the story. It may not change the minds of public officials or influence them to act or vote differently, but it forces them to respond on the record.

If space permits and the newsworthiness of the issue is sufficient, the position state-ment may be printed verbatim as a sidebar to the journalist's story. If the position paper is not quoted in the story or if the organization sending the communication is not pleased with the treatment it receives, it can purchase advertising space, in which case the position statement becomes an advocacy ad. Most such ads are given the heading "An Open Letter to . . . ." or "An Open Letter from . . . ."

Most position statements are sent through the mail with news releases or cover letters included to serve as introductory devices and summaries of the content. They can also be emailed, faxed, hand delivered, posted to an organization's website, or used as handouts to accompany presentations before government agencies or regulatory bodies.

When the Association of Federal, State, County and Municipal Employees (AFSCME), a labor union representing clerical workers and other civil servants, wanted to draw attention to unflattering portrayals of working women in the comic strip *Beetle Bailey,* it sent a position statement to the strip's creator and the syndicate that distributed it.

Another common format for position statement is that of an *argumentation paper.* This format is more effective than a business letter for explaining an organization's views on controversial issues because of the level of detail required. Argumentation papers are often structured like those commonly written in college English classes that argue a point using rules of logic and presenting evidence, including inductive and deductive reasoning and counterargument (stating opposing views, but then refuting them with evidence).

The format includes an introduction to set the tone, one or more body sections to explain the argument and present the evidence, and a conclusion to reiterate major points of the argument and to reinforce what the organization wants the recipients of the statement to do in response.

EXAMPLE

Introduction: State your case; tell us your concerns.
Background: How did this problem get started in the first place? Why does it persist?
Evidence: Convince us you know what you are talking about.
Call to Action: How can we help?
Consequence: What happens if we do not act?
Conclusions: Tie it all together.

Depending on the complexity of the topic, some of these elements may be eliminated, combined with others, or interchanged in position.

International Business Machines issued a complex position statement in the mid-1980s in response to criticism of its decision to maintain operations in South Africa. At the time, other U.S. businesses were pulling out of the country as a protest against apartheid, but IBM remained behind and became the target of public criticism and threatened boycotts. Its four-page position statement explained that remaining in South Africa did not mean that the company condoned the social policy; rather, it was IBM's belief that the company could better advocate the abolition of apartheid from inside rather than outside the country.

For most controversial issues, it is unlikely that public officials will receive position statements from only one side. In the late 1990s, for example, a women's gun-rights group calling itself the "Second Amendment Sisters" sent position statements to congressional leaders each time Congress was considering gun control legislation. One of the purposes of the statements was to respond to statements issued by advocates of the legislation, including another women's group that called itself "The Million Mom March."

Guest Commentaries

At first glance, **guest commentaries** are similar to the "letters to the editor" that appear in many newspapers. They are different from an ordinary letter, however, in that they are written by individuals with special credentials or who are otherwise in a position that qualifies them to comment on the issue involved, such as a professor who teaches about or conducts research on the issue, or the administrator of a nonprofit organization or special-interest group associated with the issue. Anyone can write a letter to the editor, but only authority figures can write guest commentaries. Guest commentaries can deal with politics, public affairs, education, health care, law, religion, lifestyles, or a variety of other topics. They can be either local or national in scope, but they are most likely to be chosen for publication if they are timely.

Generally, guest commentaries are persuasive in intent, but they are not as forcefully written as position statements. Sometimes they just attempt to make a point without necessarily including a "call to action." They therefore do not require as much research and documentation. Like an institutional advertisement, a guest commentary represents the communicating organization's opportunity to tell its side of the story, even in cases in which it knows the chances of changing opinions may be slim.

The idea for a guest commentary may be developed by a company, nonprofit association, or special-interest group involved in the issue. On occasion, newspapers and magazines may solicit commentaries from authority figures after receiving mail or phone calls from that organization commenting on the publication's treatment of an issue.

Publications customarily use a photograph of the person next to the copy and list the person's office or credentials, often in italics or boldface type at the end of the text, in order to give the commentary slightly more impact than that of a letter to the editor. Newspapers often use the term *op-ed piece* to describe these columns. Most appear on the editorial page, but they occasionally appear elsewhere in the paper.

The most widely read op-ed sections are found in national newspapers such as the *New York Times,* the *Washington Post,* the *Wall Street Journal,* and *USA Today.* Most news magazines carry guest commentaries, although some use other titles, such as "Guest Column" or "Commentary." *Newsweek* has a feature titled "My Turn" that runs just inside the back cover, and *Business Week* has one called "Economic Viewpoint" that runs on the first page after the table of contents.

Much like an executive's speeches, his or her guest commentaries are often ghostwritten by public relations representatives. If the company president or other executive invited to submit a guest commentary is not comfortable with persuasive writing, he or she may ask a member of the public relations staff to draft the message based on the executive's ideas or outline. In other cases, the executive might prepare the first draft and then submit it to the public relations department for revision and word crafting.

In the latter case, the two purposes of having the piece reviewed by the public relations staff are (1) to check for grammar and to polish the writing by improving the word choice, thereby strengthening the argument and (2) to suggest the deletion of anything that might be libelous or inflammatory. Even though most opinion writing is considered protected speech under the First Amendment (the legal term is *fair comment*) and cannot be the basis for libel action, a carelessly worded letter can still cause legal problems. Someone offended by a guest commentary can still sue, and even though it is unlikely he or she would win because of "fair comment" and the First Amendment, it may still tie up a company's lawyers in court and generate sizable legal bills.

Scott Berman, assistant professor of public relations at California State University–Northridge, describes the op-ed process as one involving three phases: envisioning, preparing, and marketing. In the *envisioning phase,* writers determine the key message to be conveyed and a "news hook" with which that key message can be associated. One example of this is the crafting of a university president's guest commentary about the future of higher education and asking the local newspaper to publish it prior to the anticipated debate in the state legislature on that subject.

The *preparing phase* is the actual drafting of the document. The *marketing phase* refers to the process of finding a publisher. In the example just used, it would be easy to interest a daily newspaper in publishing a university president's opinion piece because of the timeliness of the issue and the nature of higher education as a not-for-profit community asset. It is more difficult if the author is the president of a company, as an unsolicited opinion piece may be seen as an attempt for free publicity. But if the company is the subject of public criticism or is involved in some other way in a newsworthy circumstance, the public relations officer attempting to market the written product may have more success with a good news hook. Instead of an attempt at obtaining free publicity, editorial-page editors will instead look at the piece as the company legitimately responding to public criticism or otherwise commenting on current events.

Television and Radio Talk Shows

Recently, the label of "talk show" has become associated with negative images and is often used as a derogatory term. But legitimate television and radio talk shows, such as those dealing with governmental issues and community events, can be effective and inexpensive methods to reach an audience. Although few public relations professionals will have the opportunity to get a client booked on *Larry King Live, Meet the Press,* or *Face the Nation,* most local television stations have analogous programs on the local level. Producers are eager to find credible spokespersons from nonprofit organizations, governmental agencies, and special-interest groups and will be more receptive to the idea if the guest promises to discuss issues rather than blatantly promote an agenda. Local radio stations also have talk shows that discuss timely public issues and welcome credible guests.

Satellite Media Tours

A **satellite media tour** is an alternative to sending an organization's spokespersons around the country to do interviews with television networks and local stations. Contracting with a production company for a half-day can provide use of the television studio and technical personnel to make a spokesperson available for sequential interviews with television networks and affiliate stations across the country. With effective planning, a spokesperson can do 10 or 12 interviews in a matter of hours without leaving the studio. The two fields where these are most popular are in book publishing, in which publishers arrange for media interviews with their "star" authors, and Hollywood, in which studio publicity departments arrange for appearances by directors and actors promoting television shows and movies.

Video News Releases

A **video news release (VNR)** is analogous to a traditional paper news release or press kit in that it provides a summary of a proposed news story along with commentary (brief interviews instead of written quotes) and illustrations (video instead of still photographs). These releases can be distributed either on videos or transmitted by satellite. Running time can be anywhere from 30 seconds to 10 minutes.

Television news directors express a variety of opinions about video news releases. Some see them as a valuable source of video that is often not available from other sources; others look at them as superficial attempts at free publicity presented in the form of what many respondents to a *TV Guide* survey referred to as "fake news." The most common applications of VNRs are to introduce new products, to respond to crises, and to address other news stories that have a substantial need for video content.

One of the first widely known applications of a video news release in a crisis situation occurred in the late 1980s when a man in San Jose, California, drank from a bottle of Gatorade that had allegedly been contaminated with urine. Gatorade, manufactured by Stokely-Van Camp, feared a crisis of the same magnitude as the earlier Tylenol case. The company's public relations firm, Burson-Marstellar, suggested producing a VNR that showed an untainted bottle of Gatorade being popped so the viewers could see and hear what an unopened bottle was supposed to sound like. The firm then offered it on a satellite feed and many television stations in the market area showed it as part of their news stories on the incident. The video news release showed consumers how they could determine if their bottles had been tampered with because they could see it and hear it; it also showed that Stokely-Van Camp was a company concerned with its customers and was not trying to hide from the story and pretend that it did not happen (like other companies may have done in similar circumstances). As a result of responding quickly and effectively, the story disappeared from the media within 24 hours. If the company had tried to hide from the story, it may have snowballed and lasted for days or weeks.

Another success story took place at the National Aeronautics and Space Administration (NASA) in the late 1980s, when the agency was struggling to recover from the *Challenger* tragedy that killed seven astronauts, which triggered a setback in the space shuttle program and threatened the future of space exploration. Because a massive overhaul in the design and construction of the shuttle was necessary before the program could resume, the agency's public affairs staff worked with shuttle contractors to produce VNRs that explained the process to both the media and the public and emphasized the thoroughness of the overhaul.

Despite success stories such as Gatorade and NASA, many television news directors are still skeptical about video news releases, mainly because of the lack of objectivity. Even though news directors are reluctant to use them, in many cases they have to because it is newsworthy and the only available source for the video. In 1982, when Barney Clark became the first human recipient of an artificial heart at the Humana Heart Institute in Louisville, Kentucky, for example, major networks and hundreds of local television stations around the country showed footage from the operation on their nightly newscasts. No television stations or networks were allowed to bring cameras into the operating room; the video was coordinated by the hospital's public relations department and transmitted by satellite. The result was a newsworthy story for the media and significant public relations benefit for the hospital because it positioned it as a leader in that field of medicine.

In the Humana case, the urgency of the story did not allow for production of a complete, packaged video news release with music, narration, and titles (which might have taken several days). Instead, the content of the satellite transmission was raw video with a minimum of titles or sound. The industry term for that is **background video** or *B-roll,* which is quicker to produce and less expensive than a polished video news release. In addition to crisis situations, another popular application is in the introduction of new products.

Video shown on television news is often identified on the screen by subtitles such as "Video courtesy of XYZ" or "Video supplied by XYZ." That is the news directors' way of letting their audiences know that they did not produce that video themselves.

Some of the criteria to use in deciding whether to spend the time and money for video rather than paper include the following:

- *The Technical Capability to Produce Quality Material.* Public relations representatives should offer to TV stations and networks the same quality of video they would produce themselves. Companies that produce a lot of VNRs will have their own in-house production facilities and full-time technical personnel. But if a public relations department produces VNRs only occasionally, it is more practical to hire an outside production company instead of buying the equipment and hiring the technical people. In either case, the process is an expensive one. That is why it is mainly government agencies and major corporations that do VNRs; it is seldom that a nonprofit organization can afford to produce them. (Public service announcements are a different matter; nonprofit organizations can sometimes get those services donated, whereas video news releases are usually beyond the budget of nonprofits.)

- *News Value.* As with their traditional paper counterparts, video news releases must be based on news rather than promotion.

- *Enough Action to Justify Video.* Some news stories require video to be understood, but many others do not. When two International Business Machines researchers discovered a way to reduce electrical resistance to absolute zero, a few minutes of B-roll showing a magnet floating in mid-air gave the story enough "gee-whiz" quality to earn time on the evening news. Don Harrison, a media relations representative for the company, commented that if he had shown up at a television station trying to explain such a scientific discovery without the video to illustrate it, "someone would have shown me the door."

Although the IBM story and many others require video to be understood, many others are simply better told on paper. If the only available visual is that of someone standing behind a podium giving a speech, for example, a video news release is a waste of time and money. Many corporate public relations departments videotape the CEO's annual state-of-the-company address to stockholders and then offer it by satellite and hope the networks will use it on the evening news. But unless the featured speaker is a well-known CEO making a major announcement concerning the future of that company (which is seldom the case), the networks will not be interested. Therefore, the annual speech to the stockholders or similar speech (or any story lacking significant action) is more effectively told either by providing the transcript on paper, with a summarizing news release on top, or posting it on the company's website.

Radio Actualities

Radio actualities provide sound bites to accompanying news releases sent to radio stations. The most common example is interviews, but actualities may also include music clips or other sound effects. They can be distributed on CDs, via telephone transmission, or through an organization's website.

Sponsored Pages, Sections, or News Segments

One trend at local newspapers and television stations is to negotiate special rates for major advertisers who pay to sponsor, and often provide content for, special pages (and sometimes entire sections) in the newspaper or segments on evening news broadcasts. Called **sponsored news** or *news look-alikes,* these pages, sections, or television segments are popular and effective communication tactics for advertisers who want to do more than just purchase straightforward display advertising.

One example involves hospitals that sponsor and provide content for newspaper features and television segments about health topics while indirectly promoting their services. Newspapers often publish "special sections" to promote community events and offer major advertisers the opportunity to sponsor the sections and generate community goodwill by associating themselves with the event. Other newspaper advertisers are invited to sponsor weekly "theme pages," such as those targeted at children or seniors. Traditionalists in the newsroom or newspaper management offices often criticize this form of promotion because it blurs the lines between news and advertising. There is less concern at television stations, however.

INSTITUTIONAL ADVERTISING

Public relations professionals seldom deal with conventional advertising (unless an organization's public relations and advertising functions are combined), but they often deal with special types of advertising in which the communication is designed to promote an image or idea rather than a specific product or service. **Institutional advertising** is one of the areas of mass communications in which the dividing line between advertising and public relations becomes blurry.

Advertising is a costly form of persuasion, but it is the favorite of many organizations because the sponsor can control the content and frequency of the message and choose, with some degree of certainty, the audience that it reaches. That is different from news coverage, which is basically free but not as certain; a communicator distributes a news release or arranges a news conference and hopes for the best. This "purchased" form of persuasive communication has many names and variations, including *institutional advertising, corporate advertising, identity advertising,* and *issues advertising.*

Despite the opinion of many observers that public relations and advertising are separate functions, the lines between the two disciplines are often indistinguishable (and in some cases, almost imperceptible) because of the trend of integrated marketing communications. The major categories of advertising include commercial advertising, reputation advertising, response advertising, and advocacy advertising. Such tactics are employed to complement other public relations activities, not take the place of them.

Commercial Advertising

Commercial advertising, sometimes referred to as *conventional advertising,* may be handled by an autonomous advertising or marketing department, by a separate department working closely with the public relations staff, or by a department that performs both the advertising and traditional public relations duties. Entire books have been published on this topic, and this chapter will not attempt to condense the body of knowledge into these few pages. But here are some general guidelines:

1. The goal of the advertisement (or series of ads) must be matched with the readership of the media used. Newspapers, magazines, and broadcast outlets can provide demographic information on their audiences that help advertisers target their messages to specific groups based on age, income level, entertainment preferences, and purchasing habits.

2. The relative costs of advertising and other methods must be determined. Advertising costs considerably more than most communications tactics, but in some cases may be the most effective method of reaching certain audiences and addressing certain goals. As discussed earlier, however, many companies find that combining or integrating advertising and public relations efforts are often more effective than using one method to the exclusion of the other.

3. If both advertising and public relations tactics are used, the two efforts must be coordinated. Journalists who cover the company will take notice and point out to their audiences if messages from the two efforts appear to contradict each other.

Included in the category of commercial advertising is the *infomercial.* Even though they are often the butt of jokes, infomercials (sometimes known as *program-length commercials*) are an effective way to sell merchandise by encouraging customers to call a 1-800 number or visit a website.

Reputation Advertising

Sometimes called "image advertising," **reputation advertising** is an important part of an overall campaign for an organization. It can be developed as a response to a short-term crisis, but is more likely to be used to counter a long-term decline in an organization's public reputation or standing. In the latter case, the design of the overall communications campaign—and specifically the advertising component—should not begin until the image problem has been thoroughly researched and analyzed. Too often, companies with large public relations budgets will launch massive campaigns without conducting the proper opinion research first, and, as a result, will waste a great deal of money on unnecessary or misdirected communications.

Reputation advertising is not directly aimed at selling products, services, or organizational memberships. After a crisis or long-term image problem, the communications campaign repairs the reputation, which then allows the marketing department to capitalize on its success.

Advertising executive David Ogilvy, an expert in the use of reputation advertising by corporations, is quoted in William F. Arens and Courtland L. Bovee's textbook, *Contemporary Advertising,* as stating that "defensive" advertising is becoming necessary for corporations because of the antibusiness sentiment in the United States. "Big corporations are increasingly under attack—from consumer groups, from environmentalists, from governments, from antitrust prosecutors who try their cases in the newspapers," Ogilvy said. "If a big corporation does not take the initiative in cultivating its reputation, its case goes by default."*

In addition to helping an organization recover from a crisis, image advertising can help:

1. Build awareness for a new or little-known company.
2. Defend a company against criticism by competitors or consumer groups.
3. Respond to inaccurate media coverage.
4. Make a good impression on current and potential stockholders.
5. Brag (tastefully) about accomplishments.
6. Position the company in a competitive field.
7. Announce a change in corporate philosophy.
8. Apologize to consumers and accept responsibility for problems related to the company's products and services, including problems caused by factors beyond the organization's control.
9. Attract job candidates.
10. Motivate current employees by making them feel good about their employer (good public relations begins internally, many experts say).

Reputation advertising has grown as part of corporate public relations in the last three decades. In the 1970s and 80s, the major theme of most reputation ads was equal opportunity employment—the improvement in workplace diversity through the hiring and promotion of more African Americans, Hispanic Americans, and women—at the companies sponsoring the ads. In the late 1980s and early 1990s, that theme was replaced with two others: concern for the environment ("We're environmentally friendly") and support for education through the sponsoring of scholarships and other school programs.

In many cases, companies associated with controversial products, such as tobacco and alcohol, or organizations that deal with controversial issues, such as abortion or gun control, know the odds are stacked against them before they start, and that not even the most effective campaign will change public perception. So why spend the money? Because it is their opportunity to tell their side of the story. In the case of a corporation, its stockholders like to see it make the attempt, no matter how long the odds.

Reputation advertising is not limited to companies; nonprofit organizations and special-interest groups also use them to address reputation problems. An example of a reputation campaign for a special-interest group is one funded by the National Rifle Association (NRA), which realized that its opposition to proposed gun control legislation had led to being misperceived by the public (other than its members and supporters). Its reputation advertising campaign, which included both print media and television, centered on celebrity spokespersons who said that in spite of its negative image, they were proud to be members of the NRA. The theme of both the print and television series was "That's the NRA that I know." One of the television spots featured actress Sally Struthers, who explained NRA's gun safety classes; another featured actor Gerald McCraney, who talked about NRA and its sponsorship of the American shooting teams in the Summer Olympics.

---

*William F. Arens and Courtland L. Bovee, *Contemporary Advertising* (New York: McGraw-Hill, 1989), p. 586, © The McGraw-Hill Companies, Inc. Reprinted with permission.

Officials at NRA realized that it was unlikely the advertising series would change minds about the organization or the gun control issue, but proceeded with the campaign because it provided an opportunity to tell their side of the story. On the surface, it appeared that the organization was speaking to its critics, but it also addressed two other important audiences—the organization's current and potential members and supporters—reminding them about the organization's priorities and how it spends its money.

The NRA series won numerous awards within the advertising industry and is still discussed today as an example of an effective reputation advertising campaign. Over the next two decades, it has been followed by series-promoting industries such as cable television, oil and gas, and health care.

Response Advertising

Response advertising resembles reputation advertising in that its objective is to improve how the company or organization is perceived. But instead of dealing with long-term reputation problems, response advertising addresses short-term conflicts and problems. One example is Delta Airlines' response when the nation's air-traffic system was in chaos for two days during a winter storm in 1993, causing airports in the Northeast to close and thousands of passengers to be stranded in terminals. Even though Delta was not the only airline affected and could not be faulted for an act of nature, it purchased full-page ads in *USA Today* and other national newspapers that apologized to passengers for their inconvenience and thanked them for their patience. United Airlines employed a similar tactic in the summer of 2000, when a combination of labor conflicts, bad weather, and air-traffic control problems caused many of its flights to be delayed or cancelled. For more than two weeks, United aired a 60-second television spot in which its president apologized to customers. Many observers of the advertising industry refer to such gestures as "apology ads." In 2007, discount airline JetBlue produced a series of response ads, in both print and broadcast form, following an incident in which bad weather forced one of its planes to sit on an airport runway for more than 12 hours, stranding passengers without food or working bathrooms. Although seldom successful by themselves, they can be effective when used to announce changes in company policies or other substantive actions. But many times they are seen as too self-serving and shallow, and, if they come after other public relations efforts have failed, they are seen as "last-ditch efforts" or "signs of desperation."

Although apology ads have met with varying degrees of success, other companies have been successful in using paid advertising to explain their role in or position regarding major news events. In the week following the terrorist attacks of September 11, 2001, for example, numerous businesses purchased full-page response ads in *USA Today* and other national newspapers. Some were purchased by businesses (such as American Express) that were located in the World Trade Center; their goal was to reassure customers that their financial records were intact. Other ads were purchased by companies not directly affected by the tragedies; they simply wanted to praise the rescue workers at the World Trade Center and at the Pentagon crash site in Arlington, Virginia.

The tone of a response ad sponsored by discount retailer Target was not as positive. When competitor Wal-Mart was found to be using misleading and deceptive advertising that compared prices at the two chains, Target responded with a magazine ad that explained the company's objections. The text accused Wal-Mart of employing lower ethical standards following the death of its founder. The attention-getting headline read "This Never Would Have Happened if Sam Walton Was Still Alive."

Advocacy Advertising

Advocacy advertising picks up where reputation advertising leaves off. Whereas reputation advertising often carries with it only an informational objective, it does not ask readers or viewers to do anything other than to think more highly of the organization sponsoring the message. But advocacy advertising carries with it a motivational objective; it asks readers and viewers to act in ways other than purchasing a product or service. It asks them to conduct their lives differently, to write to one or more public officials to advocate or oppose something, or to vote for or against a certain issue.

Research shows more powerful arguments can be made with quantitative or statistical evidence than with information that is qualitative or anecdotal. The most effective public relations programs use both forms of persuasion whenever possible.

Advocacy ads are most effective when used as part of a comprehensive public relations or legislative issues campaign. Much like objectives developed for an overall campaign, the objectives for advocacy ads should be concrete, realistic, and measurable rather than vague or abstract. Occasionally, unethical forms of advocacy advertising use "scare tactics," such as exaggerated predictions about what will happen if a certain law is passed, if a labor union is victorious in negotiations, or if environmentalists are successful in forcing a manufacturer to change its operating procedures. Research indicates that most consumers are intelligent enough not to be persuaded by misleading ads, and that many such ads backfire against their sponsors.

Advocacy advertising is primarily print oriented; the broadcast media are reluctant to carry it because of the controversy it creates and because of the limited amount of response time they are able to provide for opposing points of view.

Newspapers usually label such advertising from special-interest groups (or sometimes individuals) as "paid opinion advertising" to separate it from other display advertising. In addition to attaching that label, publications will insist that the group or individual sponsoring the message be clearly identified within the ad. For a sponsor to advocate something in an ad and then insist on anonymity is highly unethical, and few newspapers or magazines would allow it.

In order to support or oppose changes in the law—as in those cases in which the campaign includes statutory objectives—nonprofit organizations, professional associations, industry consortiums, and other special-interest groups occasionally sponsor advocacy ads. This effort is usually aimed at encouraging target audiences to write to elected representatives or other public officials to express their opinions. In these cases, the advertising copy should mention the proposed federal or state law (or in local cases, a city or county ordinance) by name or number so that letter-writers will be able to mention it in their correspondence.

Advocacy ads are also known as "issue ads" or "advertorials," the latter label being attached because they are paid for the same as a traditional advertisement, yet they discuss public issues in the same way as a newspaper editorial.

DONATED MEDIA

Donated media is a term for promotional space or time that is given free of charge by newspapers, magazines, television stations, and radio stations. On the local level, nonprofit associations can obtain free space or time either through persistence or by having the proper contacts at the media outlets at which they are asking for help.

On the national level, the most effective way of obtaining free space and time is to work through the Advertising Council, an organization that helps match nonprofit groups with advertising agencies willing to help in their communications efforts. The company also helps get those messages in print and on the air. Generally, the nonprofits pay for production costs of advertising campaigns, while the agencies donate their creative services. Over the years, the Advertising Council has helped develop relationships that culminated with memorable and award-winning campaigns for organizations such as United Way ("Thanks to you, it works for all of us") and United Negro College Fund ("A mind is a terrible thing to waste"), and issues such as crime prevention ("Take a bite out of crime") and drunk driving ("Friends don't let friends drive drunk"). The council was also responsible for the development of the United States Forest Service's campaign, "Only You Can Prevent Forest Fires," and the creation of its Smokey Bear character.

Newspaper and Magazine Advertising

It is rare for newspapers and magazines to donate free advertising space—they never do it for profit-making businesses and seldom do it for nonprofit organizations. Exceptions are those cases in which a newspaper will offer the local chamber of commerce free space to promote an upcoming event. Another is the donation of ad space for the annual United Way fund-raising drive or other communitywide programs. But both of those examples would be limited to a few times per year at the most.

National publications occasionally provide free advertising space to charities and other worthy causes, but that is usually limited to those times in which the magazine is preparing its layout and has a half-page or quarter-page space left over it is unable to sell. In such cases, the magazine editor has a variety of ads already prepared in various sizes that it can plug in at the last minute. It is not practical for a public relations department to expect such space to be available in advance.

The main reason it is so difficult to get newspapers and magazines to donate advertising space is because there is little incentive for them to do so. Television and radio stations customarily donate airtime because they can include such services in the license-renewal applications as evidence that they are operating in the "public interest." But since newspapers and magazines do not have licenses to renew, they do not feel the obligation to the same degree.

Television and Radio Public Service Announcements

A **public service announcement** is basically a news release written in broadcast style. Public service announcements come in two forms: *spot announcements,* which an announcer reads with no music, sound effects, or other features; and *recorded,* which is provided to the station in a prepared, polished format.

Prior to the early 1980s, the Federal Communications Commission required radio and television stations to demonstrate their plans to serve the needs of the communities in which they operated. Many did so by donating large amounts of airtime for public service announcements so that nonprofit organizations can promote themselves and make announcements about events and other news items. Public relations representatives for non-profit organizations capitalized on this opportunity.

Deregulation of the broadcasting industry eliminated this requirement for radio in 1981 and for television in 1984, but most stations still do so voluntarily because of the license-renewal process and the FCC mandate that they operate in the "public interest." But the broadcasting industry does not provide nearly as much time now as it did when it was required to do so.

TRENDS AND ISSUES

The Future of the News Release: Does It Have One?

When Mark Twain was age 74, newspapers carried rumors that he had died. Still very much alive, he responded that the reports of his death had been "greatly exaggerated."

And so it is with news releases. Many observers say the printed news release will soon be extinct, but for now, it remains a basic communications tool. Still, news releases have their advocates and their detractors among the media. Some journalists swear by news releases; others swear at them.

Criticism of news releases and the skepticism that surrounds them is nothing new. As far back as 1981, in an article in *Public Relations Review,* Professor Bill Baxter of the University of Oklahoma questioned the effectiveness of the news release. But his comments had nothing to do with changes in technology. Instead, he claimed the use of news releases by the media was declining because of the quality and focus of the writing. Many, according to the results of his survey conducted in the late 1970s, were rejected because they were either too general or were obviously promotional rather than newsworthy.

So have news releases gotten better or worse in the 25-plus years since Baxter's observations? Their quality has probably remained the same, with the criticisms revealed by Baxter's survey just as applicable today. But with the popularity of overnight mail,

faxes, email, and the Internet—methods of transmission that the public relations industry was either not using or had just begun to use 20 years ago—the volume of news releases sent has increased exponentially.

The Argument against News Releases

It is estimated that public relations professionals distribute more than 1.5 million news releases every week, the majority of them targeted at newspapers and magazines. Each day, those newspapers and magazines receive hundreds of news releases by mail, in-person delivery, messenger services, email, overnight mail, and fax. Sorting through them is often a journalist's least-favorite job, and many identify news releases as a major source of wasted paper and junk mail.

Research studies in public relations and journalism publications often list the most common reasons for the rejection of news releases as:

1. Poorly written
2. No news value
3. No local interest
4. Too much fluff
5. Arrived too late (sometimes the morning of the event or the day after)
6. Too long

Other sources of irritation for journalists include stories unrelated to a journalist's area of interest, unsolicited or unreadable attachments to email, and the contact person's inability to answer follow-up questions about issues raised in news releases.

Some journalists are skeptical about news releases because they are often seen as an organization's quest for free publicity. They are also annoyed by flowery, long-winded writing and exaggerated or self-congratulatory claims.

EXAMPLE

In yet another industry-leading accomplishment, scientists at the XYZ Corporation made another amazing breakthrough this week, producing a product that will change the lives of millions of Americans and . . . .

It does not matter what the release says after that, because it is already in the trash can. In addition to the problems caused by the overall tone of a release, public relations representatives should also avoid individual words and phrases that irritate serious journalists, such as *astounding, extraordinary, incredible, miraculous, phenomenal, remarkable, tremendous,* and perhaps the worst of all, *unique.*

The Argument for News Releases

Despite what the more vocal journalists say, most would reluctantly admit that they are dependent on news releases and would miss many good stories if they stopped coming. Daily newspapers would be unable to keep up with what is happening with local school systems, universities, hospitals, and nonprofit organizations if they did not receive releases from them. Business-oriented publications such as the *Wall Street Journal* would be much thinner without news releases to inform staff writers about mergers, acquisitions, expansions, and major personnel moves. Entertainment magazines would be unable to fill their pages without Hollywood and Broadway publicists sending them releases and news kits about upcoming movies and plays.

According to national media directories, nationwide there are more than 2,700 daily newspapers, 2,100 weeklies, and 1,700 magazines. Those newspapers and magazines simply do not have the staffs necessary to find stories without public relations representatives pointing them out, and the news release is the best way to bring story ideas to their attention.

In addition to the dependency of the print media on news releases and other public relations materials, the expansion of television news from 30-minute to 60-minute formats and television's growing interest in business news increases the assignment editor's interest in news releases from corporations.

But for both print and broadcast media, public relations professionals should not take the journalists' dependence on news releases for granted; they are still obligated to prepare releases with care and precision. On a slow news day, an editor may be willing to take the time to salvage a poorly written release, but that is rare. An editor seldom has the time or inclination.

The best news releases are those that are simple and straightforward. Even though one does not expect a newspaper to run a news release "as is," the public relations professional still has the responsibility of preparing the information in a style and format that is standard in the profession and therefore easy for an editor to handle.

CASE STUDY 6

Two Controversies, Ten Years Apart

Throughout its history, the National Association for the Advancement of Colored People (NAACP) has become one of the most successful and influential civil rights organizations in the country. Much of its success has been its assertiveness in public debate and effective advocacy of its positions. The following are two examples of such advocacy, occurring 10 years apart.

When the organization wanted to express its objection to the Professional Golfers' Association's (PGA) selection of a private country club (with a membership policy that excluded African Americans and other minorities) as the site of its 1990 championship tournament, one of its officials crafted and sent a business-letter position statement to the leadership of the PGA. The official wrote that the organization was "extremely concerned and dismayed that the PGA, with its reputation for promoting the highest ideals of sportsmanship, would agree to stage its annual championship at a country club that maintains exclusionary membership policies and/or practices on the basis of race."

The letter added that "the NAACP feels very strongly that public and private institutions have a compelling obligation to foster and promote the very best values and leadership of the American ideal of equality of opportunity and democracy" and that tournament organizers and sponsors should "consider whether they want their products associated with places that blatantly state that African Americans are not wanted."* Copies of the letter were also sent to the media, and excerpts appeared in newspapers across the country.

Even though its objective of having the tournament moved to another venue was not realized, the NCAAP was successful—largely because of a well-written position statement and the public response it generated—in drawing enough public attention to the issue that the PGA announced a policy that future tournaments would not be held at clubs with discriminatory policies.

Ten years later, the NAACP was in the news again, this time advocating the removal of the confederate battle flag from the flagpole at the South Carolina state capitol building in Columbia. The association and other civil rights groups contended that the flag was a symbol of hatred toward and oppression of African Americans, whereas supporters of the flag wanted it to remain as a "historical artifact."

The NAACP organized a boycott of the state's tourism industry, aimed at both individual vacationers and organizations planning conventions in the state. The NAACP promoted its boycott through news releases, media interviews, and statements on its website. The organization emphasized the economic impact generated by African Americans traveling to South Carolina for vacations, family reunions, and business meetings.

In early summer 2000, approximately six months after the boycott began, the state assembly voted to

Dr. Benjamin Hooks was chairman of the NAACP in 1990 when it became an outspoken critic of the PGA of America for holding its annual championship tournament at a private country club accused of discriminatory membership practices.

*The publisher wishes to thank The National Association for the Advancement of Colored People for authorizing the use of this work.

remove the flag from the capitol flagpole and place it instead at a nearby memorial. The NAACP and other opponents responded that the move was not sufficient to overcome their objections, and the controversy is unresolved as of this writing.

TRACKING THE CASE: COLLEGE STUDENTS AND CREDIT CARD DEBT

Chapters 3 through 10 each include segments of a hypothetical student-produced public relations campaign proposal. The student team, as part of an advanced public relations class, spent the semester researching the problem of credit card debt among college students for a fictional nonprofit organization, Credit Counselors of Mason County.

As mentioned in the previous chapter, the team conducted five focus groups among students and administered an email survey. The results not only provided the team with insight as to students' existing knowledge of and attitudes toward the issue of credit cards and credit card debt but they also provided clues as to what forms of media would be most effective in reaching students.

Implementation: Traditional Media Channels

News Media

As an obvious starting point, the team put together a list of campus media outlets through which the CCMC could spread its message, including the student newspaper and radio station. The team prepared two news releases that were each approved by the CCMC. The first provided an overview of the campaign and included general information (based on background provided by the agency and additional

research). The second release provided more detailed information on the problem and an overview of the services provided by the agency. A cover letter encouraged student journalists for both the campus newspaper and radio station to contact the director of the agency directly to arrange for interviews. The team followed up with the radio station to arrange for the director and another agency employee to be a guest on the station's public affairs program.

Because focus group research indicated that many nontraditional students pay more attention to off-campus media than the student media, the team sent the same news releases to journalists who cover the university for the local daily newspaper as well as those representing radio stations and television stations.

Donated Media

The team also persuaded the advertising department of the student newspaper to donate the back page of the newspaper for an advertisement to promote the availability of the agency's services. The radio station also donated time for public service announcements written by the team and read by on-air talent.

The team's written product for this section included written descriptions for each of the above items, and the appendices submitted included drafts of the news releases and print advertisement.

DISCUSSION QUESTIONS

1. Look at Case Study 6. What are some of the positives and negatives of the NAACP's persuasive efforts? If you were assisting the NAACP in this matter, what would you have done differently?

2. Read the business section of your daily newspaper in its entirety. Look for evidence of news items either taken directly from news releases or that had their origins with news releases but were augmented with additional reporting.

3. Find a variety of websites sponsored by consumer product companies. Look for those that

offer feedback opportunities such as guest books, listservs, or mailing lists. Contact the companies (asking questions about their products and services) using these methods and share the responses with the class.

4. Find a variety of websites sponsored by nonprofit organizations. Look for those that offer feedback opportunities such as guest books, listservs, or mailing lists. Contact the organizations (asking questions about their services or volunteer opportunities) using these methods and share the responses with the class.

5. Look through a week's collection of national news and business publications such as *Time, Newsweek, USA Today,* and the *Wall Street Journal* and examine the display advertise-ments. Which ones are examples of institutional advertising? What are the clues that help you make that determination?

GLOSSARY OF TERMS

Advocacy advertising. A form of institutional advertising that addresses an organization's advocacy of or opposition to a business, legal, social, or political issue.

Background video. Raw, unedited video including only video and sound, without narration, music, or titles. Faster and less expensive (than a video news release) to provide to broadcast media, who can then use only the segments they need. Also called *B-roll.*

Broadcast fax. A method of faxing a document to multiple recipients, but feeding it through the machine only one time.

Commercial advertising. Advertising that focuses on products or services, as opposed to issues or ideas. Also called *conventional advertising.*

Datebook. A calendar of upcoming business and community events; service provided in most communities by the Associated Press.

Editorial meeting. A formal meeting between a specific news media outlet and representatives of a company or organization concerned about news coverage related to itself or an issue.

Fax-on-demand. Faxing information to news media after making arrangements in advance for specific materials or documents.

Freelancer. An independent writer, photographer, or artist who works on a per-piece or per-project basis for a variety of employers rather than having only one full-time employer. The legal term is *independent contractor.*

Guest commentary. An opinion piece submitted to a newspaper or magazine. Similar to a letter to the editor, but it carries more weight because it is written by an "expert" or other person with special credentials to comment on public issues. Also called *op-ed piece.*

Institutional advertising. Advertising that focuses on issues or ideas as opposed to products and services. Also called *public relations advertising* or *issue advertising.*

Inverted pyramid. A model for structuring a news story or news release that places the most important information at the top, followed by supporting details, and last, the least important information.

Media advisories. Brief statements advising media of event cancellations, schedule changes, or the days and times of news conferences or other news events.

Media availability. As an alternative to a news conference, this means simply to make organization officials available for a certain length of time and invite local media to visit during that specified time.

Media guide. A publication that an organization provides to journalists assigned to cover it; it includes information on the organization's history, purpose, philosophy, and leadership, as well as a list of media contacts.

Media kit. Once called a *press kit,* a media kit is a package of information, presented in a pocket folder or other device that includes news releases, background information, photographs, and other supporting information.

News conference. A formal meeting during which a news source makes an announcement and/or answers questions posed by journalists.

News release. A formal instrument used to suggest a story idea to the news media; it includes background information and suggestions on who can be contacted for further information or interviews.

Position statements. Formal documents used to communicate an organization's opinion on business, legal, social, or political issues.

Prepared statement. A news release issued in an emergency or other fast-breaking situation, such as an environmental crisis or a transportation or industrial accident.

Public service announcement. A broadcast spot, donated by a television or radio station, that nonprofit organizations can use to promote events and causes.

Radio actualities. A form of audio news release designed to provide sound bites to accompany news releases sent to radio stations.

Referral service. A service designed to help journalists find sources for interviews through a published directory, toll-free telephone number, or website.

Reputation advertising. A form of institutional advertising directed at improving an organization's reputation. Occasionally called *image advertising*.

Response advertising. A form of institutional advertising produced in response to a specific event or short-term problem rather than a long-term reputation problem.

Satellite media tour. An interview format in which a spokesperson remains in a television studio and conducts sequential interviews by satellite with various broadcast media.

Sponsored news. Features in the newspaper or on television that resemble news stories but are paid for by advertisers. Also called *news looka-likes*.

Target-topic poll. A survey released with the intent of generating a news story.

Video news release. The electronic version of a paper news release; it includes background information, interviews, narration, titles, and sometimes music. Also called *electronic news release*.

■ ■ ■ ■ ■

CHAPTER 7

IMPLEMENTATION

Interactive Media Channels

Many social scientists and media researchers call the Internet the greatest advancement in communication since a German engraver named Johannes Gutenberg invented the printing press in 1439.

In slightly more than a decade, the Internet has grown from a little-known curiosity used mainly by scientists and the military to a worldwide phenomenon used by educational institutions, government agencies, businesses, nonprofit organizations, the media, and ordinary consumers. Researchers estimated in late 2007 that there were more than 400 million Internet users worldwide, with about half of those being in the United States. The most popular uses of the Internet (by individuals) are email, shopping, banking and paying bills, discussion groups related to hobbies and interests, personal information gathering (news, weather, sports, and other topics of personal interest), airline and hotel reservations, and social networking and dating. For corporations, government agencies, and nonprofit organizations, the Internet is an effective venue for communicating with current and potential customers and stockholders, recruiting new employees, communicating with current employees, and communicating with the media. Like many other technological advances, its potential for future growth is nearly unlimited.

With Internet use on the rise by both the public and media, it should be considered an important aspect of any public relations campaign. According to media researchers, each year the number of Americans getting their news from Internet news sources grows, while the numbers decline slightly for newspapers, magazines, and television and radio news.

The Internet is used often as a marketing and research tool during political campaigns. Politicians can directly access the public without paying costs of campaigning on radio, television, or mail.

Journalists are also finding that the Internet is an effective way to research stories. In recent studies, editors responded that they or their staff used the Internet or other on-line sources daily. That number will likely grow as a new generation of journalism school graduates enters the workforce after having being exposed to those techniques in college. Younger journalists use the Internet to research stories, locate and contact potential interview sources, and receive news releases.

The Internet is one of the fastest-growing communications methods used by public relations professionals and is often the most effective way to reach younger audiences.

Nicholas Negroponte, an author, futurist, and professor at the Massachusetts Institute of Technology, wrote in the mid-1990s that the growing popularity of the Internet was based on the practicality of working with "atoms" rather than "bits." Negroponte uses the parable of contrasting visiting the public library in person as opposed to finding the same material on the Internet. He describes the in-person visit to the library as transporting his atoms to the library, perusing the collection of atoms, and then checking out a specific arrangement of atoms. While he has those atoms checked out, no one else will have access to those atoms. But if that same information was stored in the form of bits, Negroponte contends, he can access those bits without limiting access to those same bits for other interested persons.

In addition to contrasting atoms and bits, Negroponte also contrasts the older idea of a source "pushing" information to the receiver with the newer idea of the receiver "pulling" information from the source. Not only will that change the nature of the publishing business, Negroponte points out, but also the nature of libraries. Libraries of the future will handle more information electronically and less in hard-copy form. The book publishing industry, which Negroponte describes as "squeezing ink onto dead trees," will survive only if it is able to adapt to the public's new preferences for receiving information.

One of the disadvantages of the Internet has always been that information does not pass through the same editorial or "gatekeeping" process as it might in the traditional media, resulting in a lower level of credibility of the information provided. But some companies look at the lack of gatekeepers as an advantage, as they can provide information to support their point of view on their website or the websites of industry associations and not have it subject to arbitrary actions by biased or uninterested editors.

Another disadvantage is that not all of an organization's key audiences will have access to the Internet because of what sociologists refer to as "the digital divide." Some lower-income families may not subscribe to Internet service at home and may be reluctant or simply not motivated enough to seek Internet access at libraries and other public venues.

Just as new college graduates entering journalism fields must learn to gather, write, edit, and disseminate news in various formats—print, broadcast, and on-line—those entering the public relations field must be just as versatile. As always, well-prepared public relations professionals must be able to write clearly and concisely, but now they must also be able to take digital photographs, upload communication materials to their organization's website, and work with employees, journalists, stockholders, and customers who prefer to communicate via the Internet.

The Internet has allowed the formation of publics that are drawn together by mutual interests rather than geographic proximity. As a source of research information, the Internet is a double-edged sword. Although information can be gathered very quickly and from a wide variety of sources, the results of such research must be treated with caution. In many cases, the information on websites is either outdated or outright inaccurate. In addition, the recent proliferation of discussion groups and blogs allows anyone to establish himself or herself as an "expert" and express opinions—educated and otherwise—on a variety of topics. Much of this information, however, is based on anger, intolerance, paranoia, and distrust of the establishment.

Although the information must be treated with some degree of skepticism, the report card on the Internet as a research tool is far from being all negative. Internet searches can, for example, provide the researcher with connections to other sources that can verify the information found on-line.

As discussed in Chapter 4, the Internet can also be a valuable tool not only for research in a general sense but also for the research that comprises the evaluation stage of a public relations campaign. Examples include postcampaign surveys, on-line focus groups, and other methods of evaluating perception of an organization or issue via the organization's website.

EMAIL

As discussed in Chapter 6, email is a fast and efficient method for distributing news releases and other publicity materials. A great deal of research has been done on how journalists prefer to receive such materials, and the results of that research are contradictory, mainly because most studies failed to account for the demographics of the journalists themselves.

Many senior journalists who have worked much of their careers before the advent of email prefer the old-fashioned way of receiving publicity materials: first-class mail. The advantage is the ease of reading it quickly and scribbling notes in the margin. Younger journalists who attended college during the 1990s and early 2000s are likely accustomed to communicating electronically, and in most cases are open to receiving public relations materials that way. Still other journalists prefer the fax machine, which combines the quick delivery of mail with the tangibility of a hard copy.

There is no simple answer to the question of how to disseminate your information, such as always using one method over another. Much depends on your previous experience with the media and your knowledge of their preferences. Another factor is timeliness—a simple news item carrying no sense or urgency might best be sent by regular mail, while materials related to breaking news stories are better suited to email or fax.

Professional communicators should also be aware that many journalists have two email addresses: a public one (that appears either below their by-lines or below their name on the television screen) and a private one shared only with public relations representatives and other potential news sources with whom they work on a regular basis. Many reporters are too busy to check their public email, so unsolicited communication, including news releases, sent to their public email addresses will likely be lost among the junk email and reader comments.

THE WEB

Organizations of all sizes and types have found the Web to be an effective method of communication to customers, potential customers, and other important audiences. A phenomenon born in the early 1990s, the Web has drastically changed how advanced cultures deal with both products and causes. Consumer-product companies have found the Web to be an effective venue for both direct sales and encouraging potential customers to purchase their products on their next visit to the shopping mall or grocery store. Amazon.com, which began as a book retailer but now deals with nearly every product manufactured in the United States, is often credited as the leader in on-line shopping, or "ecommerce."

In addition to product sales, corporations also use websites to provide information on their missions, products, services, management structures, corporate history, and investment opportunities. Potential audiences for such a site would include employees, customers and potential customers, stockholders, market analysts, and journalists. A nonprofit organization can use a website to provide information on its mission, services, leadership, and volunteer opportunities.

Although one could argue that such commercial applications of the Web are more accurately described as "marketing" rather than "public relations," the public relations applications of the Web are apparent in the arena of public issues and debate. Special-interest groups—such as the National Rifle Association, the National Abortion Rights Action League, the Campaign for Tobacco-Free Kids, the Sierra Club, and other groups involved in public issues—have found the Web to be the most effective method for reaching current and prospective supporters. These groups can promote their causes, recruit new supporters, respond to requests for information, and raise money—all through links on their homepages. Such sites can be time consuming to maintain, but cost effective, considering the difficulty of accomplishing the same results with a combination of paid advertising and direct mail.

One of the major advantages of using the Internet is its immediacy. When Alaska Airlines needed to provide a source of timely information on the crash of one its aircraft in January 2000, it used its website to provide official information and timely updates that could be accessed by employees, media representatives, and family members of affected passengers. More recently, many large universities have developed emergency communication systems, based on employee and student email accounts and cell phone numbers, to notify employees and students in the case of campus emergencies. Those systems were developed in response to the 2007 shootings at Virginia Tech University.

In addition to being easy to navigate, an effective website must also provide a clear explanation of what the company does without depending only on mission statements consisting of clichés and industry buzzwords. A well-designed website should provide information on the organization's history, structure, and purpose. Appropriate links to the homepage might include a list of job openings, copies of position papers or other opinion-based documents, as well as the most recent annual report in a format that can be easily downloaded or printed.

Another important link, obviously, takes the visitor to the public relations department's page. In addition to providing an archive of news releases, newsletters, and annual reports, the public relations page should provide links to external sources, such as press clippings. Articles from newspapers and magazines are often considered more credible than the company's own news releases. Many of the visitors to a company's website will be journalists who cover that company or the industry in which it operates. Nearly all print and broadcast journalists use the Web for both background research and locating experts to serve as interview sources.

There are numerous advantages to the Internet, many of them related to the speed and accuracy of collecting and managing large quantities of information in a short period of time. The interactive nature of the Internet provides a two-way platform through which one can communicate and gather feedback instantly. Two-thirds of all websites include some type of survey or feedback device, such as a "guest book" or a link labeled "Click here to contact the company."

Weaknesses and limitations include the problem of the limited audience, which will change over time as more companies and individuals subscribe to Internet service. The rapid growth has led to other problems, one of them being clutter. A Google keyword search for information on "environmental regulation," for example, produces millions of items on the topic, perhaps less than 1 percent of which will include useful information.

One of the interesting aspects of the Web is a phenomenon that researchers refer to as "dueling websites." Just as companies, government agencies, and nonprofit organizations find their websites an effective way to promote their products, services, and causes, opposition groups are quick to counter those claims with websites of their own—in some cases, so specific that they target only one organization. Examples include a website titled "Stop ExxonMobil Alliance," which criticizes the public relations tactics of the oil company, and "Public Employees for Environmental Responsibility," which criticizes the operation of the Environmental Protection Agency.

SOCIAL MEDIA

The term *social media* was coined in 2006 to refer to the proliferation of websites for which the content is provided by individual contributors rather than organizations. As of late 2007, the most popular social media sites include YouTube, a video sharing site; Wikipedia, an on-line encyclopedia for which entries can be created and revised by users; and social networking sites such as MySpace and Facebook. The latter two services began as networking opportunities for teenagers and preteens, but quickly expanded their audiences—first to college students, and then to older adults. Many of these sites are also used to distribute news items and other promotional material.

The potential for social media as communication channels is enormous, but such applications are not without controversy. Ethical challenges are considerable. One example is the 2006 parody of former Vice President Al Gore that appeared on YouTube. At first, the brief skit that showed Gore lecturing penguins on the dangers of global warming was believed to be the work of a 29-year-old contributor from California who simply wanted to poke fun at Gore's campaign against corporate polluters. It was eventually determined, however, that the parody was created by a public relations agency on behalf of one of its clients, Exxon-Mobil, an oil company often criticized for its alleged role in air pollution. When the deception was exposed, the agency was publicly embarrassed, but the message for the public relations industry was apparent: The potential for the impact of social media was considerable.

THE BLOGOSPHERE

The term **blog** is a contraction of *web logs*, a phenomenon that began in the early 2000s when individuals began appointing themselves as "experts" and pontificating on their own websites about politics, sports, consumer affairs, or a variety of other topics.

According to a 2006 study conducted by the Pew Research Center, one-third of all Internet users in the United States (and one in six of all Americans) reported reading blogs on a regular basis. The same study found that almost a quarter of blog readers also participate in the discussion. As of 2006, the number of blogs was 60 times greater than it was in 2003. According to a study published in 2007, a new blog was being created every 7 seconds. Although the largest demographic group found in the blogosphere are baby boomers (between the ages of 40 and 60), the fastest-growing demographic category represented are Generation X, also known as "twenty-somethings."

Blogs allow individuals with a variety of credentials—or in some cases no credentials at all—to publish daily or weekly news and opinion content and invite readers to respond. At first, the common term for publishers of web logs was "citizen journalists." Soon, the term was shortened to "blogs" and the content providers became known as "bloggers."

When such sites were first introduced, they were viewed as novelties that would likely have short life spans and have little impact on the public relations profession. Then, when bloggers began using their platforms to scrutinize and comment on the performance of governmental agencies, major corporations, and nonprofit organizations, the public relations profession recognized the phenomenon as a potential source of negative information that would require new policies about how and when organizations should respond, if at all.

More recently, however, the public relations profession has began to look at blogging as a potential communication channel to add to an already full array of cyberspace tactics.

With no editorial supervision or scrutiny, bloggers or on-line journalists become self-appointed consumer advocates or social commentators with little or no professional training and no obligation to adhere to ethical standards regarding news gathering and dissemination. They may also feel no obligation to follow journalistic principles such as fairness, balance, and fact checking. As a result, unscrupulous competitors and disgruntled former employees can spread rumors and generate half-truths about a company's labor policies, the integrity of its finances or operating procedures, or the quality of its products, and angry consumers can use the technology to organize boycotts over frivolous issues.

In addition to the absence of an editorial process, another shortcoming of blogs is their short life span, as numerous studies have found that nearly half are abandoned within six months of their creation, with many falling idle after only a few entries.

Although many personal blogs are not taken seriously by anyone other than their authors, **corporate blogs** are another matter. One of the pioneers in the field of corporate blogs is the Microsoft Corporation, which in 2005 authorized one of its employees, Robert Scoble, to use the company's computer resources (as well as company time) to publish a daily blog on topics related to the company's products and services. Within a year, the blog had more than 24,000 daily readers. Instead of simply promoting the company's products (as in the case of its website), Scoble uses the blog to discuss new products, company policies regarding warranties, service contracts, and upgrades; respond to customer comments and complaints; and "debunk" false information about the company posted on other blogs.

Many consumer product companies—especially those that sell big-ticket items such as automobiles and home electronics—provide blogs linked to their websites. The content includes both company-provided news about current and soon-to-be-released products and consumer questions and comments. Such blogs are largely more sophisticated versions of consumer bulletin boards and discussion groups. In the early days, discussions on such venues would be shut down at the first sign of negative comments, but companies eventually realized that the sites would carry much more credibility if they allowed the negative comments alongside the positive. If they allowed only the positive comments, consumers would become skeptical and view them in the same light they view commercials.

PODCASTS

In 2001, Apple Computer, Inc., introduced the iPod, an electronic device that allows users to download digital music files from the Internet. At first, the technology was expected to be used mainly for entertainment purposes, but within a few years, journalists and marketers began to take advantage of the technology. Broadcast journalists began offering highlights of lengthy interviews in their traditional television broadcasts and longer, unedited versions (via the Internet) in a form that could be easily downloaded to iPods, a trend that gave birth to the term **podcasting**. Consumer product companies then began using the technology to provide more detailed information on their products than could easily be provided by conventional advertising. As of the end of 2007, Apple had sold more than 100 million iPods.

MONITORING CYBERSPACE

Many of the same companies that once monitored only traditional media ("clipping services" or "media monitoring services") have expanded their services to include cyberspace. Although not cheap, the services are effective ways to monitor public opinion and provide an earlier opportunity to respond to false, derogatory, or inflammatory information. Subscribing to such services also relieves company employees from the time-consuming and sometimes technologically overwhelming task of attempting to do it themselves.

Locating news items affecting your organization's public relations efforts is made easier by the Internet, but a major weakness of the Web is the lack of an accurate method by which a media researcher (or professional communicator attempting to measure the impact of a campaign) can determine the size of the audience for a message communicated through cyberspace. Although the number of visitors or "hits" on a specific website can be measured, there is no way to determine the length of time they remain on the site, the quantity of information obtained, or the degree to which members of the audience retain the information or are motivated to act on it. For banner ads, Internet service providers can provide advertisers with the total number of users who click on each item (known as "click through rates"), but the reliability of that information is also suspect. Although there has been some discussion of a system by which Internet usage could be measured and audited for accuracy (analogous to the newspaper industry's Audit Bureau of Circulation), no such system was under development as of early 2008.

The importance of monitoring the content of blogs that affect an organization or the industry in which it competes is obvious. The question of how to respond—or even if you should respond—is open for debate. Falsehoods that are widely disseminated should be addressed and corrected regardless of the venue—newspaper, magazine, television, talk radio, Internet chatroom, or industry bulletin board. The same could be said about responding to derogatory or inflammatory comments made by the most influential bloggers. It is the proper role of the public relations representative to correct falsehoods quickly and replace erroneous information with the facts. But what about small-time bloggers with limited followings? From a practical standpoint, attempting to respond to every issue raised on a blog with a limited readership may not be worth the time. In addition, beginning a back-and-forth "he-said, she-said" with bloggers will often make the organization appear to be the bully or the bad guy, regardless of who is right and who is wrong.

TRENDS AND ISSUES

Writing for the Cyberspace Audience

When developing public relations messages for the cyberspace audience, professional communicators must realize how the electronic venue is different from the print and broadcast media. People *read* the newspaper, *watch* television, and *listen to* the radio. But they *use* the Internet. The Internet is appropriate for messages that are short and concise. Messages that are long and complicated belong on paper, not on the computer screen. Although one can deliver complicated information on a website that includes hypertext links, it's not as practical as presenting the information in hard copy form. In a series of 2005 experiments involving college students and test preparation, for example, those who studied by reading material on a computer screen performed much better when the material was in one long document rather than separate documents connected by hypertext links, but those students who read the material in hard-copy form performed even better. It is dangerous to assume that younger audiences will automatically prefer receiving information on-line and older audiences will prefer it on hard copy. Researchers have found that audience preference and effectiveness is associated more with the nature and complexity of the information than with the age of the audience.

Although much of the material on the Internet comes in the form of either text or still photographs, most computers are equipped with programs that allow for the transmission of audio and video clips. The quality of the clips depends largely on the sophistication of the users' equipment and the speed with which the equipment processes the transmission. As the technology improves, the inclusion of audio and video clips within public relations materials will become more popular and effective.

Whether writing copy for an organization's website, blog, discussion group, or on-line news release, the basic principles of professional writing still apply: (1) use correct spelling and grammar; (2) avoid "puff" words, clichés, and unsubstantiated claims; (3) use phrases that are active rather than passive; and (4) avoid industry jargon.

There are important differences in the two writing styles, however. Short sentences, although important for any form of writing, are even more highly valued in cyberspace, with the ideal length for sentences being 12 to 16 words. Whether communicating by email to coworkers, clients, customers, or journalists, basic rules of common sense and courtesy apply, made even more important by the speed with which information can be transmitted. Those rules include avoiding writing in all caps (that's the equivalent of shouting) and being cautious in the use of functions such as "CC," "BCC" (blind copy), and "reply all." In addition, communicators with the tendency to dash off quick and sometimes sarcastic responses find the function labeled "save as draft" especially helpful, as writing a first draft of an angry, forceful, or sarcastic response and then waiting 24 hours to send it (or decide against sending it) may spare the writer from having to apologize later.

CASE STUDY 7

We Are Marshall

Most sports fans over the age of 50 know the story of the 1970 Marshall University football team. On November 14 of that year, the Thundering Herd played a Saturday afternoon game at East Carolina University in Greenville, North Carolina. On the return flight, the chartered DC-9 crashed into a West Virginia hillside, killing all 75 on board, including players, coaches, fans, and flight crew. According to the National Collegiate Athletic Association, it was the worst tragedy in the 100-plus-year history of intercollegiate athletics.

Today, the university and surrounding community continue to mourn the loss. Numerous memorials are found on campus and in the surrounding community, but the most poignant may be the fountain at the center of campus. Each year on November 14, the foun-

tain is turned off for the winter in a brief but touching ceremony that draws a mixture of university faculty and students, as well as local politicians and family members of those killed.

But despite the story being so well known, university officials and residents of the surrounding community of Huntington, West Virginia, are protective of the legacy of the 1970 team. So they were understandably concerned when Hollywood came calling in 2005. Warner Bros. Studio producer Basil Iwanyk and director Joseph McGinty Nichol (better known as McG) wanted to turn the story into a major motion picture titled *We Are Marshall*. Not sure how the story would be told, townspeople were skeptical about outsiders coming to town to "Hollywoodize" an important time in the community's history.

From the beginning, the crew and cast—which included stars Matthew McConaughey, Kate Mara,

David Strathairn, Matthew Fox, Ian McShane, and Anthony Mackie—realized the importance of respecting the memory of the crash victims and the feelings of family members during the production process. They took the extra time and extra steps necessary to earn the trust of the community. Members of the cast and crew were often seen at local restaurants and at public events. They were friendly and caring. They listened. They took time to answer questions and tried to place many students and community members as extras. They also made sure that representatives of the university and the community were involved in each step of the production process.

The title of the film is based on a crowd chant heard several times at each home game. After fans on one side of the stadium chant, "We are," fans on the other side respond, "Marshall." The film depicts the chant being used at home games and other occasions, including during an impromptu pep rally staged to save the football program from being scrapped. But in reality, the chant was not developed until the 1980s. As a result of the film, however, the phrase is now everywhere on campus and in town—on apparel, banners, and the university website.

"Sexiest Man Alive" Becomes the "Big Man on Campus"

McConaughey, named *People* magazine's Sexiest Man Alive in 2005, drew a lot of attention during the filming of the movie. He became the subject of many "celebrity sightings" and drew attention—both positive and negative—everywhere he went on campus and in the community.

No stranger to media scrutiny, McConaughey learned that everything he said and did while in a small town would make news—even an offhand remark about the challenge of finding a safe place to jog. And the media attention continued long after the cast and crew left town. For example, after a local television station did a story on the hotel room McConaughey used, the room was immediately booked for 45 days continuously.

Busy Times in the Public Relations Department

For the university's public relations team, the time was frantic and resulted in many nights with only a few hours of sleep. Before and during the filming, the team worked with publicists for Warner Bros. and individual cast members, as well as public relations professionals employed by state government agencies. More than 40 different media organizations—from small community newspapers to national entertainment publications to online journalists—wanted access to the campus.

"The *We Are Marshall* experience shows this is a tremendous time to be a journalist and see the changes in media relations and how entertainment media covers events," said Bill Bissett, the university's vice president for communications and marketing. "This coverage is really what public relations is all about. It is an incredible time to be involved."

Keeping track of the information, requests, and coverage was an overwhelming task. Bissett tracked media hits through Google Alerts, which sent him daily summaries of media coverage. He was pleased that comments and coverage were all favorable. "This is our time to shine," Bissett said. "We did not receive a single negative comment."

Long-Term Benefits?

Although publicity generated by the movie resulted in a significant increase in the number of hits on the university's website and an increase in the number of requests for admissions information received by regular mail, email, and telephone, it is not clear what the overall long-term effect will be on university enrollment.

After the movie, the university saw an opportunity to capitalize on the national publicity generated by the movie, without "losing who we are," Bissett said. The movie title has been augmented into marketing outreach and recruiting efforts such as through the alumni magazine, the website, and various printed materials.

"We are more than that chapter [in our history]," Bissett said. "We are a growing research university. We are new structures on campus. While the movie is a strong reference and an important chapter in our history, much has happened since the tragedy. This is not 1971. This is 2007. We have filled in many blanks."

TRACKING THE CASE: COLLEGE STUDENTS AND CREDIT CARD DEBT

Chapters 3 through 10 each include segments of a hypothetical student-produced public relations campaign proposal. The student team, as part of an advanced public relations class, spent the semester researching the problem of credit card debt among college students for a fictional nonprofit organization, Credit Counselors of Mason County.

As detailed in the previous section, the team chose a variety of traditional media channels with which it planned to reach its audience. Next, the team selected interactive media channels.

Implementation: Interactive Media Channels

The team designed a page for the university's website that offered background information on the problem of credit card debt and reiterated the key messages about (1) students not needing to feel embarrassed for seeking help and (2) the potential negative impact of credit card debt on the employment search. The page could be accessed by a link on the university's homepage as well as the homepage of the student counseling service. In turn, the page included a link connected to the homepage of the CCMC.

The written product submitted for this section included a description of the new website, and the appendix featured a visual representation of the site and a schematic diagram illustrating the links.

DISCUSSION QUESTIONS

1. This chapter, as well as Chapter 4, pointed out some of the strengths and weaknesses of the Internet as part of a public relations program. As the Internet becomes increasingly more important in business and society, will these shortcomings become greater or worse? What steps can professional communicators take to overcome or work around those shortcomings?

2. Consider how officials at Marshall University used the Internet (Case Study 7) to take advantage of publicity associated with the movie *We Are Marshall*. If you had been in charge, how might you have approached this challenge differently?

GLOSSARY OF TERMS

Blog. A contraction of *web log*, a feature of the Web that allows individuals to host their own discussion forums in which they express opinions about politics, sports, consumer affairs, or a variety of other topics.

Corporate blog. Typically written by an individual employee who uses the company's computer resources (as well as company time) to publish a daily blog on topics related to the company's products and services.

Podcasting. A method of transmitting digital files over the Internet that can be downloaded to portable electronic devices. Used for entertainment, marketing, and journalistic programming. The term is derived from the Apple Computer product, the iPod.

CHAPTER 8

IMPLEMENTATION

Nonmedia Channels

EVENTS

Events or "special events" have long been standard tactics employed by public relations professionals to communicate indirectly to audiences other than the media. Successful events can bring together an organization's members and financial supporters, as well as outsiders such as government officials, prospective members, and, in many cases, the media who cover the social issues with which the host organization is associated.

From a theoretical standpoint, the effectiveness of events is partially based on the proverb "Tell me and I will forget; show me and I will remember; involve me and I will understand." Translated into public relations vocabulary, that means a written or spoken announcement has a certain level of effectiveness; photographs and other visuals represent an improvement; but an activity that requires a higher level of involvement by the participant increases the effectiveness even more. An excellent example is "Take Our Daughters to Work Day," an annual event, sponsored by the Ms. Foundation for Women, in which mothers are encouraged to take their daughters to their workplaces in order to encourage them to begin thinking about career paths. The foundation has recently expanded the idea to include sons by renaming it "Take Our Daughters and Sons to Work Day."

Basics of Event Planning

Regardless of which category an event falls in, here are six guidelines for effective event planning:

1. Do not depend on a single event to carry more than its share of the workload. Because events are so visible, there is often a tendency to put too much of a burden on them and expect them to carry the whole load of a public relations program.

2. Have realistic expectations for media coverage. Even though media coverage is not the main purpose for producing an event, work supervisors and clients still like to see the media attending and covering the functions. But the problem is that reporters—especially business reporters—get invited to many such events, and they cannot possibly attend every corporate dinner, awards luncheon, groundbreaking ceremony, and open house to which they are invited. Many have the attitude that "if you've been to one rubber-chicken awards luncheon, you've been to all of them."

Public relations representatives often find this a difficult concept to explain to clients or superiors who do not understand that reporters get invited to several such events each week. To a boss or client, the event in question is the only one that matters. Public relations counselors therefore have to become proficient in "managing expectations" and telling their clients or CEOs that they will let the reporters know about an event ahead of time, send the reporters news kits or background information, and then make the follow-up calls to make sure reporters have not forgotten, but they cannot guarantee the reporters will attend. Aside from all the other events reporters may have been invited to, more urgent news stories may be happening that day. Media coverage should therefore not make or break an event; the event should have enough merit to stand on its own.

Company representatives, whether they work for the public relations department or not, should treat reporters as though they are there to cover a story and not to socialize. Reporters very seldom attend events to socialize, not only because they are too busy, but many newspapers and television stations have policies that prohibit them from going to social functions if there is not a significant news story associated with it. A public relations representative new to a community and not sure about the local "media culture" should watch local television news and scan the local newspapers to look for the types of events that get media coverage in the community.

Even though the emphasis of an event should not be on media coverage, it is a bonus when it occurs. One way of increasing the likelihood of media coverage is to offer something visual for both newspaper photographers (thinking in terms of still photos, usually in black and white) and television videographers (thinking in terms of moving video in color).

The Wilmington Children's Museum, a nonprofit organization in Wilmington, North Carolina, sponsors an annual sandcastle-building contest each fall at nearby Wrightsville Beach. Each year it earns a large color photograph the following day on the front page of the local daily newspaper. The visual nature of the contest, combined with its novelty, are the reasons for the detailed coverage.

3. Involve as many people as possible. Employees like to be included in company activities and events. They like to be asked to help organize and execute the event. Likewise, in nonprofit organizations and charities, volunteers should be involved as much as possible.

4. Pay attention to detail. Experienced event planners become skilled at anticipating problems and challenges, especially those involving people from outside the sponsoring organization. One example is local government officials, whose cooperation will be necessary because of factors such as street closings, permits to use public parks or other meeting areas, clean up, security, and liability insurance. Even if the event is on one's own property, off-duty police officers and other security personnel may be necessary for traffic control at entrances and exits.

5. Make sure the safety of employees and guests is a priority. Accidents resulting in injury or death are tragic, as well as harmful to one's reputation, costly in terms of legal fees and insurance costs, and emotionally draining to employees.

6. Evaluate the event immediately, and keep the results where they can be easily found. Even though the overall campaign (of which the event is only a small part) will be evaluated at its conclusion, specific events should be evaluated immediately after their conclusion, so the positives and negatives of the event are not forgotten or lost while looking at the larger picture. This is especially important in cases of annual events, so those planning the event in subsequent years can learn from successes and failures of the past.

Types of Events

Most events fall into one of four categories, although many are actually combinations of two or more. Those categories are commemorative or celebrative events, educational activities, meal functions, and contests or competitions.

Commemorative or Celebrative Events. Activities that commemorate or celebrate certain events include ribbon-cuttings, grand openings, and awards programs.

Educational Activities. Educational activities include national events, such as "Take Our Daughters and Sons to Work Day," as well as local events, such as public debates, forums, and teachers' workshops, which are covered in a later section titled In-Person Communication.

Meal Functions. Sponsoring events that are little more than opportunities to eat and socialize are common tactics, either as stand-alone activities or as part of a formal public relations campaign. One popular idea for community organizations such as chambers of commerce is to plan events around breakfast instead of lunch or dinner. The advantages are numerous: No alcohol is served, minds are more alert, and there is a built-in deadline for wrapping it up (people have to get to work). Breakfast functions also attract those who have a difficult time getting away from their offices to attend afternoon events, and those who do not want to take time away from their families to attend evening events. Officials at the Greater Tampa Chamber of Commerce in Tampa, Florida, noticed that many members showed up "a minute or two" late for 8:00 A.M. breakfast meetings, so they found humor in the situation by changing the start time to 7:59. Other organizations in the area did likewise.

Outdoor meal functions such as picnics and barbecues are another option; they are popular because they are generally informal and allow family members to attend. Contingency plans must be in place, however, for inclement weather. Menus must be chosen carefully, with consideration given to the special dietary needs of those attending. For example, some attendees expect a "meat and potatoes" meal, while others may be vegetarians or want a lighter healthier lunch. Choices can keep everyone happy but may add to an event's costs.

Contests and Competitions. Many events organized by public relations staffs take the form of contests or competitions. Contests appeal to nearly everyone, as evidenced by the popularity of television game shows. Therefore, if a program planner can develop a contest or competition that has some relevance to at least one of the program's designated audiences and at least one of the program's objectives this tactic can be cost effective because most competitions are fairly inexpensive to implement.

When companies or nonprofit organizations want to make children one of their target audiences—because they want to start young people thinking about an issue—they might include in their campaigns the sponsorship of a school essay contest for students in grades K–12. When the children need help with their essays, they will ask their parents, so program planners are effectively reaching two audiences with one communication tactic.

Another example is a contest once sponsored by the American Lung Association in many of its chapters around the country. The contest was put into the framework of a challenge—a $500 bet that contestants cannot quit smoking for 30 days. Contestants signed pledge cards at their nearest ALA office and then returned in 30 days for a blood test that determined the level of nicotine or other evidence of tobacco usage. Contestants who passed the blood test became eligible for a drawing for a $500 cash prize. Each chapter provided the cash prize and spent perhaps another $500 to promote it, but if 1,000 individuals entered the contest and 100 are able to permanently quit smoking as a result, the association achieved those results for the cost of $10 each. The same $1,000 spent on printed materials or newspaper or television advertising would not have gone very far. In addition, the association's efforts received coverage in the local news media, because the idea of a contest appealed to journalists as well.

When Virginia Power wanted to promote the concept of electric cars as the logical replacement for those powered by gasoline engines, the company announced plans for an electric vehicle race at Richmond International Speedway and challenged science classes at 25 local high schools to build the cars. Not only did the company meet its objectives of promoting the potential of electric vehicles but also its engineers picked up some useful ideas to incorporate into future designs.

Contests and competitions often benefit both the sponsor and the participants. The Public Relations Student Society of America's annual J. Carroll Bateman Competition, for example, provides sponsors with input and usable ideas, while providing participants the opportunity to gain firsthand experience in working for real-world clients. One of the most successful public relations programs in the country started as a simple contest—the Pillsbury Bake-Off.

Public relations representatives should consult an attorney if the contest involves the purchase of a product. Even if a purchase is not required, contests are still subject to regulation by the Federal Trade Commission.

SOCIAL RESPONSIBILITY AND PHILANTHROPY PROGRAMS

Public relations pioneer Edward L. Bernays often described public relations as "good work understood by the public"; other observers have observed that public relations consists of "doing good things and getting credit for it." Social responsibility and philanthropy programs help contribute to an organization's reputation in a community and across the country. On both local and national scales, companies have found that becoming involved in helping others often contributes to an enhanced reputation and, as a result, to financial success. On the national level, companies support charities through direct financial contributions and less direct forms of assistance, such as sponsoring events and providing volunteer talent. On the local level, companies not only support specific charities but also the community as a whole through the sponsorship of events and social programs.

Today, community involvement is more important than in past history because today's lifestyles do not especially promote connections with people. In years past, families knew their neighbors, their postmasters, and their local storekeepers. But as society has become larger and more complex, involvement in issues important to employees' families have become more important. Also important today is to let community members see businesses as groups of individuals rather than as "the big bad company on the other side of the fence."

Public relations expert Robert Dilenschneider wrote in his book *Power and Influence* that "people measure a company's ethical performance by comparing what it says to what it does." Paraphrased, that means it is not sufficient to just talk about being socially responsible—a company must have a verifiable track record to match the reputation it desires. As other observers have commented, "What a company does will scream so loud that people cannot hear what it says."

Social responsibility is a relatively new concept in public relations that refers to the pairing of profit-making companies with nonprofit organizations or causes. In addition to tax benefits and positive publicity, another benefit to the company is improved ability to recruit and retain quality employees. If the salary and benefits a company offers are similar to those offered by its competitors, one might have an edge if one has a reputation for being socially responsible. The same can be said about potential customers, as a reputation of being socially responsible helps a company differentiate itself from its competition: If price and quality are the same, the difference may be the level of social responsibility it exhibits.

National Sponsorships

On a nationwide scale, corporate sponsorships are best known in sporting events such as college football bowl games and professional golf and tennis tournaments. In exchange for the money invested, many corporate sponsors have their names incorporated into the name of such events. In other cases, a sponsor may be designated as the "official airline" or "official soft drink" of an event, and the result may be an increase in airline ticket sales or beverage sales for the short term. There is often a long-term benefit in terms of name recognition and product sales, although the results are difficult to quantify.

The term **cause-related marketing** has been credited to American Express, which used it to describe its involvement in the 1986 renovation of the Statue of Liberty. Other examples include Ronald McDonald's Children Charities, which include the well-known Ronald McDonald Houses, a network of facilities that house parents of hospitalized children; Avon, a cosmetics company that started the pink ribbon program in support of breast cancer research; and Bayer Aspirin, which has formed a sponsorship with the Arthritis Foundation.

In some cases, it is the company's idea to seek out the worthy cause; in other cases, the nonprofit organization takes the initiative to seek a sponsoring company. There are even some advertising and public relations firms that claim to be specialists in cause-related marketing and matching profit-making companies with worthy causes.

The Philip Morris Company, one of the country's largest manufacturers of tobacco products, is well known for its philanthropic efforts. Through its subsidiaries, such as Kraft Foods and Miller Beer, the company encourages its employees to participate in worthwhile community projects, such as after-school tutoring and mentoring programs for children at risk.

The company made a more visible effort shortly after the September 11, 2001, terrorist attacks on the World Trade Center, which once stood less than three miles from the

Philip Morris corporate headquarters. In addition to a $10 million commitment to the American Red Cross, the company also pledged $1,000 each to relief organizations on behalf of employees who volunteered 25 hours of their time to those organizations.

In addition, the Philip Morris Company's employee fund gave $100,000 to the fund for Public Schools/World Trade Center School Relief Fund to specifically help families from lower Manhattan, District 27 in Queens, and District 31 in Staten Island. Those were areas where many of the victims, notably firefighters and police officers, lived. The money went to support counseling for children, parents, and teachers, to provide safe transportation for children who were displaced from their schools, and to make available programs to teach antibias/conflict resolution and diversity education with community leaders and national organizations. The company shut down its Miller brewery in Albany, Georgia, in order to bottle more than 45,000 bottles of water that were shipped to relief workers at disaster sites. Kraft sent more than a dozen truckloads of snacks and beverages to relief workers, in addition to sending food to air travelers stranded at airports in Canada.

Many companies demonstrate social responsibility by donating services rather than making outright cash gifts. Goodyear often sends its blimps to areas in California devastated by earthquakes or parts of southeastern states affected by hurricanes. The message boards on the underside of the blimps, which usually carry advertising, are instead used to provide information on shelter locations and other news, as traditional media sources may be unavailable.

In 2000, Barnes & Noble, the largest retail bookstore chain in the country, teamed with the Anti-Defamation League (ADL), one of the country's leading civil rights organizations, to develop "Close the Book on Hate," an extensive campaign to combat racism, bigotry, and anti-Semitism. The campaign included informational literature distributed at Barnes & Noble locations and educational materials for parents and school teachers. The ADL had promoted such causes since its founding in 1913, but Barnes & Noble decided to help when CEO Leonard Riggio was motivated by news coverage of hate crimes of the late 1990s, including the shootings at Columbine High School in Colorado and the murder of James Byrd, an African American man who was dragged to death behind a truck by white supremacists in Jasper, Texas. First Lady Laura Bush was the keynote speaker for the October 2001 event, which by coincidence took place one month to the day after the September 11 terrorist attacks on New York City and the Pentagon.

On a national scale, some consumer-product companies "adopt" charitable causes. Examples include endorsements or "piggyback" advertising and/or the donation of a predetermined portion of the company's profits.

Paul Carringer, account services manager for Zook Advertising Inc. in Columbus, Ohio, is one of the country's leading experts in cause-related marketing. His research indicates that 72 percent of consumers are more likely to buy a company's products as a result of its association with a reputable charity, and that figure rises to 80 percent if the organization or activity sponsored involves children, such as the Boy Scouts, Girl Scouts, or Special Olympics.

Carringer suggests effective partnerships between companies and nonprofit organizations be based on a number of factors, including (1) the compatibility of the sponsor's goals with those of the benefiting organization; (2) the natural relationship between the two organizations (such as a company that manufactures a product purchased by teenagers with a service organization that helps runaways); (3) a detailed written agreement that describes objectives, expectations, and parameters; and (4) periodic evaluation and fine-tuning. He also warns against common pitfalls, such as unnatural relationships (such as a beer company with a children's charity), programs that benefit one side only, lack of clear goals and expectations, and lack of written agreements.

Local Programs

Every community in the country has four needs: social/economic needs, educational needs, recreational needs, and entertainment needs. A corporate public relations staff looking for a starting point for a community involvement or philanthropy program should begin by looking for opportunities to address one or more of those needs.

An excellent example of addressing *social/economic needs* is to become involved— either through cash donations or employee volunteer time (or both)—with social service agencies such as homeless services, food banks, or domestic violence shelters. One popular recipient of both financial support and employee volunteer time is Habitat for Humanity, a nationwide organization that works at the community level to built new homes or renovate older homes and provide them at nominal cost to low-income families. Some companies allow their employees one or more days off with pay in order to perform the construction work; architectural firms provide free architectural consulting services; lumber companies donate the lumber, tools, and building supplies; and fast-food restaurants will provide free food at lunchtime. Still other companies may not be able to provide any of the above, but may make cash donations instead.

Common examples of addressing *educational needs* include sponsoring academic competitions, providing school employment or internship programs, and encouraging employees to serve as tutors or mentors to students considered "at risk" of dropping out of school.

The most common example of addressing *recreational* and *entertainment needs* is the sponsoring of community events such as concerts, celebrations, festivals, parades, picnics, athletic events, and youth sports. The reason most of those events are either free or very inexpensive to attend is because they have sponsors to absorb the cost.

On the local level, sponsorship programs generally fall into one of three categories: community events and sponsorships, school and university support programs, and employee involvement programs.

Community Events and Sponsorships.   Many corporations have found "good neighbor policies" to be effective in promoting positive community relations. International Business Machines (IBM) was one of the first companies in the country to adopt a policy of expecting its branch offices to support local causes, and that concept has spread to IBM locations around the world. The company began emphasizing cultural organizations such as theatre groups, museums, and libraries, and over the years has expanded into the areas of education and child welfare.

If a company is interested in being a sponsor, it is seldom necessary to go looking for the opportunities—event organizers will come looking for sponsors. Although there are many positives to sponsoring such events, the downside is that once a company does one of them, many other worthy causes in the community will ask (or sometimes insist) that the company sponsor their causes as well. In order to help sort out sponsorship requests, many companies establish a cap on their annual expenditures in this area and/or choose a priority area and establish a policy that all requests for assistance fall into that area. Examples of priority areas might include children's issues, health promotion, environmental causes, and historical preservation. In addition to carefully screening applications and selecting those to be accepted, most companies have strict policies, including monitoring and accountability procedures, to ensure the financial and ethical integrity of the events or programs sponsored.

Aside from sponsoring events and programs organized by nonprofit organizations, many companies support local charities by making them partners for company events and other programs. One common example is that of company events, such as the grand opening of a retail location, new branch office, or manufacturing facility. In contrast to sponsoring someone else's event, this is an event that is under the company's control, but it takes on a local charity as a partner. Many pizza delivery franchisees, for example, have enhanced the unveiling of new locations by hosting grand opening ceremonies for which attendees purchase discounted pizza and soft drinks, with proceeds going to the charity chosen. The events are costly to produce because of the costs such as labor, security, entertainment, and clean-up (as well as the food itself), but each person leaves with a refrigerator magnet bearing the store's telephone number for pizza delivery. The franchise owners know that over the life of those franchises, they will make hundreds of thousands of dollars in those communities, so they choose to "give something back" at the front end.

Many national hotel chains employ similar strategies when they produce grand opening ceremonies for new properties. They develop mailing lists of community leaders and prospective customers and invite them to the event, but with a nominal admission fee. Some invitees are surprised to receive invitations to a grand opening event sponsored by a multinational hotel chain, but are impressed to learn that the proceeds will be donated to a local charity.

School and University Support Programs.   This category of sponsorship programs concerns getting involved in local schools, thereby helping to meet a community's educational needs. Unfortunately, many companies are prompted to get involved in local schools only after schools receive failing grades when evaluated by government agencies or accrediting bodies.

When schools have fund-raising events or other activities such as carnivals, field trips, club activities, sports teams, scholarship funds, and construction projects, local companies can help out either through financial contributions or donations of in-kind services.

In some public school districts, some of these programs have generated controversy because of fears that schools are becoming too "commercialized." As a result, many school boards have adopted policies that either prohibit or severely limit the degree to which companies can become involved. In some cases, school board policies prohibit donations or sponsorships involving specific schools, and instead require that monetary donations are made to a districtwide foundation that provides financial support to all schools in that district.

Colleges and universities do not have as many rules, and therefore it is a lot easier for companies to get involved. Examples include donations of cash, gifts of new or used furniture and technical equipment, the underwriting of scholarships, and the establishment of internship and employment programs.

Employee Involvement Programs.   **Employee involvement programs** encourage employees to do things on their own, such as work on nonprofit boards or serve as mentors or youth counselors. Many companies extend their network of volunteers by encouraging their retirees and spouses of current employees to serve as company representatives for such programs.

In addition to the time and brainpower from which the organization benefits, it often gets access to company resources as a bonus. That is why nonprofit organizations like to have corporate executives on their boards of directors; in addition to the person, they are also getting access to a copy machine, postage, computer time, printing services, and other company resources.

One extension of the employee-volunteer idea is the *executive loan* programs offered by many companies. Under this plan, the company "loans" its executives to charities who put them to work doing public relations, fund-raising, strategic planning, and other functions. The company continues to pay the employees' salaries and benefits, and the charitable organizations agree to provide a physical working space and challenging tasks. In some programs, the loan period is as short as 30 days; in others, the loan period is six months or more. Xerox has one of the oldest and most successful programs, which it calls "social service leave." Each year since 1971, the company has selected a number of its best employees and provided them with one-year sabbaticals to work for various nonprofit organizations, charities, and universities while retaining their company salaries and benefits.

In addition to providing a valuable community service, such programs provide an alternative to risking employees on the job market during layoffs and furloughs. When its greeting card business slows down, for example, Hallmark Cards often pays employees full pay and benefits to work full time for charities in the Kansas City area where its worldwide headquarters is located.

INTERNAL AND EMPLOYEE COMMUNICATIONS

This section deals with communications that are aimed at internal audiences, such as the members of an organization or employees of a company. Research studies in workplace communication consistently find that face-to-face communication is by far the most effective method for communicating with employees and the one that employees prefer. The lack of personal contact between superiors and subordinates creates an atmosphere of low morale, mistrust, and rumors.

One advantage to an effective system of internal communication is that it gets information about significant company events (mergers, acquisitions, layoffs, and new products) to the employees before they hear about it through the public media. Employees prefer to hear news—especially bad news—from their own managers rather than from peers or outsiders.

Company leaders who communicate bad news to employees through such impersonal methods as bulletin boards, newsletters, and memoranda distributed through employee mailboxes are viewed as impersonal and uncaring. When the news is bad, an effective strategy is to deliver it in person first and then follow with either a written or email version.

For both good news and bad, email is effective for communicating to large numbers of employees spread out over a wide geographic area, but it is viewed as impersonal when it comes from someone in the office next door. While new tools for such communication are constantly being developed and existing tools are improved, the importance of effective communications content remains a priority.

In a company setting, effective communications between management and employees is vital to the success of the company, regardless of the product or service being produced. Employees value personal communications, which serve to eliminate problems caused by rumors, which in turn result from a lack of information. Good public relations, it is said, begins inside the company.

In a club, nonprofit organization, professional association, or special-interest group, members are an important public because they provide much of the organization's funding and elect the leaders that guide the organization's activities.

Newsletters

An organization's internal or employee newsletters and other publications represent its first and sometimes its only impression to the publics on which its success or failure depends. Every company or nonprofit organization of any size produces publications, and they are customarily the responsibility of the public relations specialist or department. Newsletters are the most common form of organizational communication and may be the most cost effective. Corporations have publications for their employees, customers, and stockholders. Nonprofit associations and special-interest groups publish them for their members and supporters. Colleges and universities produce them for alumni.

Public relations specialists often oversee the complete newsletter cycle: writing and editing the copy, taking photographs, designing the layout, getting approvals, coordinating the printing, and supervising the mailing or emailing (many newsletters today are also distributed in portable document format, or PDFs). The schedule for a monthly newsletter (the most common frequency) is often demanding, and as soon as one is finished, it is time to start another. Quarterly newsletters allow more time for production but are less timely. Weekly newsletters can provide information on a timelier basis, but allow the editorial staff little time to perform other public relations functions.

With an adequate budget and staff, the public relations department at a major corporation may produce multiple newsletters to serve different audiences: executives, middle management, support staff, customers, and stockholders. Some companies have one basic newsletter and use inserts or theme pages to communicate with certain employee groups.

Employee newsletters are often nicknamed "house organs." Their purpose is internal communication, and a parallel can be drawn between them and news releases, which are external communications. The functions of a company newsletter are to:

1. Help employees understand their company's structure, goals, philosophies, and policies.
2. Recognize employees for good work, loyalty, and longevity.
3. Alert employees of opportunities, such as job vacancies in other departments, and new benefits, such as college tuition reimbursement or on-the-job continuing education programs.
4. Foster pride in the company and a feeling of teamwork; show employees meeting goals using innovative methods, emphasizing how all departments interrelate to achieve company goals.

5. Deflate rumors and speculation about the future of the company or specific departments.
6. Announce policy changes and the result of employee grievances. There is some question about the value of providing results of labor negotiations, as the news is unlikely to reach employees before they hear the results directly from the union. Also, some workers will question the objectivity of what they read about the negotiations in a management-controlled newsletter.

For nonprofit associations, membership organizations and special-interest groups, the newsletter serves to:

1. Recognize volunteers.
2. Acknowledge financial support of current members and donors.
3. Encourage additional financial support above and beyond membership dues.
4. Solicit new members, donors, and corporate sponsors.
5. Create awareness of the organization's purpose.
6. Improve a weak or decaying image.
7. Maintain credibility among financial supporters (e.g., "This is what we are doing with your money").

The complexity of a corporate newsletter can vary from the inexpensive one-page version produced on an office photocopier to slick, full-color magazines. One recent trend is toward the former: When communications budgets are slashed, the house organ is often the first victim. But that news is not necessarily bad. Instead of producing expensive monthly newsletters, some companies have found cheaper but more frequent publications more effective. A one-page weekly newsletter, distributed directly through interoffice email, can be quite effective because of its timeliness; the news is actually news. Clever names such as *Monday Morning Memo* (distributed early each Monday), *The Green Sheet* (the newsletter of an environmentally aware company, printed on green paper), or one involving a clever play on words with the company name help attract attention.

Although many employers still distribute newsletters by placing hard copies in employee mailboxes, it is more expedient and cost effective to distribute electronic versions via the company's email system. Likewise, many nonprofit organization still distribute membership publications by U.S. mail, but it is less costly in time and money to do so by email.

Employee communications materials are not about immediacy, but rather about providing analysis and rationale behind management decisions. Email is good for timely information, but printed publications are better for detail and in-depth information. Sending email is easier than walking to the other side of the building, but it comes at the expense of face-to-face communication.

Information Racks and Bulletin Boards

Personnel departments, health clinics, safety departments, and other offices within a company have found information racks to be effective in providing materials that employees can pick up at their convenience. To be most effective, these racks should be in high-traffic areas or other areas where materials can be accessed easily. Providing the information in this method allows employees to pick up information even though the office itself may be closed, and also spares employees the possible embarrassment of asking in person for materials that may be sensitive in nature.

Strategically placed bulletin boards are perhaps the oldest form of employee communication and are still popular. To avoid clutter, most companies either have policies about the nature of materials that can be posted or have separate bulletin boards for company announcements and personal matters, such as automobiles for sale. Even though the term *bulletin board* is commonly used to describe its electronic counterpart, the old-fashioned cork version is still popular and effective, especially for employees who do not use the company's computer system.

Staff Meetings, Briefings, and Conference Calls

These events can be effective in cases in which large numbers of employees are working on the same issue. They are also effective in meeting other members in one's department, finding common ground, and brainstorming for new ideas. If not managed correctly, however, these methods can consume large quantities of time and money and not produce the results expected.

Employee Advisory Committees

Forming a committee that represents a cross-section of employees can be a valuable form of two-way communication in that it allows for both the gathering and disseminating of communication. Training and safety issues are common examples of areas for which this is effective.

Informational and Training Videos

Informational videos must be short and to the point in order to be effective, keeping in mind that employees may be distracted and the video will have to compete for their attention.

INVESTOR RELATIONS MATERIALS

The two principal methods by which publicly held companies communicate with their investors are *quarterly reports* and *annual reports*. These materials serve both a legal function and a communications function. Their legal function is to provide stockholders with accurate and timely information about the company's financial status. The most important legal component of the annual report is a 10K report, which publicly held companies are required to file with the Securities and Exchange Commission. In addition to this legal requirement, however, the annual report is an opportunity to communicate to potential stockholders, job candidates, and business journalists.

Nonprofit organizations are required to submit annual reports to the Internal Revenue Service. In addition to that legal function, the reports also provide a communications opportunity, as nonprofits can use them to provide general information and recruit new members and volunteers. Many nonprofits combine their annual report, which tends to be a backward-looking document, with a forward-looking document called a *program of work* or *action plan* that previews the year ahead and establishes priorities. In other cases, however, the program of work may be a separate document.

MARKETING ACTIVITIES

Even in corporate workplaces in which there are solid dividing lines between public relations and marketing staffs and their activities, those working on the public relations side of the organization still need to be familiar with the most common tactics involved in traditional product and service marketing.

Direct Mail

One of the oldest forms of communication is direct mail, but its effectiveness varies according to the product or issue being promoted. Mail falls somewhere between face-to-face communication and advertising. Unlike face-to-face communication, direct mail is mass produced and delivered, but unlike advertising, it can be individually tailored to specific audiences.

Despite the popularity of email, direct mail is still preferred by many marketers because it allows them to better target specific audiences based on zip codes. Similarly, many consumers find direct mail less intrusive than email messages, and even important messages may blend in with commercial messages or fall victim to spam filters.

Nonprofit organizations can distribute direct mail pieces at lower costs than corporations because of their eligibility for bulk mailing permits. Second-class permits are used for newsletters and magazines that are published on a regular schedule, with rates determined by the publication's dimensions and weight. The cost is somewhat higher if the organization sells advertising in the publication. Third-class permits are used for mailings other than periodicals, with the cost being much less than first-class mail. In addition to the per-piece mailing costs, both second- and third-class mailing permits require advance payment of an annual fee. Companies are eligible for a similar category of mailing permits, but their costs are higher and rules regarding presorting and minimum number of pieces limit its practicality.

Although direct mail tends to be less expensive than advertising and is more effective at reaching specific audiences, it carries with it a disadvantage: the "junk mail" stigma that readers often attach to anything that arrives bearing anything other than first-class postage.

Sales Pieces/Point-of-Purchase Brochures and Displays

As the name indicates, a **sales piece** or point-of-purchase brochure is used to provide information to consumers about specific products or services. It can take the form of a sales piece when distributed at a location other than that where the product or service is sold, or a point-of-purchase brochure when distributed in the store. Because of the cost of reprinting brochures that contain errors, these items must be proofread in detail. If a brochure includes a phone number, the most effective way to verify it is to ask someone from the public relations staff to call it to make sure it works.

A **point-of-purchase display** is one used to attract attention to a product. It often features attention-getting devices such as product samples, flashing lights, oversized cardboard replicas of the product, or cardboard cutouts of a celebrity spokesperson with whom the product is associated.

Specialty Items

Specialty items include hats, t-shirts, plastic cups, key chains, coffee mugs, bookmarks, calculators, notebooks, computer mouse pads, computer screen-savers, and a variety of other items that can be mass produced and used as giveaways, prizes, or thank-yous for employees, visitors, customers, and volunteers.

Product Placements

Product placement refers to having a company's product appear in movies and on television as a prop or as part of the scenery. Products such as clothing, soft drinks, or other food items and automobiles often have their actual brand names visible because those companies have paid to have that product appear. The usage of this form of "indirect advertising" increased more than 50 percent between 2000 and 2005. The phenomenon started in the 1970s. Prior to that, any time a soft drink was used in the movie, it was just a red-and-white can with no visible logo. Today, on both television programs and in the movies, audiences see real products.

One of the first television programs to use such a device was NBC's hit comedy *Cheers.* When the show debuted in 1982, producers collected a substantial fee from Nike in exchange for having lead character Sam Malone, played by Ted Danson, dressed in the company's clothing with the familiar "swoosh" logo. After the Nike contract expired, competitor Dockers took over as Danson's wardrobe provider. A more recent example can be seen in the hit television program *American Idol*, where the judges of the singing competition are often seen drinking Coca-Cola on the set.

One of the first feature films to include product placement was the 1982 movie, *ET: The Extraterrestrial.* Reese's Pieces were the candy of choice for the lovable alien, for which the company paid a fee.

When law-enforcement officers Sylvester Stallone and Wesley Snipes patrolled their route in *Demolition Man,* a futuristic crime drama produced in 1992 but set in the year 2032, they did so in an Oldsmobile—a placement for which the company paid. General Motors executives claimed their objective was to send a message to film audiences that their brand would be "alive and well" in 2032.

A more recent development in product placement is the addition of real product images to scenes in video games.

Consumer Information Publications

Many consumer-product companies offer free booklets that provide information on their products or more general consumer issues. When well done, these are not blatant advertisements or sales pieces, but instead information that consumers can use in making purchasing decisions. One of the obvious goals of the publication, however, is that customers will remember the name of the company when making the actual purchase. Some publications have a less direct connection, such as Shell Oil Company's series of booklets titled "Shell Car Care Books."

Many industry groups distribute similar publications that provide information to consumers on how to evaluate and compare products in that field. These publications may mention a specific product, but are careful not to recommend one over another. Examples include the National Association of Home Builders booklet, *The Home Buyer's Guide,* and the Manufactured Housing Institute's publication, *How to Buy a Manufactured Home.*

Professional service providers produce similar publications. Examples include insurance companies that produce booklets on how businesses can curtail employee theft and how individuals can prevent automobile and home accidents, and banks that produce brochures on how consumers can protect their credit ratings and use credit responsibly.

1-800 Customer Assistance Lines and Help-Desks

This tactic is most popular in the computer and home electronics industries, as manufacturers provide the toll-free lines through which customers can get help via the telephone rather than by asking a technician to visit the home to demonstrate the product's features. Although often associated with computers and home electronics, the idea actually began many decades before in the appliance industry. Long before Apple, IBM, and Hewlett-Packard set up their customer assistance lines, Maytag, Frigidaire, and Amana established these for customers who wanted more information about how their products worked.

In the last decade, the customer help-line idea spread to the food industry, with many product labels featuring a toll-free number on it that consumers can call with either a question or a complaint. Prominent display on the label is important, as such a service can be effective only if the audience knows where to find the number.

This is a good example of two-way communication; the company can use help-lines not only to disseminate information but also as a form of ongoing market research. Skilled operators can help a company measure public reaction to its products, based on how many calls are received and what the customers are saying—both the positive comments and the negative.

One advantage to the 1-800 number is that it provides a captive audience. When customers call, the company has the customer's undivided attention for the length of the phone call. One disadvantage of 1-800 numbers is their limited audience; the company has to wait for the customers to call.

Conventions and Trade Shows

Conventions and trade shows are standard in many industries, as companies that send marketing or sales representatives to these meetings find them effective in reaching prospective customers and specific audiences. The main purpose of trade shows is to find new customers and generate sales leads, but a secondary benefit is media coverage. Journalists who cover a specific industry on a regular basis are likely to attend such events and develop stories on the most newsworthy companies or products they find.

Companies that participate in trade shows on a regular basis develop traveling exhibits and assign members of the public relations or marketing staffs the responsibility of identifying and attending the most appropriate events. In technical fields, such as computers, a company will never be a major competitor unless it participates in the industry's major trade shows.

Such events are usually coordinated by industry groups or trade associations, with part or all of the planning responsibilities being assigned to the public relations staffs. Even though many participants pay their own expenses when attending these events, organizing such large events is one of the most expensive and labor-intensive marketing activities an industry group can attempt. As soon as one year's event is concluded, planning begins for the following year.

Conventions and trade shows work well in industries in which business customers gather to see what is new in the field. It is a business-to-business marketing function and an effective method for generating new customers and reaching undecided customers before competitors do. Each year, industry groups and the public relations and marketing firms that represent them organize thousands of conventions and trade shows that attract the attention of not only distributors and retailers but also the media who cover that industry.

Product Sampling Events and Giveaways

When introducing a new product for which the future is in doubt, marketers have found that giving away a small number of samples at the beginning of a campaign is effective in generating awareness of and interest in the product. In the case of a consumable product, such as a food item or household product, the goal is that consumers will be impressed enough with their samples that they become permanent users of the product on a paying basis. With items such as toys and other nonconsumables, the hope is to get a small number of the items in use or circulation so that others will be exposed to it and want to own one as well. Examples of this strategy are found at beach resorts, where marketers distribute free samples of beach toys, tanning products, and sports drinks; and at shopping malls, where they give away free samples of cosmetics, snacks, and other consumer products.

Restaurant Items

Fast-food restaurants, coffee shops, and mid-priced cafeterias often provide opportunities for nonprofit organizations to promote programs and events. Examples include place mats, tray liners, and tent cards. In some cases, the restaurant will print promotional items at their own expense; in other cases, the nonprofit organization provides the materials and the restaurant agrees to use or display it. The cardboard tent cards (or "table tents") often promote fund-raising activities and events. On college campuses, food service contractors limit the opportunity to campus organizations, whereas off-campus restaurants limit the length of time that one group can display its tent cards in order to allow as many groups as possible to take advantage of the opportunity.

IN-PERSON COMMUNICATION

Information Booths

Many shopping malls and other public buildings provide information booths that nonprofit organizations can use for free or at a nominal cost to station representatives to provide information using a combination of conversation and written information. Many vendors make portable displays that can easily be transported and set up by one or two employees.

Speeches

If a company or nonprofit organization has leaders (or public relations representatives) who are skilled at oral communication, their speeches may be one of the organization's most effective communication tactics. But just as effective speeches can contribute to the success of your campaign, speeches that are poorly written or delivered can damage the overall process.

Spokesperson Tours

Spokesperson tours can be used in issues management campaigns (with organizational representatives qualified to comment on the issue) or in product campaigns (with celebrities who endorse the company's products).

Speakers' Bureaus

A **speakers' bureau** is a service that provides company representatives to speak to school or community groups. These are very common in public utilities and other companies that have large numbers of employees. Many electric companies, for example, use a number of spokespersons to visit elementary schools to talk to classes about electrical safety. Many telephone companies will send their employees out to do seminars for other companies on basic telephone courtesy. If a local company has a problem with a personnel matter, such as sexual harassment or retirement planning, a local company can provide a qualified representative from the personnel department to provide a one-day or half-day workshop.

Just as public relations representatives must convince journalists that their organizations' spokespersons are credible sources of information, they must also convince prospective audiences that the speakers being offered are worthy of their attention. This can be done by providing written biographies and other supporting materials that outline a person's experience and credentials. Simply identifying the speaker as one of your company's employees is seldom enough.

In large companies, speakers can be active employees or retirees looking for a way to remain involved with the company. In nonprofit organizations, speakers can be either staff members, members of the board of directors, or volunteers.

Face-to-Face Communication

Face-to-face communication is often one of the least expensive methods of communication at the disposal of public relations professionals, but it may also be the most limiting in terms of the number of audience members reached. Although the audience may be small, the impact on audience members may be great. Politicians have known for decades that personal contact with voters carries far more weight than paid advertising. Few voters may have the opportunity to meet a candidate in person, but those who do are more likely to be influenced by that meeting than by the candidate's advertising.

In addition to candidates seeking office, another application of face-to-face communication in the political arena is in the discussion of public issues. Special-interest groups or other political organizations that sponsor public debates or "town hall meetings" often find them both inexpensive and effective in reaching audiences concerned about specific issues. These are similar in nature to the editorial meetings discussed in the previous chapter. Personal contact meetings can be used not only with newspaper editorial boards but also with any other group with which one is in conflict. Meetings may be conducted on neutral ground, such as the local school where community members send their children or where a business partnership is located.

Health communication is another area in which face-to-face communication is both inexpensive and effective at reaching specific audiences, especially seniors. Health fairs, screenings, and information sessions—usually taken "on the road" to shopping malls, community centers, and other venues—have become a standard part of hospitals' outreach efforts. At most hospitals, such events are cooperative projects of the public relations and health education departments.

Lobbying

Entire books have been written on the topic of **lobbying**, and this chapter will not attempt to provide great detail on the subject. It is unlikely that entry-level professionals would get involved in a client's or employer's lobbying efforts, as that task is customarily assigned to senior members of the public relations agency or department. In fact, public relations representatives who are assigned to lobby are required by law to register as lobbyists with the federal government prior to contacting congressional representatives and with the state government prior to contacting state legislators or other officials.

Lobbying comes in two forms: direct and grass roots. As the label indicates, *direct lobbying* involves face-to-face meetings with elected government officials or other decision makers in order to persuade them to act in the interests of a client or employer. Methods employed by lobbyists may include a combination of oral presentations, written position statements, and audiovisual presentations.

In addition, lobbyists often appeal to decision-makers' interests by bringing along third parties for support or endorsement, such as celebrities or scientific experts. Lobbyists attempting to secure increased federal funding for medical research have found success by having professional athletes or entertainers affected with a specific disease to accompany them when they meet with congressional representatives. Such tactics often mean the difference between being seen and not being seen. When lobbyists for diabetes research wanted to meet with congressional leaders to discuss funding issues in 1998, for example, they found it easy to get the attention of those leaders when they took along a former Miss America. Other lobbyists for equally important medical causes were unable to secure meetings because they lacked the glamour of celebrity endorsement.

One extension of direct lobbying occurs when an individual or organization is invited to provide testimony at governmental meetings. Viewers of C-Span can often see organizational representatives providing such testimony before congressional committees, but similar opportunities exist with meetings of state legislatures, administrative agencies, and local bodies such as county commissions, city councils, school boards, and zoning boards.

Such presentations often include carefully crafted opening statements, audiovisual presentations, and supporting comments by third-party experts. Scientific presentations by experts are often effective, but the impact of celebrities cannot be overlooked. Examples of effective congressional testimony in the 1990s included professional golfer Arnold Palmer's appearance in support of prostate cancer research funding and actor Michael J. Fox's appeal for funding for Parkinson's Disease funding.

Regardless of the amount of information at one's disposal or the number of persons speaking, most governmental bodies will give notice in advance of the time limit, so a presentation should be carefully edited to fit and rehearsed numerous times. And nearly every presentation will conclude with a question-and-answer session, so just as one would prepare for a media interview, one must prepare oneself and/or the presentation team for the questions most likely to be asked.

Indirect or grass-roots lobbying refers to the strategy of communicating to the citizens to be affected by an issue or constituents of a specific governmental representative to enlist their help in the organization's persuasive efforts. This often takes the form of public events or letter-writing campaigns designed to demonstrate to public officials the level of public concern connected to the issue. This process can be effective, but it takes much longer to see the results.

Community Advisory Boards

Community advisory boards represent an expansion of a focus group. Sometimes a focus group works so well that the moderator will want to keep it going. The resulting "community advisory board" may consist of either experts on a subject or ordinary people, or a combination of both. Having them meet once a month or several times a year to discuss issues provides another opportunity to gather information and test ideas among representatives of one or more target audiences. Even though it is an indirect method of communication and the results are long term and often difficult to measure, many companies involved in controversial issues find it an effective and relatively inexpensive activity.

INSERTS AND ENCLOSURES

In addition to the direct mail tactic discussed earlier in the category labeled Marketing Activities, companies and nonprofit organizations use the mail for less direct forms of persuasion and promotion. Common variations include bill and statement stuffers, payroll stuffers, and greeting cards and invitations.

Bill and Statement Stuffers

Banks, department stores, and public utilities—or any company that communicates to large numbers of people through the mail—use **bill and statement stuffers** to communicate to customers. Banks will include information with monthly statements about money management and other services the bank may offer. Electric companies include information with bills about electrical safety. Other utilities will include information with bills about telephone rates and other matters related to telephone, water, or cable television service. Bill and statement stuffers are a relatively inexpensive form of communication. Even though the companies have to pay for the printing, there are no additional mailing costs because they were going to pay the postage anyway to mail the bill. This method may be on the decline, however, as more and more Americans have their paychecks deposited directly into their bank accounts and pay their utility bills either on-line or have charges deducted directly from their bank accounts.

Payroll Stuffers

This is the same idea as used with a bill and statement stuffer, except the vehicle involved is a paycheck envelope rather than a bill. Many companies find it effective to communicate to employees by including information in the envelope with their paychecks. Instead of a separate piece of paper inside the pay envelope, some employers print brief messages on the bottom of the paycheck stubs that read, "Don't forget to get your flu shot" or "Sign up for United Way."

MISCELLANEOUS TACTICS

Greeting Cards and Invitations

One example of effectively using mail is the holiday greeting card or formal event invitation because it is personal and stands out from what may be considered "junk mail."

Compact Disks and Digital Video Disks

Once used primarily for entertainment purposes, compact disks (CDs) and digital video disks are today used for educational programs. Recent advances in digital recording technology has allowed organizations to produce programs that are less expensive and of a higher technical quality than those provided on videotape.

Kiosk Programs

A **kiosk** is an unstaffed booth located in areas that generate high rates of pedestrian traffic—such as shopping malls, airports, or hotel lobbies—to provide a database of information for persons passing by. Most kiosk presentations are based on CD-ROM programs and display information on monitors that resemble television screens (or from a distance, video games). One common example are those used in tourist communities to offer information on nearby hotels, restaurants, and attractions. Many are equipped with printers that can provide discount coupons, maps, and other information upon request. Others include built-in communication devices (resembling telephones) that connect users to businesses listed on the screen. Although the technology behind such devices continues to improve, many sponsors find them ineffective because of the high incidence of breakdowns and vandalism. They also require frequent maintenance, such as cleaning and refilling the printers with paper.

TRENDS AND ISSUES

Tips for the Newsletter Editor

Here are some tips for the newsletter editor:

1. *Keep the Editorial Quality High.* Concentrate on those news items of interest to the largest number of readers. Do not fall into the trap of printing bowling league results, wedding news, birthdays, gossip, and items about what employees' children are doing. Nobody cares. The writing style in a newsletter or any other internal publication should be less formal than that of a daily newspaper, but not so informal that it becomes silly or folksy.

2. *Newsletters Should Look Forward, Not Backward.* A little attention paid to last month's events is necessary, but keep it brief. The emphasis should be on what is expected to happen in the next month. If the January newsletter is circulated January 3, readers will be more interested in reading a preview of the month (or year) ahead than a December 18 Christmas party.

3. *Proofread It to Death.* Whenever possible, have various members of the public relations staff proofread the newsletter.

4. *Use Only High-Quality Photographs.* If the public relations staff lacks the skill or equipment for good photography, consider hiring a freelance photographer for occasions such as awards presentations and open houses.

5. *Use Reader Feedback.* The most effective newsletters are those that periodically provide readers with the opportunity to provide feedback in the form of questionnaires, reader-response cards, or other measurement devices. Readers can comment on the publication's content, style, tone, frequency, and method of delivery.

CASE STUDY 8A

Prudential's Global Volunteer Day

Businesses customarily offer employee benefits such as health care, fitness programs, child care, and stock options. Following a popular trend, Prudential Financial Inc. is one of hundreds of American companies that offers another reward: the good feeling that comes from helping others.

Although volunteerism is ingrained in the Prudential culture, a unified opportunity to help comes once a year on its Global Volunteer Day. The annual event began as Prudential's National Volunteer Day on October 28, 1995, when 5,000 employees donated their time to 100 volunteer projects. Employees were encouraged to participate in community service projects or volunteer for organizations that interested them.

More than a decade later, the event continues to grow, receive media coverage, and make an impact every first Saturday in October, drawing not only employees but also friends, family members, and clients. The volunteers participate in more than 800 projects, including building homes, tutoring students, running marathons, and feeding the homeless.

Prudential's mission for the Global Volunteer Day is to use company-sponsored volunteerism to strengthen communities where its employees live and work.

"Global Volunteer Day gives us a chance to give back to the community and fulfill our employees' desires to volunteer. But our commitment doesn't stop there," says Gabriella Morris, vice president of Prudential Financial's Community Resources Division and president of the Prudential Foundation. "Prudential Financial encourages volunteerism year round by sponsoring ongoing volunteer programs with corporate donations as well as recognizing individuals who make our neighborhoods better places to live."

Decline in Corporate Volunteerism

According to a national poll conducted by Prudential Financial's Global Market Research division in 2002, U.S. workers believe the number of companies offering volunteer opportunities is decreasing. The poll, "Company Sponsored Volunteerism," questioned roughly 650 U.S. residents, age 18 and older, on their employers' volunteer involvement. Findings were compared with a 1998 study and showed a decrease in

Prudential Chairman and CEO Arthur F. Ryan working with fellow employees to make patriotic lapel pins for distribution to families impacted by the tragic events of September 11, 2001.

Children at Quitman Street School in Newark, New Jersey, plant fall flowers to help beautify their environment.

company encouragement to volunteer. Fewer than half of the employees surveyed said that their employers sponsor volunteer programs.

Even though the number of opportunities to volunteer has decreased, 80 percent of employees polled said that they participate in volunteer programs when offered. "Many companies offer volunteerism opportunities. But our research shows there is still a gap in mobilizing even more employees," Arthur F. Ryan, chairman and CEO of Prudential Financial said in a news release. Ryan has participated in every Global Volunteer Day since its inception.

The poll results were released as part of a communications campaign for the eighth annual Global Volunteer Day that targeted the company's global workforce, existing and potential customers, stockholders and stakeholders, and private and nonprofit business communities.

Prudential Responds

In response to the perceived decline in corporate volunteerism, and to promote the company's eighth annual Global Volunteer Day, Prudential Financial organized a public relations campaign with a budget of $67,500. The company strategically used press releases, audio/video news releases, editorials, and on-line resources to target all forms of media. Prior to the campaign, the company conducted research to support its message of corporate responsibility. Media markets were identified and prioritized based on coverage area and format.

Implementation of the campaign included distributing materials to print, broadcast, and on-line media that positioned Prudential Financial as an industry leader in corporate volunteerism, even at a time when corporate opportunities were declining, according to the 2002 poll.

Prudential volunteers coordinate truck-loads of supplies at a local food bank.

Prudential volunteers work with children on cultural and arts programs.

A daycare center in New Jersey receives a fresh coat of paint.

Location-specific news releases and media advisories were distributed before, the day of, and after the Global Volunteer Day to national, regional, and local media. The releases promoted projects occurring directly within specified communities. National media attention was also achieved by providing a news release across news wires.

Pitching to the media was planned and executed using email, fax, and phone. Local angles were possible since the Global Volunteer Day included over 800 projects around the globe. In conjunction with the localized news releases, audio/video news releases were distributed and placed on the Prudential Financial website. Opinion-editorials written by Prudential chairman and CEO and the Prudential Foundation's president were distributed to regional and national newspapers. A website was created that included a Global Volunteer Day overview with volunteerism study results as well as a Global Volunteer Day fact sheet and growth chart. As part of the website, an on-line media kit was made available that included news releases, media advisories, video/audio news releases, and sound bites. Contact information, a photo gallery, and frequently asked questions were also available.

Prudential Financial evaluated the effectiveness of its campaign and discovered it was successful in generating coverage in key markets. The evaluation confirmed coverage on television broadcasts, the Internet, hundreds of radio placements, and in local weekly/daily publication press.

Responding to September 11, 2001

In response to the terrorist attacks on September 11, 2001, Prudential Financial donated money and volunteers to help with disaster relief efforts. The company donated $3 million to the American Red Cross and $2 million to New York City rebuilding efforts. More than $2 million in additional donations were made through the Prudential CARES Disaster Relief Fund, with $900,000 in employee donations matched by the Prudential Foundation. This donation also included funds from a one-time Global Volunteer Day Dollars-for-Doers program and a company contribution made in lieu of holiday parties. Prudential employees responded with increased focus during the seventh annual Global Volunteer Day as it took place less than one month after September 11, 2001. Employees donated their time to New Jersey food banks, the Salvation Army Emergency Center on the Rutgers Newark campus, blood drives, fix-up/clean-up projects in lower Manhattan, and various fundraisers for relief efforts.

CASE STUDY 8B

Hobet Mining Promotes Community Relations through Local Schools

Hobet Mining, Inc. found that some of its most effective programs were those involving local schools. In rural areas of West Virginia, where education was quickly replacing coal mining, employees cared about helping their children prepare for school. One of the most successful projects included a simple visit to the high school from Santa Claus. Santa, accompanied by the public relations manager who was recognized in the community, gave students candy bars and encouraged good study habits. High school students usually do not respond to visits from Santa, but did so enthusiastically in this case. Before the day was over, workers were stopping by the company president's office, thanking him for caring about the students through the Santa visits.

Because the school became Hobet's focal point, the school auditorium served as a neutral site for public hearings on environmental and zoning matters in which the company held a stake. This location worked better than hearings located on company property. Because the two groups worked together for the good of the community, it appeared to be easier to work on the harder issues at the common site. Later, when the coal company wanted to put trucks on the roads with the school buses, the school board agreed, based on the trust built between the company and the community.

TRACKING THE CASE: COLLEGE STUDENTS AND CREDIT CARD DEBT

Chapters 3 through 10 each include segments of a hypothetical student-produced public relations campaign proposal. The student team, as part of an advanced public relations class, spent the semester researching the problem of credit card debt among college students for a fictional nonprofit organization, Credit Counselors of Mason County.

As detailed in previous sections, the team conducted background and primary research, developed goals and objectives, chose communication channels, and selected both traditional media tactics and interactive media tactics.

Implementation: Nonmedia Channels

In-Person Communication

The team believed that although traditional media and interactive media would be somewhat helpful, the most effective way to reach the student audience would be in person and face-to-face. Toward that end, the team served as the liaison between the agency and the university in developing informational programs that could be presented in new student orientation pro-

grams, residence hall programs, and 100-level freshman classes (such as UNI 101, Introduction to College Life) and 300-level personal finance classes. In addition, agency representatives were encouraged to send reminder letters to university contacts at least once per semester reminding them of the availability of agency speakers to make on-campus presentations.

Restaurant Items

Realizing that posters would blend into the background and be lost on most campus bulletin boards, the team assisted the agency in developing tray liners and table tents to be placed year-round in university dining halls. Because of the short attention span for reading such items, the material was purposely kept brief, providing background information along with the phone number and Web address of the agency.

The written product for this section included descriptions of the items above. The appendices included a list of source material for instructors agreeing to include the topic in the class meetings and other programs, as well as mock-ups of the restaurant items.

DISCUSSION QUESTIONS

1. Think about the last event you attended that you suspect may have been organized or sponsored by a public relations representative or department. Did you see any evidence of the sponsoring organizations following the guidelines listed in this chapter? What were the public relations goals for those events? Did attending the event change your opinion of the sponsors? Why or why not?

2. Think about your experiences in high school and college. What do you remember about external sponsorships of school activities? Did participating in these events influence you to buy that company's products or services? Why or why not?

3. Bring in the last piece of direct mail you received. Analyze its strength and weaknesses.

4. What specialty items do you have at home? Which do you use or wear? Does having them around remind you of the organization or influence decisions you make? Bring some of your favorites to class.

5. Call the 1-800 number provided by a consumer product you have purchased and either make a comment (either a compliment or a complaint) or ask for additional information. Report to the class how your call was handled.

6. Think about the last speech you attended (other than going to class). What do you remember about it?

GLOSSARY OF TERMS

Bill, statement, and payroll stuffers. Information enclosed with mailed items such as bills, bank statements, and paychecks.

Cause-related marketing. The practice of linking one's company with a charity or other worthy cause for the mutual benefit of both.

Employee involvement programs. Programs that encourage employees to get involved in worthy causes by volunteering to assist with event planning or fund-raising or by serving as youth mentors.

Kiosk. Unstaffed electronic booths or stations located in areas with high pedestrian traffic—such as shopping malls, airports, and hotel lobbies—that provide information on nearby activities or services.

Lobbying. Advocacy of a point of view in an attempt to influence decision-making governmental bodies or officials. Direct lobbying involves meeting with officials in person; indirect or grass-roots lobbying involves generating public support and encouraging contact with agencies and officials through letter-writing campaigns and similar means.

Point-of-purchase display. A display in a retail store or similar location that draws attention to the product or service being promoted.

Product placement. Paying a fee to television and movie producers to have a product visible in the background or foreground of the action on the screen.

Sales piece. A brochure used to promote a product or service at a location other than that where the product or service is sold.

Speakers' bureau. A service through which a company or nonprofit organization provides representatives to speak to school groups, civic groups, and other audiences on topics of mutual interest.

Specialty items. Low-cost items such as t-shirts, key chains, cups, coffee mugs, calculators, notebooks, refrigerator magnets, and computer mouse pads that are mass produced and given away to promote a company or nonprofit organization.

CHAPTER 9

IMPLEMENTATION

Logistics

After the implementation section has described the traditional media, the interactive media, and the nonmedia tactics being proposed, it concludes with a subsection titled logistics, which provides the detail as to how those tactics will be executed. It includes steps titled *staffing, budgeting,* and *timing* (timetable or calendar).

STAFFING

In the case of a public relations agency developing a proposal for a client, the first version of "staffing" makes general assignments of responsibilities: which will be done by employees of the agency and which will be done by employees of the client company or organization. When the proposal is developed by an internal public relations department, the first version of staffing details which responsibilities will be carried out by members of the department and which will be assigned to employees from other departments such as marketing and human resources.

Because of the downsizing of internal public relations departments, outside contractors or freelancers are often hired for tasks such as writing, graphic design, photography, and video production. Subsequent revisions of the written proposal will list specific persons who will carry out these assignments.

Staffing assignments may include doing any additional research to be conducted, writing and distributing news releases and other publicity materials, planning news conferences (including who will be the organization's spokesperson), designing and producing publications, purchasing of advertising, planning of events, and all duties related to the evaluation. For any written materials, such as news releases and brochures, indicate who will be involved in the approval process.

This section should also explain if and how any of the staff assignments will change over time. For example, if the campaign includes development of a website on behalf of a client or employer, planners should indicate not only who will be responsible for the original design but also who will be responsible for the ongoing maintenance and periodic updating of the site. Will that task be assigned to the same contractor who did the original design work, a different contractor, or a staff person?

Of all the channels of communication typically used in public relations work, events are the most labor intensive. They can seldom be executed with the full-time staff available; often, clients or the agencies that represent them must hire temporary workers as ushers and tour guides and for jobs such as envelope stuffing, security, and clean-up. Companies with large numbers of retirees living in the area often find them a valuable resource. They can be used as tour guides, ushers for special events, or speakers for the speakers' bureau.

With nonprofit associations, charities, and other organizations run by volunteers, those volunteers are often involved in public relations campaigns, especially those involving event planning. Committee chairs are often appointed to carry out various parts of the plan, and they report to an event chairperson, who is also likely to be a volunteer. If the organization employs a paid staff, those staff members will function in supporting roles.

Working with Freelancers

A **freelancer** is an independent professional communicator who works on a part-time or intermittent basis for multiple employers. Some freelancers identify themselves as either journalists or public relations specialists, but many work on both sides of the fence. Although freelance writers are interested in placing their work in newspapers and magazines, many will also consider working for public relations departments and agencies. In addition to copywriting duties, freelancers can also be employed for photography, graphic design, and other communications tasks.

The best freelancers can be identified by the organizations to which they belong and the publications that employ them. Most states and some large cities have freelance writers associations that publish membership directories. In some communities, freelancers belong to organizations such as Public Relations Society of America or the International Association of Business Communicators, and they can be located through those organizations' membership directories. Another way to locate freelancers is to call local newspapers and ask for the names and phone numbers of freelance writers they work with on a regular basis.

BUDGETING

No matter how much a client or work supervisor is impressed by a presentation or how sincere he or she is about implementing an program, at some point the question will be asked: *How much is this going to cost?*

Public relations professionals are often unprepared to deal with the financial side of their work, as their college degree programs seldom include any coursework in accounting. Proposals must take into account the cost of program ideas, but the emphasis should always be on the expected results. One of the chief complaints of company leaders is not the total amount of money spent, but the lack of results when considering the money spent.

Developing the Campaign Budget

Budgets to implement public relations campaigns are developed in a variety of ways. The most effective sequence of events is to decide which tactics will be most effective, then determine how much the entire program will cost. If the client is unwilling or unable to promise the necessary resources, agency representatives should first explain the importance of the overall program and attempt to persuade the client to allocate the necessary financial resources. If the client does not agree, alternative tactics (to achieve the same results) can be discussed. Only as a last resort should specific tactics be deleted in their entirety in order to adjust to the smaller budget. A far less effective method is to choose communication tactics based on the resources available.

Because nonprofit organizations have limited budgets for public relations activities, they often depend on vendors to provide products and services at no charge or at a substantial discount to support an event or public relations program. In most cases, the vendor providing such a donation will be identified as a "sponsor" in related publications. The "budget" subsection must therefore specify which products and services will be paid for directly and which will be donated. At the preliminary planning stage, potential sponsors may have been contacted but have not yet committed, so that must be indicated in the written document and updated as the plan is revised.

Donated products and services fall into two categories: direct donations and third-party donations. With **direct donations**, vendors such as printers, caterers, photographers, video production companies, or advertising agencies agree to provide their products or services for free or at a discounted rate. Another term often used to describe such a donation is *pro bono*, which is a Latin term meaning "for the public good." Although most nonprofit organizations cannot produce successful events without accepting such sponsorships, they are well aware of the pitfalls and in many cases are willing to accept the trade-offs.

One such pitfall is time; when a printer agrees to do a job for free, the project has fairly low priority, as customers paying full price will have their work done first. The second potential problem is the likelihood that work performed for free might not be of the same quality as work done for full price, and the awkwardness of complaining or asking that the work be done over again. When accepting donations, therefore, nonprofit organizations must (1) submit their work far ahead of time and be prepared to wait and (2) be willing to accept work of a lower quality. Most vendors deny that work done for free is not performed at the same pace or quality as work that is paid for, but most experienced public relations professionals for nonprofit organizations can provide one or more "horror stories" to contradict that claim.

The second category is called a **third-party donation**, in which case the vendor charges full price for the products and services provided, but instead of sending the bill to the nonprofit organization, the vendors sends the bill to an individual or company that has agreed to pay for that product or service.

In tough economic times, with many potential sponsors struggling themselves, non-profit organizations will find it more difficult to obtain donations of products and services.

In addition to that problem, many potential sponsors are the target of so many requests for direct donations that they either agree to a large number of sponsorships but limit the extent of each, or reduce the number of causes they support in order to fund each one fully.

Many companies establish priority areas for sponsorships. For example, some companies support only education causes. Others support only the local causes closest to their corporate headquarters or branch offices. Many large companies work so far ahead in their sponsorships that requests for funding must be submitted up to a year in advance.

In addition to direct and third-party donations, most nonprofit organizations are eligible for grants from government agencies and foundations, but those are not consistent from one year to the next and cannot always be counted on in advance. Nonprofit organizations such as chambers of commerce and tourism development councils can also apply to state and local governments for funds originating from tourism or hospitality taxes (taxes charged on hotel rooms, rental cars, restaurant bills, and other travel-related expenditures).

When promoting events, nonprofit organizations can also stretch their budgets with donated media (discussed in Chapter 6).

Categories of Budget Items

Budget items are organized into three categories: personnel costs, program costs, and administrative costs.

1. *Personnel Costs.* The number of staff hours is estimated in the staffing section, but regular salaries of staff are not included in the budget section as an expense because employees would be paid those salaries whether working on this campaign or not. The costs of overtime compensation, and hiring of temporary employees and freelancers would be included, however, because those costs would not be incurred if not required for the campaign.

2. *Program and Production Costs.* This part of the budget includes all expenses involved in designing and producing communications materials and planning and producing events. Examples include advertising, printing, photography, audiovisual services, prizes for contests and competitions, and event costs such as entertainment and catering.

3. *Administrative Costs.* This part of the budget, **administrative costs**, lists the estimated costs of behind-the-scenes expenses, such as office supplies, photocopies, travel (hotel, meals, air fare, rental cars, and personal car mileage), and liability insurance for events.

In addition to those three categories, it is customary to provide an additional 5 or 10 percent above the estimated total as a contingency fund in order to allow for cost overruns or unanticipated expenses. Also, within each section, planners should mention which items, if any, will be donated, such as catering, printing, and prizes for contests and competitions.

Client Billing

The costs of a public relations campaign generally fall into the same three categories as those just mentioned, but the costs are computed differently. Staff time is likely to be the largest budget item. Because agency employees are often working on more than one account at a time, they must keep separate time sheets to record the number of hours worked for various clients, as well as keep separate records for expenses such as travel, meals, hotels, and photocopying. Expenses such as printing, catering, and other contracted services are typically paid for by the agency and then billed to the client, with an additional mark-up or **handling fee** of 15 to 20 percent.

After the total cost of the program is determined, the method of billing can take one of three forms. One method is for the agency to divide the total cost of the campaign by the number of months it is expected to run in order to determine a uniform monthly billing schedule. Another way is to bill the client various amounts each month as costs are incurred. A third method is to bill clients in advance for anticipated costs, then adjust subsequent monthly bills either up or down to compensate for differences between projected and actual expenses. By doing so, agencies can avoid having to finance work undertaken for clients and the risk of getting "stiffed" by clients who close their businesses, file for bankruptcy, or simply change their minds about investing in the programs.

Only in rare cases does an agency wait until the completion of the campaign to submit a bill to the client. Doing so means that the agency becomes a creditor and risks not being paid at all if the client goes out of business or otherwise finds itself unable to pay the bill.

When billing a client, an agency's profit does not appear as a separate item on the bill. Instead, it is built in to the listed costs. With costs such as the purchase of advertising space, the production of communications materials, and the hiring of freelancers and other independent contractors, the agency charges the client a "handling fee." In terms of staff time, the agency bills the client an hourly fee that is much higher than the staff members are actually paid. Included in that surplus amount are "soft" costs such as benefits and training. In most cases, personnel and administrative costs will constitute approximately 70 percent of the program budget, with the remaining 30 percent reserved for programming and production costs.

Competitive Bidding

Competitive bidding is a procedure in which numerous potential service providers are given specifications for a certain project and invited to submit bids that state not only the price but also other details, such as estimated completion time. Most government agencies are required by law to use such a process in order to make sure the taxpayers' money is spent wisely and that government officials are not arbitrarily awarding contracts to their friends and political supporters. Private companies and nonprofit organizations are not legally required to use the competitive bidding process, but often do so as a way to reduce their costs for contracted services. In public relations work, the process is most often used for services such as printing and catering.

In addition to encouraging lower prices, another advantage of the competitive bidding process is increased quality of service and attention to detail. Printers will not be as likely to take a customer for granted; they know that one can take their business elsewhere if not pleased. If a printing job takes three days, for example, printers know they have to do it in three days or one of their competitors will.

The only drawback to the competitive bidding process is that it creates more bureaucracy and paperwork. It may save money, but in some cases it may not be worth the extra work.

Freelance Fees

Rates for freelance writers, photographers, and graphic artists vary greatly according to the region of the country and the experience of the person hired, but here are some general ranges.

Freelance writers who are hired to produce work involving background research typically charge a fee of $100 to $300 per hour for both the research time and copywriting time. Freelancers hired simply to write copy based on research conducted by others base their fees on the number of words (or pages) of completed text.

Work requiring more complex skills such as event planning, photography, graphic design, or Web page design charge similar hourly fees, along with charges related to materials used.

Some freelancers may reduce their fees by 25 to 50 percent for nonprofit organizations. If specific freelancers are not yet under contract and their costs determined, such costs can be estimated using a reference table in *Writer's Market* or similar publication. Although not under obligation to do so, one can enhance a professional relationship with freelancers by reimbursing them for travel, meals, long-distance telephone calls, or other costs.

TIMING

Timing is a critical aspect of public relations programs, especially if the employer or client places a high value on media coverage. Proposals must take into account the deadlines of the various media being targeted. Monthly news magazines, for example, have deadlines six to eight weeks ahead of their publication dates, and specialty publications, because of the lack of "breaking news," work even farther ahead than that. Popular radio and television public affairs and talk shows book their guests several weeks or months ahead of time.

Timetables or calendars take two basic forms: a chronological listing of program highlights or a Gantt chart. A *chronological listing of program highlights* begins with the initial client interview and ends with the evaluation stage. In between, it includes dates for portions of the program already completed (such as secondary research and verification research) and tactics scheduled for the implementation phase (see Figure 9.1).

The **Gantt chart** was invented in the early 1900s by advertising executive Henry L. Gantt. It was first used in proposals for advertising campaigns, but it is just as applicable for public relations programs. It helps clients, the agency staff, and other persons involved in the execution of the campaign to visualize how various stages of the process relate to each other, especially when those stages overlap. Office supply stores sell wall-mounted planning calendars in various formats that can be adapted for use as Gantt charts (see Figure 9.2).

For both formats, the most effective way to approach the timetable is first to choose the target date for completion of the campaign (except for the evaluation stage), then work backward toward the start date. The evaluation stage is then penciled in to take place after the implementation stage has been completed (i.e., the target date for completion of the goals).

FIGURE 9.1 **Sample Chronological Calendar**

March 12	Initial client meeting (identify staff members to participate).
March 13–31	Conduct secondary/background research (identify staff members to design research plan and conduct research).
April 3	Second meeting with client.
April 4–10	Plan focus groups: Write questions, determine method for drawing sample, book hotel conference room, and arrange for catering (identify which staff members will be responsible for each of these details).
April 11–12	Conduct focus groups (identify who will moderate and who will take notes and be responsible for other details).
April 13	Staff meeting to determine goals, objectives, messages, themes, channels, and strategies (identify all participants).
April 14–30	Staff work to develop implementation section, including tactics and logistics (identify participants).
May 10–15	Request meetings with mayor's staff and members of city council to discuss environmental impact of construction (identify participants).
May 15–20	Approximate date for editorial meetings with local newspapers (identify who will coordinate and attend meetings).
May 21	Begin series of issue advertisements to explain benefit of construction project to community (identify who will design ads and who will be responsible for placement).
May 28–30	Approximate dates for public forums at high school auditorium to address community concerns (identify who will coordinate these events).
June 10	Approximate date for groundbreaking at construction site (identify who will coordinate this event).
June 15	Issue advertising cut-off date.
June 20–30	Begin working on evaluation, including focus group research and analysis of media coverage (identify who will conduct evaluative research).
July 2	Follow-up meeting with client to discuss results of evaluation (identify participants).

When scheduling tactics, especially those involving the media, keep in mind that it is the public relations professional's responsibility to work within the time frame of the media involved, rather than expecting the media to adjust to a given timetable. Once a timetable has been agreed upon, copies should be circulated to all employees involved. In addition, copies should be posted at visible places within the company in order to serve as visual reminders of what needs to be done.

FIGURE 9.2   Sample Gantt Chart

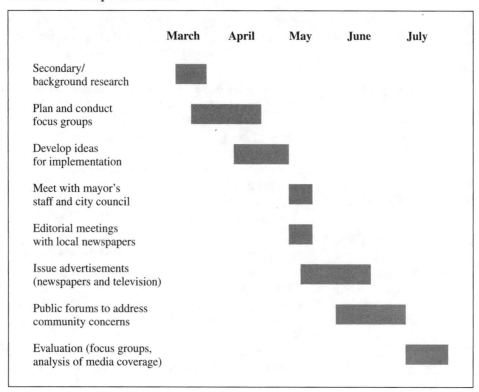

TRENDS AND ISSUES

Working with Volunteers

Volunteers represent a valuable but often overlooked source of help. There are four categories of volunteers who typically donate their services to nonprofit organizations: individuals, college students, those participating in corporate citizenship programs, and those working through professional communications organizations.

Individuals

Individual volunteers can be located through word of mouth, newspaper advertisements, and organizations such as the Service Corps of Retired Executives (SCORE).

Many nonprofit organizations have two pools from which to draw individual volunteers. The first pool consists of those individuals who identify themselves as "professional volunteers" and who immerse themselves in causes that are important to them. They tend to make themselves available on a year-round basis and can show up on short notice. Many can do so because they are retired or have flexible work schedules and employer support for their volunteer activities.

The second pool consists of those individuals who do not have large quantities of free time, but are willing to volunteer for short-term projects in their areas of expertise, such as helping to design an organization's annual report or plan its annual fund-raising event.

One key to motivating individual volunteers is to give them something meaningful to do based on their abilities and potential. Failure to do so will cause problems with retention. A volunteer with many years of practical business experience that remains untapped will become bored if assigned menial tasks. Likewise, an inexperienced volunteer will become frustrated if assigned a task above his or her head. Both individuals quickly become candidates for an early departure.

Public relations planners can determine volunteers' abilities and potential through written questionnaires (sometimes called "talent inventories") and informal interviews. Supervisors should also follow up on preliminary assignments by observing volunteers at work. The best strategy is to find the level of responsibility at which volunteers are the most comfortable and make job assignments accordingly. When time permits, their potential to accept additional responsibility should be assessed.

Occasionally, volunteers will find themselves in positions in which they are underqualified or incompetent, and someone in a position of authority has the awkward duty of addressing the issue. Despite the joke among nonprofit organizations that "you can't fire volunteers," there are occasions in which a well-meaning volunteer must be terminated. A much better strategy, however, is to reassign the individual to a responsibility for which he or she is better suited. Instead of being offended, many volunteers will be relieved to be reassigned.

College Students

Another valuable source of volunteer help is the nearby college or university. Either individually or as classes, students can get credit for assisting with research projects or event planning. In most cases, a match can be found between the needs of the client or employer and the learning objectives of public relations or other communications classes. In addition to students enrolled in relevant courses, many universities have Public Relations Student Society of America (PRSSA) chapters or student-run public relations agencies that can help.

Corporate Citizenship Programs

Many major corporations require or strongly encourage their employees to perform volunteer work, and the communications staffs of these organizations can be a valuable source of volunteers for detailed work as well as advice or consultation. At the encouragement of a hospital's management, for example, employees in its public relations department often volunteer for health-related nonprofit organizations such as the Ronald McDonald House, a facility that provides temporary housing for the parents of children who must remain in the hospital for long periods of time.

Professional Organizations

Other possible sources of volunteers are the local chapters of professional groups such as the Public Relations Society of America, the International Association of Business Communicators, and the American Advertising Federation. Many of these chapters have "public service committees" that provide free help in event planning and development of communications programs and materials.

CASE STUDY 9

Memorial Events Help a University Deal with Tragedy

On March 15, 2002, six students from Bowling Green State University were killed in a collision with a tractor-trailer on Interstate 71 in Verona, Kentucky, 25 miles south of Cincinnati. The minivan carrying six 19-year-old female students went out of control around 9 P.M., crossed the median, and collided with a semi-truck that was unable to avoid the collision. Severe winds and heavy rain were reported in the area and may have contributed to the accident, reports said. Neither alcohol nor excessive speed was suspected.

The college friends were returning to the university in northwestern Ohio from a week-long spring break trip to Panama City, Florida. They lived together in Founder's Residence Hall on the BGSU campus. Five of the six lived together in a suite; the sixth lived two floors above. All were studying to be teachers or nurses.

Officials at BGSU immediately took steps to help students deal with the tragedy. Counselors were made available in the residence hall where the students lived. Bouquets of flowers were delivered to the dormitory where the women resided. A sign was posted in the lobby, listing the names of the victims. Professors encouraged students to share their feelings in class or cancelled classes altogether. Using university stationery, students and faculty expressed their condolences to the students' families.

On March 22, one week after the accident, BGSU students assembled at 9:00 P.M. to observe a minute of silence for each student who died. The students were also commemorated during the 2002 Sigma Chi Bike Ride that benefits the Children's Miracle Network. Bikers wore black armbands to commemorate the students lost in the traffic accident and observed a moment of silence before the 180-mile charity bicycle trip. More than 50 cyclists and supporters, including BGSU students and Sigma Chi Fraternity officials, participated in the event.

Implementing the Crisis Plan

This was the first time the Office of Marketing & Communications at Bowling Green State University had to deal with a tragedy of this nature. At the same time, the office was dealing with the anticipated announcement of the elimination of several men's sports from campus.

The Office of Marketing & Communications immediately implemented the crisis plan for dealing with student deaths, which mapped out a notification system for the appropriate staff members to manage the crisis. Officials relied on the campus dispatcher in the Public Safety office for its information on the accident itself. The university police were the first ones notified from the Kentucky State Highway Patrol, who found the students' college identification cards.

Dealing with Students

The first issue addressed by the university crisis committee, chaired by Jill Carr, associate dean of students, was assisting students living in the same residence hall of the victims. Since the event occurred over spring break, many of the students' friends did not know about the deaths when they first returned to campus. A roommate who originally was to go on the spring break trip had already found out about the deaths. To handle the residence halls, the committee notified the residence hall advisors about the deaths. Counselors and the campus ministry were also made available to students in the dorms for four days after returning from break.

Dealing with the Media

The next task was responding to the media. When Kimberly McBroom, associate vice president of university advancement and director of the BGSU Office of Marketing & Communications, learned of the accident on Saturday morning, she, along with Media Relations Director Teri Sharp and the Student Affairs staff, used news sources on the Internet to obtain available information about the accident. The Cincinnati news media had already begun running television coverage of the accident Friday night. By Saturday, the tape was distributed throughout the state. The news media began contacting BGSU at mid-day on Saturday.

The first media inquiry received by the university was from the Ohio News Network at 11:30 A.M. Saturday. Although the university could confirm the victims were BGSU students, the names of victims could not be confirmed until family members were notified. The Kentucky State Highway Patrol announced the victims' names at about 4:00 P.M. that day. Complicating the identification process was that a graduate student had the same name as one of the deceased, which delayed both the identification and notification processes.

On Sunday, when students began returning from spring break, reporters were already on campus. The Office of Marketing & Communications handled reporters by limiting their access to student residence halls. The media relations director, working with the crisis team, identified key people in the residence halls who were willing to speak to the media and to avert reporters from bothering students who did not want to be interviewed. The head of the BGSU Counseling Center staff, a professor of one of the students killed, and the associate dean of students also spoke with the media.

Marketing & Communications staff members urged reporters to go to the student union to find students willing or eager to speak about the incident with the news media. Still, some reporters, to the annoyance of a number of students in who lived in the same residence hall as the deceased, made random phone calls to students to get their reactions.

To curb the news media from "in-your-face"

Bowling Green State University officials immediately took steps to help students deal with the tragedy.

reporting of the campuswide memorial service, media credentials were issued and reporters and photographers were contained in specific, upper-level sections of Anderson Arena, the university's basketball arena, where the event took place. The goal was to give the media fair treatment in covering the story while being sensitive to the needs of the grieving families, faculty, and students. As a result, the Office of Marketing & Communications enhanced its good working relationship with media across the state.

"It is important to remain available and responsive. We found the media to be respectful of the students' privacy and most reporters kept their distance from the students' residence hall as we requested. We explained that that's the students' home," Sharp said.

Memorial Services

Two memorial services were scheduled in memory of the students. The first was a "moment of silence" dedication presented at the Education Building. At 9:00 P.M., the approximate time of the accident a week earlier, one minute of silence was marked for each of the women. The second was a larger service for family, friends, and classmates held at Anderson Arena.

A committee of administrators that included the crisis committee and students on the Residence Hall Council planned the memorial services. The committee wanted students to be satisfied with the service plans. A series of meetings were scheduled every other day for a week to plan the service, which occurred the following Tuesday night.

A private dinner was served for parents and family prior to the main service at the university's student union. Families could bring as many guests as they wanted with them. The dinner was the first time the parents of the students had seen each other since the accident. The university president attended and expressed his condolences. Reserved seats were made available for family members in the arena. An estimated 2,200 students attended the memorial service.

Memorial Funding

The Six Students Memorial Fund was an idea created by the students' families and the university. The completed project included a park-like setting on campus, with concrete benches to represent each of the six students killed. In total, more than $4,500 was raised for the project.

One of many commemoratives for the six students killed on March 15, 2002.

To assist in the memorial fund-raising, Cathy Black, a singer-songwriter and relative of one of the students who died, wrote and recorded a song titled "I'm Still Here." Black peformed the song at the memorial service and at the women's funeral. She provided BGSU with 500 copies of the CD with proceeds from sales donated to the memorial fund. Scholarship funds were created in memory of two of the students and were designated for graduates of their high schools.

The Aftermath

By the end of spring semester, students were still talking about the accident, but it was not the main focus anymore. The university continued to receive condo-lences in the mail to pass on to the families. University employees also continued to maintain contact with the families of the deceased.

The university's crisis committee and the Office of Marketing & Communications both held evaluative/debriefing sessions about their experiences. The meetings evaluated decisions made through the crisis and also served as a way to bring a sense of closure. "You realize the momentum on an issue like this builds and you realize the important thing is to remain calm and maintain your ability to think clearly. We held meetings a few times a day just to make sure we were continuing to touch all of the bases and handling things appropriately," McBroom said.

TRACKING THE CASE: COLLEGE STUDENTS AND CREDIT CARD DEBT

Chapters 3 through 10 each include segments of a hypothetical student-produced public relations campaign proposal. The student team, as part of an advanced public relations class, spent the semester researching the problem of credit card debt among college students for a fictional nonprofit organization, Credit Counselors of Mason County.

In previous sections, the team selected tactics that involved traditional media channels, interactive chan-nels, and nonmedia channels. Next, the team finishes the implementation section by completing the logistics subsection.

Implementation: Logistics

Staffing

For the short term, most of the work of the campaign was carried out by the team, based on information provided by the agency. According to an agreement reached before the beginning of the project, all communications materials were approved by the agency director before being disseminated. Following the conclusion of the spring semester (and Advanced Public Relations class), much of the project had not yet been implemented, so the team passed the project off to the student-run public relations agency who would carry out the implementation and evaluation phases. The agency also agreed to work with the staff of the agency to develop a plan to maintain the relationship between the agency and the university.

Budget

The news media aspect of the campaign was essentially free, with only minimal expense involved in the preparation and mailing of media materials. The cost of the restaurant items were incurred by the agency, but the campus food service contractor agreed to waive its customary fee because of the nonprofit nature of the project.

Timeline

The team prepared a Gantt chart showing the various phases of the project. The chart showed the project beginning with background research conducted in the middle of the spring semester (as part of the Advanced Public Relations class) and extending through the following fall semester. As mentioned earlier, the class ended in mid-May, but much of the implementation phase, as well as the evaluation, took place in the fall semester.

The written product for this section included written summaries of the above information.

DISCUSSION QUESTIONS

1. Reread the section on budgeting, paying close attention to the potential pitfalls of accepting donations of products and services. If you are a public relations professional working for a nonprofit organization with a limited budget, do you believe this tactic is worth the trade-off? Are there steps you can take to deal with these potential problems?

2. Consider the response of the Bowling Green State University officials and staff in response to the tragedy described in Case Study 9. What were some of the keys (from this chapter or previous chapters) that made their response so successful?

GLOSSARY OF TERMS

Administrative costs. Expenses incurred in the planning and implementation of a program, such as office supplies, photocopies, travel, liability insurance, and similar items.

Competitive bidding. A procedure in which numerous potential service providers are given specifications for a certain project and invited to submit bids that state the price, estimated completion time, and other details.

Direct donations. Financial donations given directly to a nonprofit organization to fund public relations programs.

Freelancer. A professional communicator who works on a part-time or intermittent basis for multiple employers. The legal term is *independent contractor.*

Gantt chart. A visual representation of the highlights of a public relations program.

Handling fee. The mark-up or additional fee charged by a public relations agency for handling the subcontracting of work to printers, caterers, and other vendors.

Third-party donations. The process of having vendors involved in a public relations program send their bills to one or more outside sponsors instead of to the organization conducting the program (by prior arrangement).

CHAPTER 10

EVALUATION

Professional fund-raiser and motivational speaker Jerold Panas often uses the following anecdote to illustrate to audiences the value of learning from mistakes. He tells audiences at his fund-raising seminars about a promising young executive at International Business Machines who made a mistake on a major project that cost the company more than $10 million. Thomas Watson, IBM's founder and president, called the young man into his office. Certain he was about to be fired, the executive was quite nervous when he met the CEO. "We can't fire you now," Watson told him. "We just spent $10 million training you."

Learning from your mistakes is one of the important benefits of the evaluation stage—the final part of a public relations campaign and perhaps the most misunderstood and least appreciated. But an effective evaluation also takes into account what went right. Although clients and employers may tend to dwell on the negative, documenting what worked well in a campaign is just as important as documenting what did not.

THE IMPORTANCE OF EVALUATION

Even though managers often talk about the need to measure the results of public relations campaigns, they are often reluctant to allocate the necessary resources to do it. In a survey of corporate public relations departments, researcher Walter K. Lindenmann found that the majority of companies spent less than 3 percent of a public relations campaign's total budget on the evaluation stage.

Although most professionals acknowledge the measurement and evaluation of public relations programs and activities as being important, some admit that the concept is talked about far more than it is practiced. As one observer pointed out, it is like Mark Twain's comment about the weather: "Everyone talks about it, but nobody does anything about it."

One reason why organizations place such little emphasis on evaluation is that it is often difficult to determine the economic benefit of the public relations function. But contrary to common belief, communication can be tied to the bottom line. For example, if a company has problems with employee injuries caused by improper work techniques or misuse of equipment, a communications program with the goal of enhancing employee safety will affect the bottom line by improving productivity, reducing work time lost to injuries, lowering insurance premiums, and preventing lawsuits.

Perhaps more than any other unit, public relations departments are constantly under pressure to justify their existence and expenditures to financial decision makers. Because many public relations programs require substantial expenditures of both money and staff time, departments carrying out those programs must be able to show results in order to keep getting money and staff time allocated for future efforts.

In all types of organizations—businesses, nonprofit associations, government units, and universities—departments compete for both recognition and resources. In such competition, public relations departments have always been at a disadvantage because the results of their work cannot be easily tied to the organization's financial standing.

There is also the larger issue of survival. The departments or functions that can prove their value to the organization are the ones that will be most valued. Those departments and functions that cannot be measured or evaluated in ways meaningful to the organization are likely to be the first to be cut back or eliminated in times of financial crisis.

THE DIFFICULTY OF EVALUATION

Throughout the history of the profession, the idea of evaluation or measurement has always been a difficult concept. That is because many public relations programs produce "soft" benefits that are intangible and difficult to measure. One example is a company's speakers' bureau; it is nearly impossible to prove that it resulted in an increase in the company's product sales or enhancement of its image, yet company leaders still cite **anecdotal evidence** to support the bureau's importance.

Others point out that organizations that emphasize the research component of their public relations efforts do so to gather information at the "front end" of a program, but rarely at the "back end" in order to measure the results. Reasons for the lack of evaluation range from lack of money—spending so much of the budget on planning and implementation that little is left for evaluation—to simple fatigue. By the time a program has advanced through the implementation stage and the time comes to measure its effectiveness, many staff members are so tired of dealing with the product or issue that it is difficult to motivate them to continue to deal with it.

The effectiveness of public relations campaigns has always been difficult to measure empirically. That is because persuasion is mostly a subtle process and people rarely remember how they received information on which they base their decisions. Organizations with active public relations programs, but do no advertising, frequently receive telephone calls or other forms of inquiry from interested persons who say they learned about a product or service from an advertisement.

Many professionals are reluctant to conduct research because of the once-common misconception that public relations deals only with intangibles that cannot be measured. But with increasing pressure on public relations departments to justify their existence and demonstrate their value to the organization, new ways are being found to gather the necessary evidence. Just because the results are difficult to measure does not mean the task is impossible.

If one of the objectives of a public relations program was to have 3,000 or more people attend an open house, that is a result that is relatively easy to measure. The company either counted 3,000 people or it did not. What is considerably more difficult to measure is the effectiveness of the open house. Of those 3,000 individuals who attended, how many were actually motivated to purchase that company's products or services as a result?

THE EVALUATION PROCESS

There is no one simple, all-encompassing method by which public relations programs can be evaluated. Usually, the most effective approach is to combine a number of different methods. The results of public relations programs can most effectively be measured when an organization's priority audiences, key messages, and desired outcomes are established in advance.

Like all sections of a proposal, the evaluation section goes through a gradual transformation in verb tense as planners rework it throughout the process. Every section of the proposal is rewritten into past tense, but the evaluation section is the one with the most drastic revisions.

At the proposal stage, the evaluation section is written in future tense—projecting into the future and explaining what steps will be taken to evaluate the program after its conclusion. That should be accompanied by appendices, such as lists of focus groups questions and/or drafts of questionnaires, comment cards, and other research instruments.

After the program has run its course and the evaluation has been conducted, planners revise the evaluation section by converting the verbs to past tense: "We evaluated the program by. . . ." That is followed by a list of research methods used (revised if different from those listed in the preliminary version) and a brief summary of the information gathered. Appendices would include not only the blank questionnaires or list of focus group questions used but also detailed versions of the results in either narrative or tabular form for the finished version of the final program book.

In the preliminary proposal, the evaluation section may be divided into subsections labeled ongoing evaluation and summative evaluation. **Ongoing evaluation** describes the methods used to adjust or fine-tune the program while it is in progress. Ongoing evaluation is not possible in all cases, but planners should look for the opportunity. The longer the program runs, the more likely planners will be able to do this type of preliminary evaluation and make those adjustments. **Summative evaluation** describes how planners will evaluate the program after its completion. In the preliminary version or any revision developed before the execution of the campaign, this is a listing of the methods by which one plans to measure results, written in future tense.

There is a third phase of evaluation, labeled **formative evaluation**, found only in the final version of the program book. It describes what was learned from the program, especially during the summative evaluation, and serves as the starting point for future programs.

One of the weaknesses of many evaluation sections—especially those in student projects—is that they only recap what was done without explaining how effective it is.

In professional competitions, such as those sponsored by the Public Relations Society of America (PRSA) and the International Association of Business Communicators (IABC), judges often give high marks to campaigns that make good connections between objectives and evaluation, even if the specified results and objectives were not fully achieved.

Judges in PRSA and IABC competitions also consider how effectively a campaign's budget was used. Exceeding the preapproved budget is not necessarily a negative so long as the program's objectives were met or surpassed. Conversely, coming in under budget is not a plus if some of the campaign's goals were not met. Judges in competitions sponsored by PRSA, IABC, and other organizations often consider the use of resources as a significant factor contributing to the success (or failure) of a program. The *amount of money spent* is not the deciding factor; it is *how wisely the money is spent.*

It is important to select the criteria for evaluation and research methods before the campaign begins so that everyone involved in the project can agree on the program's expectations. This step is needed because clients' and supervisors' reactions are often difficult to predict. Planners may be pleased with the number of people calling the company's 1-800 number, but the client may place more importance on the number of visits to the organization's website. If planners are pleased with the response to the website, the client will want to know why there was not adequate media coverage. If planners are pleased with the media coverage the client receives, the client may complain about the lack of sales leads generated from participation in trade shows.

ONGOING EVALUATION

There is no need to wait until the end of the program to begin the evaluation process. Although not possible in all public relations programs, the written proposal should list ideas for evaluating the program while it is still in progress. By conducting such an evaluation, campaign organizers can use the results to fine-tune the elements of the program, or postpone or cancel certain components. Being able to make adjustments during the course of a campaign can increase the likelihood of success and save money that might otherwise be spent continuing to use ineffective tactics.

Such evaluative information can be gathered through focus groups, analyzing the responses from comment cards or other questionnaires, and analyzing feedback from staff and participants in the process. Communications programs are always easier to evaluate if at least part of the mechanism is built in. An organization's newsletter can include comment cards to solicit feedback, while registration materials for an event can ask those responding to indicate how they heard about the event.

If a program is scheduled to last only a few months, attempting ongoing evaluation is impractical because planners are likely to be so focused on the program itself that they would not have time to stop and conduct a survey or a focus group that is going to take time away from their main mission. But programs that run 12, 18, or 24 months will allow time to do some type of ongoing or preliminary evaluation in order to make those adjustments.

SUMMATIVE EVALUATION

The largest part of the evaluation section is titled "summative evaluation." In the preliminary proposal, it is written in future tense and describes how planners intend to evaluate the effectiveness of the implementation stage. It should describe (1) the criteria to be used to determine the success or failure of the campaign and (2) the research methods by which these criteria will be measured.

After the evaluation has been performed, the section is revised into past tense and describes how the evaluation was performed and what was learned. The summative evaluation focuses mainly on the effectiveness of the implementation, but it is not uncommon also to mention successes or failures of the planning stage, including the chosen audiences, objectives stated, and research methods selected.

Purposes of the Summative Evaluation

An accurate summative evaluation has both short-term and long-term benefits. For the short term, the summative evaluation should determine if the correct channels of communication were used, if key messages were received, and if audiences have taken or intend to take the desired actions. For the long term, the summative evaluation process has three important benefits, discussed next.

The "Prove It" Factor.   Public relations agencies and departments are constantly under pressure to demonstrate the value of their work. Agencies must prove the value of their services in order to retain clients, and internal public relations departments must evaluate campaigns to ensure the proper credit is given. In the absence of such evidence, many senior executives may assume success resulted from luck or coincidence.

Your Own Performance Review.   In addition to demonstrating the value of their department, employees of the public relations department can use the results of campaign evaluations as evidence of their contribution as individuals, with the importance of the evaluation being proportional to their participation in the campaign. That becomes even more important in those cases in which the public relations staff consists of only one person. Some professionals in those situations refer to their collection of program evaluations as their "Why I Deserve to Keep My Job" files.

Improvement of Future Programs and Events.   One must know what went wrong in order to avoid similar mistakes in future programs. This is especially important for programs that are dependent on scheduled events. Persons attending events can be surveyed to determine how they learned about the event, why they attended, what they liked and disliked about it, and whether their perceptions of the sponsoring organization were affected by what they learned at the event.

Evaluation Criteria and Research Methods

A number of criteria can be used to measure the results of public relations campaigns. There is no one simple, all-encompassing method by which results can be measured. More often, a combination of several methods provides the most meaningful results. The criteria may include a combination of the following items.

Anecdotal Evidence.   Examples of anecdotal evidence include informal discussions with journalists, industry analysts, and other professionals in a position to evaluate the organization's performance.

Analysis of Media Coverage.   Media coverage is the oldest of the most traditional methods by which to measure the results of public relations activities, but it may also be the least meaningful. Clippings show only media activity, but not progress toward a goal. Because the goals of public relations are associated more with changes in attitudes and behaviors than with exposure to messages, the true value of a campaign can be measured only in terms of those changes. Analyzing media coverage, often referred to as "counting clips," is therefore considered by many to be a superficial and sometimes misleading method by which to evaluate public relations campaigns. Clippings can indicate only the audience's potential exposure to a message; it cannot measure actual exposure, reception, reaction, retention, interpretation, or motivation to act.

Another limitation of counting clips is that media coverage reflects mainly short-term results; the long-term effects will not be realized for a long time. Another drawback is the assumption that recipients of the publication, as well as the pass-along readers, read the article in question.

Despite these drawbacks, however, many public relations agencies and departments collect clippings of newspaper and magazine stories and videos of television news stories that result from their public relations efforts. Some employ media monitoring services to do such work for them, based on either verbatim mentions of a company's name or the name of one of its products. A less precise method is to provide the monitoring service with a list of key phrases and synonyms to include in their searches.

In addition to simply counting the number of times a company, product, or issue is mentioned in the mass media, a more meaningful method of analysis is to look for key messages, such as product attributes (low price, reliability, environmentally safe, physically safe, easy to use, etc.) and company attributes (environmental responsibility, good labor relations, good community citizen, etc.). Messages can be contained in the text of the news story or in quotes provided by customers, stock analysts, or other observers.

Many organizations employ media monitoring services to clip newspaper stories and provide monthly packets of copies organized either chronologically or by subject matter. These packets of "what they are saying about us" are distributed internally to keep key departments informed.

Factors to consider in analyzing media clips include:

1. *Where in the publication or broadcast it was found:* on the front page of the newspaper or inside; as the lead story on the evening news or an item stuck between the sports and the weather; 6:00 P.M. or 11.00 P.M. news; etc.
2. *Tone:* positive, negative, or neutral
3. *Potential audience:* circulation of the newspaper or size of the television or radio audience
4. *Length:* print stories measured in column-inches; broadcast stories are measured in minutes/seconds
5. *Context:* news story, feature, investigative piece, editorial, column, or letter to the editor
6. *Content:* inclusion of key messages and the mention of competitors

Advertising and public relations professionals often use the term **media impressions** to describe the number of audience members exposed to the message. It is determined by multiplying the number of times a message appears in a medium by that medium's readers, viewers, or listeners. For example, if a newspaper with a circulation of 130,000 publishes two stories about a company or client, the result would be 260,000 media impressions.

One common yardstick used to measure the results of a public relations program is an analysis of media coverage generated. Public relations representatives can either do this themselves or employ media monitoring services. Regardless of who does it, the central idea is to look for and code key messages. Those come out of a program's objectives; evaluators scan news articles and broadcasts to detect the key phrases in the clips and keep track of how often the message is repeated and in which media outlets.

Key messages may not be repeated verbatim: They can be paraphrased or implied. Whether the key messages are there is much more important than counting the number of column-inches of print media coverage or the number of minutes of broadcast coverage. Examples of key messages include qualities such as reliability, environmental safety, physical safety, and company integrity. It could be in the form of a quote picked up from a news release or obtained by a journalist from either a customer or a stock analyst.

Many observers are critical of public relations professionals who consider stacks of newspaper clippings or videos of television news stories as the results of their public relations efforts. Lacking even more credibility is the idea of basing the evaluation on the volume of publicity materials produced rather than the number of stories generated by those materials. Public relations executives Frank Wylie and Simeon Slovacek describe this phenomenon as attempting to evaluate communications efforts by counting "the number of news releases thrown at the media."

For elements of public relations campaigns conducted on the Internet, results can be measured in part by determining the number of hits on the organization's website and determining to what extent the increase in hits was a result of the campaign. For a more complete evaluation, however, campaign organizers should consider hiring a media-monitoring firm specializing in Internet messages.

Advertising Equivalency.   One form of measurement that is popular but controversial is **advertising equivalency**. That means if a positive story about a company or client appears in the newspaper that is 2 columns wide and 13 inches deep, its value could be measured by determining how much it would have cost to purchase a display advertisement that same size. The same can be done with magazine stories.

A similar technique can be applied to television news. If an organization was the subject of a 45-second story on television, the advertising equivalency would be based on the cost of a 45-second commercial during that same time period, taking into consideration the time of day because of the difference in advertising rates between the 6:30 A.M. news and the noon news, as well as the news broadcasts that begin at 5:00 P.M., 6:00 P.M., 10:00 P.M., or 11:00 P.M. Instead of calling the newspaper or television station each time, advocates of this method use rate cards provided by the advertising departments of local media outlets.

Although some advocates of this method apply a 1:1 ratio, many others apply mathematical formulas or "multipliers" to reflect their belief that news coverage is more valuable than a paid advertisement of the same size (in print journalism) or length (in broadcasting). In addition to the credibility issue, some researchers believe that multipliers are appropriate in evaluating the impact of newspaper stories because of the pass-along rate—the likelihood that most newspapers are read by more than one person. The most common formula is called the **one-and-a-half rule**, which states news coverage is one-and-a-half times more valuable than advertising for the same length of time.

The most common mathematical formula is to multiply the size of the print story or time of the broadcast story by 1.5, but other public relations professionals claim a more reliable multiplier is 2, 3, or 4; some claim as much as 8. Other researchers have established separate formulas for print and broadcast media, with some even claiming a reverse formula applies in the case of broadcasting, as many viewers simply find advertising more interesting to the casual viewer.

Although anyone with experience in the field can attest to the value of news coverage over paid advertising, reputable media researchers believe that reducing the relative value to a mathematical formula is misleading at best and unethical at worst. Moreover, none of the commonly used formulas have any basis in scientific research.

Reputable media researchers claim that there are numerous shortcomings to such a technique. One problem is the inability to deal with negative stories: If a 10-column-inch story on page 7 is negative, how can that be compared to a 10-column-inch positive advertisement? Another problem is the inability to determine the value of a front-page new story, with the exception of a few trade publications that one cannot buy advertising space on the front page. It also does not take into account mentions of an organization or issue on the editorial page or in letters to the editor, and the relative value of positive and negative views expressed in those forums.

No one has determined whether such a formula has a broadcasting equivalent. If a newspaper story is 1.5 times as valuable as a newspaper advertisement the same size, does it follow that a 60-second television news story carries the same weight as a 90-second advertisement?

Audience Feedback.   This includes an analysis of sales leads or "nibbles" and feedback gathered from customers and event participants through comment cards, toll-free telephone lines, and the organization's website. To measure the effectiveness of trade show activities, public relations representatives can ask visitors to the company's booth to complete registration cards; those cards can later be matched against sales in order to determine how many sales actually resulted from attendance at the trade show. Responses to trade show participation may indicate only superficially the level of interest in the company's products; only by following up on the requests can the company truly assess the impact of participating in the trade show.

Not all organizations deal in "sales leads" per se, but they keep track of other forms of response. As an example, an electric company sponsoring a program to encourage energy conservation may measure effectiveness in terms of how many inquiries its customer service department received asking for more information about low-flow shower-heads, attic insulation, or heat pumps or other home improvement methods.

Marketing specialists working for retailers and restaurants include code numbers or bar code information on newspaper and magazine coupons in order to determine which publications are most effective in reaching their audiences.

Customer comment cards and warranty registration cards also ask customers to provide such information. Hotels, office supply stores, and other retailers and service providers often ask customers to indicate why they chose a certain business from a list that offers choices such as "newspaper advertising," "television advertising," "billboard advertising," "friend's recommendation," or "just drove by."

Food companies and other providers of consumer products encourage customers to call comment lines by offering help with recipes or related information. Manufacturers of computers, printers, microwave ovens, and other electronic devices provide "help desks" to assist customers with setting up and using the products for the first time. Both cases are examples of two-way communication because, while on the surface they appear to help only the callers, they are also a source of valuable feedback for the companies. Operators staffing the phone lines customarily ask where the callers found the telephone number.

Information gathered through the website can include the number of **hits** or persons visiting the site and the number of sales leads or customer inquiries received through the site. Customers may also be asked to sign a "guest book" or complete a voluntary on-line questionnaire that asks them to assess the quality of the website and to suggest how it can be improved.

Message Recall.   In **message recall**, viewers of a television program are asked to describe which commercial messages, if any, they remember after the program's conclusion. Many advertisers are disappointed when viewers recall the circumstances or story line of an advertisement, but cannot recall the specific product being promoted. The drawback of this method is that it is often applied in private settings, such as a focus group, when attention level is high. The reality is that typical television viewers are less likely to recall details of a product message when viewing television at home, surrounded by distractions.

Financial Indicators.   A company that looks merely at product sales or a nonprofit organization that looks only at donations is missing the big picture. Although such assessment is a good starting point, it does little to determine motive: Why are customers buying or not buying the products? Why are donors increasing or decreasing the level of their gifts?

Customer Response Data.   Many organizations will ask individuals who consume their products, use their services, or attend their events to fill out comment cards or on-line questionnaires that can be used in the evaluation process. This technique is called **customer response data**. In order to motivate audience members to respond, they offer weekly or monthly prize drawings.

Results of direct mail can be tracked using a variety of coding systems. When retailers or marketers run multiple promotions concurrently, they often use different 1-800 numbers for each promotion or provide different fictional names of company employees that respondents are to request when they call. When direct mail recipients call and ask for "Susan Jones," for example, the employee answering the phone knows immediately which promotion or direct mail piece prompted the call. In other cases, direct mail pieces include identification numbers that help sort incoming calls.

Clues in Cyberspace.   In addition to gathering feedback from customers through a website, one can also learn what customers (and, unfortunately, former customers) are saying about a company's products, services, and advertising campaigns (or those of competitors) by accessing a variety of other sites. Yahoo.com offers links to more than 140 consumer-comment sites. Another information source is the website of *Consumer Reports,* which allows respondents to comment on specific products and companies but is monitored more closely.

These sites vary greatly in their credibility and in the degree to which they are moderated; thus, opinions need to be viewed with caution. As with any application of the Internet, information or opinions posted on-line are subject to hype, exaggeration, and falsity. As one example, disgruntled former employees may attempt to damage former employers' reputations by posting multiple negative comments using different screen names.

Most Internet service providers can provide information on the number of visits to a website, and monitoring services such as E-Watch can measure the quantity and quality of comments found in chat rooms, newsgroups, or mailing lists. It will be up to the public relations professional, however, to determine if there is a correlation between those activities and changes in public opinion or an increase in sales.

Before-and-After Comparisons.   This process can involve measuring changes in either "attitudes and behaviors" (if the campaign proposal featured informational objectives) or "observable behaviors" (if the proposal featured motivational objectives).

For *attitudes and behaviors,* campaign designers can use the same research methods used in the planning stage of the campaign (such as focus groups or surveys) to measure changes after the conclusion of the campaign. For *observable behaviors*—such as sales, share price movements, conservation of water or electricity, wearing of seatbelts, consumption of harmful foods, and so on—quantitative information can be gathered at the conclusion of the campaign to be compared with information gathered prior to the campaign.

Social scientists refer to this more formally as a pretest/posttest study. Public relations professionals can use this concept as well, but must observe the formal rules that govern the process. In social science research, the independent variable (what is controlled by the researcher) is labeled X and the dependent variable (the measured result) is labeled Y. In measuring results of a public relations campaign, this model can be used by applying the X label to "exposure to the message" and the Y label to changes in "attitudes and opinions" or "observable behaviors."

The "rules of variables" used in social science research are (1) X must have occurred before Y, (2) X must be shown to have caused Y, and (3) there must have been no Z variables. A **Z variable** is an unexpected factor that may have been responsible for part or all of the change in the Y variable, in addition to or instead of the effect of the X variable.

An example of a Z variable is found in the case of measuring public awareness of the problem of drunk driving. If one were to conduct surveys or focus groups prior to the campaign to measure awareness of the problem and conduct similar research after the campaign, a substantial increase in awareness may be detected and one might assume it was the campaign that was responsible. It may have been responsible for part of it or most of it, but if there was considerable news coverage of a drunk driving arrest of a famous politician, movie star, or professional athlete during the course of the campaign, that is a Z variable that must be taken into account. How much of the increase in awareness can be attributed to the campaign, and how much happened because of news coverage of the arrest?

Although the most reliable form of evaluation, making before-and-after comparisons is difficult for several reasons:

1. It is expensive to conduct before-and-after comparisons. Formal social science research methods such as surveys are costly, and since many clients are reluctant to pay for just one survey, they are even more reluctant to pay for two.
2. Surveys using well-designed instruments require a great deal of time, and many clients want results right away. Focus groups are cheaper and faster than surveys, but are not as precise or quantifiable.
3. Some public relations agencies and departments have staff capable of conducting such research, but more often those projects are assigned to outside research firms, which further increases the costs.
4. Before-and-after results can be compared, but there are often intervening variables involved that cannot be detected or measured. The evaluation may indicate that audience members may have indeed changed their attitudes or behaviors, but it may be due to factors other than exposure to the campaigns.

FORMATIVE EVALUATION

One of the by-products of an effective evaluation is the unexpected or serendipitous information received. Well-designed evaluative research can uncover trends, attitudes, and problems (while there is still time to do something about them) that may have gone unnoticed until it was too late. The section titled Formative Evaluation in a public relations program therefore lists the problems or opportunities that should be addressed in future campaigns. Because the information to be contained in this section is not known until after the summative evaluation is completed, this section does not appear until the final version of the program book is produced.

When local chapters of national nonprofit organizations complete communications and evaluate communications programs, they often submit evaluation reports to their national headquarters. Reports on the more successful programs are compiled into a "sourcebook" or "compendium" that can be shared with other chapters or branch offices.

TRENDS AND ISSUES

With No Fear of Failure

In 1981, entrepreneurs Tom Fatjo and Keith Miller published *With No Fear of Failure,* a motivational book in which they used their own success stories as models for others to emulate. In a chapter about learning from mistakes, Fatjo uses a number of analogies to make their points:

A shining new bank building, theater or cathedral, filled with sharp-looking men and women, looks almost perfect. But anyone on the inside of such a project knows that, unseen by the public, dozens if not hundreds of errors in judgment were made along the way, as the project was being built and developed. I'm convinced that this is true of the work of every entrepreneur or manager who builds or operates a large institution.

There is a commonly held belief that people who do something well make almost no errors. But that is simply untrue. I remember clearly the jolt I felt as a young man when I realized that the greatest professional baseball players in history were put out before they reached first base more than 60 percent of the time. How many great quarterbacks have completed more than six out of ten passes during their careers? Or how many basketball players hit more than half of their shots? And contrary to much public opinion, many of the most outstanding businesses in the world operate with a clear understanding that only a very small amount of their efforts will be successful.

For example, even with the best geologists, major oil companies only find producible oil in one wildcat well out of nine or ten drilled; the rest are "failures." In the direct mail business, with all its market research, a response of 4 percent is considered great. That means that 96 percent of those contacted failed to respond. And highly trained insurance salesmen chalk up many failures for every successful sale.

These kinds of "failures" are most generally attributed to unknown factors or unforeseen circumstances involved in finding oil, selling by direct mail, and locating good insurance prospects. But many failures come from simple errors in judgment. And often in a creative enterprise, whether or not the overall dream of the originator is successfully realized depends on how these errors are faced and dealt with.

CASE STUDY 10A

Evaluative Research in the Travel and Hospitality Industry

Companies in the travel business (such as hotels and rental car companies) seek feedback from customers in the form of comment cards or brief questionnaires. Even though research methodologists often criticize such research instruments as being poorly designed and not quantifiable with any degree of accuracy, they can provide valuable information.

Because customers are usually in a hurry when checking out of a hotel or turning in a rental car, they are seldom asked to complete questionnaires or comment cards at the time. If such instruments are administered at the conclusion of the transaction, they must be kept as brief as possible. But even if customers are willing to complete a brief questionnaire or comment card at the scene, if they are in a hurry or otherwise seeking to "get it over with" they will simply mark all positive answers.

More common approaches are to provide departing customers with more detailed questionnaires and ask them to complete them at a later time and return them by mail, or mail the questionnaire to the customer's home or business address. Although the response rate to such a follow-up mail survey is much lower than a brief comment card, the depth, breadth, and sincerity of the information will make it much more reliable.

The timing of such follow-up surveys is critical. If the questionnaires arrive too soon, customers may not have yet resumed their regular work and home routines and would not be prepared to reflect on their experiences in order to offer meaningful opinions. But if too much time has elapsed, customers may not have clear recollections of their experiences or may have taken subsequent trips in the interim.

In the case of restaurant comment cards, there is a tendency to get responses from only those who were highly satisfied or highly dissatisfied, with most falling into the latter category.

CASE STUDY 10B

Selling the Lottery in the Bible Belt

Between 1999 and 2002, three traditional "Bible Belt" states grappled with proposals for state-run lotteries. In Alabama, South Carolina, and Tennessee, politicians looked to generate funding for a variety of education-related projects and compete for a share of the lottery market with their common neighbor, Georgia, which since 1993 had one of the most successful education lotteries in the country. In all three cases, however, provisions in the state constitutions (in place for more than a century) prohibited both private and public lotteries, meaning that before a lottery could be established, the voters of that state must first pass a referendum amending the state's constitution. The political battles and marketing campaigns leading up to those referenda generated considerable public debate and media attention. Both pro-lottery and anti-lottery groups executed costly and labor-intensive campaigns aimed at generating the involvement of the media, politicians, and voters.

In Theory: Support and Opposition to State Lotteries

There are five major areas of contention in the debate over state lotteries.

1. *Support for Education.* There is considerable anecdotal evidence to support the advocates' claim that a well-run state lottery can generate additional money for public education, including college scholarships. The most popular model is found in Georgia, where a lottery-funded scholarship program is popular among students, their parents, and university administrators. In other states, lotteries have generated funding for new school construction, hiring new teachers, and equipping schools with new computers.

Of all a lottery's selling points, this one is the most difficult for opponents to argue against. However, they have generated some discussion, and opposing votes, by pointing out that in most cases, the lottery money is not new money for education, but rather money that replaces the original education allotment that was taken away and spent elsewhere. In addressing the popularity of college scholarship programs, opponents point to studies that show that the majority of the scholarship recipients were students from high-income and middle-income families and were headed for college anyway; they were not the students from low-income families for whom college would not have otherwise been possible.

Closely associated with the education argument are the issues of "bandwagons" and "border crossers." Many state legislators feel compelled to offer their citizens a lottery simply because others states have them. Political journalists and other observers refer to this as "lottery as self-defense." Sometimes this argument is supplemented with statistics that show the loss of potential lottery revenue to neighboring states.

When a proposed lottery was debated in South Carolina in 1999, Senator Robert Ford claimed that residents of his state were spending $115 million a year on the Georgia Lottery and posed the riddle: "What is green and travels at seventy miles per hour?

Your money on its way to Georgia." That riddle was later the basis of a television commercial sponsored by lottery advocates. A related argument is that "people are going to gamble anyway, so the state might as well benefit." When the bandwagon appeal was raised in Tennessee in 2002, one lottery opponent posed the question, "It's like your mother used to ask you . . . if everyone else jumped off the bridge, does that mean that you have to?"

Lottery opponents contend that the perceived benefits to a state's education system are overstated. In many states, voters approved state lotteries because of campaign promises that the proceeds would go to education, but legislators then funneled the revenue into the state's general fund. In other states, lottery proceeds were earmarked for education and voters believed it was "bonus money," but once the lottery was running at full speed, the lottery funds were used to replace education money taken away and spent elsewhere.

2. *Long Odds.* Lottery opponents are fond of pointing out that the chances of winning the lottery jackpot without buying a ticket are zero—and that buying a ticket improves those odds only slightly. In his 1994 book, *Legalized Gambling: America's Bad Bet,* John Eidsmoe used the following scenario to illustrate the odds. "Flip a coin; the odds of heads or tails are 50-50," Eidsmoe wrote. "If you win, I pay you a dollar, if I win, you pay me two dollars. Would you take that bet? Of course not, but that's essentially what the lottery does."

A Massachusetts Institute of Technology professor calculated that the odds of winning a lottery jackpot were the same as visiting a casino poker table and being dealt four straight royal flushes, then walking out into the lobby and meeting four complete strangers who had the same birthday. Still others say that if a lottery customer lives one mile from a ticket retailer, he or she is 16 times more likely to get killed in an automobile accident driving there to buy a ticket than win the million-dollar jackpot. Yet another researcher has estimated that the odds of the average lottery player winning the jackpot are the same as that person living to the age of 115.

The most popular analogy regarding lottery odds, however, remains the lightning strike, but the origin and scientific validity of the comparison is in dispute. Without citing a specific source, lottery critics claim the odds of getting struck by lightning are 400,000 to

1, as compared to 13 million to 1 of winning the typical state lottery jackpot.

Lottery advocates counter with their claim that the majority of lottery customers understand the long odds and that few of them play with the hope of getting rich; instead they play for fun. In addition, they contend, opponents citing the long odds are referring mostly to jackpot prizes, whereas most state lotteries offer a number of intermediate prizes ranging from $5 to $100,000, for which the likelihood of a win is more reasonable.

3. *Religious Objections to Gambling.* Many lottery critics believe, as Saint Augustine did in the fourth century, that the devil invented gambling. Today, many social conservatives and religious leaders are concerned that within a few decades, state governments have gone from prohibiting gambling to permitting gambling to promoting gambling. The religious and moral opposition to lotteries is strongest in the Bible Belt and is voiced by groups labeling themselves as conservative Christian and pro-family.

Such objections are the hardest for lottery advocates to overcome. Not only do many Christian conservatives hold their anti-gambling beliefs so strongly, but they also vote in large numbers. Many lottery advocates choose not to address the religious objections and instead emphasize the potential for benefiting public education.

4. *Effect on the Poor and Gambling Addiction.* Critics argue that lotteries prey on the poor and point to a number of studies showing that low-income individuals play the games in greater numbers than individuals in higher income brackets. They further claim that lottery agencies not only know about the demographic disparity in lottery sales, but perpetuate it in their advertising with pitches such as "All It Takes Is a Dollar and a Dream." They also cite the "slippery slope" argument and warn that if a state passes a lottery, the next step would be legalized casinos and prostitution.

Some lottery critics believe, but cannot prove, that lottery advertising is timed to coincide with the delivery of welfare and social security checks, a charge that lottery agencies deny. Other critics chastise lottery agencies for allowing tickets to be sold in bars and liquor stores. "People already have one bad habit, now they have two," says one lottery critic.

Advocates downplay the potential harm of lotteries by claiming that a state lottery represents a "voluntary tax" that serves as an alternative to an increase in sales, income, or property taxes. Critics argue against the "voluntary tax" metaphor because of anecdotal evidence that many low-income lottery customers believe that winning a multimillion-dollar lottery jackpot is their only way out of economic despair.

Lottery opponents also contend that the games either contribute to gambling addiction (although some prefer the term *problem gambling*) or lure players into more serious forms of gambling, and there is anecdotal evidence to support that belief. And problem gambling, they contend, leads to an increase in domestic violence, homicide, and suicide. Sponsors of gambling hotlines set up to help problem gamblers report that lottery players represent the smallest segment of their callers, but they are the segment that is growing the fastest.

The concept of "benign gambling" or "gambling lite" is also popular among lottery advocates. Because the lottery is a slow and passive form of gambling, they contend, it is not as likely to produce gambling addicts as the faster-moving, more interactive games found in casinos and horse tracks and huge underground industries such as sports betting and off-track betting parlors.

In addition, many lottery agencies urge problem gamblers to seek help; in some cases toll-free phone lines and websites referring players to counseling programs are printed on lottery tickets and play slips. Lottery advocates counter the concern over teenage gambling by promising to impose age limits (in most states, age 18), but opponents respond by predicting that underage purchasers will find a way to obtain lottery tickets, just as they do cigarettes and alcohol.

5. *Political Corruption.* Lottery opponents are quick to point out that lotteries have a long history of creating opportunities for political corruption. Across the United States, state lotteries have been plagued by scandal, with a number of lottery officials being fired, paying heavy fines, or serving time in prison for crimes related to the bidding process.

Lottery advocates, however, point out that the potential for political corruption is no more than it is in any other area of state government. "Any time a state government puts work out for bid, potential vendors are going to cut corners in order to be competitive," says one former lottery official. "What's happening with the lottery contracts is different only because a lottery is such an easy target for criticism."

There's an old expression that when some government contractors have a choice between making ten dollars straight or one dollar crooked, they would rather make one dollar crooked because that's all they know."

In Practice: Wins and Losses in the Bible Belt

In 1999, newly elected Alabama Governor Don Siegelman hoped to ride the momentum of his victory and pass a referendum that would amend the state's constitution and allow for the creation of an education lottery. Advocates pointed to the success of the Georgia Lottery and brought in Georgia Governor Zell Miller and Lieutenant Governor Mark Taylor to testify about what the lottery had done for the education system in their state. Lottery ads argued that millions of Alabama dollars being spent on Georgia and Florida lotteries should stay in the state to benefit Alabama's school children. One such ad showed a group of Georgia college students gathered at the state line saying, "Thank you, Alabama" for helping pay for their education.

Lottery opponents based their campaign on two appeals. The first was on moral grounds—that gambling was immoral and inconsistent with the state's conservative Bible Belt values. That theme was promoted in campaigns organized by the Alabama Baptist Convention and other statewide church groups. The campaigns included church sermons and bulletins, prayer rallies, and get-out-the-vote efforts. Some churches mailed pledge cards to their members urging them to reject the college scholarships if the lottery was approved.

Siegelman, already unpopular among Christian conservatives as a result of the lottery campaign, further angered religious leaders by encouraging Alabama voters to "ignore their church leaders and get in line with other southern states that are bucking the Bible Belt image and cashing in on gambling to help pay for schools and college scholarships."

The second anti-lottery appeal was based on the potential for political corruption. In a state with a long and well-known history for corruption in state politics, opponents believed that voters would not allow lawmakers to create a new state program that would be ripe for further corruption. They promoted that theme through advertising in newspapers and on television and radio. Several of the television ads showed stereotypical "good ol' boy" politicians dividing lottery dollars in a smoke-filled room.

In the end, the lottery opponents won. That fall, following the most expensive and contentious issue campaign in the state's history, Alabama voters rejected the constitutional amendment by a vote of 54 to 46 percent. The state's editorial writers and political pundits gave the credit to the state's church groups and individual religious leaders who persuaded their congregations to vote in favor of their moral convictions and reject the superficial promises of generating money for education. Many religious leaders, however, declined taking credit for the defeat, and instead praised voters for checking the facts and making an informed decision.

Less than a year after the lottery defeat in Alabama, South Carolina's democratic Governor Jim Hodges, also newly elected, began pushing for the lottery referendum to pass in his state. And much like advocates in Alabama, South Carolina lottery supporters looked at the success of the Georgia Lottery as their biggest selling point. They also stressed that the lottery would improve education without raising taxes.

From the beginning, opposition groups saw the opinion polls and believed that defeating the lottery would be difficult but not impossible. Anti-lottery efforts in South Carolina included organizing committees in more than 2,000 of the state's Baptist churches for education, prayer rallies, and turn-out-the-vote efforts. Conservatives indicated they opposed the lottery as generally an immoral way of raising public money.

On November 7, 2000, the lottery passed by a vote of 54 to 46 percent—identical to the margin by which it was defeated a year earlier in Alabama. Hodges and other lottery advocates believed they won because voters saw the success of the Georgia Lottery and rejected the critics' claim that lotteries violated Christian morals. In addition, they believed the opponents' scare tactics—claiming that lotteries would open the door to casino gambling and lead to an increase in gambling-related crime—backfired.

In Tennessee in 2002, lottery advocates tried to emulate the success of the South Carolina campaign and began by hiring many of the same political consultants who had worked on it. They based much of their campaign on pointing to the success of the Georgia Lottery and downplaying the lottery's potential negatives.

For lottery opponents, focus group research indicated that the voters' objections to gambling on

State lotteries were a hot topic for political debate throughout the 1990s and the early years of the new century. Public relations strategies were used on both sides of the debate.

religious grounds would not be sufficient to outweigh the appeal of the lottery's potential to generate money for education. Focus groups also told opponents that arguments about lotteries and their effect on the poor would not resonate with the state's voters, nor would arguments about the potential for the increase in gambling addiction or gambling among teenagers.

Instead, the research indicated the argument with the most potential to persuade voters would be the potential for political corruption. As a result, lottery opponents pointed to a 1990–91 political scandal related to the regulation of bingo parlors as evidence that the government of Tennessee could not be trusted to properly regulate any form of gambling. In addition, the opponents pointed to the scandals associated

with the formation of lotteries in Tennessee and South Carolina.

That fall, the lottery passed by a vote of 58 to 42 percent. Exit polls indicated that those who voted for it did so mainly on the appeal of the Georgia Lottery and its college scholarship program, whereas those who voted against it did so because of religious objections and the potential for political corruption. In evaluating their respective campaigns, pro-lottery forces found their campaign was successful largely because of the education appeal, whereas lottery opponents realized they had failed because they spent too much time and money communicating to voters already on their side and not enough time and money on the large numbers of voters who were undecided.

TRACKING THE CASE: COLLEGE STUDENTS AND CREDIT CARD DEBT

Evaluation

Chapters 3 through 10 each include segments of a hypothetical student-produced public relations campaign proposal. The student team, as part of an advanced public relations class, spent the semester researching the problem of credit card debt among college students for a fictional nonprofit organization, Credit Counselors of Mason County.

When the public relations campaign had run its course, the team evaluated its work using the following methods.

Ongoing Evaluation

Every two weeks during the implementation phase, representatives of the student agency (who assumed responsibility for the program after the conclusion of the class) met with the agency director to discuss the status of the program and any minor adjustments that were required.

Summative Evaluation

Achievement of the process objectives was measured by developing a list of the new student orientations, residence hall programs, and other meetings conducted either by university employees or representatives of the CCMC.

The achievement of *informational objectives* was measured by compiling the clips from student newspaper stories as well as a summary of the interviews with agency representatives on the campus radio station.

The achievement of *outcome objectives* was measured by conducting surveys and focus groups (concerning student knowledge of the issue and attitude toward seeking help) and comparing the results to those of the research done during the planning stage.

The written product for this section included written summaries of the information above.

DISCUSSION QUESTIONS

1. Think about a public relations activity that you are aware of that may involve "soft benefits" (those that cannot be measured). Are those activities still worth doing? Why or why not?

2. As explained in this chapter, the idea of measuring the results of public relations activities is often controversial. Discuss some possible solutions to these controversies.

3. Discuss another example of a *Z* variable that provides misleading information or public perception.

4. What can public relations professionals learn from Fatjo's examples in *With No Fear of Failure?*

5. What were some of the keys to the lottery defeat in Alabama and its victory in South Carolina and Tennessee? If you were leader of a pro-lottery group in your state, what could you learn from the two cases? If you were leader of an anti-lottery group, what could you learn?

GLOSSARY OF TERMS

Advertising equivalency. A form of measurement that is popular but controversial. It means if a positive story appears in a newspaper, its value is measured by determining how much it would cost to purchase a display advertisement of the same size.

Anecdotal evidence. A form of criteria that can be used to measure the results of public relations campaigns. An example could include an informal discussion with a journalist or professional who is in a position to evaluate an organization's performance.

Customer response data. The responses used for evaluations individuals provide through comment cards or on-line questionnaires.

Formative evaluation. An evaluation form found only in the final version of the program book. It describes what was learned from the program.

Hits. The number of visits to a website.

Media impressions. The total number of potential opportunities to reach the audience. If an advertisement appears twice on the evening newscast with an audience of 250,000, the number of media impressions is 500,000.

Message recall. A form of measurement in which viewers are asked to describe which commercial messages, if any, they remember after the program's conclusion.

One-and-a-half rule. The formula that news coverage is one-and-a-half times more valuable than advertising for the same size or length of time.

Ongoing evaluation. Describes the methods that will be used to adjust or fine-tune the program while it is in progress.

Summative evaluation. Describes how one will evaluate the program after its completion.

Z variable. An unexpected factor that may have been responsible for part or all of the change in the *Y* variable when using rules of variables.

CHAPTER 11

LEGAL CONSIDERATIONS

INDIVIDUAL RESPONSIBILITY IN PUBLIC RELATIONS

There are few actions that an individual public relations professional can take that will result in legal consequences such as a monetary fine, prison sentence, or lawsuit. Two exceptions to this principle are insider trading and obstruction of justice. **Insider trading**, described later in this chapter, is a problem for public relations representatives because in most publicly traded companies they have access to valuable information that is not available to other employees. **Obstruction of justice** may occur when a public relations representative or other individual either fails to cooperate with a law-enforcement investigation or attempts to hinder that investigation.

What is much more common is for clients or employers to find themselves in legal trouble—required to pay a fine or settle a lawsuit—because of something the public relations representative did or failed to do.

There are two general principles regarding the legal obligations of public relations professionals:

1. *A practitioner's obligation to the law always takes priority over his or her obligation to a client or employer.* This means that practitioners must cooperate with law-enforcement or other legal investigations of a client or employer.

2. *Communication between a practitioner and his or her client is confidential in a general sense, but not privileged in a legal sense.* Although practitioners have a general obligation to maintain the confidences and privacy rights of clients or employers, that does not mean they can claim privilege in a legal proceeding. The court system recognizes the need for confidentiality in relationships such as doctor–patient and lawyer–client, but does not extend it to the relationship between public relations representatives and their clients or employers.

PUBLIC RELATIONS AND THE FIRST AMENDMENT

Political Advertising

Court rulings have drawn distinctions between **commercial advertising** that promotes products and services, and opinion or **political advertising** that deals with issues and ideas. Generally, commercial advertising is subject to greater regulation than political advertising. On the national level, commercial advertising is regulated by the Federal Trade Commission in the form of "truth in advertising laws," whereas many attempts to regulate political advertising are ruled by the courts to be unconstitutional.

For many years, profit-making corporations had no First Amendment rights, as their views were considered self-serving and unlikely to make meaningful contributions to public discourse. That changed in 1988, when the United States Supreme Court ruled in *First National Bank of Boston* v. *Bellotti* that companies have the same free-speech rights as individuals. The court ruled in that case and other similar cases that not only do companies have the right to disseminate their views to the public but also that the public has the right to receive those messages.

In the *Bellotti* case, the Commonwealth of Massachusetts attempted to punish a bank for violating its law prohibiting regulated companies from using their advertising to become involved in legal, political, or regulatory issues. But after the Supreme Court ruled in favor of the bank, the case became a precedent for other cases in which state governments attempted to regulate political advertising. The case also gave birth to the term *corporate free speech.*

In *Central Hudson Gas & Electric* v. *Public Service Commission* (1980), the Supreme Court ruled that a state ban on the advertising of utilities services was unconstitutional. During the Arab oil embargo of the late 1970s, the Central Hudson Electric Company in New York developed newspaper and television ads advocating the wise use of electricity, which the New York Public Service Commission claimed was in violation of its regulation that prohibited public utilities from advertising their services. After the Supreme Court judged the regulation to be unconstitutional on First Amendment grounds, the Public Service Commission dropped its objections to advertising by all public utilities in the state. The Supreme Court did, however, leave the door open for the government to regulate advertising in the future, emphasizing that government would bear the burden of proof to demonstrate why it needed to regulate it.

Bill Stuffers

Many state governments have attempted to regulate the manner in which banks and public utilities communicate to their customers by including informational items or **bill stuffers** when mailing statements and bills. When challenged in the court system, however, such laws are often declared unconstitutional because they infringe on the company's First Amendment free speech rights.

In a 1980 case, *Consolidated Edison Co. of New York* v. *Public Service Commission of New York,* the court ruled that the electric company could use bill stuffers to communicate with its customers regardless of their content. The ruling invalidated a state law that allowed banks and utilities to include noncontroversial information in bill stuffers, but prohibited information that dealt with legal, political, or regulatory matters.

In the 1986 case of *Pacific Gas & Electric Co.* v. *Public Utilities Commission of California,* the court invalidated a state law that required public utilities to provide an opportunity for their critics to respond with bill stuffers of their own. The law, called a "right of reply" rule, stated that any individual or group who objected to the content of a bill stuffer could produce its own stuffer, at its own expense, deliver it to the utilities company, and the company would be required to include it in the next month's bill.

The Supreme Court, however, ruled that the utilities do not have to provide such an opportunity. The state's Public Utilities Commission claimed the rule was analogous to the broadcasting industry standard of "equal time," but the court ruled that bill stuffers are more like print journalism than broadcasting, and therefore could not be regulated.

Contributions to Political Candidates and Causes

The courts have generally ruled that in political campaigns—either those involving candidates running for an office or a public referendum on an issue—spending money is analogous to speech, and is therefore worthy of First Amendment protection. Most of the laws dealing with political campaigns and contributions came out of federal election laws that resulted from the Watergate scandal of the early 1970s. Those laws draw careful distinctions, however, between contributions and expenditures. A contribution is what is given to a candidate, whereas an expenditure is what the candidate, political party, or other entity spends.

Contributions can be limited under state and federal campaign laws, but expenditures cannot. If an organization purchases an advertisement on behalf of a candidate, but does so without the candidate's knowledge or approval, that is considered an expenditure and is therefore not subject to regulation. But if the purchase is coordinated between the candidate and the organization, it is considered a contribution to the campaign and is subject to campaign financing rules.

The first case to test the new campaign laws was *Buckley* v. *Valeo* (1976), in which the Supreme Court reinforced the distinction between expenditures and contributions. The Court ruled that the government could legally place limits on contributions, but not on how people and organizations could make expenditures supporting or opposing political causes, because the latter is considered speech. The rationale in the *Buckley* decision was that (1) contributions are more damaging to the integrity of the election process than expenditures and (2) limits on contributions are less intrusive on free speech than limitations on expenditures.

FUNDING OF GOVERNMENT COMMUNICATIONS ACTIVITIES

Because of a 1913 law known as the **Gillett Amendment**, government agencies and units cannot spend public money on promotional activities or legislative advocacy unless they are authorized to do so by law or congressional mandate. The rationale behind the law is to prevent government agencies from spending taxpayer funds to implement advertising and public relations campaigns related to political issues in which they have a vested interest. The law does not prevent government agencies and branches of the military from employing public information officers, as those functions are authorized by law and there are no conflicts of interest.

Although the Gillett Amendment is part of federal law and does not apply to states, many state legislatures have created similar laws restricting the expenditure of state funds. One example is found in the case of state universities that use public money to support campaigns to increase the amount of funding the university receives. In essence, a university involved in such an activity is using taxpayer money to generate more taxpayer money, creating an inherent conflict of interest. Universities wanting to conduct such persuasive activities must therefore do so using privately raised funds.

PUBLIC RELATIONS REPRESENTATIVES AS LOBBYISTS

When public relations professionals represent their clients in advocating or opposing political or regulatory issues at the federal level, they are required to register with the federal government as **lobbyists**. Most states have similar regulations for public relations professionals working on state issues. Also, in most states, the attorney general or secretary of state is the official in charge of the registration process. For example, if a public relations representative is working in the public relations department at a public utility and wants to meet with state legislators in an attempt to influence government regulation, it is not as easy as making appointments and then showing up at their offices.

Registration has always been a requirement for full-time political operatives, but for public relations professionals, it was unheard of until a 1950 court case. In *United States* v. *Slaughter,* the court took away the dividing line between full-time lobbyists and public relations professionals. Even if lobbying is only a small part of their job duties, public relations representatives are required to work under the same rules as full-time lobbyists if they represent their clients in the political arena.

LEGAL PROBLEMS IN INVESTOR RELATIONS

Public Disclosure

Public disclosure refers to the requirement that information about a company that may affect how its stock is evaluated by stockbrokers, analysts, or potential investors must be released in a manner that is timely, accurate, and in its correct context. There are numerous cases of stockholders suing companies because information was not provided in a timely manner, was deemed to be misleading, or was not in its correct context. Examples include quarterly or annual earnings, potential mergers and acquisitions, changes in leadership, new products or services, pending litigation, major expansion plans, employee layoffs, and defaults on loans.

Public disclosure is a large and complicated area of the law that is subject to frequent change. It is often difficult to keep up with the changes, meaning that when in doubt, public relations representatives should not hesitate to contact their legal departments for guidance. Attorney and public relations expert Frank Walsh wrote, "There is a great deal for the public relations professional to know, but perhaps the most important is when to turn to the corporate attorney."

In a 1972 case, *SEC* v. *Pig 'n' Whistle Corporation,* a public relations agency distributed news releases for its client, a Chicago-based restaurant and motel chain. When the releases were found to include inaccurate and misleading information, the question arose as to who was responsible—the agency or the client. The court ruled that the responsibility belonged to both, and the agency's claim that it was only "doing what the client asked" was not a sufficient defense. The Securities and Exchange Commission (SEC) claimed, and the court agreed, that the agency was responsible for knowing enough about the client's business and SEC regulations to verify the claims made in the releases before they were distributed. The SEC requirement that public relations representatives are responsible for the accuracy of news releases does not mean those representatives must cross-examine clients in detail about the information they are asked to disseminate, but they should avoid blindly releasing nebulous or questionable information without some level of scrutiny.

In addition to the *Pig 'n' Whistle* case, other major cases in this area are *SEC* v. *Texas Gulf Sulphur* (1968), *Zucker* v. *Sable* (1976), *Staffin* v. *Greenberg* (1982), and *Stockholders* v. *Apple Computer* (1984). These cases are discussed in the Trends and Issues section of this chapter.

Insider Trading

Members of a company's public relations staff as well as employees of public relations agencies that represent publicly traded companies are in a unique position because they have access to a great deal of company information. If an employee of a company or the agency that represents that company uses such information to illegally trade that company's stock, however, they may be in violation of the Securities and Exchange Act of 1934, a law to prevent insider trading. An individual becomes an "insider" if he or she is in a position to learn of business information that affects that organization's stock before that information becomes public knowledge. Rules established by the SEC prohibit such individuals from purchasing or selling stock until after the information becomes public.

Because of the complexity of SEC rules and the possibility of "honest mistakes" resulting in criminal charges, many public relations agencies take the added precaution of prohibiting their employees from owning stock in the companies the agency represents. Although not a widespread problem at present, a 1986 case—*SEC* v. *Franco*—is a constant reminder of the danger. Anthony Franco was owner of a public relations agency and at one point in the 1980s was president of the Public Relations Society of America (PRSA). He was found guilty of violating insider trading laws because he bought stock in one of his client's companies based on information that was not generally available to other stockholders. He never admitted any wrongdoing, but he did pay a fine and was forced to resign as president of PRSA.

PUBLIC RELATIONS MATERIALS AND LIBEL LAW

Libel is a legal term that refers to the defamation of a person's character or reputation in a published or broadcast form. Libel is most often associated with media such as newspapers, magazines, television, and radio, but it can also be found in news releases, internal publications, and other public relations materials. One notable example is the 1979 case of *Hutchinson* v. *Proxmire,* in which a United States senator was sued by a research scientist because of defamatory comments in the senator's news releases and newsletters. The case did not involve public relations practitioners, but it caught the attention of practitioners because it involved materials commonly used in the profession.

The only aspects of the First Amendment that do serve to protect news releases are libel defenses of "truth" and "fair comment." In the 1986 cases of *Karp* v. *Hill and Knowlton* and *Parks* v. *Steinbrenner,* courts considered the "fair comment" defense that is customarily applied to editorials and other forms of opinion writing and applied it to opinions expressed in news releases.

Other specific examples of legal problems caused by public relations materials can be found in employee newsletters. Numerous companies have been sued by employees for either libel or invasion of privacy because of defamatory or embarrassing information in the company's publications.

Complicating this problem is the fact that although the definition of libel applies to public relations material, the defense of "freedom of the press" does not. Courts have ruled that news releases and employee newsletters are "tools of the trade" and are not fully protected by the First Amendment's press freedom clause. Therefore, companies who allow defamatory or embarrassing information to be printed in a company newsletter can be sued by the employees affected and cannot claim "press freedom" or "newsworthiness" as a defense.

APPROPRIATION

Appropriation is the use of a person's name, photograph, image, likeness, or voice to endorse or promote a commercial product or service without the individual's consent.

For nonemployees, the rule is simple: Organizations may not use that person's name, photograph, image, likeness, or voice to endorse a product or service unless that person provides his or her consent in writing. If a public official, professional athlete, show business personality, or other celebrity attends a company's event and a member of the communications staff takes photographs of the event, it is safe to use those photographs in the company newsletter or other publication provided they are presented in their correct context (for instance, the individual attended the company's event and shook hands and/or signed autographs for employees). But the company cannot use those photographs in print or broadcast advertisements to promote that company's products or services without written permission of the individual involved.

Nonprofit organizations must also be careful when using photographs of celebrities to endorse their causes. A celebrity attending an event and consenting to photographs should be regarded as a short-term endorsement. Just because a famous person agrees to have his or her photograph taken and used in the next issue of the newsletter does not mean the photograph can be used beyond that. Most celebrities who agree to attend such events will insist on written agreements that spell out for how long and for what purposes their photographs may be used.

When photographs of crowds are used in a news context, individuals appearing in the photograph have no legal rights to demand compensation because they are outside their homes and voluntarily taking part in a news event. But when individuals pose for photographs that will be used for promotional purposes, written agreements should be used to specify how the photos will be used and what compensation will be provided.

For employees, the rules are even simpler. Organizations may not use employees' names, photographs, images, likenesses, or voices to endorse a product or service unless they provide their consent in writing. However, companies who frequently use photographs of employees in their internal publications or advertisements will have new employees sign consent forms as a condition of employment so they will not have to do them individually at the time they are used. This process also gives the public relations departments consent to provide photographs to the media of employees who earn recognition within the company or industry. In many cases, courts will recognize the concept of *implied consent*, meaning that if a photographer asks an individual or group of people to pose for a photograph and explains that it is for the employee newsletter, written permission from the person or persons being photographed is not required. But if the photographs are candid or not posed, it is better to obtain written permission.

Common law provides an important distinction regarding the nature of the photograph in question. If a tour group visits a manufacturing plant or other privately owned property, the event is considered "news," and therefore the permission of those individuals is not needed to take photographs or use those photographs in a company publication, but only if those photographs and the accompanying captions are kept within the context of "news." But if one or more of the photographs (or video) is used in an advertising context, that usage is considered "promotional," and the individuals involved must give their written permission and, if appropriate, be compensated. Not all courts apply the legal precedents consistently, however, so legal problems can be avoided by obtaining written permission of the individuals involved, even if you have reason to believe it is not necessary.

When minors are involved, a higher standard applies, as they cannot legally give permission to have their photographs used. When employees bring their children to a company event, for example, the public relations department must have the parents' written permission to use their children's photographs in company publications.

INTELLECTUAL PROPERTY

Intellectual property is a field of law with numerous areas, but the one of most concern for public relations professionals is copyright. **Copyright** laws protect works that are creative in nature and often intangible. Prior to 1976, authors and publishers claiming copyright infringement must have formally registered it with the U.S. Copyright Office. Although registration is still recommended and is legally advantageous, it is not absolutely required to make a copyright claim. A 1976 revision of copyright law recognizes that an author's work is legally protected as soon as it is completed, even if never registered.

To receive an official copyright, the holder must submit a form to the government and pay a small fee. For most items, two copies must be submitted—one for the copyright office to keep on file, and the other to be on file at the Library of Congress.

Under current law, last revised in 1998, copyright protection for work owned by an individual lasts for 70 years past the life of the author. For work owned by an organization, copyright protection lasts for 120 years after its creation or 95 years after its first usage, whichever comes first. When a copyright expires, or if the work was never copyrighted to begin with, it is said to be in the **public domain** and can be used by others without permission or compensation.

Another important part of copyright law is the **works for hire** principle as it applies to the employment of independent contractors. The works for hire doctrine, first introduced with the 1909 revision of the copyright law, deals with the difference in legal relationships that companies have with their regular employees as opposed to those between companies and independent contractors. The basic difference is that in the case of regular employees, the materials they create belong to the company, not the individual. In the case of freelancers or independent contractors, whatever they create belongs to them after the first usage unless a written agreement or contract with a "works for hire" clause has been signed by both parties. The works for hire principle was the key issue in the 1989 case of *Community for Creative Nonviolence* v. *Reid* (see Trends and Issues later in this chapter).

RELATIONSHIPS WITH CLIENTS

There are no specific laws regulating the relationship between public relations agencies and their clients. Therefore, clients or agencies that feel they have been cheated, mistreated, or misled during the agency-client relationship have no specific laws under which they can file lawsuits. Some, however, have been able to use the common-law principle of **unfair business practices** to file suit against the other party. One example is a scenario in which a prospective client invites numerous public relations firms to submit competing proposals for a project. If the client likes one proposal, but hires another agency to carry it out, the agency on the losing end can pursue legal action under the unfair business practice principle. In most such cases, courts tend to rule in favor of the agency on the losing end of the transaction. To avoid such problems, many agencies attach copyright protection to their written proposals, or require prospective clients to agree in advance to compensate the agency for its time if all or part of the proposal is accepted, but the agency is not hired to carry it out.

TRUTH IN ADVERTISING

Professors and practitioners often emphasize the difference between the fields of advertising and public relations, but the Federal Trade Commission (FTC)—the government body that enforces laws regarding advertising—makes no such distinction. Communications programs that promote a commercial product or service are therefore subject to FTC rules, regardless if the tools used are advertising or public relations.

One of the FTC's main responsibilities is the enforcement of "truth in advertising" laws that deal with messages that are false, misleading, or deceptive. What is the difference between an advertisement that is "false" and one that is merely "misleading or deceptive"? The dividing line is difficult to detect. But here are some examples that may help to clarify the difference.

An advertisement is clearly false if it makes claims that are not true, such as a product's ability to achieve a certain result that in practice it clearly cannot. In order to substantiate such a claim of false advertising, however, the FTC or other government agency attempting to do so would have to prove that the advertiser knew the product's limitations but published or broadcast the advertisement nevertheless. Other examples of outright false advertising include the mention of fictional endorsements or test results, such as "The American Cancer Society recommends eating XYZ daily" (if no such recommendation was ever made) or "Scientists at the University of Illinois tested our product and found that . . ." (if no such tests were actually conducted).

Conversely, an advertisement is merely "deceptive" if it makes no false statements, yet leaves out important information or is otherwise misleading. For example, an advertisement would be ruled deceptive if it claims that product A costs less than product B, yet omits the fact the product A is sold in 32-ounce bottles while product B is sold in 48-ounce bottles.

To determine if an advertisement is deceptive, the FTC uses the **reasonable consumer standard**, meaning that each advertisement in question would be evaluated according to the likelihood that a "reasonable consumer" would be deceived. An advertisement would not be deemed to be deceptive if only a few gullible consumers would be misled. The FTC admits that a company "cannot be liable for every possible reading of its claims, no matter how far-fetched," and that the law "could not help a consumer who thinks that all french fries are imported from France or that Danish pastry actually comes from Denmark."

Truth in advertising laws can be enforced by either barring it from being broadcast or published, or by a fine, or both.

CONTESTS AND COMPETITIONS

If a company sponsors a contest, its attorneys should review contest materials such as entry forms, posters, news releases, and advertisements. Even if a purchase is not required, any contest that is merely associated with a commercial product or service is subject to Federal Trade Commission rules. To avoid legal problems, many companies hire experienced outside consultants to administer sweepstakes or other contests for them.

TRENDS AND ISSUES

Public Relations on Trial

A significant number of public relations professionals responding to a 1996 survey admitted that they were either "not at all familiar" or only "somewhat familiar" with the legal principles involved in public relations work. Results for specific legal issues included Securities and Exchange Commission regulations (86.7 percent either "not at all familiar" or "somewhat familiar"), commercial speech (86.7 percent), copyright (78.5 percent), access to information (75.6 percent), and libel (71.8 percent).

Public relations professionals who do not consider the potential legal consequences of their actions can learn a great deal by examining some of the major cases that have shaped the law in this area.

News Releases and Investor Relations

Numerous court cases and Securities and Exchange Commission actions have established rules and guidelines under which publicly traded companies must communicate with stockholders. Significant court cases include *SEC* v. *Texas Gulf Sulphur* (1968), *Zucker* v. *Sable* (1976), *Staffin* v. *Greenberg* (1982), and *Stockholders* v. *Apple Computer* (1984).

Texas Gulf Sulphur was an American-owned chemical company that had drilling rights in a remote region in eastern Canada. One of its operating units discovered large deposits of copper, zinc, and other valuable minerals, but wanted to keep the discovery a secret for as long as it could so it could purchase additional land to expand its operation.

Rumors of the discovery leaked out and eventually reached Wall Street, so the company issued a series of news releases that admitted the find but downplayed its value. Meanwhile, the company officials who knew how valuable the minerals were bought additional stock, so the SEC prosecuted the company for releasing misleading information and omitting other pertinent details from the news releases. The company was found guilty and fined.

In the *Zucker* case, the defendant was the Sable Corporation, the manufacturer of contact lenses and other health-related items that issued a news release about a new type of soft contact lens that it was developing. Based on the news release, new investors purchased stock in the company, and existing stockholders bought additional stock. Both groups expected the stock price to rise as a result of the new product.

What was omitted from the news release was the fact that the product had not yet been submitted to the Food and Drug Administration for its approval—a process that often takes two years or more. By leaving out that important detail, the release implied that the product would be on the market immediately.

One angry stockholder sued the company, claiming the omission misled him and other stockholders. A federal district court ruled that although the company should have been more specific, that omission did not constitute an inaccuracy. Even though the company was found not financially liable, it spent thousands of dollars in legal fees and the prolonged litigation damaged it in the eyes of stock analysts and current and potential investors.

In the early 1980s, two more cases generated national attention. *Staffin* v. *Greenberg* (1982) and *Stockholders* v. *Apple Computer* (1984) involved stockholders suing companies because their public relations departments either failed to make information available on a timely basis or released information that was misleading.

In *Staffin* v. *Greenberg*, a company was able to defend itself against a stockholder lawsuit, but not before spending thousands of dollars in legal fees. Robert Staffin was a stockholder in a Pennsylvania company called Bluebird, Inc. that dealt in wholesale meats. For many years, its stock price had remained stable, selling for about $10 per share—the same price that Staffin and other investors had paid for it. What Staffin and other stockholders did not know was that the company was about to be taken over by a British wholesale company, and the stock price was expected to take a significant jump.

There had been some rumors that the acquisition was going to take place, but each time the stockholders tried to find out information from the company, its public relations department either denied the meetings were taking place or responded with information that made it look like the merger was less likely than it actually was. The company issued news releases and stockholder advisories that used phrases such as "still a long way off" and "may happen in the distant future."

Staffin and the other stockholders grew tired of waiting and in July 1979 sold their stock for $10 a share—about what they paid for it. Less than a month later, Bluebird was taken over by the British company, and the stock jumped from $10 to $15 a share overnight. Staffin and the other stockholders sued the company, claiming that it violated SEC rules by releasing false and misleading information. A Federal District Court and Circuit Court of Appeals both ruled that it was a "close call," but decided in favor of the company.

The SEC punished the company with a nominal fine and said that although some of the information was misleading, there was no "smoking gun" to indicate a conspiracy to hide the truthful information. Even though the company did not lose the suit, it was nevertheless damaged in the eyes of current and potential investors.

An opposite situation took place in the *Apple Computer* case. Instead of misleading information skewed toward the negative that influenced stockholders to sell, it was a case of misleading information skewed toward the positive, and it influenced stockholders to buy more stock based on positive and overoptimistic comments by company leaders. The case involved a new software program called "Lisa," which was overpromoted in the company's stockholder communications, influencing outsiders to begin investing in the company and existing stockholders to purchase additional stock. The software program was a failure, and stockholders later learned that company leaders knew it would fail but continued to promote it, hoping it would somehow work out. The case was settled out of court, with Apple paying the stockholders an undisclosed amount.

News Releases and Libel Law

In two 1986 cases, the courts applied the **fair comment** defense (typically used by defendants in libel cases based on opinion and editorial writing) to opinions contained in news releases.

The case of *Karp* v. *Hill and Knowlton* began when Steven Karp, an executive with the Buckingham Corporation, left the liquor and wine distributing company and formed his own competing company. Buckingham, a Hill and Knowlton client, filed a lawsuit against Karp, claiming that the former employee used confidential business information and conspired with the company's distributors to form the new venture. After a court ruled in favor of the company, but before a financial award was determined, Hill and Knowlton issued a news release that repeated the company's claim of fraud and expressed its view that "substantial relief should be granted." Karp filed a libel suit against the public relations firm, but the court ruled that all statements in the release were either factual (as based on the findings of the court in the initial case) or were protected as opinion or "fair comment."

In *Parks* v. *Steinbrenner*, the New York Supreme Court ruled in favor of the New York Yankees in a libel suit filed by Dallas Parks, who served as a replacement umpire when major league baseball's full-time umpires were on strike. The news release quoted the team's owner as calling Parks a "scab" who "had it in" for the Yankees and "misjudged" plays. The release added that Parks did not "measure up" to American League standards for umpires and criticized his decision to throw two Yankee players out of game. A trial court ruled in favor of Parks, but the New York Supreme Court overturned, examining the news release and determining that, like in the *Karp* case, all of its components were either statements of fact or opinion, both of which were protected.

Works for Hire

The works for hire principle was the key issue in the 1989 case of *Community for Creative Nonviolence* v. *Reid.* The CCNV was a nonprofit organization dedicated to drawing attention to and reducing the problem of homelessness. In the fall of 1985, the organization hired sculptor James Earl Reid to design a display that would combine a biblical manger scene with a modern-day portrayal of a homeless family. The parties did not sign any written agreements, and neither mentioned copyright.

After the finished product was displayed at a month-long CCNV event in Washington, DC, the organization announced plans to take it on a nation-wide tour. Reid objected, fearing it would be damaged in the process. He requested that it be returned to him, and that started a four-year dispute that began in Federal District Court and ended in the United States Supreme Court.

The lower court ruled in favor of Reid, claiming that because Reid was not an employee and that no works for hire agreement was executed, the artwork belonged to him. The U.S. Court of Appeals for the District of Columbia and the U.S. Supreme Court agreed, and the case set the standard for how organizations would deal with freelance writers, photographers, and other independent contractors for the next decade and perhaps beyond.

CASE STUDY 11

Free Speech and Selling Shoes

Like many U.S. companies that outsource the manufacturing process to overseas labor markets, sporting goods manufacturer Nike is often accused of violating child labor standards and condoning "sweatshop" conditions. In 2002, the company struck back at its critics, claiming in news releases and letters to newspapers that its products were not produced under such conditions. It also wrote letters to university administrators on campuses where students had called for their institutions to boycott the company, a major provider of athletic equipment.

Consumer advocate Marc Kasky of San Francisco accused Nike of conducting a "misleading" public relations campaign that violated California's truth-in-advertising law. California's unusual advertising statute not only prohibited companies from disseminating false information (a determination usually left to the Federal Trade Commission) but also allowed individuals to file charges against violators, even though they may not have been personally harmed. The case centered not on whether Nike's statements were true, but whether they were protected as free speech and whether individuals such as Kasky should be allowed to pursue such cases.

A California trial court sided with Nike, ruling that its messages aimed at responding to public criticism were statements of opinion rather than commercial messages. But the California Supreme Court reversed that decision, claiming that every message a company disseminates is to some degree a commercial message and was therefore not fully protected by the First Amendment.

Nike appealed the decision to the U.S. Supreme Court. Harvard Law School professor Laurence Tribe, representing the company, argued that the suit should be thrown out because of the company's First Amendment right to defend itself in matters of public interest. He and other Nike supporters pointed out that the company was merely using the same communications methods as its critics, and therefore deserved an equal level of free speech protection.

Organizations lining up to help Nike by filing *amicus curiae* ("friends of the court") briefs included Microsoft, the Public Relations Society of America, ExxonMobil, the American Civil Liberties Union, and national news organizations that worried that if Nike lost the case, many companies would be reluctant to communicate with the media for fear of violating the law. Siding with Kasky were the Sierra Club, Public Citizen, and several consumer groups.

In the spring of 2003, the Supreme Court refused to hear the case, meaning that Kasky could continue to pursue it in the California court system. In declining to hear the case, Justice John Paul Stevens wrote that "the speech at issue represents a blending of commercial speech and debate on issues of public importance," and Justice Sandra Day O'Connor added that "none of this speech was advertising in the strictest sense of the term."

Later that year, Nike agreed to settle the case for $2 million, with $1.5 million being paid to Kasky's organization and $500,000 being spent to provide after-hours educational programs and other benefits for Nike's overseas employees.

DISCUSSION QUESTIONS

1. Consider the scenario in the section titled Relationships with Clients in which a client accepts multiple proposals, selects one of them, but hires another firm to carry it out. Do you agree with the court rulings that this is an unfair business practice? Or should the firm on the losing end of the deal be forced to accept the outcome as one of the risks of being in a competitive business?

2. Look at the legal cases of *Parks* v. *Steinbrenner, Karp* v. *Hill and Knowlton, First National Bank of Boston* v. *Bellotti, Consolidated Edison Co. of New York* v. *Public Service Commission*, and *Pacific Gas and Electric Co.* v. *Public Utilities Commission of California.* With which of the court decisions do you agree, and why? With which do you disagree, and why?

For each of the following, answer with either yes or no, provide any necessary qualifiers (such as "but only if . . ."), and cite one or more cases to support your answers.

3. Can my public relations materials such as news releases and newsletters be the subject of libel action? Do any First Amendment principles apply?

4. If my company hires a freelance writer or photographer to help out in the public relations department, do we own the permanent rights to what they produce?

5. My company wants to get involved in political issues by purchasing newspaper advertisements to explain our position on public issues. Do we have the First Amendment right to do this?

6. The public utility company I work for wants to use "bill stuffers" to communicate to our customers about political issues. Do we have a First Amendment right to do this?

7. If my news releases include inaccurate or misleading information that affects our company's stock prices, will the company (or I) get in trouble?

8. One of my clients is involved in a court case, and I have been called to testify about what I know. Does our confidentiality agreement prohibit me from testifying?

GLOSSARY OF TERMS

Appropriation. The use of a person's name, photograph, image, likeness, or voice is used to endorse or promote a commercial product or service without the individual's consent.

Bill stuffer. A way to communicate with customers by including informational items in with statements and bills.

Commercial advertising. Advertising that promotes products and services.

Copyright. Protects works that are creative in nature and often intangible.

Fair comment. A defense used in libel cases in which the material in question is deemed to be based on opinion rather than fact.

Gillett Amendment. A federal law that prohibits government agencies and units from spending public money on promotional activities unless they are authorized to do so by law or congressional mandate.

Insider trading. If an employee of a company or agency that represents that company uses information about the company to trade illegally that company's stock, the person may be in violation of the Securities and Exchange Act.

Intellectual property. A field of law with numerous areas but the one of most concern for public relations is copyright.

Libel. The defamation of a person's character or reputation in a published or broadcast form.

Lobbyist. A role in which public relations professionals represent their clients in advocating or opposing political or regulatory issues. Lobbyists are required to register.

Obstruction of justice.   Failure to cooperate with a government or law-enforcement investigation or other intentional act intended to delay or impede an investigation.

Political advertising.   Advertising that deals with issues and ideas rather than products or services.

Public disclosure.   The Security and Exchange Commission requires that information that may affect how a company's stock is evaluated must be released in a timely manner and must be in its correct context and not misleading.

Public domain.   Works that can be used by others, such as work that was never copyrighted or when a copyright expires.

Reasonable consumer standard.   A standard applied in cases of advertising accused of being deceptive; an advertisement is deemed to be deceptive if a "reasonable consumer" would be deceived.

Unfair business practice.   When there are no specific laws under which to file lawsuits, some have been able to use the common-law principle of unfair business practices to file suit against the other party.

Works for hire.   A part of copyright law that deals with the difference in legal relationships that companies have with their regular employees as opposed to those between companies and independent contractors.

CHAPTER 12

ETHICAL CONSIDERATIONS

GENERAL PRINCIPLES

Nearly every discussion of public relations ethics begins with the concepts of honesty, integrity, and credibility, and they apply both to the individual and the organization.

Ethics and the Individual

Public relations professionals have an obligation to protect the reputation of the profession as well as their own reputations. There is a good reason why many journalists dislike and distrust public relations representatives. Some reporters' loathing of the profession is a result of merely being annoyed by unsolicited news releases about trivial events, but many other journalists tell stories of being misled, deceived, or lied to by someone claiming to be practicing public relations. When one public relations professional crosses the line, the entire industry suffers. Individually, a professional communicator's reputation and credibility lies not only with individual reporters but also with newspapers and television stations as a whole. Even though there may be turnover as reporters assigned to cover an organization come and go, those reporters have already talked to their editors and coworkers about which public relations representatives in the community can be trusted and which cannot. Just because one reporter leaves an assignment and another takes over does not mean that a public relations representative who has deceived that reporter in the past can expect to start over again with a clean slate.

Another key to personal and professional integrity is to avoid conflicts of interest—real or perceived. One frequently discussed example of the conflict of interest issue is the giving and receiving of gifts with journalists, vendors, or other parties. In general, the codes of ethics of professional associations in the public relations field discourage public relations representatives from giving or receiving gifts that are out of line—especially when there is an agreement between the parties as to what will be received in exchange for the gift. The Latin term is **quid-pro-quo**, the translation of which means "something for something." This is in contrast to the media culture of many foreign countries, where paying bribes either to reporters or directly to newspaper management is an accepted way of seeking positive publicity.

Decision making in public relations is a popular area for hindsight. Decisions may eventually turn out to be black and white, but they do not always look that way when they first arise. In many cases, a public relations representative may not realize he or she has made a bad decision until it is too late to do anything about it. Edward L. Bernays, for example, is considered to be one of the pioneers of public relations ethics, yet he did work for the American Tobacco Company and designed persuasive campaigns to encourage people to start smoking. That was in the 1930s, and shortly before he died in 1995, he referred to that as his "only professional regret."

Public relations representatives come to the table with a built-in bias, and there is nothing wrong with that. Practitioners have the right to promote the point of view of clients or employers without having to apologize for doing so. And although the public's expectations of professional persuaders are different from the profession's expectations of journalists, they must still adhere to principles such as honesty and truth.

Critics of the public relations professionals are fond of referring to public relations work as *spin*, a term coined by *Time Magazine* in 1988 to refer to the ability of politicians to position themselves cleverly on complex and controversial issues. Most professional communicators object to the term. Author Robert Dilenschneider labels "spin doctors" as "purveyors of deception, manipulation, and misinformation" and claims that "spin is antithetical to legitimate public relations. . . . Spin is to public relations what pornography is to art."

But confidential surveys of those who work in the field provide some alarming statistics. In a 2001 study by *PR Week,* for example, 43.9 percent of respondents reported feeling uncertain about the ethics of a task they were asked to perform, and only 31.1 percent believed the ethical boundaries of their job had been clearly defined. More than 25 percent of the respondents reported having lied on the job, and more than 38 percent said they had exaggerated information about a client or product—and those are just the ones who admitted it.

Ethics and the Organization

Bad ethics is bad for business. Companies that shade the truth or participate in other illegal or unethical activities may see some short-term benefit, but most will suffer in the long run. Even if wrongdoings are not publicly exposed, simply knowing about them among insiders damages employee productivity and results in cynicism and low morale. One need look no further than the newspaper headlines of the last decade to see how getting caught in a public deception affects a company's reputation. In the 1980s and 1990s, giant companies such as Exxon and Texaco became targets of public disdain over environmental problems and race relations, respectively. In 2001 and 2002, company names such as Enron and WorldCom became synonymous with corporate wrongdoing for their misdeeds in accounting and securities issues.

Publicity serves a cleansing and illuminating function. When a company or nonprofit organization seeks visibility, it must also accept the scrutiny (by both the public and the media) that comes with it. Organizations with no appreciation for how public relations works want to emphasize the positive while attempting to cover up or explain away the negative. Organizations that understand how public relations works do not overpromote their positive attributes; they simply make them known and allow human nature to take its course. As for the negative, these organizations do not attempt to cover them up, but instead work hard to correct them.

WHAT PROFESSIONAL ASSOCIATIONS
SAY ABOUT ETHICS

Voluntary Codes of Ethics

The Public Relations Society of America and the International Association of Business Communicators—the two major professional associations serving the public relations industry—each has its own code of ethics, and there is little difference between the two. One factor they have in common is that they are both criticized for being watered-down with vague and imprecise language.

In addition to that criticism, there are two other weaknesses or limitations of both the PRSA and the IABC codes. The first weakness is that neither carries the force of law. They are not like the American Bar Association (ABA) code or the American Medical Association (AMA) code that both carry quasi-governmental authority. If the ABA decides that a lawyer cannot practice law, he or she cannot do so. If the AMA decides that a doctor cannot practice medicine, he or she cannot do so. Neither the IABC nor the PRSA, however, has been given that level of authority over the public relations profession—and neither of them wants it. Neither group has the staff nor the resources that would be necessary to set up the bureaucracy and due process that would be required to take away someone's job. Instead, the major professional groups use the term *voluntary compliance*. They expect members to comply voluntarily with their ethical codes and admit that they do not have the staff nor the procedures in place to detect or investigate code violations. The toughest penalty that IABC and PRSA can administer to members who violate their codes of ethics is to revoke the offender's membership. There is no license to take away like there is in law or medicine.

The second limitation of the ethical guidelines of both organizations is that they apply only to the members of those organizations. Both IABC and PRSA admit that only a small number of people practicing public relations are members of one of those two groups—only about 15 percent belonging to one or the other. So, if the professional associations have only minimal authority over the 15 percent of the practitioners who are members, how much do they have over the 85 percent who are not? None.

The codes of ethics established by the professional organizations have both merits and shortcomings. Advocates of professional codes contend that codes help newcomers by educating them about moral guidelines and sensitizing them to ethic problems in their field. Critics of professional codes point to the vagueness of codes and the lack of enforceability. One such critic is Donald K. Wright, professor at the University of South Alabama, who wrote in a 1993 article that the codes "are more cosmetic than anything else. . . . They're warm and fuzzy and make practitioners feel good about themselves, but they don't accomplish much. They don't even come close to being meaningful tools for ensuring accountability. They don't achieve what they're set out to do and most are filled with meaningless rhetoric and are not taken seriously by the majority of those who practice public relations."

Formal Licensing

Numerous times in the history of the organization, the leadership of PRSA discusses the potential for a formal licensing procedure for public relations professionals. Edward L. Bernays was the leading advocate for licensing from the 1950s until his death in 1995, but since his death, no individual has stepped forward to advocate licensing with the same level of enthusiasm. If the field was licensed, Bernays claimed, it could require more educational preparation, enhance the image of the field, and provide a mechanism for removing those guilty of dishonest or unethical conduct.

Those opposing such a plan counter with two arguments of their own. The first is that before there could be a formal licensing program, there would have to be a universal definition for public relations—one on which all the major professional groups could agree. As mentioned earlier, a second problem is that none of the professional groups want to take on the responsibility for setting up the bureaucracy and the due process that would be necessary to administer such a program.

WHAT THE EXPERTS SAY

A number of notable authors and other public relations experts have attempted to deal with the topic of public relations ethics in their writings and public comments. In addition to his admission of regret over once working for a tobacco manufacturer, Bernays often addressed the topic of professional conduct when he attended professional meetings and visited college campuses across the country during the last 20 years of his life. Bernays was often critical of the PRSA and IABC codes for their dependence on voluntary compliance to their ethical codes.

In *Public Relations: Strategies and Tactics* (2000), a popular textbook for introductory-level public relations classes, authors Dennis L. Wilcox, Phillip H. Ault, Warren K. Agee, and Glen T. Cameron describe a practitioner's four ethical obligations: to society and the public interest, to his or her client or employer, to the interests of the public relations profession, and to his or her own personal value system. "In the ideal world, the four would not conflict," they wrote. "In reality, however, they often do."

Faced with assignments that call for unethical or questionable conduct, a public relations representative has a number of options. The first is to advise the client or employer that the actions being considered are not in the best interests of the organization. To do so, it is helpful to provide examples of how such conduct resulted in negative results in the past. Public relations textbooks, especially those used in case studies classes, contain many such examples. The second approach is simply to refuse to participate and explain the reasons for doing so. The practicality of this tactic depends on the nature of the relationship between the individual and the client or employer; professionals new to their positions may lack the confidence to do so.

A third option—to be considered only in the most serious cases—is to sever relationships with the client or employer in question. The justification for such a drastic step is clear, however. A public relations professional forced to act in a way that conflicts with accepted ethical standards will lose confidence in the client or employer and would therefore be unable to provide appropriate counsel or serve as a credible spokesperson. But in his 1993 book, *The Credibility Factor: Putting Ethics to Work in Public Relations,* Lee Baker writes:

> When asked to violate ethics by a boss or client, I do not take the arbitrary position that a practitioner should immediately quit, or threaten to. First, that is a bad negotiating technique. Second, it implies that all ethical issues are black and white. . . . Some hard-liners say that we must have the courage to stand by our principles, and if necessary, walk away from a client. But how does an individual with two children in college, a mortgage, a three-thousand dollar orthodontist bill, and a wife thinking about divorce walk away from a high paying job on a matter of principle?

In a speech to public relations executives, Baker summarized his view on the importance of integrity by saying, "Do what's right, be fair, tell the truth, be open, and assume responsibility. Avoid conflicts of interest, misrepresentation of facts, lying, cover-ups, deceit, and subterfuge."

Robert L. Dilenschneider, former president of Hill & Knowlton, wrote in his book, *Power and Influence: Mastering the Art of Persuasion,* that the public often judges an organization's ethical performance by comparing what it says to what it does. His point is that employees, government regulators, journalists, current and potential customers, and current and potential stockholders will compare an organization's actual conduct with what it says about itself in news releases and television interviews, and the discrepancies will be conspicuous. "I have never seen a truly unethical company elude being found out for long, especially these days," Dilenschneider wrote. "In our trade, we learn about the likely ethics soft spots in a business long before they become public knowledge."

PUBLIC RELATIONS AGENCIES AND UNETHICAL PRACTICES

Relationships with clients represent an ethical minefield for public relations agencies. Common practices for which agencies are criticized include:

1. *Bait and Switch.* Experienced senior account executives make the presentation and land the account, but then the detail work is assigned to younger, less experienced staffers. In another variation, agencies send attractive young women to make new business proposals to male clients. The clients are likely unaware that once they hire the firm, they are unlikely to ever see those women again, much less have the opportunity to date them.

2. *Churning.* Unnecessary work is created or the amount of staff time actually involved in a project is exaggerated in order to "pad" the client's bill.

3. *Unrealistic Expectations.* The agency hints that there is more publicity potential in a project than there actually is, or drops titles of publications such as *Time Magazine* and the *Wall Street Journal* into the conversation in order to land a prospective account, even though the agency representative already knows that such publicity is unlikely. One of clients' chief complaints about public relations agencies is that they overpromise and under-deliver.

Other unethical practices of agencies include having employees pose as reporters at a client's news conference and ask friendly setup questions to influence the tone of the event, or having them attend a competitor's news conference to ask hostile questions. Even more extreme tactics include gathering information on a client's opponents, such as by infiltrating meetings of an opposition group, or by posing as a college student gathering information through the mail. Leise L. Hutchison, assistant professor of communication at St. Louis University, suggests that agency owners should insist on high ethical standards for their employees by either adopting the PRSA code of ethics or developing their own, requiring employees to sign the code, inserting the code into requests for proposals, and then setting the example by demonstrating ethical conducts themselves.

A CONDENSED VERSION OF THE PROFESSIONAL CODES

Rather than present both the IABC and PRSA codes in this chapter, we have chosen to consolidate the two codes and add some general principles of business ethics and common sense to produce a list of "shalls" and "shall nots" that is easier to grasp than the formal organizational codes.

The "Shalls" of Public Relations

A public relations professional SHALL:

1. Conduct his or her professional life with respect for the best interests of the client or employer as well as the interests of the public relations profession, but giving even higher priority to the best interests of the public.
This principle comes mainly from the PRSA Code of Professional Standards (in place from 1988 through 2000) that required members conduct their professional lives "in the public interest." In its official interpretation of the Code, PRSA explains that "in the public interest" refers to the rights and privileges guaranteed by the U.S. Constitution and its amendments.

2. Ensure that all communications on behalf of a client or employer are made with the highest regard for honesty, integrity, accuracy, and timeliness.
Professional communicators should be honest with everyone they come into contact with, including clients, the media, and other professional communicators. One of the hardest parts of the agency–client relationship is telling a client bad news. It is especially difficult for those who have just started their own agencies and worked hard to get their telephones ringing and to get clients to walk through their front doors. Early in an agency–client relationship, there may be a temptation to tell clients what they want to hear in order to keep them as clients. In the old days of Greek mythology, messengers who delivered bad news were often executed. In public relations work, clients rarely kill the messengers,

but they sometimes fire their agencies if they become the messengers that deliver bad news on a regular basis. An agency that holds back bad news, however, is not serving the client's best interests. Effective public relations counselors do not tell their clients what they want to hear, but rather what they need to know.

In addition to not lying to a client, a public relations representative should not lie to anyone else on behalf of a client. Clients will remember that the representative lied for them in the past and may expect them to lie bigger and better for them in the future. It is better to be labeled as uncooperative than labeled as a liar.

3. Respect the intellectual property rights of others and acknowledge the sources of information obtained from others.

In theory, public relations professionals should have more respect than the general public for laws concerning plagiarism and copyright because so many of those professionals entered the field after working in journalism. The reality, however, is that plagiarism and copyright violation are serious problems in the field, and they are becoming larger problems because of the availability of information from the Internet. Many of the violations are not intentional, but instead result from public relations professionals not being as familiar with intellectual property law (see Chapter 11) as they should be.

4. Act promptly and in good faith to correct erroneous communications for which he or she is responsible.

A communicator is obligated to correct errors once they have been recognized. If the communicator realizes a mistake has been made and acts quickly to correct it, the original mistake is not considered a violation of any ethical code.

One common example occurs in the case of annual reports, which is often the largest and most expensive printing project of the year. After the report goes to the printer, the responsible employee may find a typographical error that changes perception of the company's financial performance. If the employee acts in good faith and corrects it before it goes into print, or arranges for a corrected page to be printed and included in the report, the original error is not considered false and misleading information. But if the employee were to say, "It's too late now" or "It will cost too much to reprint it," that does not meet the requirement. In order to meet the requirement, however, the original mistake must have been unintentional.

5. Deal fairly with clients and employers—past, present, and potential—including the safeguarding of confidences and privacy rights.

In an agency setting, employees cannot share information from one client with another client or with anyone else. In general, employees are expected to keep information secret until the client directs them to release it. However, although the PRSA and the IABC expect agency representatives to honor confidentiality agreements with their clients, such agreements do not prohibit professional communicators from "blowing the whistle" on a client or employer who is doing something illegal or testifying in court about a client or employer's illegal activity.

In terms of whistle-blowing or voluntarily providing information to law-enforcement or regulatory agencies, this clarification is significant not only for what is says but also for what it does not say. Although it says a public relations representative *may* blow the whistle, it does not say that he or she *must* blow the whistle. If a public relations representative wants to voluntarily provide information about a company doing something illegal, but is not sure if such action is appropriate, he or she could find justification in the professional association's concept of "serving the public interest."

Public relations representatives must also be prepared to deal with situations in which providing information about the illegal activities of clients or employers is *not* voluntary. Many receive subpoenas to testify in court or grand jury hearings, in which case they are required to provide information and cannot claim "privilege" (see Chapter 11).

6. Be prepared to publicly and truthfully identify clients or employers on whose behalf communication is made.

This provision is based on what the PRSA once called the "mystery client clause." Public relations representatives are not required to identify their clients at the front end of every communication (even though they should in most cases), nor do ethical codes require them to do so. But codes do require public relations representatives to identify their clients or employers when asked, especially when the inquiry comes from the media. Put simply, there is no such thing as a confidential client. Public relations representatives are required to keep their clients' information secret, but cannot keep their identities secret. As soon as someone requests that information, the representatives are ethically required to identify for whom they are working.

Another example is the fictional client. Organizations involved in controversial public issues sometimes create fictional organizations to which they can attribute position statements or research data to support their view. Neither the PRSA nor the IABC would approve of such a tactic, however, and in nearly every case media scrutiny would eventually uncover the deception and the organization's credibility would suffer long-term damage.

A third example is found in public relations representatives failing to identify themselves when they participate in on-line discussion groups. Monitoring and participating in email discussions and on organizational bulletin boards can be a valuable method of gathering information about how an organization is perceived by the public. There are ethical considerations, however. For example, if a public relations representative simply monitors discussions without participating (the slang term is *lurking*), that person is under no legal or ethical obligation to inform participants of his or her on-line presence. But if a public relations representative contributes to the discussion in a manner that may pose a conflict of interest, that person is obligated to identify himself or herself. For instance, if the public relations representative for a consumer product company participates in a discussion group, he or she should not recommend the company's products without also disclosing the fact that he or she is employed by that company. Disclosing that fact is not only the ethical thing to do but it is also advantageous. Many participants will not consider it an intrusion, but will instead appreciate the fact that an "expert" is available to answer their questions. The same principle of self-identification applies to the issue of corporate blogs and other opportunities to deceive others in cyberspace. Through the late 1990s and early 2000s, for example, many Hollywood movie studios were caught by movie critics and consumer advocacy groups posting fake movie reviews (all positive, of course) on the Internet. In 2005, for example, a major cosmetics manufacturer was embarrassed when it was revealed that a blog published under the name of "Claire"—supposedly one of its loyal customers who had nothing but good things to say about the company's products—was actually published by its public relations agency.

7. Sever relationships with any client or employer if such relationship requires conduct contrary to ethical guidelines.

Earlier in this chapter, Lee Baker provided a scenario about a public relations representative with orthodontist bills, a mortgage, and a wife thinking about divorce. Recent graduates may not have mortgages, orthodontist bills, or spouses thinking about divorce, but they do often have apartment rent, car payments, and student loans.

The "Shall Nots" of Public Relations

The public relations professional SHALL NOT:

1. Take any action that interferes with the processes of government or law enforcement.

Public relations representatives must cooperate with any regulatory agency or any type of legal investigation of their clients or employers, and in doing so they are not violating rules about the release of confidential information. In addition to being unethical not to cooperate with law-enforcement investigations, it may also be labeled as "contempt of court" or "obstruction of justice" and may result in a criminal prosecution.

2. Take any action that harms the integrity of a constructive working relationship with the news media.

Examples of conduct that would violate this clause include (a) giving to media representative gifts of more than nominal value, (b) providing journalists with trips or travel opportunities that are unrelated to legitimate news interests, and (c) attempting to secure media coverage by connecting it to the organization's advertising activities.

With respect to the first example, the dividing line between souvenirs associated with a news event (such as hats, t-shirts, and other specialty items that most journalists readily accept) and gifts (such as golf balls and desk accessories) is often blurry. Even though there may not be a quid-pro-quo involved, what must be avoided is the *appearance* of any impropriety. Allen Parsons, executive editor of the *Wilmington Star News* in Wilmington, North Carolina, has a simple rule about his reporters accepting such gifts: "It is easy to sell your integrity, but impossible to buy it back," he says.

One business editor of a daily newspaper recalled a previous employer's rule that accepting food from a news source was permissible provided the quantity was small enough to be consumed in one day. That policy presented a dilemma for the newspaper staff when one news source provided a quart of whiskey.

The second example occurs frequently in travel and tourism marketing. Resorts and theme parks are often criticized by competitors, journalism critics, and media watchdog groups for paying for airline tickets and hotel accommodations for travel writers in order to influence them to write favorable stories. Although some acceptance of these expenses falls within the guidelines of "legitimate news interest," such as the opening of a new resort or theme park, the conflict centers on the degree of excess. The marketing departments at Disneyland in California and Walt Disney World in Florida are frequent targets for such criticism because of the lavish nature of their press gatherings.

Most media organizations have policies dealing with the potential problems caused by employees from accepting gifts or meals from potential news sources. Some policies forbid the acceptance of even nominal gifts; others leave it up to the employees' judgment but caution that gifts should be nominal and infrequent.

One example of the latter is the policy of the New York Times Company; the policy applies not only to the flagship paper but also to all of the local newspapers the company owns. The policy acknowledges that courtesies such as gifts and meals have an important place in American business, but that the role of the journalist requires a higher standard. "Gifts accepted from or given to anyone with whom the company does business should be promotional in nature and nominal in value," the policy states. "A business courtesy should not be accepted if it does not fall within the guidelines described above or if the donor expects something in return, may be attempting to gain an unfair advantage, may be attempting to influence the employee's judgment, or if acceptance creates the appearance of any of the foregoing. Employees should also avoid a pattern of accepting frequent gifts or business courtesies from the same persons or companies." To clarify the terms *promotional* and *nominal,* the policy states that "a ballpoint pen with a company logo would satisfy the test of being promotional in nature and of nominal value. An inscribed gold wristwatch may be promotional in nature but would unlikely be nominal in value and, therefore, would not be acceptable."

In his broadcast news textbook, Mitchell Stephens wrote, "Reporters shouldn't accept any gifts from the people they may have to write about—no bottles of Scotch, vacations, fountain pens, or dinners. Reporters don't even want to be in a position of having to distinguish between a gift and a bribe. Return them all with a polite thank-you."

The Radio and Television News Directors Association's Code of Ethics admonishes members to "strive to conduct themselves in a manner that protects them from conflicts of interest, real or perceived," and "decline gifts or favors which would influence or appear to influence their judgments."

In addition to being unethical for journalists to accept free travel or other considerations, it is also unethical for public relations representatives to make such an offer.

Even newspaper executives who establish such policies for travel sections disagree on what can be accepted. On one extreme are the more traditional journalists who forbid the acceptance of any travel assistance, claiming that if the story is worth covering, it is worth paying the travel expenses of the reporters who cover it. On the other extreme are those who claim that a newspaper cannot produce a good travel section without accepting assistance from the resorts and theme parks they cover.

In addition to the travel sections of daily newspapers, travel magazines are another source of media coverage for resorts and theme parks, and a variety of philosophies can be found among their editorial policies.

Prominent travel magazines, such as *Conde Naste Traveler* and *Travel & Leisure,* employ experienced full-time staff writers and established freelancers who are not allowed to accept subsidies in any form. But other travel publications allow their staff writers to accept free travel and purchase stories from freelancers without asking about how much of their travel was subsidized. In between the two extremes are those publications that allow staff writers and freelancers to accept free transportation and accommodations, but only under certain conditions, such as accepting only those arrangements that are available to all media representatives attending the same event, and agreements that no promises as to the content or tone of resulting stories is expected or implied.

Resort destinations, such as Walt Disney World and other major theme parks, are common targets for criticism because of their extravagant spending on media events in which they pay the travel expenses and provide free hotel rooms and food for reporters covering events. The New York Times Company, which may have the most rigid ethical guidelines in the journalism business, deplores the practice and claims it "debases the profession" and "creates the impression that the entire press is on the take."

The Associated Press provides specific guidelines for its newspaper sportswriters who travel to cover college and professional sports teams. Those rules include a requirement that newspapers pay all expenses up front for writers' transportation, accommodations, and food; or if that is not practical, the newspaper will reimburse the team for such expenses. Newspapers are also expected to reimburse the team for media room services such as long-distance telephone calls or facsimile service. The guidelines also warn against the potential conflicts of interest that occur when reporters are asked to contribute articles to media guides or other team publications, or when they appear as guests on television and radio talk shows.

The third example is the making of an advertising commitment to a publication in exchange for news coverage: The news source agrees to purchase a minimum amount of advertising, and in exchange the publication produces only positive stories. The strategy of "buy an ad, get a story" was once common among trade publications, but the idea of purchasing advertising space in exchange for new coverage is outdated. Some less-reputable publications may suggest such an arrangement, but those who do are unlikely to be the most respected in a field. Serious news publications and television stations would never agree to such an arrangement, and most reporters and editors resent the suggestion that major advertisers are entitled to special treatment.

The phenomenon may still be found in some travel and recreational publications. Typical examples are found in the annual "Top X" lists that some publications publish, such as a travel publication's list of the top 10 resort destinations in the country, or a golf magazine's list of the top 50 golf courses in a certain state. What they are implying (and what most readers infer) from these lists is that they have sent reporters to check out those resorts and golf courses in order to make the comparisons and then vote on how to rank-order entries on the list. In reality, in most cases, a Top X list is not based on merit, but more likely is a list of the publication's Top X advertisers.

An important clarification of this clause dealing with "the integrity of a constructive working relationship with the news media" is that it does not prohibit the reasonable giving or lending of products or services to media representatives who have a legitimate news interest. The emphasis here is on the key phrases "reasonable giving or lending" and "legitimate news interest." Examples of allowable behavior would include:

a. Loaning an automobile to an automotive writer who has been assigned to write a story about that car would be allowable because the car is not being given to the writer, but instead it is being loaned for a short period of time. Because the writer has been assigned to write the review (most public relations representatives confirm such assignments with an editor), it is considered "legitimate news interest."

b. Allowing a theater critic to attend the performance of a play would be considered legitimate news interest, although most theater critics, like movie critics and restaurant critics, prefer to do their work anonymously in order to avoid extra attention.

c. In the case of a consumable product such as toothpaste—a circumstance in which it would be impractical to ask for it back—the public relations or marketing representative should provide the journalist only with enough of a sample for them to make a judgment.

3. Use misleading or manipulative communications tactics on behalf of a client or employer.

Deceptive or misleading information can influence audiences to make bad decisions, and when they discover the deception and its source, they will be resentful and will likely become more negative toward the cause than they were before. Public relations professionals who are caught releasing false or misleading information, whether it is intentional or unintentional, suffer from damage to their credibility and typically find such damage difficult to repair.

During war time, the U.S. military often engages in "disinformation," which is the deliberate release of false information in order to deceive or mislead the enemy. Few media outlets would knowingly go along with such a strategy, but they occasionally are fooled themselves and find themselves as accomplices. When businesses attempt such a strategy, they will find the media much less likely to be fooled into participating in the deception. When reporters catch on to the disinformation, not only will they expose it but they will also be less likely to trust information from that organization in the future.

When asked a question they cannot answer for legal or competitive reasons, public relations representatives should explain the reason or reasons they cannot respond and indicate when they might be able to respond. Most reporters will understand and respect the legal reasons, but they will not understand nor respect "no comment" or deception in any form.

4. Condone any illegal or unethical behavior on the part of their clients, employers, superiors, or subordinates.

Although they are seldom qualified to provide specific legal advice, public relations professionals have an obligation to their clients to advise them about the ethical implications of their actions. By not providing such advice at the appropriate time, public relations representatives may be viewed as supporting or endorsing such activity. On a larger scale, public relations professionals have an obligation to society to act in the public interest by not condoning the unethical behavior of others.

In matters involving law enforcement, such as fraud, insider trading, or misleading or deceptive advertising, individuals need not be directly involved in a criminal activity to find themselves in legal trouble. Having knowledge of illegal activity and failing to report it may result in an individual being charged with obstruction of justice or being an "accessory after the fact."

5. Guarantee the achievement of specified results beyond the public relations representative's direct control.

It is permissible to guarantee to clients such conditions as quality of service, degree of effort, and methods utilized, because those are examples of conditions within the control of the public relations agencies. Agencies can, for example, guarantee their clients that a research project will be done ethically and responsibly, will use the most up-to-date technology or methods, or will achieve a certain sample size. The agencies cannot, however, guarantee what the results of the research project will reveal.

As for the outcome of communications activities, the agency cannot promise that the client will be profiled in an industry publication, that a client will see an increase in product sales, or that proposed government legislation with the potential to affect the client will be passed or defeated. All of those conditions can be listed as objectives, but they cannot be guaranteed because they are largely outside of the agency's control.

6. Perform work for any client or employer that causes a conflict—real or perceived—with the interests of another client or employer, unless full disclosure is made to and approval is given by all parties involved.

In agency work, this means that an agency cannot represent clients that compete against each other. Some agencies wishing to keep two competing clients will attempt to skirt the issue by appointing separate account teams and forbidding them to discuss details of their work with each other. Such a strategy may sound good in theory, but even though they have separate account executives and they do a good job of not talking to each other about those two clients, the agency has only one art department, one media department, and one research department. The prospects of complete confidentiality between the two account teams is unrealistic.

7. Perform work for any client or employer that causes a conflict—real or perceived—with the professional's own personal interest.

One example of this conflict involves the employee who works full time in the public relations department of a company (or a public relations agency) and performs freelance work in his or her spare time. The individual should not accept as a client any organization that competes with his or her full-time employer unless both the client and the employer are aware of the situation and both agree to it.

This would also apply to the case of an independent public relations consultant or employee at a public relations agency whose personal interest—such as membership in a special-interest group—is in conflict with the interests of a client. An example would be a consultant working for a chemical company who is also an officer of an environmental watchdog group. If the watchdog group is involved in litigation against or is otherwise targeting the chemical company, the consultant must either cease working for the chemical company or resign his or her position in the watchdog group. As much as he or she may claim the ability to remain neutral, at some point he or she will be caught in the crossfire between the two parties and will be forced to choose which loyalty is more important. It is best to make such a decision before a conflict arises.

8. Accept financial consideration from anyone other than a client or employer without the knowledge and approval of the employer and/or affected clients.

This provision eliminates the concept of kickbacks, meaning that all the money a public relations professional makes should be made "above the table." An example that often occurs in agency work is that a regular client will ask the agency to do something that it cannot do because it lacks the staff or the technical expertise, so the agency refers the client to another agency or an independent consultant. At some point in the future, that other agency reciprocates by referring different clients back to the first agency. Although there is a great deal of competition in agency work, there is also much cooperation, and such referrals back and forth are quite common. What the ethical guidelines frown on, however, is the offer or acceptance of commissions, kickbacks, or other financial consideration in exchange for referrals. This restriction also applies to printers, independent contractors, or any other vendors involved in the development of communications programs.

Another example is in an organization's relationship with publications. Newspapers seldom publish news stories as they are written by public relations representatives, but specialty magazines with limited staffs often ask public relations representatives to write feature articles that are basically expanded versions of news releases. But because the public relations representative is already being paid by his or her employer or client for writing such an article, he or she could not later accept the same fee the magazine would pay one of its freelance writers. Accepting the fee is an example of **double-dipping**—being paid twice for the same work. A similar example would be accepting a speaker's fee in exchange for a presentation at a professional or industry conference if the presentation was associated with the representation of a client or employer. But accepting fees for writing an article or speaking to a group would be acceptable if both the client/employer and party providing the fee were aware of the compensation arrangement and neither stated an objection.

9. Intentionally damage the professional reputation of another professional communicator.

One example of this scenario occurs when public relations agencies are competing for a new account and the representatives of those agencies are asked to comment on the abilities of competing firms. "What can you do for us that the other agencies can't?" is a tricky question but it can be safely addressed if the person responding speaks only of his or her own agency's ability and does not mention other agencies by name. He or she can respond that the agency "has the best research staff in town" or "has the widest range of staff talent" and still remain on solid ground. But if the client asks specific questions about the competency of a specific competitor, it is best not to say anything at all. There is little to be gained and much to be lost by launching specific criticisms at competitors.

TRENDS AND ISSUES

Hacks versus Flacks

Historically, public relations professionals and the journalists with whom they work have had an adversarial relationship, but often the negative feelings are stronger on the side of the journalists. Although some public relations professionals tend to dislike and distrust journalists, it is more common to find journalists who dislike and distrust public relations professionals. Many experienced journalists, especially business reporters, look at public relations representatives as "hired guns" who use misleading and deceptive tactics in order to promote their clients' positives and downplay their negatives. The perception is one that lingers from the previous century, when the connotation of the public relations profession was that of highly paid media consultants who were hired to protect clients by disseminating half-truths and misinformation.

Journalists Sound Off about the Public Relations Profession

Why do journalists continue to dislike and distrust public relations professionals today? Their criticisms fall into two major areas:

1. In crisis or "bad news" situations, journalists complain that public relations representatives will stonewall and not release information that the journalists believe they have a right to access and report. Many times, journalists are operating in a "people have a right to know" mindset, and they expect public relations representatives to answer every question they ask or take them to someone who can answer those questions. They often look at the public relations representatives as barriers standing between them and higher-ranking organizational leaders. That complaint is sometimes a valid one; public relations representatives may appear to be stonewalling and not releasing information that should be released and serving as barriers between the media representatives and organizational leaders.

But other times, public relations representatives cannot answer questions for legitimate reasons. They might have the information the media seeks, but for legal or ethical reasons cannot yet release it. In other situations, public relations representatives cannot answer media questions—not because they do not want to, but because they do not yet know the answers themselves. One veteran government spokesperson, speaking to reporters on this subject, explained, "You want what you want when you want it, but I'm going to give you what I have when I have it."

When journalists or other individuals pose questions that are "loaded," inflammatory, or include incorrect information, spokespersons should avoid responses such as "That's nonsense" or "That's so ridiculous I won't dignify it with a response." A more

rational response is "That is untrue" or "That is not correct." When asked a question he or she is unable to answer, the spokesperson should avoid the standard "no comment" and instead provide the reason for not being able to answer the question and, if possible, the day or time at which more information might be available, such as "after the families have been notified," "next week," or "after the investigation is concluded." Some journalists claim that public relations representatives lie to them, engage in misleading or deceptive tactics, or provide them with "misinformation." That does happen, but not nearly as often as the first scenario in which the public relations representative stonewalls or provides no information at all.

2. The other major criticism that journalists have about public relations representatives is that they exaggerate the importance of an organization's products, services, or sponsored events or programs. Some cynical journalists use the derogatory term *flack* to refer to public relations representatives guilty of such conduct, and, as mentioned in Trends and Issues section of Chapter 1, they use verbs such as *flack* and *hype* to describe the work of the profession.

Most experienced public relations professionals know better than to be guilty of either of the above violations; they understand that the working relationships they have with the journalists who cover their organizations are too valuable to risk with questionable conduct. The problem is that many journalists lump together the good public relations professionals with the bad and paint all of them with the same broad and negative brush.

Public Relations Professionals Sound Off about Journalists

What criticisms do public relations professionals make about journalists? The first is that journalists sometimes ignore or underreport positive stories about the representative's client or employer, while emphasizing or overreporting the negative. As an example, public relations representatives may be frustrated by the media's lack of interest in a client's charitable contribution or worthwhile community project, but if the client faces an environmental crisis, journalists are more than willing to report that story.

The second criticism that public relations representatives often launch at journalists is that even when they do cover the "good news" stories, they get the facts wrong. Even consumers of news who have never worked in the public relations profession can recall cases in which they have attended a public event and then seen the media coverage on television or in the newspaper and asked, "Was that reporter at the same event I was at?" While little more than annoying to a consumer of news with no connection to the story, inaccurate or misleading news coverage of an event is very frustrating to the public relations representative who planned or promoted the event.

What Research Reveals

Taking those criticisms into consideration and examining the anecdotal evidence, the research indicates the reality is quite different. Numerous research efforts concerning the working relationships between the public relations and journalism professions indicate that the animosity or distrust the two parties exhibit for each other is more likely to be based on conditioning and role expectation than on experience or substance. When asked why they dislike or distrust public relations professionals, many journalists are able to provide examples of being lied to or stonewalled, but those examples are often exaggerated. Some say, "I'm a journalist; it's in my job description that I'm supposed to dislike public relations people." They look at it as part of the role they play to dislike public relations representatives and to be skeptical about what they say and do. Public relations professionals would respond similarly if asked to explain why they dislike and distrust journalists. But on both sides of the relationship, the animosity is more likely to be based on conditioning and role expectation than on substance or experience.

The working relationship between journalists and public relations professionals is one that is interdependent, but not necessarily reciprocal; at times the relationship appears to be unbalanced. To a large degree, each side depends on the other. Public relations representatives depend heavily on the journalists—especially the business reporters—to communicate to their external publics. And although journalists depend on public relations representatives, it is not a balanced relationship. Part of the job of a public relations representatives is to help the journalists do their jobs better, but it is not the responsibility of journalists to assist public relations representatives.

Public relations professionals often find themselves in a position in which they must choose between the interests of two parties for which they work: a client or employer, and the media that cover that client or employer. Likewise, journalists also find themselves conflicted between two sets of interests: those of his or her employer, and the audiences that depend on the media for information.

Although the relationship between a public relations representative for a nonprofit organization and journalist can sometimes be adversarial, the problem is much more serious in the cases of corporate public relations professionals and business journalists. Journalists covering business issues tend to have a lower opinion of the public relations industry than other categories of journalists.

They are reluctant to admit it, but business reporters also depend more than other journalists on public relations representatives. Without public relations representatives to provide story ideas, publications such as the *Wall Street Journal* and *Business Week* simply could not fill all of their pages. Rebecca Madiera, the public relations director for Pepsi, describes the relationship as being similar to a game of tennis: "You're on opposite sides of the net, but it's the only way to play the game."

What Public Relations Professionals Can Do to Help

What can a public relations professional do to improve the relationship? The list is a simple one:

1. Be thoroughly knowledgeable of how their clients or employers operate. With such knowledge, public relations representatives will be in a better position to speak confidently about their clients or employers and will be more trusted by journalists with whom they work. In highly technical fields, public relations representatives may not be able to become experts on the technical side of what the company does, but they need to know who the company's experts are and make them available to media.
2. Make themselves available to respond to media inquiries, regardless of how busy they are or how inconvenient the timing. By making sure a qualified spokesperson is always available, an organization can avoid reading in the newspaper or hearing on the television news that "representatives of the XYZ Company were not available to comment."
3. Have a working knowledge of how the media operates and understand the difference in how

print media and broadcast media approach stories and their differing deadlines.

4. Hold a limited number of news conferences—only when necessary. As explained in Chapter 6, simpler methods such as news releases are often more practical.

5. Anticipate crises and know what is going on in the organization. Public relations representatives must be "in the loop" and be aware of potential problems. They should know what keeps the company's CEO awake at night and constantly be anticipating what might happen next.

6. Avoid playing favorites among media or taking any action that creates the perception of playing favorites. A public relations representative who leaks a story to a friend or favored journalist risks alienating other journalists, and journalists who are embarrassed by competing newspaper or television stations may harbor that resentment and strike back later. A public relations representative should avoid making personal friendships with journalists who cover his or her organization, or if one does develop, make sure it does not affect the working relationship. Although it is advantageous to have a respectful and cordial relationship with the journalists who cover their clients, it is more important to maintain some degree of professional distance.

CASE STUDY 12A

Hill and Knowlton and the United States Catholic Conference

Public relations firms are often criticized when they accept clients involved in public controversies. In the early 1990s, for example, Hill and Knowlton was criticized for accepting the United States Catholic Conference as a client for one of its antiabortion campaigns. Many of the firm's employees objected to the idea, and two felt strongly enough to resign.

After months of media criticism, the agency established a policy that any employee who objected to the campaign did not have to work on it. That was an easy situation to resolve for a large organization such as Hill and Knowlton, a worldwide firm with thousands of employees; it could easily find enough workers to staff the account. The situation would be far different for a small firm that may only have five or six employees and requires every staff member work on every account.

CASE STUDY 12B

The Wall Street Scandals That Changed America

Any study of ethics must include a detailed look at Enron. The mention of the name Ken Lay can cause emotion, and former Enron employees expressed "feeling cheated" when the former Enron Chief Executive Officer and Chairman, Kenneth Lee Lay, died on July 5, 2006, months before his scheduled sentencing. He died of a heart attack while vacationing in Colorado.

Lay was found guilty of 10 counts, each with a 5- to 10-year sentence in the company's corporate abuse and accounting fraud case that has been called the largest in history and perhaps the most complex. The company that had employed 21,000 employees collapsed with the former blue chip stock shares reduced to pennies in the Enron Creditors Recovery Corporation. The result included directors paying personal sums of money and the dissolving of the Arthur Anderson accounting firm.

The Enron story became the subject of a best-selling book, *The Smartest Guys in the Room*, and a feature film of the same name, and University of Wisconsin Professor of Business Denis Collins wrote the book *Behaving Badly: Ethical Lessons from Enron*. Business journalists continue to discuss the collapse and what it means to us today and what it means to us tomorrow.

American viewers were shocked in 2002 and 2003 when television news programs showed images of men and women in handcuffs and other suspected criminals testifying in courtrooms and congressional committee hearings.

The Enron Story

Starting as a pipeline company in 1985, Enron grew quickly to be the world's largest and most powerful energy broker in electricity and commodity trading. Following the deregulation of the electrical power markets, Enron found new ways to make money through contracts that made promises as the middleman. By being a part of the contract, Enron collected money by predicting and using the difference between the selling prices and the customers' prices.

As the contracts became more complex, stock soared and customers were pleased to avoid the problems associated with weather and interest rates. When the contracts to deliver the commodities could not meet the demand of the Enron contracts to buy the products, Enron creatively found ways to manage the risk and growing debt. Although Enron did have safeguards in place and although some of the losses may have eventually been paid, the company ignored basic business and accounting rules and found ways to form and maintain a culture that allowed corruption and greed to exist. The company created a system of extensive bonuses and hired aggressive employees who pushed for brutal competitiveness and continued growth. Questions from employees and auditors were considered disloyal and resulted in demotions, fear, and loss of jobs. This same method of growth caused the company to collapse under the growing hidden debt and increasing sales of promise. Executives covered up false records and continued to earn large, inflated, up-front bonuses.

One method that covered debt included the creation of partnerships that shifted Enron's growing debt off the books. Taking a loan would have reduced profits, but creating partnerships, without complete ownership, allowed the company to avoid reporting the debt information. The loan from the partners was used to report a profit. This allowed the company to take all the profit now without concern for the debt growing in the created partnership companies. If required to cover its positions with cash, the company did not have enough money, but the public continued to be unaware of the financial picture and continued to support the company.

Vice President Sherron Watkins served as an anonymous whistleblower, warning that future accounting scandals could cause the company to ruin. Warnings were ignored by companies such as Arthur Anderson, at that time one of the largest accounting firms. Anderson's job as auditor was to guarantee investors they could trust the information on Enron's financial reports. At the time, Anderson had other business deals with Enron, including finding and selling consulting services and performing accounting services. Because of these conflicts, the Securities and Exchange Commission (SEC) ruled that companies may no longer perform these services.

Anderson made headlines as the company shredded Enron documents. It became the first accounting firm convicted of a felony obstruction of justice. The company is barred from doing audit work. Banks, including J. P. Morgan Chase and CitiGroup, had loaned Enron money and lost hundreds of millions of dollars. As Enron continued to report losses and overstated earnings, a future possible merger with another company was dropped.

Thousands of Enron employees were unemployed as a result of the scandal. Employees lost money invested in the company and matched with company stock. Employees had been encouraged to invest their 401(k) plans in the company and felt betrayed by company executives when they lost their retirement funds. The company froze the plan, which prevented employees from saving their money, as Enron stock continued to decline to its final junk status.

Even as executives told a positive company story to employees, reporters, and others, they began cashing their stock. Each executive earned millions in addition to their salaries and cashed large amounts in stock before the decline. Lay resigned but reportedly had millions in protected investments. Former Chief Financial Officer Andrew Fastow was ousted from Enron when the SEC began its conflict of interest search into the partnerships Fastow created and controlled. He was indicted on wire and mail fraud, money laundering, and conspiracy to inflate profit. Others faced charges, including charges that executives created ways to make illegal millions in contract promises, including ones that worsened the California energy crisis.

Following the initial disclosure, reporters looked at all areas as contributors to the problem. This included the executives, company culture, board members, auditors, investors, securities analysts, the SEC, and employees.

WorldCom and ImClone

Enron was far from alone in the scandals. WorldCom, a large long-distance and data provider, helped the company's bottom line through improper accounting methods that hid debt.

The ImClone scandal was another example of fraud, obstruction of justice, and insider trading. In addition to the ImClone executives, Martha Stewart served 5 months in jail for selling her stock before the Food and Drug Administration announcement was public that it was rejecting the drug Erbitux.

After a ruling separating parts of Merrill Lynch, the SEC now requires analysts to disclose conflicts of interest. A new federal statute, the Sarbanes-Oxley Act, was signed into law in July 2002. The law makes it harder for corporations to mislead their stockholders and employees, and makes it easier for government agencies to hold individual executives accountable.

Lessons Learned

Leaders of many other major U.S. companies—and the public relations executives who advise them—learned a number of lessons from the Wall Street scandals. Many of them are scheduling more in-house training for their communicators, dusting off previously neglected ethics policies, and watching out for possible red flags in annual reports and other financial documents.

CASE STUDY 12C

Another Black Eye For FEMA

In October 2007, a series of wildfires swept across southern California, causing billions of dollars in property damage and leaving thousands of families homeless. The Federal Emergency Management Association planned a news conference at its Washington, DC, offices to brief reporters on the agency's response to the disaster, but due to the short notice and other miscommunications, FEMA officials found themselves talking to an empty room. Rather than cancel the briefing, FEMA official Pat Philbin gathered agency employees to pose as journalists and ask softball questions, such as, "Are you pleased with FEMA's response so far?" Reporters were invited to listen to the news conference by telephone but not allowed to ask questions, and television stations were later given videotaped copies of the news conference without being told about its artificial nature.

Once the deception was exposed, FEMA claimed it was Philbin's idea alone and that Deputy Director Harvey Johnson, who conducted the briefing, did not recognize FEMA employees as the individuals asking the questions. FEMA Director David Paulison, Homeland Security Secretary Michael Chertoff, and President George W. Bush all condemned the event as "unacceptable."

The fake news conference fiasco came just two years after a much bigger FEMA fiasco—the botched reaction to Hurricane Katrina. The Category 5 storm was one of the most expensive and deadly to hit the mainland United States, coming ashore near New Orleans in late August 2005.

The storm killed more than 1,800 people (including those killed on Caribbean islands in the storm's path) and caused $86 billion in property damage. Americans were horrified by media reports of human tragedy and suffering as well as reports of damage, plundering, and rapes. Many of these reports were later reported to be false and misleading. Communication systems were down and reporters were at a severe disadvantage going into the damaged and dangerous areas. There was a series of miscommunications between FEMA, city government officials in New Orleans, and state officials in Louisiana. Although all of the parties shared in the blame, FEMA took most of the criticism, and critics used the scenario to portray the Bush administration as callous and uncaring toward the people effected. The slow and ineffective response led to the resignation of then head of FEMA, Director Michael D. Brown.

For two years following Katrina, ongoing news coverage of the FEMA mistakes and oversights, most of them related to unnecessary bureaucracy, created the agency's new organizational structure. FEMA was once an independent agency, but after becoming part of the Department of Homeland Security following the September 11, 2001, terrorist attacks, many of its new leaders were political appointments with little or no previous experience in disaster recovery.

Following the Katrina disaster and months of negative media coverage, many congressional leaders called for the agency to be removed from underneath the Homeland Security umbrella and once again made an independent agency. The fake news conference faux pas in 2007 made the agency's public image even worse.

DISCUSSION QUESTIONS

1. Professional organizations such as the Public Relations Society of America (PRSA) and the International Association of Business Communicators (IABC) have rejected suggestions that they develop formal licensing programs for public relations professionals. Should they reconsider this possibility? Why or why not? If you were a member of one of these organizations, would you support an effort to develop such a program, even if it meant the organization would have to expand its office staff and increase annual membership fees? Explain your answer.

2. Read Case Study 12A, Hill and Knowlton and the United States Catholic Conference. Was this situation handled fairly and ethically? Support your answer. What would you have done differently if you were in a leadership position in the agency?

For each of the following scenarios, consider the list of "shalls" and "shall nots" provided in this chapter.

3. You are the communications manager for a local bank, and in your spare time you are also a freelance writer specializing in designing corporate annual reports. You receive a phone call from the representative of another bank in the same city and he asks if you will contract with his bank to design its annual report. Is this permissible under the ethical guidelines explained in this chapter? Why or why not? Are there any circumstances under which you could accept this client?

4. You have been hired as executive director of a political action committee formed to lobby in favor of legalized abortion. The PAC is funded by the National Federation of Hospitals, but the association insists that you do not reveal its participation in or funding of the PAC for fear of negative public reaction. Can you represent that PAC within the ethical guidelines explained in the chapter? Why or why not?

5. You are a student majoring in public relations at Enormous State University. During the course of your studies at ESU, you accept an internship at a large downtown public firm. Your supervisor asks you to call local businesses, identify yourself as a student working on a research project for a class, and ask those companies what public relations services they would be most likely to use in the following year so that she can call them later and solicit their business. Would that be a violation of the ethical guidelines? Why or why not?

6. You are working for a public relations agency called MegaHype. One of your clients is a small computer software company. You find out from one of your contacts at the company that it is about to be bought out by a larger national software manufacturer and that the stock value is expected to double overnight. You call your broker and buy 1,000 shares. Have you committed any ethical violation? Explain.

7. You are working for a national chain of discount stores. The company has been the subject of numerous news stories that report that its clothes are made by child labor in sweatshops located in developing countries. The company claims to have improved working conditions for the children in the factories and is now being endorsed by a watchdog group called the Worldwide Child Labor Coalition. The company wants you to organize a news conference to announce the changes and the endorsement. The day before the news conference, you discover that the company has made no changes in its labor conditions and that the sweatshop conditions are actually worse than the news reports have indicated. You also find out that the Worldwide Child Labor Coalition does not exist—it is just a name that someone in company headquarters has made up. If you continue to go forward with the plans for the news conference, will you be violating ethical guidelines? Explain.

8. You are a freelance public relations consultant. A major computer company asks you to bid on a short-term project to promote a new software program. The public relations director calls you and says she will get fired if the software program is not mentioned in the next issue of *Computer Age* magazine. She says the job is yours, but only if you can say with certainty that the story will appear. Can you accept this job under these conditions? Why or why not?

9. You are the public relations director for an automobile manufacturer. A writer for a major automotive magazine calls and says he is writing a review of your company's newest sports car models for an upcoming issue and wants to borrow a demo model for two or three days.

   a. Is this permissible under the ethical guidelines? Why or why not?

   b. The writer returns the car, calls you a few days later and says he has a "hot date" that weekend and wants to borrow the car again. He says, "And by the way, I've written a very positive review about the car, but I haven't turned it in to my editor yet." Do you loan him the car?

10. You have a job interview to be the public relations director for a large company. The company has an unwritten policy that it prefers married persons for executive positions. You are single, but a friend offers to loan you her wedding ring for you to wear to the interview. Would that be a violation of the ethical guidelines? Why or why not?

11. You own a nationwide public relations firm that is preparing to expand into a new city. You buy out a smaller public relations firm in that city to establish that as your new branch. The larger firm has had Delta Airlines as a client for many years. The smaller firm you have just acquired has had American Airlines as a client for many years.

    a. After the merger, can you keep both clients? Why or why not?

    b. Are there any conditions under which you could keep both clients? Explain.

12. You work for a public relations firm with an award-winning video production department. You are working on a series of reputation advertisements for one of your clients that will not be shown on television until next year. You are invited to be a "Career Day" speaker at your son's high school to talk about what public relations people do. Can you take a preliminary version of the advertisement to show the high school students? Why or why not?

13. You have recently changed jobs. A student who worked with you as an intern at your previous job calls to ask you for a letter of recommendation. But the student asks you to write the letter on the previous company's stationery because he believes it will be more prestigious than the stationery of your new employer. When you tell the student that you do not have any of the old stationery, the student says, "That's OK; I do." Will you write the letter on the stationery of the company for which you no longer work? Why or why not?

ETHICAL DILEMMA 1

The Golf Weekend

You are the public relations manager for a small non-profit organization. Part of your job is to oversee a variety of publications, such as newsletters, annual reports, and other similar items, including oversight of a competitive bidding process involving four local print shops. Unlike other nonprofits, you have a large and generous budget for these publications. Since all of the print shops do similar work in terms of quality and price, you attempt to spread out the jobs in order to be fair to all.

A sales representative for one of the four printing companies invites you to spend a weekend with him and other members of the sales staff (no funny business is implied here) at a golf resort a few hundred miles away. Greens fees at the resort are $175 per round and hotel rooms are $275 per night. The sales rep tells you that all of the golf, accommodations, and meals will be paid for by his company as a business expense.

1. Which of the following courses of action do you take?
   a. Accept the offer and show your gratitude by making sure that that company is the lowest bidder on all future printing contracts.
   b. Accept the offer but inform the sales rep that the competitive bidding process will continue and work will continue to be spread among the four printers.
   c. Accept the offer without saying anything.
   d. Decline the offer.
2. Is there a fifth alternative?

ETHICAL DILEMMA 2

Focus Groups and Date Rape

As part of a research project in an advanced public relations class, students organize focus group sessions to gather students' perceptions on the problem of sexual assault on campus. Because of the sensitive nature of the discussions, students are segregated into male and female focus group sessions. Before each session begins, the moderator informs the participants that the identities of the participants and content of the discussions are confidential.

During one of the focus group sessions for female students, several of the participants tell about a specific bar in the community at which they believe employees spiked their drinks with date-rape drugs. Although none of the women were assaulted as a result, they did recall being nauseated and were dizzy for several days.

The students' experience becomes part of the written record of the session. When the students prepare their final report, they mention the women's experience but do not elaborate on it. Several weeks after the conclusion of the research, the professor who supervised the research submits copies of the final report to the Dean of Students' office, not thinking about the impact of the information related to the date-rape drug.

The Dean of Students' office notices it, however, and is now insisting that the professor turn over the names of the students participating in the focus group sessions so he can question them, find out which bar they were referring to, and notify local law enforcement.

1. What should the professor do—turn over the names of the students (which means violating the agreement that their identities would remain confidential) or stick to the promise of confidentiality given to the participants at the beginning of the session?
2. Even though information revealed in social science research may be confidential in a general sense, it is not legally protected (such as in cases of doctor–patient privilege or lawyer–client privilege). In this case, does the interest of possibly uncovering illegal activity (such as use of a date-rape drug) take priority over the moderator's promise of confidentiality?

ETHICAL DILEMMA 3

Big Problems in Brookwood

You work in the public information office for the city government in Brookwood, a mid-size community in southeastern United States. The town is named after John Brookwood, a patriarchal figure who was one of the state's leading agricultural pioneers. He founded the town in 1848.

A representative from the mayor's office has approached you for help in planning a public event to be held in conjunction with a larger annual celebration of the town's anniversary on October 10. The purpose of the event is to name a new street and public park in honor of Mr. Brookwood.

Today is October 8. Your contact in the mayor's office provides you background information about the event and a list of the invited guests so that you can prepare a news release for local media. Among the guests will be members of the Brookwood family and several descendents of the slaves who worked on Brookwood's farms and in his home in the 1840s and 1850s. The mayor's office, however, suggests you refer to them in your news releases as descendents of Brookwood's "personal staff." Before making a decision as to which term to use, you interview a local historian who tells you that even though Mr. Brookwood was a slave owner, he was not a tyrant such as those portrayed in television documentaries about the period; he was respected and beloved.

1. Do you refer to the guests in question as "descendents of slaves" (the more accurate description) or "descendents of Mr. Brookwood's personal staff" (the mayor's preference)?

2. Can you avoid the issue by leaving them out of your news release altogether (while not dropping them off the list of guests)?

3. To what extent should you explain the historian's point of view about Mr. Brookwood being loved and respected?

4. Suppose you use the term "descendents of his personal staff" and a reporter who receives your news release calls and asks, *Does that mean they were his slaves?* How do you answer that question?

ETHICAL DILEMMA 4

Get Your Can to the Game

You're president of the Public Relations Club at your university. Your group has worked for several weeks to plan an event to benefit the food bank that feeds low-income families in your community. The event, which takes place two weeks before Thanksgiving, involves club members working with players from a minor-league hockey team to collect cans of food outside the arena before a game. Fans who bring two or more cans of food may exchange them for coupons that give them a discount on tickets for the game. Fans who already have their tickets when they come to the arena will receive discount coupons for a local restaurant. Fans will also receive one raffle ticket for each can of food they bring.

In addition to providing the discounts, the hockey team allows you to use its name in promoting the event, provides prizes for the raffle, and helps you obtain an insurance waiver required by the company that manages the arena. The night of the game, the team gives you part of the first intermission to present the raffle prizes and make a brief announcement explaining the year-round needs of the food bank.

Your goals for the event are to:

- Generate donations for the food bank.
- Create awareness of the year-round needs of the food bank.
- Get some practice in planning the event and developing publicity materials.
- Generate publicity and recognition for the Public Relations Club.

Your faculty advisor helps you prepare news releases to promote the event. The afternoon of the game, your members are busy collecting cans outside the arena. The hockey players, who were supposed to be there to help collect cans and sign autographs, are nowhere in sight. Reporters from the local daily newspaper and television station arrive and start to interview chapter members. Then three hockey players show up, and the reporters end their interviews with members and begin to interview the players.

On the 11 o'clock news that night, the television reporter who was there provides a report that does not mention the students, the Public Relations Club, or even the name of your university. Instead, the story consists mainly of interviews with the hockey players and makes it appear as though they were solely responsible for the food drive. The next morning, the daily newspaper carries a story that includes some quotes from the players, but also quotes the students and gives the Public Relations Club the majority of the credit for the event.

How should you respond, if at all, to the television news story that gave all the credit to the hockey players?

GLOSSARY OF TERMS

Double-dipping. Being paid by two different sources for the same work; unethical unless both sources are aware of the situation and neither objects.

Quid-pro-quo. A Latin term meaning "something for something." When applied to ethical situations, it refers to an agreement to exchange one product or service for another.

CHAPTER 13

INTERNATIONAL, MULTICULTURAL, AND GENDER ISSUES

GENERAL PRINCIPLES

The American workforce, predominantly white and male throughout history, has become more diverse. Women now comprise half of the workforce, and the percentage of African American, Hispanic American, and Asian American employees is increasing rapidly. The U.S. Census Bureau predicts that by 2050, there will be no ethnic majority in the United States. Although many companies report having benefited from **diversity** in terms of increased productivity and a better understanding of their customers, the phenomenon has also created problems such as resentment and the so-called white male backlash. Nevertheless, as the population of the United States continues to become more diverse, the need for what experts call **multicultural** thinking becomes even more important in the management of businesses and nonprofit organizations. That is especially true for an organization's communications professionals, who should be the leaders and advocates for multicultural thinking within an organization.

In a business, respect for diversity is important for two reasons. First, an increasing number of employees are likely to be from other cultures; and second, an increasing number of customers are likely to be from other cultures. In a nonprofit organization or social service agency, these same trends can be seen among membership and the constituents who benefit from programs and services. Professional associations, such as the Public Relations Society of America (PRSA) and the International Association of Business Communicators (IABC), are encouraging their members to become advocates for multiculturalism and diversity within the organizations for which they work.

The benefits of a diverse workforce are especially important to public relations agencies. Those benefits include enhanced ability to service accounts that require a multicultural approach and, prior to that, making the agency more attractive to potential clients that prefer business partners that share their philosophies about diversity.

Successful diversity programs benefit not only employees but also customers and potential customers. Coca-Cola, for example, sponsors an annual "Share the Dream" scholarship competition to honor Dr. Martin Luther King Jr. Kraft Foods produces a cookbook featuring African American recipes. McDonald's annually recognizes Black History Month with in-store displays honoring African American scientists and inventors. In the early 1990s, Philip Morris Companies sponsored a series of public radio documentaries on the history of blues music and a number of other topics of interest to African American audiences.

Many large organizations fail in their diversity programs when they limit the responsibility to the human resources or personnel functions. Certainly, it is commendable for organizations to follow principles such as "affirmative action" and active recruitment of minorities when they hire new employees, but the responsibility for diversity does not stop there. Other departments within the company, especially public relations and communications, must expand the concept until it is companywide. The benefits include improved morale, an increase in employee retention, and greater external recognition.

Diversity often creates conflict, but that conflict may be used for constructive purposes if it is properly channeled. A moderate degree of conflict often produces better decision making and more creative thinking. The lack of diversity (or an excess of homogeneity) in an organization's workforce leads to an excess of "group think" and the avoidance of risk.

People tend to work harder, are more productive, and will be more loyal to their employers when they feel valued. "An elephant will never feel at home in a house designed for a giraffe," says Dr. Roosevelt Thomas Jr., founder of the American Institute for Managing Diversity in Atlanta.

Without training in this area, organizational leaders make decisions based on their own cultural identity and references, assuming that others within the organization share the same values and priorities. As a result, employees from different cultural backgrounds may react differently and be viewed as uncooperative, incompetent, or unmotivated. Management consultants consistently identify a company's failure to understand cultural differences as the primary reason for the failure of companies attempting to expand into international markets. The negative outcomes of a poorly executed diversity initiative (or making no effort at all) include absenteeism, poor performance, hostility, low morale, and high turnover.

Those are only the personnel-related costs. The more serious problems include public criticism, boycotts by civil rights and other advocacy groups, and costly lawsuits. In the mid-1990s, for example, Texaco reached a $115 million out-of-court settlement of a racial discrimination lawsuit filed by former and current employees. In addition to the financial consequences, the company was subjected to intense media and public criticism for years thereafter. Similar financial penalties were incurred by restaurant chains such as Shoney's ($100 million) and Denny's ($46 million) in the 1990s.

Traditionally, executives of companies making decisions on how to communicate in other countries relied on their intuition, which often proved to be wrong. One common mistake is to assume that advertising or public relations programs that are effective with English-speaking audiences will be equally successful when translated into other languages. Because cultural barriers are often more difficult to overcome than language barriers, some companies have lost large sums of money on campaigns that turned out to be ineffective.

But to take the opposite approach is equally as faulty. Companies that look at international communications as being so different that it requires a separate communications program or staff risk losing part or all of the identity that made them successful. For example, McDonald's and Nike have distinctive logos known around the world, even in non-English–speaking countries. To abandon those graphic images in international markets would result in the loss of brand recognition.

The solution, therefore, is to find a balance between the two approaches. Many U.S. companies that send employees on long-term assignments in other countries provide **cross-cultural training** for them as well as family members who travel with them. J. Stewart Black, professor of business administration at Dartmouth College, was quoted in a *Wall Street Journal* article as claiming that American businesses lose more than $2 billion on failed assignments in foreign countries. One of the most common complaints about employees of U.S. companies operating overseas is their apparent lack of punctuality, especially in cultures that place great importance on arriving at business meetings and social events on time. Planning meetings and other events present additional problems, as business leaders in other countries are often perplexed about Americans' insistence on business meetings over breakfast and social events in the evening. In many European cultures, for example, breakfast is viewed as a leisurely activity, and evenings are to be spent at home with the family. When questions arise about customs or protocols, public relations representatives should consult the embassy or consulate representing the country in which they are working.

Another common mistake is to generalize based on demographic categories that are too broad. For example, there is no such thing as a "Hispanic culture," as individuals from Spain, Cuba, and Mexico may all speak Spanish, but they differ in many other ways. Nor is there a singular "Asian culture," as individuals from China, Taiwan, Japan, Korea, and southeast Asian countries also differ greatly in cultural matters.

RESPECT FOR CULTURAL DIFFERENCES

Many Americans raised in a mainstream environment value ideals such as competition, individual accomplishment, and recognition for achievement. In some other cultures, however, more emphasis may be placed on teamwork, cooperation, and group success; modesty may be preferred over boasting and self-promotion.

Sociological research shows that most individuals born in the United States consider themselves as "Americans" first and therefore place less importance on identifying themselves by race, gender, religion, or profession. This is not always the case with naturalized citizens, however. In many other cultures, individuals identify themselves by their membership in ethnic or religious groups rather than nationality, with these values instilled from infancy.

In addition to obviously affecting the communication process, cultural differences also affect the research process. For example, *courtesy bias*—the tendency of respondents to provide answers that will please and/or not offend the interviewer—is even more of a problem when dealing with individuals from cultures that value politeness, cooperation, and a positive attitude above sincerity. In a focus group setting, issues that Americans may consider acceptable for discussion with both men and women in the group might be frowned on in other countries or with individuals from other cultures. Those rules of politeness, although the norm for many cultures, discourage the type of constructive disagreement that makes a focus group effective. In order to prevent methodological errors and problems in language translation, many international companies hire local research firms to conduct focus groups and design and execute marketing and opinion surveys.

When making in-person presentations, it is important to speak at a pace consistent with the culture. Generally, Americans are accustomed to rapid-fire presentation of information, whereas other cultures prefer a slower pace and the opportunity to assimilate information. When in doubt, speakers should pause frequently to check for comprehension before moving on. Formality is another issue. American audiences are accustomed to speakers moving into the audience to ask impromptu questions, but many European audiences would be appalled at such informality.

Public relations representatives working in other countries should also familiarize themselves with customs and traditions of local media. In Japan, for example, representatives find it effective to work through the *kisha kurabu,* which are influential press clubs that organize news conferences and greatly increase the likelihood of positive news coverage. The clubs are well connected to government agencies, political parties, business organizations, and professional societies. A representative attempting to promote a news story without working through the appropriate press club will find it a frustrating experience and most likely ineffective.

Making Assumptions That Are Wrong and Harmful

Supervisors should avoid making assumptions about the behavior or motives of an employee, client, or customer based on his or her cultural background. Many individuals make decisions and exhibit behaviors that may at first appear to be culturally motivated, but turn out later to be for unrelated reasons. For example, if an employee declines an invitation to a social event, a supervisor might assume (incorrectly) that the individual is not comfortable in social situations outside his or her culture. The real reason, however, might be that the employee simply has other plans for that evening. Another example would be a client who rejects an idea presented by an agency representative, creating the false impression that the rejection indicates prejudice against an individual based on cultural differences. Instead of cultural differences, however, the real reason might be that the client simply does not like the idea. The only way to know for sure is to ask.

Considering an Employee's Background

Supervisors should consider an employee's cultural background when evaluating his or her work. Employers should explain the company's philosophy and the department's objectives when judging an employee's role. That does not mean that the company or department has to change its approach to accommodate the cultural beliefs of its employees, nor does it mean that those from other cultures should be expected to abandon their own beliefs in order to fit in. It means that a balance can often be found in which an organization can maintain its values and goals while the cultural beliefs of its employees are still respected.

Recognizing the Significance of Ethnic and Religious Holidays

A late December event should be labeled a "holiday party" rather than a "Christmas party" out of respect for Jewish and African American employees who may prefer to celebrate

Hanukkah or Kwanzaa. Employees from other cultures may not recognize any December holidays at all. The major religious holiday for Muslims, for example, is Ramadan. Certainly, all employees should be welcome to attend a December holiday party; they should not be forced to participate, however.

Recognizing the religious holidays of other cultures is a bit trickier, as many cultures have holidays that are unique to them. Employers must find reasonable solutions to conflicts that both respect the religious beliefs and cultures of those employees and the need to continue the pursuit of organizational objectives. One example is the importance of frequent prayer for Asian, African, and Muslim employees during their respective religious holidays, few of which coincide with U.S. holidays. Many companies provide private areas where employees can gather to pray or hold other religious rituals.

For nonreligious holidays, such as Martin Luther King Jr. Day, the Mexican celebration of Cinco de Mayo, or the "independence days" of other countries, there are ways of recognizing such days other than giving affected employees the day off. Alternatives include theme lunches or dinners.

Considering All Possible Alternatives

Change should not be forced on anyone until all other possibilities have been exhausted. American companies that employ workers who speak little or no English are inviting conflict and resentment if they require those employees to speak only English while on the job. A more practical alternative is to provide English classes for those employees who are interested, and classes in Spanish (or other appropriate languages) for supervisors or other interested employees. It is preferred that participation in such classes be voluntary rather than mandatory, but employers can provide the appropriate incentives such as advancement opportunities and recognition in performance reviews.

Publishing in Other Languages

External communications may be published in languages other than English. According to a 2000 study, more than 32 million Americans speak a language other than English at home, as compared to 23 million responding to a similar survey in 1980. In Los Angeles, Miami, and San Antonio, Spanish-language radio stations have the largest audiences. Organizations serving communities with large non-English–speaking audiences should provide company publications in all appropriate languages.

INCLUDING PERSONS WITH DISABILITIES

Most people interpret the term *culture* to refer to how groups view their values, lifestyles, religious beliefs, and entertainment preferences, but many advocacy groups contend that the concept can also be applied to persons with disabilities. That population participates in many of the same activities as those without disabilities, but they share with each other unique characteristics such as physical limitations, transportation methods, and a vocabulary of unique jargon and inside jokes.

Market research into the population with disabilities indicates that they purchase consumer products in the same quantities as persons without disabilities, but for many of these products they have specific needs, such as books printed in large print or Braille, food items to meet dietary restrictions, and automobiles that can be fitted to accommodate their physical limitations. The research also indicates that persons with disabilities tend to be brand-loyal; they find products that fit their needs and continue to purchase those brands throughout their lives.

Despite their advocacy for laws such as the Americans with Disabilities Act, many persons with disabilities do not seek special treatment; they desire only to be treated on an equal basis with others. Some are offended by what they perceive as an artificially sympathetic or patronizing attitude of persons without disabilities. As one example, some object to the modifier *challenged,* such as descriptions of persons as "mentally challenged" or "physically challenged." A person who uses a wheelchair, for example, might look at a set of concrete steps and say, "That's not a challenge—that's an impossibility." On a television sitcom, an adult who never grew beyond the height of four feet was complaining to another character about the patronizing attitude of some persons of standard height. "Do you mean when they bend over to talk to you?" the other character asked. The reply: "No, I mean when they *pick you up* to talk to you."

PAYING ATTENTION TO COMPANY PUBLICATIONS

Companies should use their employee handbooks or policy manuals as opportunities to emphasize the company's policies regarding tolerance, diversity, and equal opportunity. Annual reports and other company literature should identify multiculturalism and diversity as a business goal. Employee publications should list ethnic and religious holidays, regardless of whether they are days off.

There is some disagreement over terms used to refer to ethnic groups. Some individuals refer to themselves as *black,* whereas others prefer *African American.* The same level of disagreement exists with pairs of terms, such as *Hispanic* and *Latino,* and *Native American* and *American Indian.* There is little dispute about the term *Asian,* however, as it is always preferred over *Oriental.*

When writing about employees in company publications, public relations staff members should consult the organization's personnel department or ask the individuals involved which term they prefer. When referring to outsiders, staff members should use whichever is the prevailing term within the community or industry.

Sexism, Racism, and Other "Isms"

Words hold the language together, but they can sometimes push people apart. Editors of both internal and external publications should watch for possible problem words and phrases during the revision process. Internal and external publications should avoid, for example, words and phrases that exclude one gender or the other. When writing about concepts that apply both to men and women, the best way to structure the sentence is to combine a plural subject with a plural pronoun, such as *their.* Instead of writing "An XYZ employee is proud of his company," one should write, "XYZ employees are proud of their company." Instead of writing that the seminar "will help the employee improve his time-management skills," one should write that the seminar "will help employees improve their time-management skills."

A person's gender should not become an adjective in front of his or her title unless pertinent, so in most cases it is best to avoid references to "female engineers" or "male secretaries" unless there is some significance to the person of that gender holding that position. Also, refer to females age 18 and over as "women," not "girls."

Publications should use the terms *artificial* instead of *man-made, workforce* instead of *manpower,* and *letter carrier* instead of *mailman.* But editors should not invent silly titles or terms such as *person power.*

When writing about individuals outside of your organization, the rules may have to be bent occasionally. Most journalistic style manuals suggest following the custom of the organization about which you are writing. If an organization refers to its chief officer as "chairman," "chairperson," or "chairwoman," that is the one that outsiders should also use. Some organizations use the title "chairman," even though it may be a woman. One trend is to avoid the title and use *chair* as a verb: "Professor John Smith, who chairs the committee, said that . . . ." Failing to use gender-neutral language is not only bad public relations, but it may also be dangerous from a legal standpoint. Job descriptions that use only male pronouns have been introduced as evidence in sexual discrimination lawsuits.

The same rule about the inappropriate use of gender adjectives also applies to race. When a publication identifies someone as a "black lawyer" or a "Hispanic doctor," it is implying that it is unusual for someone of that race to achieve that professional position. Since one would seldom write "white lawyer," one should not write "black lawyer."

In choosing words, it is also important to avoid condescension. Business communication consultant Kitty O. Locker contends that comments such as "He is an asset to his race" suggests that excellence in the race is rare, and that "She is a spry 70-year-old" suggests that the writer is amazed that anyone that old can still move.

Care should also be taken in the selection of photographs. Although it is not critical that individuals shown in company newsletters and magazines reflect the demography of the organization to a precise percentage point, the general impression created should not exclude either gender nor any racial or ethnic group, but should instead suggest that diversity is the norm.

MONITORING COMPANY ADVERTISING

Watching for Stereotyping, Whether Intentional or Not

Both print and broadcast advertising should avoid **stereotyping**, which is the portrayal of members of racial or ethnic groups in an unflattering manner based on generalizations or outdated perceptions. In prime-time television, for instance, African Americans were once depicted mainly in menial occupations such as janitors or bus drivers, while Asian

Americans were often shown in scientific or technical jobs. Most ethnic stereotypes have been eliminated in entertainment programming, but they occasionally surface in advertising. In the early 1990s, for example, Irish Americans objected that the beer companies—specifically Coors, Budweiser, and Miller Brewing—producing television commercials portrayed their ancestors as heavy drinkers. Letter-writing campaigns organized by advocacy groups resulted in many of the ads being withdrawn.

In 1993, Taco Bell produced a series of television advertisements urging consumers to "run for the border." Mexican Americans called the series insulting because it added to the stereotype of Mexicans being responsible for illegal immigration and unemployment. As a result, many of the chain's restaurants were targets of consumer boycotts.

Being Careful with Translations

When translating advertising or any other materials into another language, the best method to test the accuracy of the translation is to ask a person fluent in the other language (but not the same person who did the original translation) to translate it back into English.

Many advertising and marketing textbooks include samples of famous gaffes caused by inaccurate translations of slogans and product messages. When Pepsi entered the Chinese market, its phrase "Come alive with the Pepsi generation" was translated as "Pepsi brings your ancestors back from the dead." In Germany, it read as "Come out of the grave with Pepsi." Colgate-Palmolive had to change the name of its Cue toothpaste when it was marketed in France after the company discovered that *Cue* was the title of a popular pornographic magazine in that country.

In the early 2000s, British sporting goods manufacturer Umbro named its new running shoe the "Zyklon," which market researchers believed to be the German word meaning "cyclone." Although that etymology was mostly true, the company was unaware that during World War II, the Nazis used a gas called Zyklon-B to exterminate millions of Jews in concentration camps. Needless to say, the shoes sold poorly in Germany, and after the faux pas was exposed, the company executed an expensive and embarrassing worldwide product recall and spent much of the following year apologizing.

Automobile manufacturers have also had their share of translation problems. When attempting to market automobiles in Latin America, executives at Chevrolet did not understand why the Nova would not sell, until they eventually learned that Nova in Spanish means "no go." Ford Motor Company's "Caliente" was translated into "prostitute" in Mexico, and its Fiera model was interpreted as "ugly old woman."

OTHER STEPS TO TAKE

Companies should encourage their employees to learn about the cultural backgrounds of their superiors, subordinates, and peers. Public relations departments should suggest that the company sponsor community events of a multicultural nature, rather than only those associated with the mainstream. If a company sponsors a brown bag lunch series for its employees, it should include topics of a multicultural nature. Decorators should avoid making decorating decisions that reflect the preferences of only one group.

TRENDS AND ISSUES

Women in Public Relations

In 1986, the International Association of Business Communicators (IABC) published a three-part research report titled *The Velvet Ghetto: A Report of the Increasing Percentage of Women in Public Relations and Business Communication.* The report was the culmination of a two-year study that examined the status of women in the field, including job duties, salaries, and advancement opportunities. Through the use of in-depth interviews with senior practitioners, focus group sessions with practitioners from the United States and Canada, and psychological testing of communication majors at eight U.S. universities, the researchers found that women were paid substantially less than men and that women were more likely to perceive themselves as filling technician roles rather than managerial roles.

The study suggested three reasons to explain the difficulty that women face in seeking career opportunities on an equal footing with men: (1) the perception that they are not "tough enough" to be good managers, (2) the perception that they will be distracted from their job duties by family responsibilities, and (3) the perception that they are not involved in spectator and participant sports to the degree that it will help them "network" well enough to be successful in sales, marketing, and other communications-related job functions.

More recent studies concerning the role of women in public relations produced similar findings. Between 1970 and the late 1980s, the public relations workforce increased from 27 percent women to 58 percent, according to *Public Relations Journal.* By the late 1990s, that percentage increased to 62 percent, according to the 2001 book, *Women in Public Relations.* During that same 30-year time span, the salary gap has narrowed but is still evident.

Today, women continue to enter public relations in impressive numbers, yet their role in management has not kept pace. Like women in the U.S. workforce in general, they encounter a glass ceiling to overcome when seeking leadership positions in their organizations. Professional organizations such as PRSA and IABC estimated that the field of public relations is approximately two-thirds female, but less than half of management positions are held by women. The trend toward more women entering the field is likely to continue for many years to come, as enrollment in university undergraduate programs was 70 to 80 percent female in 2006–07, according to PRSA.

CASE STUDY 13A

NAACP and the Television Networks

For nearly a decade, the National Association for the Advancement of Colored People (NAACP) has waged a campaign against the major television networks over the lack of diversity among the characters portrayed in television programming. The effort began in 1999, when the networks unveiled their 1999–2000 programming line-ups, and NAACP leaders noticed a lack of African American, Asian American, and Latino characters in leading roles. Each television season since, the organization has examined new programs and their casts, and while some progress has been seen, the organization says the degree and pace of that progress has been too slow. In 1999, the president of the organization used the term "virtual whitewash" to describe the networks' new program line-up, and his successors have made similar criticisms in the years since.

Following the 1999–2000 season, the major networks—NBC, ABC, CBS, and Fox—all promised to do better in presenting more minority characters, while also purchasing products and services from minority-owned businesses, creating development programs for young minority talent wishing to work behind the cameras, and offering scholarships and internships for minority college students planning careers in the entertainment industry. A 2001–02 study by the Screen Actors Guild indicated that during the preceding television season, roles for African

Kweisi Mfume, president and CEO of the NAACP, addresses the audience at the organization's 1999 national convention. At that meeting and several meetings since, the NAACP has discussed the lack of diversity in network television programming.

American performers increased to slightly more than 15 percent, while Latino portrayals increased to 6 percent—both modest increases over previous seasons. Asian American portrayals remained about the same as in previous years—at 2.5 percent—while Native American portrayals decreased to less than 1 percent. But behind the cameras, the picture was even worse. A study conducted the same year by the NAACP found that for all four ethnic categories, the number of writers, producers, and directors fell to its lowest point in more than a decade, with less than 8 percent of those positions being held by minorities. And of those positions, the NAACP pointed out, most were on UPN and WB—networks with largely minority audiences and limited cross-over appeal.

The NAACP made the following position statement on the issue:

> As the nation's viewing population is estimated to rapidly grow more and more multiracial, network programmers are increasingly becoming aware that programs featuring African American, Latinos, Asians and Native Americans are simply good business. However, African Americans and other races of people are still underrepresented in almost every aspect of the television and film industry as they have, for the most part, been excluded from positions of power in Hollywood. Although there appears to be small gains in on-air roles, there is practically no representation of racial minorities in the top echelon of production, which is the nucleus of both the film

and television industry. Too often the casual viewer will confuse the presence of racial minorities in television commercials or in non-speaking and non-recurring roles as somehow equating to progress."

In addition to television programming, the organization has seen a similar lack of diversity in motion pictures. The NAACP points out that more than 30 percent of the movie audience is African American, but the characters featured in those films are largely white. And when African American characters are shown, the organization points out, in too many cases they are portrayed in stereotypically negative roles.

With progress on such issues coming at such a slow pace, the NAACP has threatened numerous times to organize boycotts of the major networks' programs and their advertisers, as well as the major motion picture studios. As of this writing, however, no such boycotts have come to fruition, as each threat is met with another round of promises from the networks and studios, followed each time by only a minimum level of progress.

Although the organization's role in the entertainment-diversity debate appears to be a recent development, it is not. As far back as 1915, the NAACP organized protests outside of movie theaters showing *Birth of a Nation*, a film often criticized for perpetuating racial stereotypes. Now almost a century later, the organization continues to work on the issue. "The NAACP will continue to monitor the state of employment in the television and film industry, including the extent to which actors, writers, and directors have been affected by unscripted programming, how the presence of reality shows can aid or impede the efforts to increase opportunities for minorities in network tel-evision, and the industry's true commitment to diversity in the face of such obstacles," concluded a recent NAACP statement.

CASE STUDY 13B

Ladies Need Not Apply

The Masters golf tournament, in the news the last several years largely because of four victories by Tiger Woods, is now drawing attention to itself for other and less positive reasons. The tournament is held each April at Augusta National Golf Club in Augusta, Georgia, a prestigious club shrouded in mystery and mystique. Historically, Sunday's final round at the Masters is one of the highest-rated sports broadcasts of the year. In 2001 and 2002, more than 40 million viewers watched the tournament's final rounds, and millions more kept track on the event's website, which was designed and maintained by International Business Machines as part of the company's sponsorship of the event.

Shortly before the 2002 event, the club came under fire for the absence of women among its membership. Critics pointed out a glaring double standard in that the tournament's sponsors—Coca-Cola, IBM, and Cit-iGroup—all have policies forbidding any type of discrimination in employment or other aspects of their operations. But when journalists asked company rep-resentatives to comment on the inconsistency between their corporate policies and their sponsorship of a tournament at an all-male club, each deferred to Augusta National and declined further comment. A media relations representative for IBM side-stepped the issue in a two-sentence statement that praised the company's Masters sponsorship as a marketing opportunity. She declined to address the membership issue. Even CBS, which has broadcast the tournament for decades, declined to comment on the membership issue.

When pressed on the issue by journalists gathered for the 2003 event, club officials repeated their position that the club's membership policies are a private issue, but insisted that it has no exclusionary policies. As a for-profit entity, Augusta National, Inc. earns millions of dollars each year from television rights fees, ticket sales, and merchandise. Until 2003, many television viewers were unaware of the Augusta National's antiwomen stance. One reason for that lack of information is the seriousness with which the club takes its privacy rights. Members are admonished not to talk about membership matters with anyone—certainly not the media.

Martha Burke, chairwoman of the National Council of Women's Organizations, led a protest outside the gates of Augusta National Golf Club during the 2003 Masters golf tournament.

Augusta National argued that as a private entity, it has the right to select its members without interference from outsiders. But Martha Barnett, past president of the American Bar Association, says that when all-male clubs host public events such as international sports competitions, they invite outside scrutiny.

Donna Shalala, former Secretary of Health and Human Services in the Clinton administration and now president of the University of Miami, was one of the first women of national stature to comment publicly on the issue. Pointing out that the companies identified as sponsors have been leaders in affirmative action, she acknowledged the double standard and called on those companies to use their sponsorship and name-recognition clout to put pressure on the host club.

Both Barnett and Shalala acknowledged the rights of private clubs to run their operations as they see fit, but agreed that the hosting of nationally televised sporting events called for a higher standard of inclusion.

The fight to admit women into membership at Augusta National was eventually taken over by the National Council of Women's Organizations. When the NCWO hinted at a potential boycott aimed at the three major sponsors, Augusta National officials announced they would take the pressure off those companies by not renewing sponsorship agreements for the 2003 event. A protest organized by the NCWO at a site near the golf course during tournament week drew only a few sincere protestors, but attracted large numbers of journalists and curious onlookers. The 2003 event was staged without disruption, and shortly thereafter tournament organizers announced that no corporate sponsors would be part of the following

year's event. Two years later, the club reversed that position and reinstated major sponsors for the 2006 tournament. While the issue is still discussed in connection with media coverage of the tournament, there are no protestors outside of the gate, and each year the topic becomes less of an issue.

The Masters controversy came a decade after another in major championship golf. In 1990, Shoal Creek Golf Club in Birmingham, Alabama, hosted the PGA Championship Tournament (see Case Study 7B). Two months before the event, club president Hall Thompson acknowledged in a newspaper interview that the club purposely excluded African Americans. Though such exclusionary policies were quite common at other country clubs, critics blasted the event's organizers, claiming that hosting such an important event meant the club could be held to a higher standard. Four major advertisers—IBM, Toyota, Honda, and Sharp Electronics—canceled more than $2 million in advertising on ABC and ESPN. As the tournament week grew closer and the critics became more vocal, ABC began to worry that broadcasting the tournament would only draw more attention to the issue, including its affiliation with the event. Shortly before the event, Shoal Creek amended its membership policies, and after the tournament, the club admitted its first black member.

In the months following the Shoal Creek controversy, the PGA Tour and other golf organizations implemented policies that clubs wishing to host their events must not have exclusionary membership practices. Unwilling to change, many clubs withdrew from consideration as host clubs and forfeited millions of dollars in potential profits from ticket sales and television revenue.

CASE STUDY 13C

Watch Your Language!

Here are some examples of words and phrases that are offensive to persons with disabilities, as highlighted in a publication by United Cerebral Palsy (UCP):

Afflicted. Too negative. Say that the person is "affected."
Crippled. This paints a mental picture no one wants to look at.

Disease. Before referring to a medical phenomenon as a "disease" or a "condition," find out which it is. There is a difference between the two terms.
Suffers from. If someone with a disability is independent and copes with life as well as most of us, this term does not apply.
Victim. A person with a disability is not a victim. Refer to him or her as a "person with cerebral

Demonstrating respect for employees and customers with disabilities is one of the many responsibilities of being a professional communicator.

palsy" or other condition, not a "cerebral palsy victim."

Wheelchair bound. Call the person a "wheelchair user" instead. Few people are truly bound to a wheelchair; they use it mainly for transportation. The same applies to "confined to a wheelchair."*

---

*Excerpt from a United Cerebral Palsy (UCP) publication, "Watch Your Language," tips describing words and phrases that are offensive to persons with disabilities. www.ucp.org. Reprinted by permission.

Paraquad, a St. Louis-based nonprofit organization dealing with the rights of the disabled, also provides literature to help employers choose their words more carefully. It encourages employers to say "a person with a disability" rather than a "disabled person" or "handicapped person."

In addition to offering much the same advice as UCP, the organization recommends saying "disabled since birth" or "born with" instead of "birth defect." Its literature also warns against using outdated or insensitive terms such as *abnormal, burden, deformed, incapacitated,* and *pathetic.*

DISCUSSION QUESTIONS

1. If you are a member of any of the groups discussed in this chapter (African American, Hispanic American, Asian American, or disabled), think for a moment about how companies market their products and services to you. Share with the class some examples of how companies have either made a special effort to reach you or disregarded your needs and concerns.

2. The National Association for the Advancement of Colored People (NAACP) in recent years has engaged in a public relations campaign to encourage the major television networks to practice diversity by casting more black char-

acters in television programs (Case Study 13A). Is it the networks' responsibility to do this, or, as private businesses, can they do whatever they want? Do you think the NAACP is doing a good job in its advocacy role on this issue? What could the organization do better or differently? If you were a network executive, how would you respond to the NAACP?

3. Read the "Trends and Issues" section of this chapter. Do you agree with the three reasons put forth in the 1986 Velvet Ghetto report to explain the lack of promotion opportunities for women working in public relations? Do these

same three reasons still exist? What, if anything, can be done to remedy the problems of job discrimination and salary inequities?

4. Case Study 13B details the issue of a private country club with no female members serving as host to a major professional golf tournament.

    a. Do you agree with the position of the club, which claims that as a private organization, it has the right to choose its own members and make its own rules? Why or why not?

    b. Do you agree with Martha Barnett and Donna Shalala, who claim that as host of an internationally televised sporting event, it should be held to a higher standard? Why or why not?

    c. Do you agree with the sponsor companies' response to media inquiries, by simply deferring to the club spokespersons and declining to comment on the membership issue? If you were the media spokesperson for one of those companies, how would you respond?

    d. Do you agree that the companies have the right to continue their sponsorship of the Masters despite the host club's membership policies? If you were an internal counselor to the CEO of one of those companies, what would your public relations advice be?

5. You are working in your company's branch office located in another country and have been invited to a business dinner at the home of your company's most important customers. Consider the following situations:*

    a. You want to bring the host a gift of flowers. Which type of flowers would be *least* appropriate?

      1. roses

      2. chrysanthemums

      3. a dozen of any type of flower

    b. You enter the home through the front door and find a receiving line that includes dozens of guests that you do not know. As you are introduced to each, how do you address each one?

      1. by their first name

      2. by a courtesy title (Mr., Ms., Dr.) and last name

      3. "sir" or "madam"

    c. During the course of the meal, when do you stop eating?

      1. when your entire plate is clean

      2. when you are full

      3. when the host or hostess stops eating

*Answers provided in instructor's manual.

GLOSSARY OF TERMS

Cross-cultural training. Training in the principles and beliefs of another culture provided for employees of U.S. companies prior to accepting work assignments in other countries.

Diversity. Differences in people that provide a mixture, including race, sex, age, religion, class, and sexual orientation.

Multicultural. An adjective used to describe respect for other cultures being represented within your employees and customers.

Stereotype. The portrayal of members of racial or ethnic groups in an unflattering manner based on generalizations or outdated perceptions.

SOURCES AND SUGGESTED FURTHER READINGS

General

Accreditation Study Guide. New York: Public Relations Society of America, 1992.

Austin, Erica Weintraub, and Bruce E. Pinkleton. *Strategic Public Relations Management.* Mahwah, NJ: Lawrence Erlbaum, 2001.

Backer, Thomas E., Everett M. Rogers, and Pradeep Sopory. *Designing Health Communication Campaigns: What Works.* Newbury Park, CA: Sage, 1992.

Baskin, Otis, and Craig Aronoff. *Public Relations: The Profession and the Practice.* Dubuque, IA: William C. Brown, 1992.

Brody, E. W. *Public Relations Programming and Production.* New York: Praeger, 1988.

Caywood, Clark. *The Handbook of Strategic Public Relations and Integrated Communications.* New York: McGraw-Hill, 1997.

Clancy, Kevin J., and Robert S. Shulman. *Marketing Myths That Are Killing Business.* New York: McGraw-Hill, 1994.

Cole, Robert S. *The Practical Handbook of Public Relations.* Englewood Cliffs, NJ: Prentice-Hall, 1981.

Crable, Richard E., and Steven L. Vibbert. *Public Relations as Communication Management.* Edina, MN: Bellwether Press, 1986.

Cutlip, Scott M., Allen H. Center, and Glen M. Broom. *Effective Public Relations.* Englewood Cliffs, NJ: Prentice-Hall, 1994.

Dennis, Lloyd. *Practical Public Affairs in an Era of Change.* Lanham, MD: University Press of America, 1996.

Ferguson, Sherry Devereaux. *Communication Planning: An Integrated Approach.* Thousand Oaks, CA: Sage, 1999.

Goff, Christine Friesleben, ed. *The Publicity Process.* Ames: Iowa State University Press, 1989.

Goldberg, Marvin E., Martin Fishbein, and Susan E. Middlestadt, eds. *Social Marketing: Theoretical and Practical Perspectives.* Mahwah, NJ: Lawrence Erlbaum, 1997.

Grunig, James E., and Todd Hunt. *Managing Public Relations.* Fort Worth, TX: Holt, Rinehart and Winston, 1984.

Guth, David W., and Charles Marsh. *Public Relations: A Values-Driven Approach.* Boston: Allyn and Bacon, 2000.

Harris, Thomas L. *Value-Added Public Relations: The Secret Weapon of Integrated Marketing.* Lincolnwood, IL: NTC Business Books, 1998.

Heath, Robert, ed. *The Handbook of Public Relations.* Thousand Oaks, CA: Sage, 2000.

Kendall, Robert. *Public Relations Campaign Strategies.* New York: HarperCollins, 1996.

Matera, Fran R., and Ray J. Artigue. *Public Relations Campaigns and Techniques: Building Bridges into the 21st Century.* Boston: Allyn and Bacon, 2000.

Mercer, Laurie J., and Jennifer Singer. *Opportunity Knocks: A Public Relations Guide for Small and Medium-Sized Businesses.* Radnor, PA: Chilton Book Co., 1989.

Moore, H. Frazier, and Frank B. Kalupa. *Public Relations: Principles, Cases and Problems.* Homewood, IL: Richard D. Irwin, 1985.

Nager, Norman R., and T. Harrell Allen. *Public Relations: Management by Objectives.* Lanham, MD: University Press of America, 1984.

Nager, Norman R., and Richard H. Truitt. *Strategic Public Relations Counseling.* New York: Longman, 1988.

Newsom, Doug, Judy VanSlyke Turk, and Dean Kruckeberg. *This Is PR: The Realities of Public Relations.* Belmont, CA: Wadsworth, 2000.

Nolte, Lawrence W. *Fundamentals of Public Relations.* New York, Pergamon, 1974.

Pavlik, John V. *Public Relations: What Research Tells Us.* Newbury Park, CA: Sage, 1987.

Peake, Jacquelyn. *Public Relations in Business.* New York: Harper and Row, 1980.

Rice, Ronald E., and Charles K. Atkin, eds. *Public Communication Campaigns.* Newbury Park, CA: Sage, 1989.

Seitel, Frasier. *The Practice of Public Relations.* Englewood Cliffs, NJ: Prentice-Hall, 1995.

Simmons, Robert E. *Communication Campaign Management.* White Plains, NY: Longman, 1990.

Simon, Raymond. *Public Relations: Concepts and Practices.* Columbus, OH: Grid Publishing, 1980.

Smith, Ronald D. *Strategic Planning for Public Relations.* Mahwah, NJ: Lawrence Erlbaum, 2002.

Wilcox, Dennis L., Phillip H. Ault, Warren K. Agee, and Glen T. Cameron. *Public Relations: Strategies and Tactics.* New York: Addison-Wesley Longman, 2000.

Chapter 1: Public Relations and Persuasion

Bernays, Edward L. *Biography of an Idea: Memoirs of a Public Relations Counsel.* New York: Simon & Schuster, 1965.

Black, Sam. "I Am Proud to Be in Public Relations." *Public Relations Quarterly,* Summer 1993, pp. 45–46.

Bleifuss, Joel. "Flack Attack." *Utne Reader,* January/February 1994, pp. 72–77.

Bleile, Paul. "PR and Propaganda: Where Do You Draw the Line?" *Communication World,* June/July 1998, pp. 26–28.

Covey, Stephen. *The Seven Habits of Highly Effective People.* New York: Simon and Schuster, 1990.

Dennis, Lloyd. *Practical Public Affairs in an Era of Change.* Lanham, MD: University Press of America, 1996.

Dilenschneider, Robert L. *Power and Influence: Mastering the Art of Persuasion.* New York: Prentice-Hall, 1990.

Dilenschneider, Robert L. "Spin Doctors Practice Public Relations Quackery." *The Wall Street Journal,* June 1, 1998.

Drinkard, Jim. "Public Relations: Selling an Idea with Distortion and Lies." *Charleston Gazette-Mail,* April 17, 1994, p. B-4.

Ewe, Stuart. *PR! A Social History of Spin.* New York: Perseus Books, 1998.

Friederich, Karl H. "The Public Relations Process." Chapter 2 in *The Publicity Process.* ed. Christine

Friesleben Goff. Ames: Iowa State University Press, 1989, pp. 10–31.

Gorney, Carole. "The Trouble With Spin." *Public Relations Tactics,* October 1999, p. 24.

Jowett, Garth S., and Victoria O'Donnell. *Propaganda and Persuasion.* Newbury Park, CA: Sage, 1992.

Kinzey, Ruth Ellen. *Using Public Relations Strategies to Promote Your Nonprofit Organization.* New York: Haworth, 1999.

Kurtz, Howard. *Spin Cycle: Inside the Clinton Propaganda Machine.* New York: Simon and Schuster, 1998.

"The Pepsi Hoax: What Went Right." Brochure produced by the Pepsi-Cola Co., 1993.

Public Relations: An Overview. PRSA Foundation Monograph Series, Vol. 1, no. 3, November 1991.

Queenan, Joseph. "Ten Things I Hate about Public Relations." *Media Writing,* authors Doug Newsom and James Wollert, pp. 408–409. Belmont, CA: Wadsworth, 1988.

Ross, Irwin. *The Image Merchants.* Garden City, NJ: Doubleday, 1957.

Rothenberg, Randall. "The Age of Spin." *Esquire,* December 1996, p. 71.

Rowe, Reg. "Public Relations Isn't as Easy as it Looks." *Kansas City Star,* October 27, 1992.

Simmons, Robert E. *Communication Campaign Management.* White Plains, NY: Longman, 1990.

"Spin Is Not the Job of PR." *O'Dwyer's PR Services Report,* January 1997, p. 7.

Stauber, John. *Toxic Sludge Is Good for You: Lies, Damn Lies and the Public Relations Industry.* Monroe, ME: Common Courage Press, 1985.

Stevens, Art. *The Persuasion Explosion.* Washington, DC: Acropolis Books, 1985.

"The Tylenol Comeback." Brochure produced by Johnson & Johnson, 1982.

Unger, Brent. "For Immediate Release." *Panama City News-Herald,* December 15, 1996.

Chapter 2: An Overview of the Public Relations Process

Fearn-Banks, Kathleen. *Crisis Communications: A Casebook Approach.* Chicago: Lawrence Erlbaum, 1995.

Larson, Wendy, ed. *When Crisis Strikes Campus.* Washington, DC: Council for the Advancement and Support of Education, 1992.

Ogrizek, Michel, and Jean-Michel Guillery. *Communicating in Crisis.* New York: Aldine de Gruyter, 1999.

Pinsdorf, Marion K. *Communicating When Your Company Is under Seige.* New York: Fordham University Press, 1999.

Chapter 3: Planning: Background Research

Antonoff, Michael. "Baby Boomer Is a Badge Whose Time Has Come and Gone." *Advertising Age*, September 17, 2007.

Berger, Arthur Asa. *Media Research Techniques.* Thousand Oaks, CA: Sage, 1998.

"Business Executives' Attitudes toward the Aging Workforce." Report from the American Association of Retired Persons, October 2006.

Cantril, Hadley. *Gauging Public Opinion.* Princeton, NJ: Princeton University Press, 1944.

Communicating Science News: A Guide for Scientists, Physicians and Public Information Officers. Greenlawn, NY: National Association of Science Writers, 1992.

Dembo, Mark. "Reaching Generation Y." *Public Relations Tactics,* May 2000, p. 20.

Dobrow, Larry. "Marketers Overlooking a Vast Audience." *MediaPost,* February 2007.

Grossman, Lev. "Grow Up? Not So Fast." *Time*, January 24, 2005, pp. 42–54.

Holtz, Shel. *Public Relations on the Net.* New York: American Management Association, 1999.

Horovitz, Bruce. "Gen Y: A Tough Crowd to Sell." *USA Today,* April 22, 2002, p. B-1.

Irvine, Martha. "Youngest Adults Represent Growing Voting Group." Associated Press report, July 7, 2004.

Jackson, Amy, and Unity Stoakes. "Monitoring Public Opinion Online." *Public Relations Tactics,* November 1997.

Jayson, Sharon. "Gen Y's Attitudes Differ from Parents'." *USA Today*, January 10, 2007, p. D-1.

Jayson, Sharon. "The Goal: Wealth and Fame." *USA Today*, January 10, 2007, p. D-1.

Jones, Dan, and Karen Lane. *Technical Communication: Strategies for College and the Workplace.* New York: Longman, 2002.

Kirk, Elizabeth. "Evaluating Information on the Internet." Baltimore, MD: Johns Hopkins University, 1996.

Lindenmann, Walter K. *A Guide to Public Relations Research.* New York: Ketchum Public Relations, 1999.

Lyman, Rick. "Life in Exurbia Often Framed by Time in Car." New York Times News Service, December 18, 2005.

Marston, John E. "Reaching Special Publics." *The Nature of Public Relations.* New York: McGraw-Hill, 1979, pp. 39–68.

Masterton, John. "Discovering Databases." *Public Relations Journal,* November 1992, pp. 12–14.

McGee, Tom. "Getting Inside Kids' Heads." *American Demographics,* January 1997, pp. 53–59.

"Monitor These Web Sites for Grievances, Corporate Attacks and Misinformation." *Bulldog Reporter's Media Relations Insider,* 2001.

Morgan, Carol M., and Doran H. Levy. "Psychographic Segmentation." *Communication World*, December–January 2002–03, pp. 22–35.

Ottman, Jacquelyn A. *Green Marketing: Challenges and Opportunities for the New Marketing Age.* Lincolnwood, IL: NTC Business Books, 1992.

Reinard, John C. *Introduction to Communication Research.* Madison, WI: Brown and Benchmark 1994.

Scanlon, Christopher. "As We May Write: The Web and the Future of Writing." *The Poynter Institute Report,* Winter 2000, pp. 6–7.

"Segmenting Publics around Issues in Hyper-Political Times." *PR Reporter,* Vol. 39, no. 15, April 8, 1996.

"Six Ways to Use Research." *Public Relations Journal,* May 1994, pp. 26–27.

Thompson, William. *Targeting the Message.* White Plains, NY: Longman, 1996.

Walker, Albert. "Anatomy of the Communication Audit." *Communication World,* September 1988, pp. 33–34.

Witmer, Diane F. *Spinning the Web: A Handbook for Public Relations on the Internet.* New York: Longman, 2000.

Chapter 4: Planning: Primary Research

"And the Survey Says." *Public Relations Journal,* May 1994, p. 24.

"Ball State Study: Americans Use Media More Than They Say." *Crisis Counselor Newsletter,* April 2004.

Berger, Arthur Asa. *Media Research Techniques.* Thousand Oaks, CA: Sage, 1998.

Brandt, D. Scott. "Evaluating Information on the Internet." *Computers in Libraries,* May 1996, pp. 44–46.

Brink, Alice. "One Simple Question." *Communication World,* December 1996–January 1997, pp. 25–27.

Broom, Glen M., and David M. Dozier. *Using Research in Public Relations.* Englewood Cliffs, NJ: Prentice-Hall, 1990.

Budiansky, Stephen. "The Numbers Racket: How Polls and Statistics Lie." *U.S. News and World Report,* July 11, 1988, pp. 45–47.

Cantril, Hadley. *Gauging Public Opinion.* Princeton, NJ: Princeton University Press, 1944.

Clancy, Kevin J., and Robert S. Shulman. *Marketing Myths That Are Killing Business.* New York: McGraw-Hill, 1994.

Crossen, Cynthia. *Tainted Truth: The Manipulation of Fact in America.* New York: Simon and Schuster, 1996.

Deacon, David, Michael Pickering, Peter Golding, and Graham Murdock. *Researching Communications: A Practical Guide to Methods in Media and Cultural Analysis.* New York: Oxford University Press, 1999.

Dillman, Don A. *Mail and Internet Surveys.* New York: John Wiley & Sons, 2000.

Finn, Peter. "Demystifying Public Relations." *Public Relations Journal,* May 1982, pp. 12–17.

Franfort-Nachmias, Chava, and David Nachmias. *Research Methods in the Social Sciences.* New York: St. Martin's Press, 1996.

Gaddis, Susanne Elizabeth. "On-Line Research Techniques for the Public Relations Practitioner." *The Handbook of Public Relations.* Robert Heath, ed. Thousand Oaks, CA: Sage, 2000, pp. 591–601.

Greenbaum, Thomas L. *The Handbook of Focus Group Research.* New York: Lexington Books, 1993.

Greenbaum, Thomas L. "Focus Group by Video: Next Trend of the 90's." *Marketing News,* July 29, 1996.

Grunig, Larissa A. "Using Focus Group Research in Public Relations." *Public Relations Review,* Vol. 16, No. 2, 1990, pp. 36–49.

Horovitz, Bruce. "Marketers Zooming in on Your Daily Routines." *USA Today,* April 30, 2007, p. 1-D.

"How the Poll Was Conducted." *The New York Times,* November 25, 1992, p. A-2.

Huff, Darrell. *How to Lie with Statistics.* New York: W. W. Norton, 1954.

Jaffe, A. J., and Herbert F. Spirer. *Misused Statistics: Straight Talk for Twisted Numbers.* New York: Marcel-Dekker, 1987.

Kaus, Mickey. "Facts for Hacks." *The New Republic,* May 20, 1991, pp. 23–25.

Krueger, Richard A., and Mary Anne Casey. *Focus Groups: A Practical Guide for Applied Research.* Thousand Oaks, CA: Sage, 2000.

Lane, Wendy E. "Logos Put to the Test." *Washington Post,* February 12, 1997.

Lindenmann, Walter K. *A Guide to Public Relations Research.* New York: Ketchum Public Relations, 1999.

Manning, Anita. "For Many Men, One Hand Does Not Always Wash the Other." *USA Today*, September 18, 2007, p. D7.

Mehta, Raj, and Eugene Sivadas. "Comparing Response Rates and Response Content in Mail versus Electronic Surveys.*" Journal of the Market Research Society,* Vol. 37, 1995, pp. 429–439.

Merton, Robert K. "The Focussed Group Interview and Focus Groups: Continuity and Discontinuity." *Public Opinion Quarterly,* Vol. 51, 1987, pp. 550–566.

Meyer, Philip. "Pollsters Switch Tactics to Foil Answering Machines." *USA Today,* November 2, 1998, p. A–19.

Miller, Mark. "The Road to Panama City." *Newsweek,* October 30, 1995, p. 84.

Nager, Norman R., and T. Harrell Allen. *Public Relations: Management by Objectives.* Lanham, MD: University Press of America, 1984.

Nager, Norman R., and Richard H. Truitt. *Strategic Public Relations Counseling.* New York: Longman, 1988.

Negroponte, Nicholas. *Being Digital.* New York: Alfred A. Knopf, 1995.

Nesbary, Dale K. *Survey Research and the World Wide Web.* Boston: Allyn and Bacon, 2000.

Neuman, W. Lawrence. *Social Research Methods.* Boston: Allyn and Bacon, 1991.

Payne, Stanley. *The Art of Asking Questions.* Princeton, NJ: Princeton University Press, 1980.

Peterson, Robert A. *Marketing Research.* Plano, TX: Business Publications, 1988.

"Polls and Surveys." *Associated Press Stylebook.* New York: Associated Press, 1998, pp. 161–162.

Rayburn, Jay. "Focusing on Focus Groups." PRSA International Conference, St. Louis, MO, 1996.

Rea, Louis M., and Richard A. Parker. *Designing and Conducting Survey Research.* San Francisco: Jossey-Bass, 1997.

Reardon, Kathleen K. "The ABC's of Research." *Public Relations Journal,* May 1981, pp. 21–23.

Reinard, John C. *Introduction to Communication Research.* Madison, WI: Brown & Benchmark, 1994.

Rubenstein, Sondra Miller. *Surveying Public Opinion.* Belmont, CA: Wadsworth, 1995.

Rubin, Rebecca B., Alan M. Rubin, and Linda J. Piele. *Communication Research: Strategies and Sources.* Belmont, CA: Wadsworth, 1986.

Sandomir, Richard. "Popularity Pays Off." *New York Times,* December 19, 1997.

Simmons, Robert E. *Communication Campaign Management.* White Plains, NY: Longman, 1990.

Sommers, Christina H. *Who Stole Feminism: How Women Have Betrayed Women.* New York: Simon and Schuster, 1994.

Stacks, Don W., and John E. Hocking. *Essentials of Communication Research.* New York: HarperCollins, 1992.

Stewart, David W., and Prem N. Shamdasani. *Focus Groups: Theory and Practice.* Newbury Park, CA: Sage, 1997.

Underhill, Paco. *Why We Buy: The Science of Shopping.* New York: Simon and Schuster, 1999.

Ward, Jean, and Kathleen A. Hansen. *Search Strategies in Mass Communications.* New York: Longman, 1993.

Williams, Frederick, Ronald E. Rice, and Everett M. Rogers. *Research Methods for the New Media.* New York: The Free Press, 1988.

Wimmer, Roger D., and Joseph R. Dominick. *Mass Media Research.* Belmont, CA: Wadsworth, 1998.

Witmer, Diane F. *Spinning the Web: A Handbook for Public Relations on the Internet.* New York: Addison-Wesley Longman, 2000.

Zikmund, William G. *Exploring Market Research.* Chicago: Dryden Press, 1986.

Chapter 5: Planning: Goals and Objectives, Messages and Themes, Channels and Strategies

Aldrich, Leigh Stephens. *Covering the Community: A Diversity Handbook for the Media.* Thousand Oaks, CA: Pine Forge, 1999.

Berk, Laurey, and Phillip G. Clampitt. "Finding the Right Path in the Communications Maze." *Communication World,* October 1991.

Bolland, Eric J. "Advertising vs. Public Relations." *Public Relations Quarterly,* Fall 1989, pp. 10–12.

Broder, David S. *Behind the Front Page: A Candid Look at How the News Is Made.* New York: Simon and Schuster, 1987.

"Corporate Web Sites Get a 'D'." *Public Relations Tactics,* June 2001, p. 6.

Duggan, Maria, and John Deveney. "How to Make Internet Marketing Simple." *Communication World,* April-May 2000, pp. 58–61.

"Facts about Newspapers." Newspaper Association of America report, 2006.

Foster, Mimi F. "Boomers Bring a Bumper Crop of New Publications." *The Atlanta Journal and Constitution,* May 20, 1994, p. F-1.

Howard, Theresa. "Lipton Ices Some Chicks Promos." *USA Today,* May 2, 2003, p. B-6.

Hvistendahl, J. K. "Using the Media to Bring about Change." *The Publicity Process.* Christine Friesleben Goff, ed. Ames: Iowa State University Press, 1989, pp. 32–43.

Janal, Daniel S. *Online Marketing Handbook.* New York: Van Nostrand Reinhold, 1995.

Kaye, Barbara K., and Norman Medoff. *Just a Click Away: Advertising on the Internet.* Boston: Allyn and Bacon, 2001.

Larkin, T. J., and Sandar Larkin. "Change the Communication Channel: Web, Paper, or Face-to-Face." *Communication World,* November–December 2005, pp. 16–18.

Levy, Dorothy. "What Public Relations Can Do Better Than Advertising." *Public Relations Quarterly,* Fall 1989, pp. 7–9.

Liles, Stinson. "A New Breed of Trade Publications." *Public Relations Tactics,* April 1997.

Liles, Stinson. "More and More Reporters are Getting Wired." *Public Relations Tactics,* April 1997.

Mansfield, Brian. "Will Criticism Prompt Chicks to Fly the Country Coop?" *USA Today,* May 1, 2003.

Marlow, Eugene. *Electronic Public Relations.* Belmont, CA: Wadsworth, 1996.

Mindich, David. *Tuned Out: Why Americans Under 40 Don't Follow the News.* New York: Oxford University Press, 2005.

Mitternight, Helen L. "Winning the Hearts and Minds of the Online Audience." *IABC Communication World,* March 1998, pp. 36–37.

Negroponte, Nicholas. *Being Digital.* New York: Alfred A. Knopf, 1995.

Newport, Frank, and Lydia Saad. "A Matter of Trust." *American Journalism Review,* July–August 1998, pp. 30–33.

Ouellette, Laurie. "War of the Weeklies." *Utne Reader,* November/December 1993, pp. 24–25.

Ries, Al, and Laura Ries. *The Fall of Advertising, the Rise of PR.* New York: HarperCollins, 2002.

Scanlon, Christopher. "As We May Write: The Web and the Future of Writing." *The Poynter Institute Report,* Winter 2000, pp. 6–7.

Stark, Phyllis. "Arbitron Studies Finds 95% of U.S. Still Hooked to Radio." *Billboard,* March 11, 1995, p. 95.

"Ten Ways to Create Feature Stories." *Ragan's Media Relations Report,* July 1, 1999, pp. 1–2.

VanSlyke Turk, Judy. "Public Relations Influence on the News." *Newspaper Research Journal,* Summer 1986, pp. 15–27.

"What a Journalist Wants." *Public Relations Tactics,* August 2000, p. 4.

Witmer, Diane F. *Spinning the Web: A Handbook for Public Relations on the Internet.* New York: Longman, 2000.

Chapter 6: Implementation: Traditional Media Channels

Arens, William F., and Courtland L. Bovee. *Contemporary Advertising.* Chicago: Irwin Publishing, 1989.

Ask the Experts. Marshall University Office of University Relations, 1996.

Backer, Thomas E., Everett M. Rogers, and Pradeep Sopory. *Designing Health Communication Campaigns: What Works.* Newbury Park, CA: Sage Publications, 1992.

Baird, John E., and Patricia H. Bradley. *Communication for Business and the Professions.* Dubuque, IA: William C. Brown, 1980.

Baxter, Bill F. "The News Release: An Idea Whose Time Has Gone?" *Public Relations Review,* Spring 1981, pp. 27–31.

Belch, George E., and Michael A. Belch. *Introduction to Advertising and Promotion Management.* Chicago: Irwin Publishing, 1990.

Berman, Scott. "Newspaper Op-Eds: A Frequently Overlooked PR Tool." *Public Relations Tactics,* April 1999, p. 22.

Bivins, Thomas H. *Public Relations Writing: The Essentials of Style and Format.* Lincolnwood, IL: NTC/Contemporary Publishing Group, 1999.

Bovee, Courtland L., and William F. Arens. "Corporate Advertising and Public Relations." *Contemporary Advertising.* Homewood, IL: Irwin, 1989.

Bowbrick, Peter. *Effective Communication for Professionals and Executives.* Norwell, MA: Graham and Troutman Publishing, 1988.

Boyd, Christopher. "Apologies in Ads Gain Popularity." *The Orlando Sentinel,* June 22, 2003.

Catacalos, Renee. "Internet Too Confusing? Why Not Send a Fax?" *Public Relations Tactics,* May 1996.

Chemicals, the Press and the Public: A Journalist's Guide to Reporting on Chemicals in the Community. Washington, DC: National Safety Council Environmental Health Center, 2000.

Communicating Science News: A Guide for Scientists, Physicians and Public Information Officers. Greenlawn, NY: National Association of Science Writers, 1992.

"Continued Job Cuts in Busy Newsrooms Make Freelancers a Golden Pitching Opportunity." *Bulldog Reporter's Media Relations Insider,* 2001.

Edelson, Edward. *A Journalist's Guide to Nuclear Energy.* Bethesda, MD: Atomic Industrial Forum, 1985.

Elfenbein, Dick. "Business Journalists Say If It's Not Local, It's Trashed." *Public Relations Quarterly,* Summer 1986.

Elsasser, John. "What Reporters Really Think of Press Releases." *Public Relations Tactics,* December 1994.

Garbett, Thomas. "The Two Worlds of Corporate Advertising." *Public Relations Journal,* November 1984, pp. 28–30.

Hall, Betty. "Demystifying Editorial Boards." *Public Relations Tactics,* July 1994.

Hendrix, Jerry A. "Know the Difference: Hang Up on Fraud." *Public Relations Cases.* Belmont, CA: Wadsworth, 1998, pp. 297–306.

Henry, Rene A. Jr. *Marketing Public Relations: The Hows That Make It Work.* Ames: University of Iowa Press, 1995.

Higbee, Ann. "How to Score Points with Editorial Boards." *Public Relations Tactics,* September 1997, pp. 5–9.

Holtz, Shel. *Public Relations on the Net.* New York: American Management Association, 1999.

Johnson, Peter. "Trust in Media Keeps on Slipping." *USA Today,* May 28, 2003.

King, Thomas R. "Director Goes On-Line to Push 'Sneakers.'" *The Wall Street Journal,* August 8, 1992.

"Know Tech Journalists' Peeves So Your Junior Staffers Don't Alienate the Press." *Bulldog Reporter's Media Relations Insider,* 2001.

Kucharski, Matt. "Are News Conferences Dead?" *Public Relations Tactics,* December 1996.

Lammers, Teri. "The Press Release Primer." *Inc.,* August 1991, pp. 34–36.

Liles, Stinson. "A New Breed of Trade Publications." *Public Relations Tactics,* April 1997, p. 7.

MacStravic, Robin E. *Managing Health Care Marketing Communications.* Rockville, MD: Aspen Systems, 1986.

"Making News." *Executive Female,* March 1991, pp. 62–63.

Marlow, Eugene. *Electronic Public Relations.* Belmont, CA: Wadsworth, 1996.

Mercer, Laurie J., and Jennifer Singer. *Opportunity Knocks: Using PR.* Radnor, PA: Chilton Book Co., 1989.

Minnis, John H., and Cornelius Pratt. "Newsroom Socialization and the Press Release: Implications for Media Relations." Unpublished paper, 1994.

"NAACP Boycott Continues in South Carolina Over Flag Issue." Associated Press report, November 5, 2001.

O'Neil, Kathleen. "Research Designed for Public Release: A Powerful Tool for Public Affairs and Public Relations." *Practical Public Affairs in an Era of Change.* Lloyd Dennis, ed. Lanham, MD: University Press of America, 1996, pp. 63–73.

Otterbourg, Robert K. "Banishing Boredom." *Public Relations Journal,* July 1990, pp. 21–24.

Rosenthal, Edmond. "Video PR Growing; Agencies Careful in Sticking to the News." *Television/Radio Age,* January 20, 1986, pp. 31–33.

Ruberry, Brian. "E-Mailing Media: A Primer." *Public Relations Tactics,* May 2000, p. 6.

Rubin, Alissa. "Whose News Is It?" *Public Relations Journal,* October 1985.

Sauerhaft, Stan, and Chris Atkins. *Image Wars: Protecting Your Company When There's No Place to Hide.* New York: John Wiley & Sons, 1989.

Sethi, S. Prakish. *Advocacy Advertising and Large Corporations.* Lexington, MA: D. C. Heath, 1977.

Singer, Kristi L. "Music Industry Press Kits." Unpublished memorandum, 2001.

Stone, Martha L. "Options Increase for Opt-in E-mailers." *Advertising Age's Business Marketing,* January/February 2000, p. 32.

Stovall, James Glen. *Writing for the Media.* Englewood Cliffs, NJ: Prentice-Hall, 1990.

Townsend, Jacqueline. "Tips for High-Tech Public Relations Writers." *Technical Communication,* August 1992, pp. 399–400.

Walers, Marilyn. "Dealing with Alternative Media." *The Public Relations Strategist,* Spring 1998.

Watkins, John J. *The Mass Media and the Law.* Englewood Cliffs, NJ: Prentice-Hall, 1990.

Wilcox, Dennis L., and Lawrence W. Nolte. *Public Relations Writing and Media Techniques.* New York: HarperCollins, 1990.

Williams, Doug. "In Defense of the (Properly Executed) Press Release." *Public Relations Quarterly,* Fall 1994, pp. 5–7.

Williams, Michelle. "Press Releases and Wasted Paper." *Editor and Publisher,* August 1990, p. 48.

Wooley, Alexander. "Experts on Demand: The Story Behind ProfNet." *Public Relations Tactics,* December 2001, p. 11.

"Writing for the Media." *Technical Communication,* November 1992, pp. 638–641.

Yaverbaum, Eric. *Public Relations Kits for Dummies.* Foster City, CA: IDG Books Worldwide, 2001.

Chapter 7: Implementation: Interactive Media Channels

Crowther, Greg. "Face-to-Face or E-Mail: The Medium Makes a Difference." *Communication World,* August–September 2001, pp. 23–26.

Fawcett, Karen. "The Care and Feeding of an Internet Site." *Communication World,* August/September 2000, pp. 18–20.

Fernando, Angelo. "Social Media Change the Rules." *Communication World,* January–February 2007, pp. 9–10.

Ha, Louisa, and Cornelius Pratt. "The Real State of Public Relations on the World Wide Web." *Public Relations Strategist,* Fall 2000, pp. 30–33.

Hocker, Thea. "Building Customer Loyalty on the Web: The 10 Commandments." Public Relations Society of America International Conference, Anaheim, CA, 1999.

Holtz, Shel. *Public Relations on the Net.* New York: American Management Association, 1999.

Kaye, Barbara K., and Norman J. Medoff. *Just a Click Away: Advertising on the Internet.* Boston: Allyn and Bacon, 2001.

Long, Richard K. "During Times of Tragedy, Alaska Airlines Turns to the Internet." *Public Relations Tactics,* July 2000, p. 16.

Mindich, David. *Tuned Out: Why Americans Under 40 Don't Follow the News.* New York: Oxford University Press, 2005.

Negroponte, Nicholas. *Being Digital.* New York: Alfred A. Knopf, 1995.

Paine, Katie Delahaye. "How Do Blogs Measure Up?" *Communication World,* September–October 2007, pp. 30–33.

Sullivan, Ruth, and Randy Bobbitt. "We Are Marshall: University Benefits from Hollywood Version of Its Story." *Public Relations Tactics,* October 2007, p. 44.

Witmer, Diane F. *Spinning the Web: A Handbook for Public Relations on the Internet.* New York: Longman, 2000.

Chapter 8: Implementation: Nonmedia Channels

Backer, Thomas E., Everett M. Rogers, and Pradeep Sopory. *Designing Health Communication Campaigns: What Works.* Newbury Park, CA: Sage, 1992.

Barks, Edward J. "Preparing for a Congressional Testimony." *Public Relations Tactics,* March 1998, p. 9.

Bivins, Thomas H. *Public Relations Writing: The Essentials of Style and Format.* Lincolnwood, CA: NTC/Contemporary Publishing Group, 1999.

Carringer, Paul T. "Not Just a Worthy Cause: Cause-Related Marketing Delivers the Goods and the Good." *American Advertising,* Spring 1994, pp. 16+.

Church, George J. "The Corporate Crusaders." *Time,* April 28, 1997, pp. 56–58.

Close the Book on Hate: 101 Ways to Combat Prejudice. New York: Anti-Defamation League, 1998.

Cole, Yoji. "One Company's Efforts in World Trade Center's Relief." DiversityInc.com, September 24, 2001.

Deep, Sam, and Lyle Sussman. *Smart Moves.* Reading, MA: Addison-Wesley, 1990.

DeLoach, Melissa. "First Lady Kicks Off 'Close the Book on Hate' Campaign in Washington." *The Dallas Morning News,* October 11, 2001.

Elliot, Stuart. "A Car Could Be Your Grandson's Oldsmobile." *The New York Times*, October 8, 1992, p. D-10.

Embly, Lawrence. *Doing Well While Doing Good: The Marketing Link between Businesses and Nonprofit Organizations.* Englewood Cliffs, NJ: Prentice-Hall, 1993.

Eppley, Garrett G. *Improving Your Public Relations.* Arlington, VA: National Recreation and Park Association, 1977.

Gammage, Jeff. "New Venue for Ads Make It Hard for Consumers to Tune Them Out." *Philadelphia Inquirer,* August 13, 2006, p. 1-B.

Grates, Gary. "Is the Employee Publication Extinct?" *Communication World,* December 1999/January 2000, pp. 27–30.

Henry, Rene A. Jr. *Marketing Public Relations: The Hows That Make It Work.* Ames: University of Iowa Press, 1995.

Hoff, Ron. *I Can See You Naked: A Fearless Guide to Making Great Presentations.* Kansas City, MD: Andrews and McMeel, 1988.

Holland, Robert. "Face-to-Face Communication Comes Face-to-Face." *Communication World,* January–February 1993, pp. 24–26.

Jackovics, Ted. "School Ties." *The Tampa Tribune,* May 21, 2001, Business & Finance, pp. 8–11.

Kennedy, Jim. "And Don't Forget to Straighten Your Necktie." *The Tampa Tribune,* May 18, 1986.

Koranda, Timothy. "Writing Speeches with Impact." *Public Relations Journal,* September 1990, pp. 31–35.

"Making News." *Executive Female,* March 1991, pp. 62–63.

McCullough, Daryl. "The Nuts and Bolts of Putting on a Special Event." Public Relations Society of America International Conference, Anaheim, CA, 1999.

Noonan, Peggy. *What I Saw at the Revolution.* New York: Random House, 1990.

Petrecca, Laura. "Product Placement—You Can't Escape It." *USA Today*, October 11, 2006, p. 1-B.

Phillips, Linda. *The Concise Guide to Executive Etiquette.* New York: Doubleday, 1990.

Pitcher, Dave. "There's No Business Like Show Business: What Every PR Pro Should Know about Trade-Show Exhibits." *Public Relations Tactics,* October 2001, p. 31.

"Senior Writers Have Considerable Influence with Top Management." *Public Relations Journal,* February 1990, p. 12.

Shaw, Stephen. *Airline Marketing and Management.* Long Acre, England: Pitman Publishing, 1990.

Shelton, Bill. "Speechless." *The Tampa Tribune,* March 31, 1991.

Sloan, Allan. "Can Need Trump Greed?" *Newsweek,* April 28, 1997, pp. 34–36.

Sower, Gene. "Promoting Special Events: How to Avoid Competing with Yourself." *Public Relations Tactics,* June 2001, p. 20.

Voss, Bristol. "Measuring the Effectiveness of Advertising and PR." *Sales & Marketing Management,* October 1992, pp. 123–124.

Yaverbaum, Eric. *Public Relations Kits for Dummies.* Foster City, CA: IDG Books Worldwide, 2001.

Chapter 9: Implementation: Logistics

Drucker, Peter F. "From Volunteers to Unpaid Staff." *Managing the Non-Profit Organization.* New York: HarperCollins, 1990, pp. 161–169.

Frankowiak, James R. "Staffing: An Overlooked Essential." *Public Relations Tactics,* March 1999, p. 24.

Wasnak, Lynn. "How Much Should I Charge?" *Writer's Market.* Cincinnati, OH: Writer's Digest Books, 2002.

Yale, David R. *The Publicity Handbook.* Lincolnwood, IL: NTC Business Books, 1993.

Chapter 10: Evaluation

Balch, George I., and Sharyn M. Sutton. "Keep Me Posted: A Plea for Faculty Evaluation." *Social Marketing: Theoretical and Practical Perspectives,* ed. Marvin E. Goldberg, Martin Fishbein, and Susan E. Middlestadt. Mahwah, NJ: Lawrence Erlbaum 1997, pp. 61–74.

Bobbitt, Randy. *Lottery Wars: Case Studies in Bible Belt Politics, 1986–2005.* Lanham, MD: Lexington Books, 2007.

Broom, Glen M., and David W. Dozier. "An Overview: Evaluation Research in Public Relations." *Public Relations Quarterly,* Fall 1983, pp. 5–8.

Cole, Larry. "To See Communication It Has to Be Measured." *Communication World,* August/September 1997, pp. 49–51.

Drucker, Peter F. "What Is the Bottom Line When There Is No Bottom Line?" *Managing the Non-Profit Organization.* New York: HarperCollins, 1990, pp. 107–112.

Fatjo, Tom, and Keith Miller. *With No Fear of Failure.* Waco, TX: Word Books, 1981.

Focusing on Program Outcomes. Alexandria, VA: United Way of America, 1996.

Freitag, Alan R. "How to Measure What We Do." *Public Relations Quarterly,* Summer 1998, pp. 42–47.

Greene, Amanda. "Gripe.com: From Airlines to Dentists, No One Is Safe From E-Complainers." *Wilmington Morning Star,* March 26, 2001, p. 1-B.

Guidelines and Standards for Measuring and Evaluating PR Effectiveness. Gainesville, FL: Institute for Public Relations Research and Education, 1997.

Hauss, Deborah. "Measuring the Impact of Public Relations." *Public Relations Journal,* February 1993, pp. 14–21.

"How Well Do Your Communications Really Work? Here's How to Find Out." Lawrence Ragan Communications special report, 1997.

Kilpatrick, James J. "Free Speech and Tennis Shoes." Syndicated newspaper column, November 30, 2002.

Klein, Pamela. "Measure What Matters." *Communication World,* October/November 1999, pp. 32–35.

Lindenmann, Walter K. "Research, Evaluation and Measurement: A National Perspective." *Public Relations Review,* Vol. 16, no. 2, Summer 1990, pp. 3–16.

Lindenmann, Walter K. "An Effectiveness Yardstick to Measure Public Relations." *Public Relations Quarterly,* Spring 1993, pp. 7–9.

Lindemann, Walter K. "Setting Minimum Standards for Measuring Public Relations Effectiveness." *Public Relations Review,* Winter 1997, pp. 391–408.

Lindenmann, Walter K. *A Guide to Public Relations Research.* New York: Ketchum Public Relations, 1999.

MacNamara, Jim R. "Evaluation of Public Relations: The Achilles Heel of the PR Profession." *International Public Relations Review,* Vol. 15, No. 4, 1992, pp. 17–31.

Mathews, Wilma. "The Heresy of Media Measurement." *Communication World,* February/March 2000, pp. 11–12.

Matthews, Downs. "Shooting for a Gold Quill." *Communication World,* June/July 1997, pp. 21–24.

Newlin, Patricia. "A Public Relations Measurement and Evaluation Model That Finds the Movement of the Needle." *Public Relations Quarterly,* Spring 1991, pp. 40–41.

Simmons, Robert E. "Evaluating Campaign Results." *Communication Campaign Management.* White Plains, NY: Longman, 1990.

Voss, Bristol. "Measuring the Effectiveness of Advertising and PR." *Sales & Marketing Management,* October 1992, pp. 123–124.

Weiner, Mark, and Don Bartholomew. "Dispelling the Myth of PR Multipliers and Other Inflationary Audience Measures." Institute for Public Relations, 2006.

Wylie, Frank W., and Simeon P. Slovacek. "PR Evaluation: Myth, Option or Necessity?" *Public Relations Review,* Vol. 10, No. 2, 1984, pp. 22–27.

Chapter 11: Legal Considerations

Biskupic, Joan. "Case Tests Limits of a Company's Free Speech." *USA Today,* April 22, 2003.

Clark, Charles S. "Clashing Over Copyright." *CQ Researcher,* November 8, 1996, pp. 987–1003.

Collins, Erik. "Public Relations and Libel Law." *Public Relations Review,* Winter 1990, pp. 36–47.

Elias, Stephen. *Patent and Copyright Law: A Desk Reference to Intellectual Property Law.* Berkeley, CA: Nolo Press, 1999.

Fitzpatrick, Kathy R. "The Court of Public Opinion." *The Texas Lawyer,* September 30, 1996, pp. 30+.

Fitzpatrick, Kathy R. "Public Relations and the Law: A Survey of Practitioners." *Public Relations Review,* Spring 1996, pp. 1–8.

Gearan, Anne. "Nike Protects Its Labor Ads as Protected Free Speech." Associated Press report, April 24, 2003.

Gower, Karla K. *Legal and Ethical Restraints on Public Relations.* Prospect Heights, IL: Waveland Press, 2003.

Jenkins, Allan. "What Would You Do? Nike v. Kasky Puts Public Relations Campaigns Under New Scrutiny." *Communication World,* April–May 2003, pp. 14–17.

Kozinksi, Alex, and Stuart Banner. "Who's Afraid of Commercial Speech?" *Virginia Law Review,* Vol. 76, No. 4, May 1990, pp. 627–653.

Mauro, Tony. "Let Nike Speak Up for Itself." *USA Today,* October 14, 2002.

McGuire, George, and Harold D. Clapper. "Intellectual Property Issues for PR Professionals." *Public Relations Tactics,* December 2000, p. 6.

McManis, Charles R. *Intellectual Property Law in a Nutshell.* St. Paul, MN: West, 1993.

Middleton, Kent R., Robert Trager, and Bill F. Chamberlin. *The Law of Public Communication.* New York: Longman, 2001.

Moore, Roy, Ronald T. Farrar, and Erik Collins. *Advertising and Public Relations Law.* Mahwah, NJ: Lawrence Erlbaum, 1998.

O'Donovan, Cheryl. "Copyright versus Copywrong." *Communication World,* October/November 2001, pp. 12–15.

Parkinson, Michael G., Daradirek Ekachai, and Laurel Traynowicz Hetherington. "Public Relations Law." *The Handbook of Public Relations,* ed. Robert Heath. Thousand Oaks, CA: Sage, 2000, pp. 247–257.

Questions and Answers on Copyright for the Campus Community. Association of American Publishers, National Association of College Stores, and the Software Publishers Association, 1997.

Sneed, Don K., Tim Wulfemeyer, and Harry W. Stonecipher. "Public Relations News Releases and Libel: Extending First Amendment Protections." *Public Relations Review,* Vol. 17, No. 2, 1991, pp. 131–144.

Walsh, Frank. "Public Relations Firm Charged with Insider Trading." *Public Relations Journal,* May 1986, p. 10.

Walsh, Frank. *Public Relations and the Law.* Gainesville, FL: Foundation for Public Relations Education and Research, 1988.

Wilcox, Dennis L., and Lawrence W. Nolte. *Public Relations Writing and Media Techniques.* New York: HarperCollins, 1990.

Chapter 12: Ethical Considerations

Alger, Grad, and Jessica Burnette-Lemon. "Ethics in the Real World." *Communication World,* March–April 2006, pp. 28–29.

Baker, Lee. *The Credibility Factor: Putting Ethics to Work in Public Relations.* Homewood, IL: Business One Irwin, 1993.

Bergman, Eric. "The Ethics of Not Answering." *Communication World,* September–October 2005, pp. 16–19.

Bernays, Edward L. *The Later Years: Public Relations Insights.* Rhinebeck, NY: H&M Publishing, 1986.

Bivins, Thomas H. "Applying Ethical Theory to Public Relations." *Journal of Business Ethics,* Vol. 6, 1987, pp. 195–200.

Budd, John F. *Street Smart Public Relations.* Lakeville, CT: Turtle Publishing, 1992.

Curtin, Patricia A., and Lois Boynton. "Ethics in Public Relations." *Handbook of Public Relations,* ed. Robert Heath. Thousand Oaks, CA: Sage, 2001, pp. 411–421.

Daugherty, Emma L. "Public Relations and Social Responsibility." *The Handbook of Public Relations,* ed. Robert Heath. Thousand Oaks, CA: Sage, 2001, pp. 389–401.

Day, Kenneth D., Qingwen Dong, and Clark Robins, "Public Relations Ethics." *Handbook of Public Relations,* ed. Robert Heath. Thousand Oaks, CA: Sage, 2001, pp. 403–409.

Day, Louis Alvin. *Ethics in Media Communications: Cases and Controversies.* Belmont, CA: Wadsworth, 2003.

Dilenschneider, Robert L. *Power and Influence: Mastering the Art of Persuasion.* New York: Prentice-Hall, 1990.

Dilenschneider, Robert L. "Spin Doctors Practice Public Relations Quackery." *The Wall Street Journal,* June 1, 1998.

Drinkard, Jim. "Public Relations: Selling an Idea with Distortion and Lies." *Charleston Gazette-Mail,* April 17, 1994, p. 4–B.

Edelman, Daniel J. "Ethical Behavior Is Key to Field's Future." *Public Relations Journal,* November 1992, p. 32.

"The Ethics of Keeping Secrets." *Communication World,* August/September 1999, pp. 31–40.

Fitzpatrick, Kathy, and Carolyn Bronstein, eds. *Ethics in Public Relations: Responsible Advocacy.* Thousand Oaks, CA: Sage, 2006.

Foss, Brad. "The Year of the Corporate Scandal." *Toronto Star,* December 26, 2002.

Goodell, Jeffrey. "What Hill and Knowlton Can Do for You That It Couldn't Do for Itself." *The New York Times Magazine,* September 9, 1990, p. 44+.

Gower, Karla K. *Legal and Ethical Restraints on Public Relations.* Prospect Heights, IL: Waveland Press, 2003.

Howard, Carole M., and Wilma K. Mathews. *On Deadline: Managing Media Relations.* Prospect Heights, IL: Waveland Press, 1994.

Hutchison, Liese L. "Agency Ethics Isn't an Oxymoron." *Public Relations Tactics,* May 2000, p. 13.

Johnson, Deborah G. "Ethics On-Line." *Communications of the ACM,* Vol. 40, No. 1, January 1997, pp. 60–65.

Johnston, Jo-Ann. "Investors, Executives Are More Wary of Corporate Fraud in Wake of Scandals." *The Tampa Tribune,* July 28, 2003.

Landler, Mark. "When a PR Firm Could Use a PR Firm." *Business Week,* May 14, 1990, p. 44.

Larson, Charles. V. *Persuasion: Reception and Responsibility.* Belmont, CA: Wadsworth, 1992.

Lieberman, David. "Fake News." *TV Guide,* February 22, 1992, pp. 10–26.

Leyland, Adam. "One Out of Four Pros Admit Lying on Job." *PR Week,* May 1, 2000, p. 1.

Mallinson, Bill. *Public Lies and Private Truths: An Anatomy of Public Relations.* London, England: Cassell Publishing, 1996.

McElreath, Mark P. *Managing Systematic and Ethical Public Relations.* Madison, WI: Brown & Benchmark, 1993.

Pratt, Cornelius. "Public Relations: The Empirical Research on Practitioner Ethics." *Journal of Business Ethics,* Vol. 10, 1991, pp. 229–236.

Radolf, Andrew. "Junket Journalism." *Editor & Publisher,* October 18, 1986, pp. 16–17.

Sachdev, Ameet. "In 2002, Scandal, Upheaval Mar Corporate America's Image." *Chicago Tribune,* December 31, 2002.

Schudson, Michael. *The Sociology of News.* New York: W. W. Norton, 2003.

Seib, Philip, and Kathy Fitzpatrick. *Public Relations Ethics.* Ft. Worth, TX: Harcourt Brace, 1995.

Seligman, Mac. "Travel Writers' Expenses: Who Should Pay?" *Public Relations Journal,* May 1990, pp. 27–34.

Shell, Adam. "Disinformation Not Justified in Corporate World." *Public Relations Journal,* February 1992, p. 8.

Stephens, Mitchell. *Broadcast News.* New York: Holt, Rinehart and Winston, 1986.

Thompson, William. *Targeting the Message.* White Plains, NY: Longman, 1996.

Vargas, Ann. "Liar, Liar, PR on Fire." *PR Week,* May 1, 2000, pp. 18–19.

"Ways to Avoid Ethical Problems." *Public Relations Journal,* June 1993, p. 9.

Wessel, Harry. "Workplace Ethics Issues Take Center Stage Again." *The Orlando Sentinel,* May 21, 2003.

Williams, Dean. "Blurred Standards." *Communication World,* August/September 2002, pp. 34+.

Williams, Dean. "Un-Spun: Ethical Communication Practices Serve the Public Interest." *Communication World,* April/May 2002, pp. 27–35.

Witmer, Diane F. *Spinning the Web: A Handbook for Public Relations on the Internet.* New York: Longman, 2000.

Wright, Donald K. "Enforcement Dilemma: Voluntary Nature of Public Relations Codes." *Public Relations Review,* Spring 1993, pp. 13–20.

Chapter 13: International, Multicultural, and Gender Issues

Adelson, Andrea. "Spanish-Language Radio Leads." *The New York Times,* January 24, 1994.

Aldrich, Leigh Stephens. *Covering the Community: A Diversity Handbook for the Media.* Thousand Oaks, CA: Pine Forge Press, 1999.

Anderson, Stephen. "Successfully Working with International Journalists." *Communication World,* September 1994, pp. 30–32.

Armour, Stephanie. "Reports of Workplace Bias Still on Rise Since Sept. 11." *USA Today,* May 10, 2002.

Aronson, Elliot. *Nobody Left to Hate.* New York: W. H. Freeman, 2000.

Baker, Gail F. "Race and Reputation." ed. Robert Heath. *The Handbook of Public Relations,* Thousand Oaks, CA: Sage, 2000, pp. 513–520.

Balbridge, Letitia. *Letitia Baldrige's New Complete Guide to Executive Manners.* New York: Rawson Associates, 1993.

Bates, Don. "Update on Japan: Tips on Dealing with the Press." *Public Relations Journal,* October/November 1994, p. 14.

Blanck, Peter David. *Communicating the Americans With Disabilities Act.* Washington, DC: The Annenberg-Washington Program, 1994.

Boutwilier, Robert. *Targeting Families: Marketing to and through the New Family.* Ithaca, NY: American Demographic Books, 1993.

Chambers, Marcia. "Ladies Need Not Apply." *Golf for Women,* May/June 2002, pp. 108+.

Cole, Robert S. "Include the Disabled in Diversity Programs—Or Else!" *Public Relations Strategist,* Summer 1995, pp. 34–39.

Del Valle, Christina. "Some of Jerry's Kids Are Mad at the Old Man." *Business Week,* September 14, 1992, p. 36.

DeMente, Boye. *Doing Business with the Japanese.* Lincolnwood, IL: NTC Publishing Group, 1993.

Dickey, Christopher. "Why We Can't Seem to Understand the Arabs." *Newsweek,* January 7, 1991, pp. 26–27.

Dolnick, Edward. "Deafness as Culture." *Atlantic Monthly,* September 1993, pp. 37–53.

Flynn, Gillian. "Accommodating Religion on the Job: Few Rules, Lots of Common Sense." *Workforce,* September 1998, pp. 94–97.

Fouke, Carol. "Asian-American Market More Important Than Ever." *Marketing News,* November 11, 1991, pp. 1–2.

Francis, June N. P. "When in Rome? The Effects of Cultural Adaptation on Intercultural Business Negotiations." *Journal of International Business Studies,* Third Quarter 1991.

Funk, Tim. "Arrivals Push 'Latino' as Their Label." *Wilmington Morning Star,* August 21, 2001.

Gallahan, P. A. "Tapping the Power of a Diverse Workforce." *Training and Development Journal,* March 1991, pp. 39–44.

Gancel, Charles, and Chilina Hills. "Managing the Pitfalls and Challenges of Intercultural Communication." *Communication World,* December/January 1997/1998, pp. 24–26.

Garcia, Tonya, and Randi Schmelzer. "Diversity from the Top Down." *PR Week,* December 11, 2006, pp. 14–20.

Geary, David L. "The PR Implications of Census 2000." *Public Relations Strategist,* Fall 2001, pp. 12–17.

Geddie, Tom. "Moving Communication across Cultures." *Communication World,* April/May 1999, pp. 37–40.

Grunig, Larissa A., Elizabeth L. Toth, and Linda C. Hon. *Women in Public Relations.* New York: Guilford Press, 2001.

Guth, David W., and Charles Marsh. "Writing for Diverse Publics." *Public Relations: A Values-Driven Approach.* Boston: Allyn and Bacon, 2000, p. 303.

Harris, Philip R., and Robert T. Moran. *Managing Cultural Differences.* Houston, TX: Gulf Publishing, 1987.

Heiss, Brian, and Edie Frasier. "Is Your Company Ready to Go Global?" *Communication World,* August/September 2000, pp. 29–32.

Henry, Rene A. "How to Target Special Markets." *Marketing Public Relations: The Hows That Make it Work.* Ames: Iowa State University Press, 2000.

Johnson, David W., and Frank P. Johnson. "Dealing with Diversity." Chapter 10 in *Joining Together: Group Theory and Group Skills.* Boston: Allyn and Bacon, 1997, pp. 443–465.

Johnson, Roy S. "The New Black Power." *Fortune,* August 4, 1997, pp. 46–82.

Jost, Kenneth. "Diversity in the Workplace." *CQ Researcher,* October 10, 1997, pp. 891–907.

Kay, David. "The Puzzles and Protocols of International Market Research." *Communication World,* December/January 1996/1997, pp. 17–19.

Kemper, Cynthia L. "Communicators, Go Global." *Communication World,* September 1998, pp. 30–33.

Kern-Foxworth, Marilyn. *Aunt Jemima, Uncle Ben and Rastus: Blacks in Advertising, Yesterday, Today and Tomorrow.* Westport, CT: Greenwood Press, 1994.

Konrad, Walecia. "Welcome to the Woman-Friendly Company." *Business Week,* August 6, 1990, pp. 48–55.

Kotcher, Raymond L. "Diversity in Today's Workplace and Marketplace." *Public Relations Quarterly,* Spring 1995, pp. 6–8.

Kranhold, Kathryn, Dan Bilefsky, Matthew Karnitschnig, and Ginny Parker. "Lost in Translation." *The Wall Street Journal,* May 18, 2004, p. B-1.

Laurie, Marilyn. "Managing a Diverse Workforce in a Changing Corporate Environment." *The Handbook of Strategic Public Relations and Integrated Communications,* ed. Clarke Caywood. New York: McGraw-Hill, 1997, pp. 231–243.

Lipman, Joanne. "Irish-Americans Attack Beer-Ad Images." *The Wall Street Journal,* March 16, 1992, p. B-4.

Locker, Kitty O. *Business and Administrative Communication.* Boston: McGraw-Hill, 2003.

Lopez, Joe T. "Communicating Outside Our Borders." *Communication World,* July/August 1989, pp. 28–30.

Lublin, Joann S. "Companies Use Cross-Cultural Training to Help Their Employees Adjust Abroad." *The Wall Street Journal,* August 4, 1992, p. B-1.

McKee, Bradford. "The Disabilities Labrynth." *Nation's Business,* April 1993, pp. 18–23.

Miller Howard Consulting Group. *The Internal Consultant's Guide.* Atlanta, GA: Towers Perrin Company, 1997.

O'Hare, William. "A New Look at Asian Americans." *American Demographics,* October 1990, pp. 26–31.

O'Hare, William. "The Rise of Hispanic Influence." *American Demographics,* August 1990, pp. 40–43.

Parnell, Myrtle, and Jo Vanderkloot. "How to Build Cross-Cultural Bridges." *Communication World,* July/August 1989, pp. 40–42.

Petrini, Catherine. "The Language of Diversity." *Training and Development,* April 1993, pp. 35–37.

Pinsdorf, Marion K. "Flying Different Skies: How Cultures Respond to Airline Disasters." *Public Relations Review,* Vol. 17, No. 1, 1991, pp. 37–56.

"Public Relations Must Pave the Way for Developing Diversified Work Force." *Public Relations Journal,* January 1992, pp. 12–13.

Puenta, Maria, and Martin Kasindorf. "The New Face of America." *USA Today,* September 7, 1999, p. A-1.

Rabin, Steve. "How to Sell across Cultures." *American Demographics*, March 1994, pp. 56–57.

Rose, Edward J. "Is the Blue I See the Blue You See? *Communication World,* July/August 1989.

Skinner, Merna. "Presenting to International Audiences Effectively." *Public Relations Tactics,* January 2001, pp. 12–13.

Stern-LaRosa, Caryl, and Ellen Hofheimer Bettmann. *Hate Hurts.* New York: Anti-Defamation League, 2000.

Swasy, Alecia. "Changing Times: Marketers Scramble to Keep Pace with Demographic Shifts." *The Wall Street Journal,* March 22, 1991, p. B-6.

Thomas, R. Roosevelt Jr. "From Affirmative Action to Affirming Diversity." *Harvard Business Journal,* March–April 1990, pp. 107–117.

Toth, Elizabeth L., and Carolyn G. Cline. *Beyond the Velvet Ghetto.* San Francisco, CA: IABC Research Foundation, 1989.

The Velvet Ghetto: The Impact of the Increasing Percentage of Women in Public Relations and Business Communication. San Francisco, CA: IABC Research Foundation, 1989.

Wakefield, Robert I. "Effective Public Relations in the Multinational Organization." *The Handbook of Public Relations*, ed. Robert Heath. Thousand Oaks, CA: Sage, 2000, pp. 639–647.

"Watch Your Language!" Fact sheet provided by United Cerebral Palsy.

"Words with Dignity and Disability Etiquette." Brochure provided by Paraquad, Inc.

Williams, Mary V. "Will Diversity = Equality for Multicultural Communicators?" *Communication World,* February 1991, pp. 26–30.

Yate, Martin. *Keeping the Best: Thoughts on Building a Super-Competitive Workforce.* Holbrook, MA: Bob Adams Publishing, 1990.

INTERNET RESOURCES FOR PUBLIC RELATIONS

Professional Associations on the Web

Broadcast Education Association: This website includes links to a number of broadcasting industry sources that provide information pertaining to the broadcasting, cable television, and related industries. (www.beaweb.org)

Public Relations Society of America: Information on the organization and its programs, publications, chapters, national and regional conferences, and other activities. (www.prsa.org)

Public Relations Student Society of America: Information on the student organization and its programs, publications, chapters, national and regional conferences, and other activities. (www.prssa.org).

International Association of Business Communicators: Information on the organization and its programs, publications, chapters, national and regional conferences, and other activities. (www.iabc.com)

Other Organizations and Services

American Institute of Philanthropy: A nonprofit organization that monitors the financial integrity and fund-raising performance of charities across the country and makes information available to prospective donors. Based in St. Louis. Summaries of reports available at no charge on the Web; detailed versions available by mail order at a nominal charge. (www.charitywatch.org).

Chronicle of Philanthropy: A nationally known journal dealing with fund-raising issues. (www.philanthropy.com).

Commercial news release services: PRNewswire and BusinessWire use the Internet to distribute news releases, charging fees to both the organization providing the release and the media outlets subscribing to the service. Both companies got their starts by faxing news releases to the media (and still do some faxing), but now do a majority of their distribution on-line. Both companies post sample stories on the Web. PRNewswire can be found at www.prnewswire.com, and BusinessWire at www.quote.com/info/bwire.html.

Diversity Inc.: A website that covers issues such as employee diversity and other international and multicultural issues. (www.DiversityInc.com)

Better Business Bureau Wise Giving Alliance: Formerly known as the National Charities Information Bureau, this organization services a similar function to the American Institute of Philanthropy. Based in Arlington, Va. (http://us.bbb.org.)

Poynter Institute: Information on media education programs in areas such as law, ethics, technology, journalism education, and diversity issues. (www.poynter.org)

Internet Discussion Groups

PRFORUM, administered by Indiana University/Purdue University at Indianapolis, is a worldwide discussion of current public relations issues among working professionals, educators, and students. (prforum@listserv.iupui.edu)

PRSSA-TALK, administered by the Public Relations Student Society of America, includes the discussion of student and professional issues, including information on employment and internship opportunities, plus news related to the organization's regional and national conferences. (www.prssa.org)

Miscellaneous

ProfNet, developed by the State University of New York at Stony Brook but now administered by PRNewswire, offers reports by more than 1,200 university professors and other experts for email interviews. For more information, contact ProfNet at profnet@profnet.com.

Similar sources include MediaNet, administered by Compuserve (www.compuserve.com) and SourceNet, administered by MediaMap (www.mediamap.com).

INDEX